The Asylum Acquis Handbook
THE FOUNDATION FOR A COMMON EUROPEAN ASYLUM POLICY

The Asylum Acquis Handbook

THE FOUNDATION FOR A COMMON
EUROPEAN ASYLUM POLICY

edited by

Peter J. van Krieken

T·M·C·ASSER PRESS
The Hague

Published by T.M.C. ASSER PRESS,
P.O.Box 16163, 2500 BD The Hague, The Netherlands

Sold and distributed in North, Central and South America
by Kluwer Law International,
675 Massachusetts Avenue, Cambridge, MA 02139, U.S.A.

In all other countries, sold and distributed
by Kluwer Law International, Distribution Centre,
P.O.Box 322, 3300 AH Dordrecht, The Netherlands

to be cited as:
P.J. van Krieken (ed.), *The Asylum Acquis Handbook* (The Hague, 2000)

ISBN 90-6704-122-X

All rights reserved.
© 2000, T.M.C. ASSER PRESS, The Hague, The Netherlands, the Röling Foundation and the authors

No part of the material protected by this copyright notice may be reproduced or utilized in any form or by any means, electronic or mechanical, including photocopying, recording, or by any information storage and retrieval system, without written permission from the copyright owner.

Lay-out and cover: Oasis Productions, Nieuwerkerk a/d IJssel, The Netherlands
Printing and binding: Koninklijke Wöhrmann BV, Zutphen, The Netherlands

SUMMARY OF CONTENTS

Preface		VII
Acknowledgements		XII
Table of Contents		XIII
INTRODUCTION		1
1	CONTRIBUTIONS	7
1.1	The EU Asylum Acquis: History and Context *Johannes van der Klaauw*	9
1.2	Harmonisation of Asylum and Immigration Policies: The Long and Winding Road from Amsterdam via Vienna to Tampere *Cornelis D. de Jong*	21
1.3	Decision-making in Justice and Home Affairs *Helen Staples*	37
1.4	Amsterdam and the Institutions *Georg Wirtz*	47
1.5	The Danish Exception Denmark's JHA Reservation and Amsterdam *Fabrice Liebaut*	57
1.6	The Enlargement Process and JHA Co-operation *Oliver Seiffarth*	61
1.7	Actors and Sources *Peter J. van Krieken*	73
2	LISTS	83
2.1	Original list	85
2.2	Chronological list	95
2.3	Topical list	99
2.4	TAIEX list	104
2.5	What is the acquis (Brussels' Commentary)	115
3	TEXTS	123
	(26 relevant instruments)	125

4. COMMENTARIES 209

Brussels' Commentaries on the most important instruments
4.1 Commission Working Document dd 3 March 1999 211
4.2 Joint Position, 4 March 1996 [JP] 224
4.3 Minimum Guarantees for Asylum Procedures [MG] 233
4.4 Host Third Countries [HTC] 245
4.5 ('Safe') Countries ('of Origin') [CoO] 250
4.6 Manifestly Unfounded Applications [MUA] 253
4.7 Unaccompanied Minors [UM] 260
4.8 Readmission Agreements 267
4.9 Dublin and Eurodac 272

5. ADDITIONAL TEXTS 281

5.1 Title IV of the Consolidated Version of the Treaty Establishing the European Community 283
5.2 Protocol on Asylum for National of Member States of the European Union 287
5.3 Convention relating to Extradition between the Member States of the European Union 288
5.4 Vienna Action Plan 293
5.5 Tampere Milestones 304
5.6 Draft Eurodac Convention 310
5.6.b Draft Eurodac Protocol 320
5.6.c Draft Eurodac Regulation 324
5.7 List ExCom Conclusions 344
5.8 UNHCR Handbook, Introduction and Conclusion 347

6. CROSS REFERENCES 353

PREFACE

February 2000, an ad-hoc body of 62 under the presidency of the former German President, Roman Herzog, began drafting a 'European Charter of Fundamental Rights'. It is to be taken for granted that such a Charter will not only pay due attention to the rights (and, hopefully, responsibilities) of the Union's citizens, but also to those of third-country nationals legally residing in the Union, as well as to the right to seek and enjoy asylum from persecution.

Quite remarkably, Europe as a continent has never unequivocally included this latter issue in a basic, legally binding instrument. Even the European Convention on Fundamental Freedoms and Human Rights (ECHR, 1950) lacks a reference to this internationally recognized principle, and it is only thanks to the flexible use of the ECHR's Article 3 (prohibition of torture, degrading treatment) that Europe has made a useful reference to the non-refoulement principle.

More striking, probably, is that Europe has never come around to lay down any proper rules and regulations for the admission, reception and status of those who flee (civil) war, whereas that same Continent has witnessed during the 1990s war and atrocities on a scale which was believed to have been consigned to the past. Those same wars and atrocities forced hundreds of thousands of people to flee and to seek protection and shelter elsewhere.

A proper foundation for a European asylum policy has hence been lacking, but recent events and developments, the Treaty of Amsterdam in particular, have resulted in Europe as a whole subscribing to the idea that the asylum principles should be clearly spelled out and embedded in proper instruments. Moreover, with the decision to move the asylum issue from the so-called Third Pillar to the First Pillar, meaning that asylum as such would be a matter for 'Brussels' rather than the respective capitals as was hitherto the case, the asylum issue has come to the fore. The Third-First Pillar transition is to be completed by May 2004 and a great many decisions hence need to be taken between now and 2004.

The underlying principles have been laid down in a so-called acquis. This acquis is meant to form the basis for further regulating Europe's asylum policy and its implementation. The acquis, however, is not easily accessible and is difficult to interpret. During the many meetings in the Union itself, in the Member States, and in particular between Union Members and the Candidate Countries, it became clear that there is a need for an 'Asylum Acquis Handbook', with above all condensed information: texts, lists, commentaries and relevant background information.

The underlying need for producing this Handbook becomes even more evident when we look at part of the keynote address delivered by the Honourable António VITORINO, the Commissioner for Justice and Home Affairs at the 4th

International Metropolis Conference, Washington DC, December 9th, 1999:

(...) Ten years have passed since the fall of the Iron Curtain, and yet uncertainty is still the main characteristic of today. We live in a period of transition. We are leaving behind a fading world order that gave birth to many of our institutions – the EU, NATO, and the UN –, and that still bears a clear influence on their development. This is a turning point, where globalisation meets an intense revolution in technology and communication. Ahead, we face an ascending cycle, the shape of which is still undetermined.

This new cycle is one where clear changes are occurring in the patterns which for so long have moulded and guided our societies – the end of the concepts of 'a job for life' and of 'continued progress'; widespread economic and physical insecurity; underlying poverty and structural unemployment; phenomena of social exclusion. To counter this, the existing regulatory framework is proving to be manifestly insufficient. Nation-states are no longer able to tackle these radical factors of change alone. This allows for the growing intervention and increasing role of institutions such as the European Union. (...)

One of the basic keys to alleviate [tension which may be the result of the introduction of the Euro, combined with a process which demonstrated some waning in intra-European solidarity and a decreased relevance of social and economic cohesion] is the strengthening of the collective understanding, among EU members, that enlargement and economic integration will make the Union's institutional reform inevitable so as to meet the challenges ahead.

What are those challenges? (And I arrive at the third dynamic of European integration). Basically, the enlargement of the Union and the re-legitimisation of the European ideal.

Enlargement is itself a challenge. It will indeed accentuate the differences in stages of development of member states, and at the same time advance the urgent revision of common policies such as the Common Agriculture Policy, institutional reform, and the redefinition of structural funds. But it stands at the very centre of our essence as Europeans: we all share the same values and vocation, and are open to the voluntary participation in the process of European construction of those willing to agree to the Union's politically-based rules.

Second, a 'refounding act' of the Union is urgently called for. There is a strong feeling, across the board, of the need to mobilise citizens' support. The very low turnouts at last June's elections for the European Parliament reflect this growing disinterest on the part of citizens to the issues relevant to Europe. Thus the need to re-legitimise our ideal. The arguments for the maintenance of the Union have changed. The main reasoning is no longer the avoidance of a war between Europeans. Nor are the goals of integration any longer supposedly 'painless', with hard political decisions being cushioned by economic integration. We have to build on a positive, pro-active, message that attracts citizen support and makes the European ideal, not a 'mal mineur', but, a true project for the future.

This re-legitimisation should cover three main issues:

– First, the need to safeguard the cultural values of European citizenship. To the economic dimension, spearheaded by the euro, and to the enlargement process, we must add a further dimension, both social and political, anchored in citizenship values.

You are all aware of the importance of the European Convention on Human Rights. Its precepts have been written into the succeeding EU treaties, starting with the Single European Act of 1986. Yet this instrument of the Council of Europe needs to be supplemented in the context of the European Union, since the Union's treaties confer certain rights on its citizens which they can exercise throughout its territory. The mechanisms are thus now in place for the drawing up, within the coming year, of a Charter of Fundamental Rights, which was given an additional impetus at the recent Tampere EU Summit.

Equally, we have to face the unpleasant fact that racism and xenophobia are, in Europe, evils incompatible with our common values and against which our fight has to be stepped up. We have evidence of this even at the level of extremist political parties. The Commission ran a European text against racism in 1997 and set up a monitoring centre on racism and xenophobia. But more needs to be done in conjunction with the Member States and other pan-European institutions such as the Council of Europe and the OSCE.

– Secondly, the Union's increased influence in the world. The EU has its place and its responsibility within a shared world leadership. We are developing a Common Foreign and Security Policy compatible with our own internal priorities. European stability cannot be dissociated from the transatlantic link, in itself a reference for our political and economic stability. NATO will continue to be the cornerstone of our security, upon which we will build, with full co-operation of our North American Allies, a European pillar of security and defence. Our Common Foreign and Security Policy is a tool to enhance that transatlantic partnership.

– Last, – and this falls under my direct responsibility –, the need to guarantee our internal security, with a full respect for human rights and the fundamental rules of political democracy. Our common effort is towards consolidating an area of freedom, security and justice for all living within the Union, bridging the gap between the citizens and the European institutions. A three-fold effort, it touches upon the free movement of persons, their access to justice, and the fight against transnational organised crime.

It is a difficult and complex task. Our navigational chart is the Treaty of Amsterdam, which came into force last May, when its ratification process was completed. This Treaty introduced major improvements in our efforts to implement specific measures for the strengthening of an area of freedom, security and justice. I can assure you that it was one of the most extensively discussed chapters of the whole inter-governmental conference.

On the one hand, it reflected an awareness of the direct relevance of these issues to the general public, and the fact that it would become a major issue in the subsequent ratification. On the other, it constituted an admission that co-operation in police and judicial affairs had hitherto failed in its objectives within the purely intergovernmental framework of the Treaty on European Union, better known as the Maastricht Treaty.

From a very early stage of European integration, Justice and Home Affairs was seen as an area where far-reaching changes were most needed, and where demand was strongest. The great innovation in the Treaty of Amsterdam was that it very clearly formulated the Union's objectives in this field, setting out a 5-year plan, to which we are now committed.

It was with these tools that we arrived at the Tampere Special European Council, which brought together the Heads of State and Government (...) Tampere's agenda

was forthright but could nevertheless be seen as a gamble, as this subject is not fully developed in terms of 'acquis communautaire'. Our main aims were:
- To send out a strong political message that the Member States are determined to make a success of the Treaty of Amsterdam's provisions;
- To introduce concrete ideas with which to catch public attention and deal with specific daily problems European citizens face when dealing with justice;
- And to strike the right balance between effective measures against criminality, and avoiding the unwanted image of a 'repressive' Summit.

The net result was an obvious success. Justice and Home Affairs were set high up on the political agenda, and the Summit's conclusions demonstrate how close this matter is to the citizens' concerns.

Those conclusions can be divided into four main areas:
- Regarding asylum, we set a target for a common European asylum system, based on the full and inclusive application of the Geneva Convention, thus ensuring that no person is sent back to persecution. This system will allow for special protection measures for those fleeing conflicts, and establish a financial reserve for situations of mass influxes, such as the one arising from the war in Kosovo.
- In the field of immigration, the need to work with the countries of origin and transit, to combat the traffic of human beings, rather than the victims themselves, and the need for fair treatment of third country nationals legally resident in Member States, with the maximum possible balance of their rights and obligations.
- In the judiciary, we aim to reduce the intermediate measures still required to enable recognition and enforcement of decisions and judgements between Member States, thus facilitating access to justice across the Union. Another objective is to attain the mutual recognition of judgements, based on the approximation of legislation and minimum standards, in both civil and criminal cases.
- And last, in the fight against transnational organised crime, there will be an intensified effort against money laundering, trafficking in drugs and human beings, as well as terrorism. The key role of Europol was confirmed, and Eurojust was established, a framework composed of national prosecutors, magistrates and police officers, from Member States, to facilitate the required co-operation in this area.

In order to keep under constant review progress made towards implementing the measures needed for developing an area of freedom, security and justice, and for meeting the Treaty of Amsterdam 5-year deadline, the Commission is currently establishing what we have called a scoreboard system, similar to the one successfully used for the Union's Internal Market.

Another important element to bear in mind is the very close connection between the creation of an Area of Freedom, Security and Justice, and the process of enlargement. Our wish is to 'enlarge with security', and for that we shall need to co-operate closely with candidate countries in implementing many of these objectives I have outlined.

We are aware of the quicksands ahead. This is an area where national sensitivities are very strong, as States tend to see the issues exclusively in terms of sovereignty. National administrations, the judiciary and the police have very little history of mutual co-operation. Nevertheless, it is my conviction that the Member States see the need for common action in an area of largely open borders. The overall objective is not to destroy the nation-state. Our aim, on the contrary, is to focus on specific issues that can be tackled through common actions. Our wish is for a Europe secure from internal and external threats, where justice is promoted for all, and where its citizens, each and every individual, may live in peace and prosperity.

Addressing an audience in Washington, DC, where the politicians and officials, and the brightest and best of the academic world, deliberate, is always a daunting experience. But equally, Washington is a place where one can always learn. This is especially true when it comes to issues of migration and asylum and the administration of justice on a continental scale. (...)

I am also sure that your deliberations will add considerable insight to issues of migration, which are of great importance in Europe. It may come as a surprise to some of you that since the early 1980's the European Union has received about six million refugees. As North Americans, you have come to expect migration from Europe, not to Europe. This, of course, reflects Europe's economic growth. But we have to learn how to handle the side effects.

In his book 'The Clash of Civilizations' (the thesis of which I do not wish to endorse), Samuel Huntington does make a true statement regarding migration, when he says that 'population movements are the motor of history'. Our, your, task is to provide the best possible environment for that motor to function, whether it is by channelling migratory fluxes, or in the optimum planning of urban development.(...)

We trust that the present Handbook is an appropriate and useful tool in that very context, and thus contributes to the important debate on Europe's future asylum policy.

Oegstgeest, The Netherlands, Spring 2000 THE EDITOR

ACKNOWLEDGEMENTS

This Handbook came about in close coordination with the Society for International Development, Netherlands' Chapter, the project on the future of asylum and migration. The Handbook is, of course, above all meant to assist the Phare Horizontal Asylum Programme, and the Editor herewith expresses his thanks for the assistance provided by UNHCR Vienna and the Nuremberg-based Bafl Phare Team. The Netherlands Ministry of Justice IND/INS agreed to provide the manpower for the task of ensuring that this Handbook sees the light of day. It should also be mentioned that the Brussels' Commentaries contain training material established by the European Commission on the basis of work prepared by Messrs. Van der Klaauw, Buchhorn and Anagnost. Funds were made available under the Odysseus Programme, for which I am grateful. Also the Röling Foundation provided financial support. The English language editor, Mr Peter Morris, should be thanked for his diligent revision of 'Euro-English' into proper English. Last but not least, I would like to commend Ms Staples and Messrs. de Jong, van der Klaauw, Liebaut, Seiffarth and Wirtz for their transparent and enlightening contributions.

TABLE OF CONTENTS

Summary of Contents	V
Preface	VII
Acknowledgements	XII
Table of Contents	XIII
INTRODUCTION	1

1. CONTRIBUTIONS — 7

1.1	The EU Asylum Acquis: History and Context *Johannes van der Klaauw*	9
1.2	Harmonisation of Asylum and Immigration Policies: The Long and Winding Road from Amsterdam via Vienna to Tampere *Cornelis D. de Jong*	21
1.3	Decision-making in Justice and Home Affairs *Helen Staples*	37
1.4	Amsterdam and the Institutions *Georg Wirtz*	47
1.5	The Danish Exception Denmark's JHA Reservation and Amsterdam *Fabrice Liebaut*	57
1.6	The Enlargement Process and JHA Co-operation *Oliver Seiffarth*	61
1.7	Actors and Sources *Peter J. van Krieken*	73

2. LISTS — 83

2.1	Original list	85
2.2	Chronological list	95
2.3	Topical list	99
2.4	TAIEX list	104
2.5	What is the acquis (Brussels' Commentary)	115

3.	TEXTS	123

(26 relevant instruments)

3.1	Council Regulation (EC) No 2317/95 of 25 September 1995 determining the third countries whose nationals must be in possession of visas when crossing the external borders of the Member States	127
3.2	Joint Action of 4 March 1996 adopted by the Council on the basis of Article K.3 of the Treaty on European Union on airport transit arrangements	130
3.3	Council Resolution of 26 June 1997 on unaccompanied minors who are nationals of third countries	132
3.4	Council Resolution of 1 June 1993 on harmonisation of family reunion	137
3.5	Council Resolution of 25 September 1995 on burden-sharing with regard to the admission and residence of displaced persons on a temporary basis	140
3.6	Council Decision of 4 March 1996 on an alert and emergency procedure for burden-sharing with regard to the admission and residence of displaced persons on a temporary basis	143
3.7	Council Recommendation of 22 December 1995 on harmonizing means of combating illegal immigration and illegal employment and improving the relevant means of control	144
3.8	Council Decision of 22 December 1995 on monitoring the implementation of instruments already adopted concerning admission of third-country nationals	147
3.9	Council Decision of 16 December 1996 on monitoring the implementation of instruments adopted by the Council concerning illegal immigration, readmission, the unlawful employment of third country nationals and cooperation in the implementation of expulsion orders	148
3.10	Joint Position of 4 March 1996 defined by the Council on the basis of Article K.3 of the Treaty on European Union on the harmonized application of the definition of the term 'refugee' in Article 1 of the Geneva Convention of 28 July 1951 relating to the status of refugees	149
3.11	Council Resolution of 20 June 1995 on minimum guarantees for asylum procedures	157
3.12a	Convention determining the State responsible for examining applications for asylum lodged in one of the Member States of the European Communities (Dublin Convention)	162
3.12b	Decision No 1/97 of 9 September 1997 of the Committee set up by Article 18 of the Dublin Convention of 15 June 1990, concerning provisions for the implementation of the Convention	171
3.12c	Decision No 1/98 of 30 June 1998 of the Committee set up by Article 18 of the Dublin Convention of 15 June 1990, concerning provisions	

	for the implementation of the Convention	178
3.13	Resolution adopted 30 November 1992 on manifestly unfounded applications for asylum	179
3.14	Resolution adopted 30 November 1992 on a harmonised approach to questions concerning host third countries	183
3.15	Conclusions adopted 30 November 1992 concerning countries in which there is generally no serious risk of persecution	185
3.16	Decision of 11 June 1992 setting up a Centre for Information, Discussion and Exchange on Asylum (Cirea)	186
3.17	Guidelines for joint reports on third countries (text adopted by the Council on 20 June 1994)	188
3.18	Circulation and confidentiality of joint reports on the situation in certain third countries (text adopted by the Council on 20 June 1994)	191
3.19	Council Decision of 26 June 1997 on monitoring the implementation of instruments adopted concerning asylum	191
3.20	Council Decision of 26 May 1997 on the exchange of information concerning assistance for the voluntary repatriation of third-country nationals	193
3.21	Council Recommendation of 30 November 1994 concerning a specimen bilateral readmission agreement between a Member State and a third country	194
3.22	Council Recommendation of 24 July 1995 on the guiding principles to be followed in drawing up protocols on the implementation of readmission agreements	199
3.23	Council Recommendation of 22 December 1995 on concerted action and cooperation in carrying out expulsion measures	202
3.24	Council Recommendation of 30 November 1994 concerning the adoption of a standard travel document for the expulsion of third-country nationals	207
4.	**COMMENTARIES** Brussels' Commentaries on the most important instruments	209
4.1	Commission Working Document dd 3 March 1999: Towards Common Standards on Asylum Procedures	211
4.2	Joint Position, 4 March 1996 [JP]	224
4.3	Minimum Guarantees for Asylum Procedures [MG]	233
4.4	Host Third Countries [HTC]	245
4.5	('Safe') Countries ('of Origin') [CoO]	250
4.6	Manifestly Unfounded Applications [MUA]	253
4.7	Unaccompanied Minors [UM]	260

4.8	Readmission Agreements	267
4.9	Dublin and Eurodac	272
5.	**ADDITIONAL TEXTS**	282
5.1	Title IV of the Consolidated Version of the Treaty Establishing the European Community	283
5.2	Protocol on Asylum for National of Member States of the European Union	287
5.3	Convention relating to Extradition between the Member States of the European Union	288
5.4	Vienna Action Plan	293
5.5	Tampere Milestones	304
5.6.a	Draft Eurodac Convention	310
5.6.b	Draft Eurodac Protocol	320
5.6.c	Draft Eurodac Regulation	324
5.7	List ExCom Conclusions	344
5.8	UNHCR Handbook, Introduction and Conclusion	347
6.	**CROSS REFERENCES**	353

INTRODUCTION

Peter J. van Krieken

Suddenly the concept 'acquis' had become a buzz-word. Many of the experts did not really dare to acknowledge that they too did not know what 'acquis' stood for, or what it really meant. Yet, the concept expanded, people started to use it in daily use, and it quickly become part and parcel of 'Brussels-speak'.

Probably the best way to describe it is by referring to it as the sum of what the Union and its Member States have agreed upon. It is the reflection, if not projection, of norms, regulations, and criteria in any given field. It might consist of binding regulations, or of 'soft' recommendations and virtually everything in between.

At the same time, the 'acquis' in its entirety is of the utmost importance for the enlargement process. The candidate countries have to adopt the acquis irrespective of the binding force of its various instruments. The complete 'acquis' now amounts to over 90,000 pages and covers virtually everything, from customs to the environment and from competition to migration.

To make matters more complicated, there is a difference between the 'acquis communautaire' and the so-called non-First Pillar acquis. The Asylum Acquis, agreed upon under the Third Pillar, is hence not part of the acquis communautaire, as it has a different standing. This also means, now that asylum and migration are in the process of being moved from the Third to the First Pillar, that new instruments will be agreed upon which undoubtedly will have an impact on the existing acquis: some instruments will be reinforced as the soft character of the particular instrument will give way to an increasingly binding force. On the other hand, some instruments will be overruled by newer ones, with, maybe, a new direction, a new conceptualization, new norms. Yet, the Acquis, as it now stands, undoubtedly forms the foundation for a common European asylum policy.

As the Commission has in mind to involve the Candidate Countries in the process of further defining the Asylum Acquis – as those Countries would otherwise be confronted with a maybe constantly changing Acquis – it is of the utmost importance to make the Acquis, as it stands per 1 January 2000, easily accessible. However, it should be underlined that the Acquis is a 'living document' which is bound to witness a great many changes.

This is particularly true, as 'Tampere' agreed inter alia on the following:

P.J. van Krieken (Ed.), The Asylum Acquis Handbook
© 2000, T.M.C.Asser Press, The Hague, the Röling Foundation and the authors

– The freedom to move freely throughout the Union should not be regarded as the exclusive preserve of the Union's own citizens. Its very existence, in combination with other freedoms, acts as a draw to many others worldwide who cannot enjoy the freedom Union citizens take for granted. It would be in contradiction with Europe's traditions to deny such freedom to those whose circumstances lead them justifiably to seek access to our territory. This in turn requires the Union to develop common policies on asylum and immigration, while taking into account the need for a consistent control of external borders to stop illegal immigration and to combat those who organise it and commit related international crimes. These common policies must be based on principles which are both clear to our own citizens and also offer guarantees to those who seek protection in or access to the European Union.

– The aim is an open and secure European Union, fully committed to the obligations of the Geneva Refugee Convention and other relevant human rights instruments, and able to respond to humanitarian needs on the basis of solidarity. A common approach must also be developed to ensure the integration into our societies of those third country nationals who are lawfully resident in the Union.

– In the context of partnership with countries of origin under which a comprehensive approach to migration addressing political, human rights and development issues in countries of origin and transit deserves to be elaborated, the European Council welcomes the report of the High Level Working Group on Asylum and Migration set up by the Council, and agrees on the continuation of its mandate and on the drawing up of further Action Plans. It considers as a useful contribution the first action plans drawn up by that Working Group, and approved by the Council, and invites the Council and the Commission to report back on their implementation to the European Council in December 2000.

– The European Council reaffirms the importance the Union and Member States attach to absolute respect of the right to seek asylum. It has agreed to work towards establishing a Common European Asylum System, based on the full and inclusive application of the Geneva Convention, thus ensuring that nobody is sent back to persecution, i.e. maintaining the principle of non-refoulement.

– This System should include, **in the short term**, [1] a clear and workable determination of the State responsible for the examination of an asylum application, **[2] common standards for a fair and efficient asylum procedure, [3] common minimum conditions of reception of asylum seekers**, and [4] the approximation of rules on the recognition and content of the refugee status. It should also be completed with [5] measures on subsidiary forms of protection offering an appropriate status to any person in need of such protection. To that end, the Council is urged to adopt, on the basis of Commission proposals, the necessary decisions according to the timetable set in the Treaty of Amsterdam and the Vienna Action Plan. The European Council stresses the importance of consulting UNHCR and other international organisations.

– **In the longer term**, Community rules should lead to [6] a common asylum procedure and [4] a uniform status for those who are granted asylum valid throughout the Union. The Commission is asked to prepare within one year a communication on this matter.

– The European Council acknowledges [7] the need for approximation of national legislations on the conditions for admission and residence of third country nationals, based on a shared assessment of the economic and demographic developments within the Union, as well as the situation in the countries of origin. It requests to this end

rapid decisions by the Council, on the basis of proposals by the Commission. These decisions **should take into account not only the reception capacity of each Member State, but also their historical and cultural links with the countries of origin.**
– *The legal status of third country nationals should be approximated to that of Member States' nationals. A person, who has resided legally in a Member State for a period of time to be determined and who holds a long-term residence permit, should be granted in that Member State a set of uniform rights which are as near as possible to those enjoyed by EU citizens; e.g. the right to reside, receive education, and work as an employee or self-employed person, as well as the principle of non-discrimination vis-à-vis the citizens of the State of residence. The European Council endorses the objective that long-term legally resident third country nationals be offered the opportunity to obtain the nationality of the Member State in which they are resident.*[1]

The Asylum Acquis is symbolic for the turn of the century: Europe is in the process of rearranging its own house, new members are welcome, new mechanisms and decision-making structures are being developed, and on top of that, new issues come to the fore and/or new opinions on certain issues are gaining force.

Asylum and migration belong to all of the above. Decision making will be moved from the respective capitals to Brussels; it is not yet known, however, whether the issue is subject to a consensus rule or rather a majority rule, and if so to what extent. Moreover, it is not known how long and how much those who opted-out can stick to their positions.

Of probably greater importance is to ensure that the acquis does not run counter to obligations under international law in general and human rights in particular. All the Union Member States have acceded to the 1950 European Convention on Human Rights and Fundamental Freedoms, as well as to the 1951 Convention Relating to the Status of Refugees. The Asylum Acquis should not run counter to the principles embedded in these Conventions, nor should the obligations and responsibilities under these Conventions be regarded as subsidiary or secondary to the Acquis. In fact, this problem has more or less been solved by including these Conventions in the Acquis, whereby, at least on paper, conflicts are supposed to be non-existent.

Much will henceforth depend on interpretation and actual implementation. A good example can be found in the principle of safe third countries, or, in 'acquis-speak', host third countries. Whereas the 1951 Refugee Convention focuses to some extent on those coming directly from the country in which they fear persecution and whereas a relevant Executive Committee Conclusion makes mention of countries where the asylum seeker had found protection, the relevant London/Acquis document refers to countries where protection *could* have been found. A number of solutions to this prima facie minor difference are possible: a) to deny any difference; b) to agree that both interpretations fall well above the minimum

---

[1] The Tampere document has been reproduced elsewhere in this Handbook (Chapter: Additional Texts). Emphasis and [number] have been added.

norms; and c) to agree to disagree. In view of the very fact that the Tampere Milestones have once again underlined that the Union shall consult as well as cooperate and coordinate with the UNHCR, it can be assumed that pragmatic solutions are to be found.

ACCESSIBILITY AND TRANSPARENCY

1. The original Asylum Acquis list (25 May 1998 and later that year updated) contains a great many documents and instruments. The list itself is in 'Anglo-French' meaning that it contains some English titles and some French titles. We have made an effort to stick to the English language only, and hence French titles have been duly translated into English.

2. Some of the documents contained in the list were originally labelled 'restraint' or 'limited'. It can, however, be assumed that once those documents become part and parcel of the Acquis, limited distribution can no longer be adhered to and indeed they are now in the public domain.[2] In as far as is useful and pragmatic, these documents have been included in this Handbook.

3. This Handbook focuses on the asylum issue. However, a great many documents which have been placed in the original list under 'external borders' or, e.g., under 'migration', have been included in this Handbook as these documents have an impact on the Asylum Acquis as such.

4. The full Asylum Acquis list is provided hereinbelow, with a list of the updated documents included in a footnote. Against some titles of documents an asterix has been added. This means that those documents have been reprinted in full in this Handbook. For easy reference a chronological and topical list have also been included as well as the TAIEX list, drawn up under the screening/enlargement exercise.

5. The **Geneva documents** have not been reproduced. To make full use of this Handbook, it should be underlined that this Handbook should be used in conjunction with **UNHCR's 'Handbook on Procedures and Criteria for Determining Refugee Status'**, be it the original 1977 edition or the re-edited January 1992 edition. UNHCR's Handbook contains the full texts of the 1951 Convention and the 1967 Protocol Relating to the Status of Refugees. The Introduction to and the Conclusion of that Handbook, however, have been included.

---

[2] See e.g. Elspeth Guild, *The Developing Immigration and Asylum Policies of the European Union*, Kluwer (1996).

INTRODUCTION 5

6 Less accessible are the **Conclusions adopted by UNHCR's Executive Committee** (ExCom). Although it does indeed concern 'soft law', the Conclusions generally contain a wealth of information on how to interpret the 1951 Convention and they hence provide a great many keys on related issues. Due attention to the value of ExCom Conclusions has been paid hereinbelow, under 'Actors/ Sources', and the Cross References also often refer to those ExCom conclusions. Most UNHCR Offices have available a fairly outdated booklet containing the ExCom Conclusions (up to 1994). More recent ExCom Conclusions can be found on UNHCR's web-site.[3] Useful as most ExCom Conclusions may appear, it has nevertheless been decided not to include them, apart from a list of numbers and topics.[4]

7. The **Dublin Convention** and its various related instruments are very much part and parcel of the Acquis. It has been decided to include the most relevant of the Convention and two related documents only. Deciding otherwise would hinder the accessibility and use of this Handbook.

8. Because of its specific character, **Schengen**, although since the entry into force on 1 May 1999 of the Treaty of Amsterdam forming part of the EU acquis communautaire, has not been included. This is mainly because of its character: it focuses on trouble-free travel among the Schengen countries, not as such on entry and/or sojourn, the asylum-related issue.[5]

9. Of great importance for future approaches to migrants and asylum seekers will be **EURODAC**, the agreement to set up a dactylo-information system. In as far as is relevant, drafts of the Convention, Protocol and (EC) Regulation have been included in the Chapter entitled 'Additional Texts'.

SET-UP

This Handbook has been set up as follows.
First, some general introductions to the issue have been provided, which include a short history of the Union's involvement with the issue of asylum and migration, an explanation of the (non-)binding force of the various instruments, the long and winding road from Amsterdam via Vienna to Tampere, the role of the institutions after 'Amsterdam', a survey of the various Actors and Sources, the special position of Denmark, and the relevance of the Acquis for the enlargement process.

---

[3] unhcr.ch/refworld/unhcr/excom/reports
[4] UNHCR is herewith urged to up-date and widely distribute its ExCom publication.
[5] See the various pp 600+ EU Schengen editions.

The main part consists of the Acquis itself, the list as drawn up by the Commission and agreed upon by Coreper, a chronological overview and the texts in full of the most relevant instruments (25 of the some 40 asylum-related documents). In Chapter 5 entitled 'Additional Texts' parts of the Vienna Action Plan, the Tampere Milestones, the relevant paragraphs of the 'Consolidated Treaties' as amended by the Treaty of Amsterdam, the Commission's Working Document of March 1999, Eurodac and some UNHCR documents have been included in order to assure access to and to stress the wider context of the Acquis phenomenon.

Some of the Acquis documents have been 'commented' upon by the Commission for the purpose of providing a training tool in the various Phare and Odysseus exercises, in Eastern Europe in particular, and especially in the Phare Horizontal Asylum Programme and Twinning activities. These 'Brussels Commentaries', although non-official in nature, carry a great deal of weight, as they provide the key to optimalize interpretation and implementation and are thus indispensable for the proper use of the Acquis. These 'Brussels Commentaries' have been reproduced in Chapter 4.

Another '*piece de résistance*' can be found in the section entitled 'Cross References' in which an effort has been made to assist the 'workfloor', those who have to apply and/or implement the Acquis, by providing under each heading the various places where relevant information has been included or contained. The 35 or so headings refer to finding-places contained in both this Handbook and also in ExCom Conclusions (not included herein) or the UNHCR Handbook (not included either).

Finally, it should be admitted that this Handbook will not be of everlasting value: the developments are manifold, the move from Third to First Pillar will result in a great many new instruments, and views and opinions are bound to develop during the following years as well. Still, it is hoped that this Handbook will fill some gaps, and will also prove to be as useful as we had in mind. The Acquis is after all a first and essential stone of the foundation of a common European asylum policy, the contours of which are now getting shape.

1. CONTRIBUTIONS

1.1	The EU Asylum Acquis: History and Context *Johannes van der Klaauw*	9
1.2	Harmonisation of Asylum and Immigration Policies: The Long and Winding Road from Amsterdam via Vienna to Tampere *Cornelis D. de Jong*	21
1.3	Decision-making in Justice and Home Affairs *Helen Staples*	37
1.4	Amsterdam and the Institutions *Georg Wirtz*	47
1.5	The Danish Exception Denmark's JHA Reservation and Amsterdam *Fabrice Liebaut*	57
1.6	The Enlargement Process and JHA Co-operation *Oliver Seiffarth*	61
1.7	Actors and Sources *Peter J. van Krieken*	73

1.1

THE EU ASYLUM ACQUIS: HISTORY AND CONTEXT

Johannes van der Klaauw[1]

TERMINOLOGY

The European integration process has been marked by the adoption of a constantly expanding body of European Community legislation, joint policies and actions which have accumulated, and been constantly revised over the past four decades. It comprises more than 100,000 pages of regulations, directives, and decisions, in addition to non-binding recommendations and opinions. This body has been expanded with the introduction, under the Maastricht Treaty, later revised by the Amsterdam Treaty, of new – mostly non-binding – instruments of common policy and joint action adopted within the framework of the common foreign and security policy and inter-governmental cooperation in justice and home affairs.

This body is normally referred to as the *acquis communautaire*, if reference is made to the Community standards developed according to the Community method within the so-called First Pillar. It represents the sum of the Community's laws, standards and practices which govern Member States' actions in matters within the competence of the Community and which cannot be disassociated from the achievements of the Community objectives. The body includes the founding Treaty of Rome as revised by the Single European Act and subsequently by the Maastricht Treaty and the Amsterdam Treaty, as well as the judgements of the European Court of Justice, which has jurisdiction over its application.

If one also includes the relatively recent results of cooperation within the Second and Third Pillar, including in asylum matters, the body of standards is normally called the 'acquis of the European Union and its Member States' (EU acquis). Most of the justice and home affairs (Third Pillar) elements of this wider set of standards are of a non-binding nature. With the entry into force of the Am-

---

[1] Senior European Affairs Officer, UNHCR Regional Office, Brussels. The views expressed in this contribution are made in a personal capacity and do not necessarily reflect the views of the Office of the High Commissioner for Refugees or the United Nations.

P.J. van Krieken (Ed.), *The Asylum Acquis Handbook*
© 2000, T.M.C.Asser Press, The Hague, the Röling Foundation and the authors

sterdam Treaty, the present non-binding EU asylum standards will be gradually codified into binding legislation and become part of *the acquis communautaire*.

THE EU ASYLUM ACQUIS: ORIGINS AND DEVELOPMENT

So far the EU acquis in asylum (and migration) has been developed as a result of inter-governmental consultations between the EU Member States. This approach was taken, in contradistinction to the Community approach involving actively all Community institutions (Commission, Council and European Parliament), since matters pertaining to justice and home affairs – among them asylum and migration – were long considered to be the sole responsibility of States, mindful of their sovereign right to establish their own policies and practices in these areas. With the adoption of the Single European Act in 1986, resulting in a programme for the abolition of internal border controls and the creation of a zone of free movement of persons, the (then) twelve EC Member States decided to start a regular consultation process with a view to improving the co-ordination of their policies in asylum and migration as part of a programme to adopt a number of flanking measures necessary to achieve the objectives of the Single Market. Earlier on, a limited number of Member States (the BeNeLux countries, France and Germany, joined by other EU Member States in the 1990s) had pioneered a form of 'enhanced cooperation' by moving forward in adopting common measures on visa policy, immigration controls at external borders, allocation of responsibility for the examination of asylum applications, police cooperation and judicial cooperation within the framework of the Schengen cooperation. The 1985 Schengen Accord was supplemented by an implementing Agreement in 1990, including a chapter on the determination of the responsibility for examining asylum claims among Contracting Parties.[2] This chapter was a first element of the developing asylum acquis, albeit prepared outside the institutional EU framework. This was also the case with other justice and home affairs instruments which resulted from dialogue and co-operation between the (then) EC Ministers responsible for immigration, including, in the area of asylum, the Dublin Convention[3] which was signed in 1990[4] and the so-called London Resolutions

---

[2] Title II, Chapter 7, Articles 28–38. This chapter was operational between 26 March 1995, when the Schengen Implementation Agreement entered into force, and 1 September 1997, when it was replaced by the provisions of the Dublin Convention.

[3] Convention Determining the State Responsible for Examining Applications for Asylum Lodged in One of the Member States of the European Communities.

[4] Denmark signed and ratified in June 1991. The Convention entered into force in the original twelve signatory states on 1 September 1997, and in the States which joined the EU in the mid-1990s on 1 October 1997 (Sweden, Austria) and 1 January 1998 (Finland).

which were adopted at the end of 1992.[5] These instruments were prepared and adopted outside any formal institutional structure, but showed the increasing interest of Member States to adopt a common approach to the implementation of some key elements of procedural asylum law. This was considered necessary as a natural complement to the adoption of a common mechanism to determine responsibility for processing asylum applications in order to avoid 'orbit' situations in which no State would assume responsibility for a claim, or 'forum shopping' where asylum applicants, rejected by one Member State, would be able to reapply in another Member State.[6] Following the signature of the Dublin Convention, Member States adopted a number of acts to prepare for the implementation of the instrument, once the ratification process would be completed, related to, inter alia, procedures for decision-making and transfer, time limits, means of proof or situations where various of the Dublin criteria would be applicable.[7] Moreover, in response to the perceived increasing need for inter-governmental consultation on legislative and policy developments in asylum, as well as assessments of situations in countries of origin and their role in refugee status determination procedures, in 1992 Member States decided to establish a Centre for Information, Discussion and Exchange on Asylum (CIREA). The decision to create this forum, which is part of the EU asylum acquis, has resulted in the monthly exchange of information and consultations, without any decision-making competences, as well as the compilation of documentation on all relevant asylum matters, and has given impetus to the harmonisation of policies and practices.[8]

Following the entry into force of the Maastricht Treaty, the Third Pillar provided the EU Member States with a single institutional framework and a number of instruments to further develop joint policy and action in the area of justice and home affairs, including asylum matters. During the 'Maastricht-era' (1993–1999) EU Member States prepared and adopted, within the Council framework, a few additional non-binding instruments, mainly related to procedural and material

---

[5] Resolution on Manifestly Unfounded Applications for Asylum [MUA]; Resolution on a Harmonized Approach to Questions concerning Host Third Countries [HTC]: Conclusions on Countries in Which There is Generally no Serious Risk of Persecution [CoO], London, 30 November and 1 December 1992.

[6] Whether this means that the Dublin Convention, as stated in its objectives (see preamble), guarantees examination by at least one Member State, remains to be seen, in so far as Article 3(5) of the Convention allows the designated State to send the asylum applicant to a 'safe' third country. Moreover, the 1992 London Resolution para. 3(a) allows the State where the application is lodged to send the applicant to a third country prior to considering whether or not the Dublin provisions need to be applied.

[7] A compilation of these guidelines was published in the OJ 1997 L 281/1 of 14 October 1997.

[8] Since early 1995, UNHCR has been participating as an observer in (part of) CIREA meetings, providing country expertise. The Justice and Home Affairs Council of 20 June 1994 adopted guidelines for joint reports on third countries to be prepared by CIREA (OJ C 274/52). Exchange, information and research on border control and immigration matters takes place in CIREFI (Council Conclusions of 30 November 1994, OJ C 274/50, 19 September 1996).

asylum law, such as a Resolution on minimum guarantees for asylum procedures[9] and a Joint Position on the harmonized application of the refugee definition of the 1951 Convention.[10] In addition, EU Member States agreed on a non-binding model for bilateral readmission agreements to be concluded between individual Member States and third States,[11] and, in the wake of the Bosnia crisis, a Resolution outlining some general principles governing a burden-sharing mechanism for the admission of temporary protected persons in situations of mass influx.[12] Also, a Resolution on the treatment of unaccompanied minors,[13] including minor asylum applicants, was added to the list of instruments. During the period 1997–1999, the EU Commission made use of its right, shared with Member States, to initiate under the Third Pillar a proposal on temporary protection. However, this proposal, including a revised version, met with strong opposition by some Member States which prevented it from being adopted.

It may be clear that the EU asylum acquis – as is the case with all other policy areas where the EU is legislating and developing common policies and practices – is constantly evolving. A first indication of what elements constituted the acquis in asylum was given in the Opening Statement delivered by the President of the Council at the Ministerial meetings launching the Accession Conferences

---

[9] Resolution on minimum guarantees for asylum procedures, 20 June 1995, OJ C 274/13, 19 September 1996 [MG].

[10] Joint Position (...) on the harmonized application of the definition of the term of 'refugee' in Article 1 of the Geneva Convention of 28 July 1951 relating to the Status of Refugees, 4 March 1996 (OJ L 63/10, 13 March 1996). This is the only Joint Position of its kind on asylum adopted within the framework of the Third Pillar – the status of the instrument is unclear as it has been copied from Second Pillar instruments; this particular instrument states explicitly that it shall not bind the legislative authorities or affect decisions of the judicial authorities of Member States.

[11] Council Recommendation of 30 November 1994 concerning a specimen bilateral readmission agreement between a Member State and a third country (OJ 274/20, 19 September 1996). EU Member States have also drawn up a set of implementing guidelines: Council Recommendation of 24 July 1995 on the guiding principles to be followed in drawing up protocols on the implementation of readmission agreements (OJ 274/25, 19 September 1996). On 2 December 1999, the Justice and Home Affairs Council adopted a standard readmission clause for insertion in partnership and cooperation agreements between the Community (and its Member States) and third countries (Council press release 13461/99 – Presse 386).

[12] Council Resolution on burden-sharing with regard to the admission and residence of displaced persons on a temporary basis, 25 September 1995 (OJ C 262/1, 7 October 1995). The Resolution was supplemented by a Council Decision on an alert and emergency procedure for burden-sharing with regard to the admission and residence of displaced persons on a temporary basis, 4 March 1996 (OJ L 63/10, 13 March 1996). This mechanism has so far not been used by the EU Member States, although some Member States wanted to invoke it during the Kosovo emergency in April 1999 when humanitarian evacuation from the former Yugoslav Republic of Macedonia had to be arranged.

[13] Council Resolution of 26 June 1997 on unaccompanied minors who are nationals of third countries (OJ C 221/23 of 19 July 1997). Although also dealing with the situation of separated children seeking entry for immigration purposes, the instrument largely deals with the various aspects of the treatment of asylum claims lodged by this group, including issues related to admission, procedural treatment, care and maintenance and return.

of Austria, Finland, Norway and Sweden in February 1993 relating to justice and home affairs. This was amplified in a similar Opening Statement by the President of the Council at the opening of accession negotiations with the candidate countries in Central Europe, the Baltic States, and Cyprus in early 1998. A full compilation of the asylum acquis was subsequently drawn up and adopted in the Council in May 1998. In a covering memorandum accompanying the list,[14] the Presidency of the Council summarizes a number of salient points related to the scope and nature of the acquis in justice and home affairs (including asylum). Pointing out the evolving nature of the acquis, the Council acknowledges that any list will require regular updating.[15] Furthermore, it stresses the need for monitoring, assistance and evaluation if effective implementation of the acquis is to be achieved. Although stated in the context of preparations for accession by applicant countries, the need for monitoring is equally important in EU Member States whose asylum systems are not yet fully developed, as is the case for instance in Greece, Portugal or Ireland.

The EU acquis in asylum includes conventions or instruments (resolutions, recommendations) established within the framework of the Third Pillar of the Maastricht Treaty (Article K 3), as well as those instruments adopted as a result of inter-governmental cooperation prior to the establishment of the Third Pillar. Although the latter are not the result of EU decision-making, such as the Dublin Convention, applicant States are nevertheless required to become a party to them 'in the same way as the Member States have done in the past'.

Part of the acquis is also a category of conventions or other binding instruments which are 'inseparable from the attainment of the objectives of the Treaty on European Union' (as now amended by the Treaty of Amsterdam). New members must accede to these instruments without reservations, in order to honour the international obligations to which all Member States are – and future ones should be – committed. In the asylum area, the 1951 Convention and the 1967 Protocol, as well as the European Convention on Human Rights, are part of the EU asylum acquis, since the elements of this part of the acquis refer to these international refugee law and regional human rights law instruments.[16]

---

[14] Council document 6473/3/98 REV 3 LIMITE, JAI 7 ELARG 51, 25 May 1998.

[15] As has been done by the Commission in early 1999 (see the Commission's website http://u-e.eu.int/ejn/vol_a3_Adhesion/06473-r3-en.html).

[16] An open question is whether the case-law related to the European Convention, as well as the interpretative guidance as contained in ExCom conclusions, needs to be considered as part of the EU acquis in the larger sense. Rulings by the EC Court of Justice are part of the acquis proper, yet this is apparently different for interpretative case-law and guidance related to instruments which are inseparable from the EU objectives but have been drafted in international, not EU fora.

THE ASYLUM HARMONIZATION PROCESS

The creation of a common area of freedom of movement and respect for the basic rights of those residing in it or seeking access to it has been the main force behind the development of the asylum acquis and the efforts of Member States to harmonize their policies and practices in this area. External factors have also contributed to this process, such as the substantial intensification of migratory movements, the increasing complexity of the refugee problem and the concomitant pressures on Member States' asylum systems. Harmonization of asylum and migration policy was initially not regarded as an end in itself but rather as a means of reorienting policies in order to equip Member States with common instruments to combat illegal immigration and the abuse of the asylum procedure, as well as to regulate admission for legal purposes (labour, family reunion) and to strengthen the position of legally residing non-EC citizens. Harmonization of asylum policy was seen more specifically as a logical step towards allowing Member States to have mutual trust in the quality and efficiency of each other's asylum systems as a pre-condition to the fair and efficient operation of the Dublin mechanism.[17] Member States therefore took a pragmatic approach to harmonization in so far as readjusting their policies could help to improve the efficiency of their cooperation and the speed of joint decision-making in order to solve common problems.

Member States were originally not primarily interested in establishing a body of binding obligations and instruments, as was the case in policy areas where Community competence in legislative and policy development had long been established, and where complete harmonization of law, policies and practice was a goal in itself. Due to an intensification of cooperation under, first, the Schengen Agreement and, later, the Dublin Convention, and as a result of the progressive development of a common understanding of key aspects of procedural and material asylum law in the mid-1990s, Member States started to change their attitude towards the harmonization process as such, as well as the level of harmonisation to be attained. In the area of asylum, Member States took an interest in the establishment of a comprehensive set of standards applicable in all Member States in a non-discriminatory manner. They also started to voice concern about the limitations to inter-governmental cooperation which was mainly serving States' interests, yet did not address the rights of the individual (asylum seekers, refugees, immigrants) – whereas the Union's vocation as an area of freedom and respect

---

[17] Similarly, the preparation of a (draft) Convention on the crossing of external borders, designed in a situation in which immigration policies were not harmonized, had to be implemented by a host of measures aimed at harmonizing Member States' admission and expulsion policies and practices in order to prepare for effective implementation of the Convention (by early 2000 still not signed, however, due to an ongoing dispute between Spain and the United Kingdom over its application in Gibraltar).

for basic rights and values needed to be given content, credibility and visibility.[18] These developments ultimately resulted in the decision to shift from inter-government cooperation to the Community method of law-making and the new conceptual framework of a common area of freedom, security and justice, which was subsequently incorporated in the revised Treaty (signed in Amsterdam in 1997). In preparing for this fundamental change, Member States started to review the piecemeal development of the loose set of non-binding (and largely ineffective) asylum policy instruments adopted so far, in order to identify the key elements of the future EU asylum acquis, with a view to laying the foundations for a coherent asylum system to be applicable throughout the Union.

The identification of these key elements resulted in the adoption of the asylum provisions of the Amsterdam Treaty (Article 63). They have been reaffirmed in the paragraph related to the common asylum system in the Tampere Summit Conclusions.[19] Under Title IV of the Amsterdam Treaty, the existing body of soft law instruments will be replaced by binding Community instruments such as Regulations, Directives, or Decisions. Their application will be subject to judicial scrutiny by the EC Court of Justice, although the competences of the Court will be limited in comparison to the Court's normal competences in ruling on Community matters.[20] The European Parliament will have increased consultation powers yet its opinions and proposals for amendments need not be followed up by the Commission or the Council.[21] Although judicial and democratic control of the implementation of the future elements of the EU asylum acquis will thus be limited, monitoring by the Council and Commission is likely to be increased and will undoubtedly contribute to the further harmonization of policies and practices. Moreover, the status of the future instruments will be clear and the present problems with the lacking, or partial, implementation of the existing soft law instruments should be overcome once legally binding instruments are in place. While existing resolutions and recommendations are likely to be used as a basis for drawing up the new binding instruments, the deficiencies of these texts must not be reproduced. Indeed, the Commission has indicated its intention, in draw-

---

[18] Article F of the Maastricht Treaty, and Article 6 of the Amsterdam Treaty stipulate that the Union is to respect fundamental rights, as guaranteed by the European Convention on Human Rights and as they result from Member States' constitutional traditions, as general principles of Community law.

[19] Presidency Conclusions, Tampere European Council, 15–16 October 1999, paragraph 14.

[20] Article 68 of the Treaty limits the Court's competences in matters pertaining to Title IV of the Treaty to preliminary rulings on a question of interpretation of a Treaty provision, upon the request of a Member State, the Council or the Commission. The ruling, however, cannot influence judgments issued by national courts or tribunals. The latter may seek a preliminary ruling from the EC Court of Justice, provided the request is submitted by a court of last instance, and such a ruling is considered necessary to enable the court or tribunal to pronounce its own judgment.

[21] Article 67 refers to merely consultating the European Parliament whose competences in Title IV matters are thus considerably limited in comparison with Parliament's general competences as laid down in Article 251 (including co-decision).

ing up a Directive on asylum procedures, to revisit some of the concepts and principles found in existing soft law instruments and to propose the removal of some of the exceptions and derogations which weaken these instruments.[22]

THE RELEVANCE OF THE EU ASYLUM ACQUIS FOR THE ACCESSION PROCESS

In addition to factors inherent to the European integration process, the requirements of the successive stages of EU enlargement have equally contributed to the development and 'codification' of the EU acquis. In order to prepare the EU for enlargement with the accession of all Central European and Baltic States, Cyprus and Malta, EU Heads of State, meeting in Copenhagen in June 1993, defined the criteria stipulating the requirements of membership. According to the 'Copenhagen criteria', States which want to be considered eligible for the opening of accession negotiations must have achieved stability of institutions, and guarantee democracy, the rule of law, human rights, and respect for and protection of minorities; have in place a functioning market economy as well as the capacity to cope with competitive pressure and market forces within the EU; and be able to take on the obligations of membership, including adherence to the aims of political, economic and monetary union. Since the EU acquis lies at the basis of the obligations of membership, concrete negotiations on accession with applicant countries have taken as a starting point ability to take on the EU acquis in law and practice.

Since the acquis is constantly evolving, its scope and contents as they exist at the time of accession will have to guide the Commission in the screening of, and subsequent negotiations on, the applicant's ability to meet the requirements of membership in practice. Whereas new Member States should be able to apply the acquis in full upon accession, transition periods of definite and reasonable duration may be necessary in certain duly justified areas, thus not putting at risk the progressive integration of the new members into the EU within a limited period of time. The Community has identified areas where transition periods should be few and brief, such as those linked to the extension of the Single Market, and areas where transition arrangements could be spread over a definite period of time – but only where the candidate country can demonstrate that alignment is underway and that it is committed to investing in the establishment of the necessary structures and the enhancement of required capacities.[23]

---

[22] Commission Working Document, Towards common standards on asylum procedures, SEC (1999) 271 fin, 3 March 1999, para. 10.

[23] The six countries with which accession negotiations were opened in March 1998 have reportedly not asked for a transition period in the area of justice and home affairs, suggesting that they will be ready to apply the acquis in this area in full by the time they are accepted as EU Member States.

The acquis is thus an essential element in the accession process: it constitutes the basis for the rights and obligations of membership and needs to be applied and enforced – some parts immediately, others gradually – upon accession. Without a clear commitment on the part of candidate countries, as well as demonstrable efforts to invest in institution- and capacity-building, membership will not be accepted. During accession negotiations, the EU regularly reviews the applicant country's progress in adopting the acquis and in preparing itself for membership. An analytical examination of the acquis with candidate countries is undertaken by the Commission ('screening') – first in a multilateral context with all candidate countries to explain the nature of EU legislation, followed by bilateral sessions following the formal opening of accession negotiations. The latter type of screening, organized around the different chapters of the acquis, including justice and home affairs, is aimed at identifying areas where there can be problems in accession negotiations.[24]

In order to prepare applicant countries to apply the acquis, the EU has adopted a pre-accession strategy for each of the applicant countries. This strategy is governed by a set of clearly defined objectives and a time-frame for the implementation of agreed short- and medium-term priorities. The transposition of EU standards into law and their effective implementation are central to this process. The strategy is also aimed at familiarizing the applicant countries with EU policies and procedures through the possibility of participation in Community programmes and training and exchange. The EU's assistance programme to Central Europe (PHARE) now includes, for each applicant country, training and assistance, as well as infrastructural support, in the area of asylum. In early 1997, a horizontal programme was established aimed at assessing the needs and priorities for capacity-building and improving inter-State dialogue and cooperation between applicant countries and with EU Member States. National PHARE programmes in support of institution-building and enhancement of practitioner capacities now also include asylum-related projects, although priorities remain primarily with border management and control and combating organized crime. Co-operation with EU Member States – through the transfer of expertise, including twinning arrangements – is of essence here, as is the involvement of competent regional and international organisations, such as UNHCR for the asylum area. Existing training and exchange programmes for EU Member States, such as the Odysseus programme in the areas of asylum and migration, are now also open to

---

[24] Whereas the Commission undertakes the 'screening' in the context of preparations for accession, EU Member States meeting in Council have set up a 'Collective Evaluation Group' tasked with collecting, analysing and evaluating information relating to the effective implementation by candidate countries of the EU acquis in justice and home affairs. The evaluation is a continuing process which will accompany the enlargement process at all its stages, and the Commission is expected to take account of the regular evaluations of the Group when reviewing priorities and objectives of the Accession Partnerships, concluded with applicant countries.

applicant countries (and certain third countries), in order to familiarize themselves with relevant parts of the EU acquis.

In all these programmes, the EU acquis is the basis for whatever policies and practices are developed and exchanged and for whatever standards there are to be introduced, applied and multiplied in the systems of candidate countries. Training on related international standards will be a useful (necessary) complement, but the minimum basis remains the EU acquis. The acquis, however, is characterized by some flexibility, allowing, as a result of the non-binding nature of the individual instruments, for the adoption of more favourable provisions in national law and procedures. It has been recommended therefore that relevant international standards be also taken into account, if only to avoid that the minimum standards of the acquis will turn into maximum standards, instead of representing a starting point for more inclusive and detailed legislative and policy development.[25]

TOWARDS AN AREA OF FREEDOM, SECURITY AND JUSTICE IN AN ENLARGED UNION

With the progressive development of a common asylum system based on the relevant provisions of Title IV of the Amsterdam Treaty (primarily Article 63) the EU asylum acquis will be further expanded and, moreover, codified in Community law instruments. This is a welcome development in so far as it can contribute to the establishment of a coherent and consistent body of standards applicable throughout the Union. This will also help to realize the establishment of a common asylum procedure and a uniform status for those granted asylum, as referred to in the Tampere Summit (paragraphs 14 and 15). Both the Amsterdam Treaty provisions and the Tampere Summit Conclusions refer to the 1951 Convention as the basis on which the future *acquis communautaire* in asylum is to be built, and this in taking a 'full and inclusive' approach to the 1951 Convention.

The question remains what level of harmonization will be achieved, and what level of standards will be aimed at in developing the future acquis. Although the Tampere Conclusions suggest that Member States want to move beyond minimum levels of harmonisation of their asylum laws and policies, whether this will be realised remains to be seen. In the context of initial discussions on a future instrument on asylum procedures, Member States have indicated their intention to favour gradual harmonization, through the adoption of common standards allowing them to retain certain particularities of their procedure, rather than a pre-

---

[25] The PHARE Horizontal Programme on Justice and Home Affairs 1996–1999 includes a Joint Support Programme on the application of the EU acquis on asylum *and related standards and practices* in the Associated Countries of Central and Eastern Europe (emphasis added), which involves UNHCR (as well as EU Member State experts).

scriptive approach which would require all Member States to apply exactly the same procedure. The ambitions of the drafters of the future acquis may therefore have to be tempered as regard the possibilities of full harmonization which will remain a long-term objective. They should rather take up the challenge to avoid the acceptance of minimum standards based on the lowest common denominator[26] and to develop for each instrument a consistent set of standards, each representing high levels of protection in accordance with existing international refugee law principles.

In adopting a coherent, protection-based strategy towards the development of the acquis communautaire in asylum the Commission and Member States should seize the opportunity to rethink the order of priority for developing the various standards constituting this part of the acquis. Whereas the existing soft law is predominantly of a procedural nature, a common asylum system should take as a starting point a common understanding of the interpretation and application of the definition of a 'refugee' and the content and legal basis of the refugee status. Once agreement on who qualifies as a refugee has been reached, a common approach to complementary forms of protection can be developed. Simultaneously, the various procedural issues can be addressed in a Community instrument developing procedural standards in accordance with principles accepted in international asylum law. Once these core elements of the common asylum system are adopted, then common standards for the reception of asylum-seekers, criteria and procedures for the allocation of responsibility for processing applications (Dublin mechanism), and a common approach to temporary protection and burden-sharing in situations of mass influx can be elaborated. However, the Vienna Action Plan adopted in December 1998 has already set the priorities for the development of the asylum instruments according to a two-year and five-year period. All procedural elements – already covered by existing soft law – have been listed under the short-term priorities, whereas issues of substantive asylum law (including a common interpretation of the refugee definition) have been put back as medium-term priorities.

The EU asylum acquis will be transformed into a body of binding Community instruments within a period of five years following the entry into force of the Amsterdam Treaty (1999). It is hoped that the future instruments will aim at high protection standards in accordance with principles elaborated by competent bodies in international fora (EXCOM Conclusions, Council of Europe/CAHAR Recommendations). This would be within the spirit of the protection-oriented language of the Tampere calling, inter alia, for the 'full and inclusive' application of the 1951 Convention as the cornerstone of a future common asylum system. This is not only important for the EU in its present composition, but also in view

---

[26] With the Treaty requirement of unanimity voting (Article 67) there is, however, a significant risk of acceptance of standards at the lowest level, as well as an emptying of their substance as a result of ongoing controversy which cannot be solved by consensus.

of its future enlargement, as well as with regard to the 'export value' of the EU standards, which States outside Europe are inclined to copy. The asylum institution came to fruition in Europe first, and Europe should be faithful to its values and traditions by giving a proper legal and political dimension to the right to asylum in the future area of freedom, security and justice.

1.2

HARMONISATION OF ASYLUM AND IMMIGRATION POLICIES
The long and winding road from Amsterdam via Vienna to Tampere

Cornelis D. de Jong[1]

1. INTRODUCTION

European co-operation in the fields of asylum and immigration policies has undergone major changes during the 1990s. Originally, these policies were a matter of purely intergovernmental co-operation between the Member States. After the entry into force of the Maastricht Treaty on European Union, on 1 November 1993, this form of co-operation was institutionalised within the European Union through the introduction of the so-called 'Third Pillar'. Although on the basis of the Maastricht Treaty the European institutions had a certain role to play, this form of institutionalised co-operation was still mainly intergovernmental, since Member States themselves took the final decisions, and this on the basis of consensus only. The Treaty of Amsterdam, which entered into force on 1 May 1999, goes a considerable step further, and no longer defines immigration and asylum policies as mere areas of common interest, but as part of Community Policies aimed at the progressive realisation of an area of freedom, security and justice. Even though consensus decision-making will persist at least during the first five years after the entry into force of the Treaty, the Council must accomplish a whole range of measures in this five-year period and co-operation is no longer *à la carte*.

These institutional changes reflect the growing importance of asylum and immigration policies. Migration pressures are high and unevenly spread over the

---

[1] From 1987 to 1999, Cornelis de Jong occupied a number of different positions in the fields of asylum and immigration policies. Up until 1993 he was head of the staff policy division of the Netherlands Ministry of Justice Aliens Affairs Department; from 1993 to 1996, he worked as Advisor to the Head of the Justice and Home Affairs Task Force of the European Commission and in 1997 and 1998 he was the Justice Counsellor in the Netherlands Permanent Mission to the EU. In 1999, he organised the first EUROMED-Seminar on migration and at the present time Mr. de Jong is the Co-ordinator of the Global Forum on Fighting Corruption and Safeguarding Integrity II, to be held in The Hague in May 2001.

P.J. van Krieken (Ed.), The Asylum Acquis Handbook
© 2000, T.M.C.Asser Press, The Hague, the Röling Foundation and the authors

Member States. The labour market situation and demographic trends differ between Member States, but in a number of Member States a discussion is emerging concerning the question of future needs for immigration, thus questioning the basis of traditional, restrictive immigration policies. Illegal immigration has become a phenomenon affecting most, if not all Member States. At the same time, the number of people seeking asylum or forms of temporary protection is still high and shows no real downward trend. On the contrary, some Member States are facing all-time highs when it comes to the number of asylum applicants. And last but not least, the integration of those legally resident in one of the Member States, continues to pose challenges.

This article is composed of three main parts. The first part contains an analysis of the present decision-making procedures, based on the Treaty of Amsterdam. The second part sets out the substantive measures that need to be taken by the Council, based on the Treaty of Amsterdam itself, the Vienna Action Plan and the Tampere Milestones. In the third and final part, I shall try to indicate the pitfalls of both the procedural and substantive arrangements and I shall try to suggest a number of measures in order to overcome these obstacles.

2. DECISION-MAKING BASED ON THE AMSTERDAM TREATY

Ideally, European decision-making is as transparent and democratic as national or local decision-making. European co-operation in the fields of Justice and Home Affairs has often been criticised as lacking such transparency and democracy. Such criticisms are partly justified, although the new arrangements under the Amsterdam Treaty have improved the situation.

Article 67 of the Treaty establishing the European Community (hereafter EC Treaty) lays down the ground rule for the first five years:

> 'During a transitional period of five years following the entry into force of the Treaty of Amsterdam, the Council shall act unanimously on a proposal from the Commission or on the initiative of a Member State and after consulting the European Parliament.'

During the first five years after the entry into force of the Amsterdam Treaty the situation remains rather hybrid. Whereas normal community law procedures reserve the right of initiative for the European Commission, Article 67 of the EC Treaty retains the shared right of initiative for both the Commission and Member States. The only slight difference with the previous arrangements is the fact that the right of initiative for the Commission now comes first, and the comparable right for Member States has been placed second.

The European Parliament needs to be consulted on each proposal, but a right of co-decision has not been introduced. The Council can therefore choose not to take into consideration the views of Parliament. Still, compared with the situation under the Maastricht Treaty, the position of the EP has been strengthened, as under the latter Treaty the Parliament was consulted on main lines of policy only.

Of course, the real decision-making process is more complicated than the wording of Article 67 may suggest. In practice, the Council hardly ever takes decisions spontaneously. These need to be prepared by bodies at technical or policy levels. In many other areas of Community policies, Coreper refers issues to a technical working group, which reports back directly to Coreper. This simple procedure has not been followed in the areas of immigration and asylum policies. Many Justice and Home Affairs Ministries have always maintained that it would not be useful to submit the outcome of technical discussions at working group level directly to Coreper. This has to do with the fact that Coreper consists of the EU Ambassadors and the influence of Foreign Offices on Coreper tends to be greater than that of JHA Ministries. In the case of asylum and immigration policies, it has therefore been agreed that the technical working groups report to a newly created Strategic Committee on Immigration, Frontiers and Asylum. The results from this Committee go to Coreper and the Council.

Although both the Commission and Member States have the right of initiative, in practice, Member States tend to rely quite heavily on the Commission. The internal Commission's organisation needs to be quickly adapted to this new workload. Although initiatives have been taken to remedy this situation, at this moment the responsible services of the Commission are still severely understaffed. It is not to be ruled out that eventually Member States will come 'to the rescue' of the Commission by submitting initiatives that the Commission could not prepare in time.

The Commission's power is not only hampered by a lack of staff, but it is also handicapped by the fact that, if the Council chooses not to accept a Commission proposal or to water it down, the Commission does not really have any power to act against the Council. Normally, the Commission can threaten the Council with withdrawing its proposal, thus threatening non-action. However, as long as Member States retain a right of initiative, the Council can act on the basis of a proposal from one or more Member States.

Despite this temporary setback, the position of the Commission has been considerably strengthened in practice by its role in the context of Community funding, by the fact that co-ordination within the Commission is easier than between various national ministries, and by the strong position of the Commission in the field of relations with third countries.

Under the Maastricht Treaty, whenever Member States felt that their co-operation required common funding, they had the choice between intergovernmental funding and Community funding. Intergovernmental funding would be a purely inter-State arrangement, perhaps supported by the Council Secretariat, but not requiring the co-operation of either the European Commission or the European Parliament. Community funding, however, automatically involves the European

Parliament, since it has to be based on a budget line, and in the end it is the European Parliament which decides whether such a budget line is created or not and if so, what the amount of that budget line will be. The Commission can become powerful, especially when it works closely together with the EP: it normally negotiates with the EP concerning the setting up of the budget line, it administers it, and it has to report to the EP concerning the use that has been made of it. Even if Member States have tried to limit the Commission's power in this respect through tight comitology arrangements, in the end the Commission retains much discretionary power, when administering a budget line. Since practically all Member States are interested in submitting proposals for funding, it is almost impossible for them to form coalitions and thus to push through certain decisions. Amidst all these opposing points of view, the Commission becomes the honest broker.

Under the Amsterdam Treaty, Community funding is the only option left for Member States. This means that the European Parliament has the final word and the Commission plays a very powerful role in administering the funds.

Although the Commission is not free from bureaucracy itself, it has to be recognised that communication between the various Directorates-General runs generally more smoothly than communication between comparable ministries at the national level. This means that often the Commission knows better what happens in other EU and EC bodies than Member States. Since asylum and immigration are multidisciplinary subjects, it should not come as a surprise that there are all sorts of linkages between these and other Union policies. Asylum and human rights are heavily interconnected. Immigration policies need to take account of, for example, international discussions on freedom of movement for service-providers, etc. The role of the Commission is considerably strengthened when it knows about such related developments.

Finally, in the field of external relations, the principle of *in foro interno, in foro externo* means that the Commission will be responsible for carrying out external negotiations relating to the acquis communautaire. This does not mean that all external negotiations in the fields of asylum and immigration policies are automatically the sole responsibility of the Commission: its negotiating competence is limited to those areas in which the Council has adopted EC instruments. Even if the Commission is responsible for the external negotiations it still needs a mandate from the Council and such negotiations often require a flexible position on the part of the Commission, which means that the mandates cannot be formulated too narrowly. In practice, therefore, the Commission has obtained an important new role in this respect.

Article 68 of the EC Treaty provides the Court of Justice with jurisdiction to give preliminary rulings concerning the interpretation of the Treaty, or the validity and the interpretation of acts of the institutions of the Community. However, these questions must have been raised in a case pending before a court or a tribunal of a Member State against whose decisions there is no judicial remedy under national law. The Court of Justice shall have no jurisdiction to rule on any measure or decision relating to the maintenance of law and order and the safeguarding of internal security. In addition to the courts or tribunals referred to above, the Council, the Commission or a Member State may also request the Court of Justice to give a ruling concerning the interpretation of the Treaty or the validity and the interpretation of acts of the institutions of the Community.

Five years after the entry into force of the Treaty of Amsterdam, further changes can be expected. One such change automatically follows from the text of the Treaty itself: the Commission will obtain an exclusive right of initiative, although it shall examine any request made by a Member State that it should submit a proposal to the Council (Article 67, paragraph 2). In other words, the Commission's position will be similar to its regular position in the EC. The fact that it has to examine Member States' requests does not mean much, for the Commission can always back by concluding that after thorough examination it does not see the need for a formal proposal.

Other changes will require further decisions by the Council. This holds true for the introduction of decision-making by qualified majority. It also holds true for strengthening the role of the European Parliament from a consultative to a co-decisive role. These changes can only be decided upon unanimously after consultation with the EP. It remains to be seen if in 2004 such unanimous decisions can be made.

Much more could be said about the provisions of the Treaty of Amsterdam: for example, the entire situation is further complicated by a number of Protocols which contain special provisions for the United Kingdom and Ireland, and Denmark. Furthermore, with the Treaty of Amsterdam the provisions of the Schengen Agreement are incorporated in EC law, including the special arrangements of the Schengen partners with Norway and Iceland. These complications do not alter the main conclusion, however, that is that the Treaty of Amsterdam firmly embeds immigration and asylum policies within an EC framework. The position of the European institutions is not yet as powerful as under normal Community law and although this will be partly redressed in 2004, voting procedures and the role of the EP can only be strengthened, if by then all Member States will agree to these steps.

3. THE IMMIGRATION AND ASYLUM AGENDA

The Treaty of Amsterdam sets a number of targets in the fields of asylum and immigration. A large number of measures need to be taken within the first five years after the entry into force of the Treaty, that is before 1 May 2004. These measures concern:[2]

a) the ensuring of the absence of any controls on persons, be they citizens of the Union or nationals of third countries, when crossing internal borders (Art. 62.1);
b) standards and procedures to be followed by Member States in carrying out checks on persons at the external borders of the Member States (Art. 62.2a);
c) rules on visas for intended stays of no more than three months (Art. 62.2b);
d) the conditions under which nationals of third countries shall have the freedom to travel within the territory of the Member States during a period of no more than three months (Art. 62.3);
e) criteria and mechanisms for determining which Member State is responsible for considering an application for asylum submitted by a national of a third country in one of the Member States (Art. 63.1a);
f) minimum standards on the reception of asylum seekers in Member States (Art. 63.1b);
g) minimum standards with respect to the qualification of nationals of third countries as refugees (Art. 63.1c);
h) minimum standards on procedures in Member States for granting or withdrawing refugee status (Art. 63.1d);
i) minimum standards for giving temporary protection to displaced persons from third countries who cannot return to their country of origin and for persons who otherwise need international protection (Art. 63.2a);
j) illegal immigration and illegal residence, including repatriation of illegal residents (Art. 63.3b).

Other measures, which are not subject to the five-year period deadline, concern:
a) promoting a balance of effort between Member States in receiving and bearing the consequences of receiving refugees and displaced persons (Art. 63.2b);
b) conditions of entry and residence, and standards on procedures for the issue by Member States of long-term visas and residence permits, including those for the purpose of family reunion (Art. 63.3a);
c) defining the rights and conditions under which nationals of third countries who are legally resident in a Member State may reside in other Member States (Art. 63.4).

These subjects are by no means new. Member States have co-ordinated their policies in these areas since the early 1990s. However, in the so-called Vienna Action Plan, adopted by the JHA Council of 3 December 1998, the JHA-Council itself notes that:

> 'most of the instruments adopted so far suffer from two weaknesses:
> – they are frequently based on 'soft law', such as resolutions or recommendations

---

[2] The full text of the relevant Articles can be found elsewhere in this Handbook (Chapter 5.1).

that have no legally binding effect;
- they do not have adequate monitoring arrangements.'

The Council further states that 'the commitment in the Amsterdam Treaty to use European Community instruments in the future provides the opportunity to correct where necessary these weaknesses'.

Thus, the Council is facing an enormous challenge: it has to adopt formal, legally binding EC instruments on each of the subjects listed. The tricky part of this exercise is that in the past many instruments have been acceptable for all Member States precisely because they were soft law. But the Treaty of Amsterdam creates a rather peculiar imbalance: on the one hand, it demands that a large number of measures be taken within five years after the entry into force of the Treaty; on the other hand, it provides for decision-making by consensus during this period of time. Obviously, this has been a political compromise necessary to reach agreement among all Member States, but it does create a real burden for the Council, since every measure will have to be acceptable to all Member States, before it can be adopted.

The entire exercise is made even more complicated by the fact that once adopted, EC instruments will be subject to further interpretation by the European Court of Justice, in accordance with the conditions outlined above. This means that Member States will have to check the proposals twice: firstly, to see whether they constitute a problem for them as such; secondly, to see whether some formulations are so vague as to give rise to additional interpretative judgements of the European Court. The traditional way-out of adopting vague formulations therefore no longer works.

The EC Treaty provides several implicit solutions for the situation whereby States do not succeed in reaching agreement on the measures to be taken, but none of these is very helpful for the harmonisation process itself.

First, the Treaty only speaks of 'measures'. It does not define this concept. It could therefore be interpreted as non-legally binding measures. According to Art. 249 of the EC Treaty, EC instruments are: regulations, directives, decisions, recommendations and opinions. Only the first three instruments are legally binding; recommendations and opinions have no binding force. Whenever it proves to be completely impossible to reach consensus on a legally binding instrument, the Council could decide to adopt a recommendation or opinion instead. However, the Vienna Action Plan seems to reject this way out. By recognising the weakness of soft law and by expressing the wish to correct that weakness 'where necessary', the Council has introduced the basic principle that the word 'measure' in the asylum and immigration related provisions of the EC Treaty should normally be interpreted as referring to a legally binding instrument.[3]

---

[3] See also elsewhere in this Chapter (1.3), the contribution by Helen Staples.

Secondly, the Treaty normally refers to 'minimum standards'. There are two ways of looking at this. Looking at it from a positive side, it means that Member States remain free to be more liberal at the national level than the European standard. Looking at it from a more negative side, it means that whenever it becomes difficult to reach a unanimous decision, the Council may decide to adopt a less humanitarian norm, since the instrument contains only 'minimum standards' anyway. This, I fear, will prove to be the solution that will be applied in most of the cases under consideration. The Vienna Action Plan also tries to establish some ranking among the most urgent measures. It stipulates in this respect that:

'Particular priority needs to be attached to combating illegal immigration on the one hand, while on the other hand ensuring the integration and rights of those third country nationals legally present in the Union as well as the necessary protection for those in need of it even if they do not meet fully the criteria of the Geneva Convention.'

The Action Plan makes a further distinction between measures to be taken within two years and measures to be taken within five years. Paragraph 36 of the Action Plan lists the following measures as those that have to be taken within two years:[4]
a) Rules on visas for intended stays of no more than three months;
b) Assessment of countries of origin in order to formulate a country specific integrated approach;
c) Continued examination of the criteria and conditions for improving the implementation of the Dublin Convention and of the possible transformation of the legal basis to the system of Amsterdam. Study concerning the issue of family members;
d) Implementation of Eurodac;
e) Minimum standards on procedures in Member States for granting or withdrawing refugee status with a view, inter alia, to reducing the duration of asylum procedures. Special attention to the situation of children;
f) Limitation of secondary movements by asylum seekers between Member States;
g) Minimum standards on the reception of asylum seekers with a particular attention to the situation of children;
h) Study with a view to establishing the merits of a single European asylum procedure;
i) Instruments on the lawful status of legal immigrants;
j) Coherent EU policy on readmission and return;
k) Combating illegal immigration through, inter alia, information campaigns in transit countries and in the countries of origin;
l) Further harmonising of Member States' laws on carriers' liability.

---

[4] The Vienna Action Plan has been included in Chapter 5.4 of this Handbook.

It should not be forgotten that in addition to these measures, the incorporation of the Schengen acquis brings with it the implementation of a number of measures, especially in the fields of external border controls and freedom to travel. Taking this into account, the list reflects the general priorities mentioned in the introductory paragraphs of the Vienna Action Plan, although asylum-related issues have been given a prominent place.

The Vienna Action Plan mentions two sets of measures to be taken as quickly as possible in accordance with the provisions of the Treaty of Amsterdam. These are:
a) Minimum standards for giving temporary protection to displaced persons from third countries who cannot return to their country of origin;
b) Promoting a balance of effort between Member States in receiving and bearing the consequences of receiving displaced persons.

The first of these instruments has to be finished within five years according to the Treaty of Amsterdam; the second has been exempted from this deadline. The fact that it is mentioned here undoubtedly reflects the need to accommodate the concerns of a number of EU Member States about the uneven distribution of the number of people in need of international protection among Member States.

Finally, the Vienna Action Plan mentions the following measures to be taken within a period of five years:
a) Identification and implementation of the measures listed in the European migration strategy;
b) Minimum standards with respect to the qualification of nationals of third countries as refugees;
c) Minimum standards for subsidiary protection to persons in need of international protection;
d) Improvement of the possibilities for the removal of persons who have been refused the right to stay;
e) Admission rules (Immigration);
f) Determination of the rights and conditions under which nationals of third countries who are legally resident in a Member State may reside in other Member States;
g) Extension of Schengen representation mechanisms with regard to visas;
h) Measures to improve security of the uniform format for visas.

On 15 and 16 October 1999, the European Council held a special meeting in Tampere, Finland, on the creation of an area of freedom, security and justice in the European Union. The Conclusions of this Council meeting, which are referred to as the 'Tampere Milestones' do not diminish in any way the significance of the Vienna Action Plan. Whereas the Action Plan indicates the various measures that need to be taken within specific deadlines, the Tampere Milestones develop these priorities in a more general way.

The conclusions relating to asylum and immigration are divided into the following chapters:
a) Partnership with countries of origin;
b) A common European Asylum System;
c) Fair treatment of third country nationals;
d) Management of migration flows.

Most of the measures which are mentioned in these chapters have also been included in the Vienna Action Plan. However, reference is also made to a new concept, i.e. 'a common asylum procedure and a uniform status for those who are granted asylum valid throughout the Union'. The European Council concluded that Community rules should lead to such a common procedure and asked the Commission to prepare a communication on this matter within one year.

4. CHALLENGES AHEAD

Considering that European co-operation in the fields of asylum and immigration policies is a relatively recent phenomenon, it must be recognised that much work has been done. However, the new EC Treaty, the Vienna Action Plan and the Tampere Milestones now put this process under enormous pressure to produce concrete results within well-defined periods of time.

The previous paragraphs show that many attempts were made to formulate priorities, each attempt following its own logic. I shall now try to deal with the challenges in each of the relevant areas, based on the lists mentioned above, but grouped together in what I consider to be a more logical order.

The development of a European migration strategy

In Paragraph 38(a) of the Vienna Action Plan the Council mentions the first of the measures to be taken within five years of the entry into force of the Treaty: the identification and implementation of the measures listed in the European migration strategy. This creates the impression that there is already such a strategy. However, in paragraph 34 of the Action Plan, the Council states that 'an overall migration strategy should be established in which a system of European solidarity should figure prominently'. This implies that the strategy referred to in paragraph 38(a) should still be elaborated. The Plan does not clarify the nature of the strategy other than the reference to European solidarity.

These contradictory statements can be explained by the fact that although the Austrian Presidency had submitted a paper which contained the basic elements of a possible migration strategy, this paper was never adopted by the Council. The Austrian document was valuable insofar as it reflected the need for a comprehensive approach, but some paragraphs created the impression that the 1951 Geneva Convention on the Status of Refugees had become obsolete and this overshadowed the entire discussion.

This means that theoretically the implementation of the Vienna Action Plan requires the elaboration and adoption of a new migration strategy. It would have been logical to see this as the main priority: the more specific measures could then be based on such an overall strategy. Once the overall objectives would have been firmly agreed upon, it would also be easier to formulate the appropriate practical implementing measures. However, Europe hardly ever works like that. In 1994, the European Commission already submitted a Communication, which contained all the necessary elements for a comprehensive approach on asylum and immigration. It addressed the root causes of migration pressures, admission policies, the issue of illegal immigration and the integration of third-country nationals legally resident on the territory of one of the Member States. Although the Council took note of this Communication, it did not consider it necessary itself to adopt a comparable document. Taking into account the more recent pressures caused by the various deadlines of the Treaty of Amsterdam, it has become even less likely that the Council will take the necessary time to formally adopt a migration strategy.

The challenge therefore becomes to build a strategy on the basis of actions that the Council does give priority to. In my opinion, a migration strategy should at least consist of the following elements:
– an analysis of the root causes and scope of migration pressures;
– monitoring Europe's immigration needs;
– a system expressing European solidarity.

The analysis of the root causes and scope of migration pressures gained momentum with the creation, in December 1998, of the High Level Working Group on Immigration and Asylum. At its meeting in Tampere, the European Council agreed to continue the mandate of the HLWG. It explicitly placed this decision in the context of the need for a comprehensive approach to migration addressing political, human rights and development issues in countries and regions of origin and transit. According to the Council, this requires combating poverty, improving living conditions and job opportunities, preventing conflicts and consolidating democratic states and ensuring respect for human rights, in particular the rights of minorities, women and children.

The mandate of the HLWG is broad: it includes the elaboration of action plans based on assessments of countries of origin with a view to, inter alia, addressing the root causes of forced migration. The action plans are multifaceted though: they can also contain material for further co-operation with transit countries and countries of origin in combating illegal immigration. And they can serve as a more common basis for the decisions of Member States' asylum adjudicators.

Step two of an effective migration strategy consists of a stocktaking exercise with regard to the immigration needs of Member States. These needs can be determined by demographic and economic developments, but they can also originate at a level of humanitarian standards that each Member State wants to defend. The Tampere Milestones seem to refer to such an exercise, when it is stated that:

> 'The European Council acknowledges the need for approximation of national legislations on the conditions for admission and residence of third country nationals, based on a shared assessment of the economic and demographic developments within the Union, as well as the situation in the countries of origin. It requests to this end rapid decisions by the Council, on the basis of proposals by the Commission. These decisions should take into account not only the reception capacity of each Member State, but also their historical and cultural links with the countries of origin.'

I think that if the Council succeeds in adopting such decisions, this will be a very important contribution to the negotiations on individual instruments. At the moment, Europe still lacks a commonly agreed philosophy with regard to immigration and asylum policies. National delegations often limit themselves to comparing their own national legislation with the European proposals, and take it for granted that their national legislation is to be preferred. It would be ideal if delegations were forced to rethink the basic assumptions on which their national policies are based.

Demographers have already pointed out that without immigration, Europe's population will quickly decrease. Normally, a decrease of the population is considered to produce major problems, especially when taking into account the rapid ageing of the population that goes hand in hand with such a development. It might therefore be most interesting to see how this relatively new trend may affect the traditionally sacred principle of a restrictive immigration policy. Similarly, the labour market situation in some EU Member States has developed from a labour surplus into a labour deficit. For economic reasons immigration may then be considered a tool to making up a possible shortage of national manpower.

Although all Member States are party to important international instruments, such as the Geneva Convention and the European Convention on Human Rights, there are still important differences between the national policies based on these international instruments. This holds true, in particular, for the right to family reunification. Despite the fact that in 1993 a soft law instrument had been adopted, Member States' policies are still fundamentally different.[5] It would therefore be vital for a European migration strategy to provide guidance with respect to fundamental principles concerning the admission of third-country nationals on humanitarian grounds.

Finally, a migration strategy should reflect European solidarity. This means that either the number of third-country nationals in need of international protec-

---

[5] The December 1999 draft regulation on family reunification has been referred to in a note to the relevant 1993 instrument as included in this Handbook.

tion or the costs relating to their reception, admission or alternatively their return should be divided evenly among Member States. In the case of asylum applicants, the existing arrangements under the Dublin Convention contain a mechanism for determining State responsibility for the examination of such applications. In the case of displaced persons seeking temporary protection through legal channels other than asylum, such a system of responsibility-sharing does not exist. Moreover, it is often argued that the existing Dublin arrangements are not fair, since they work to the disadvantage of peripheral States, because the overriding criterion is that the State where the asylum applicant entered the European Union is responsible.

I believe that eventually it will become inevitable that the Dublin arrangements will be replaced by a completely new system, in which asylum applications will be examined in special reception centres near the external borders of the EU. The decisions governing these applications could usefully be taken by a European board, and only in the case of positive decisions would the asylum applicants be referred to another Member State. However, it will take time before the Member States will be ready to place their confidence in such a European board and, moreover, such decision-making by a European board requires harmonisation through legally binding instruments of at least the main elements of refugee policy. It is therefore to be expected that for the time being discussions in the Council will tend to focus on financial forms of burden sharing. In this respect, the Commission has already submitted a proposal for a merger of the existing budget lines.

Even if in the short term far-reaching solutions to the problem of a lack of European solidarity may not be agreed upon, in the context of a migration strategy it should be possible to agree at least on the way forward: arrangements other than those under the Dublin Convention could then be usefully explored.

Harmonisation measures

Most of the actions listed in the EC Treaty, the Vienna Action Plan and the Tampere Milestones relate to harmonisation of policies. The development of a common European Asylum System, as required by the Tampere Milestones, not only relates to the Dublin arrangements mentioned above, but also brings with it the need for a common asylum procedure and a uniform status for those who are granted asylum valid throughout the Union.

As I stated before, the formal rules governing EC activity in this area during the first five years after the entry into force of the Treaty of Amsterdam are cumbersome. Without the introduction of qualified majority voting rules, it will be a major undertaking to agree on all of these harmonisation measures.

When harmonisation of asylum and immigration policies was first brought up at the level of the European Council, in 1991, one of the underlying ideas was that a European policy could easily be less restrictive and more humanitarian than individual policies of Member States. It was believed that at the European level there would be no need to fear that more humanitarian policies would constitute important pull factors, a consideration which had governed national policies for a long time.

However, both the Vienna Action Plan and the Tampere Milestones reflect a different political priority at this moment. Admittedly, reference is made to the need to respect international obligations, in particular the 1951 Geneva Convention on the Status of Refugees and its New York Protocol, but the overall tone is defensive: especially illegal immigration is seen as a major threat. The same holds true for the uncontrolled and unevenly spread numbers of people asking for international protection.

As I noted above, under these circumstances there is a real danger that Member States faced with enormous time pressures combined with the need for decision-making on the basis of consensus, will develop the most minimal of standards. As long as no agreement has been reached on a European migration strategy as outlined above, there is no objective yardstick against which the outcome of these negotiations can be measured. It will thus depend on the willingness of individual Member States to block certain measures, if, in their opinion, those measures would fall short of the humanitarian tradition as perceived by that Member State. This, however, is more easily said than done, since no Government likes the idea of being isolated by carrying the blame for blocking 'progress'.

Rights of third-country nationals legally resident in one of the Member States

The rights of third-country nationals legally resident in one of the Member States have become a real concern for the EU. Of particular importance is the following consideration included in paragraph 37c(iii) of the Vienna Action Plan:

> 'Within the competent Council bodies discussions could be held, taking account of the consequences for social equilibrium and the labour market, on the conditions under which, like Community nationals and their families, third country nationals could be allowed to settle and work in any Member State of the Union;
> ... although the Amsterdam Treaty does not request action to be accomplished in a five year period, efforts should be made towards an improvement of the situation in due time;'

In the Tampere Milestones, even more far-reaching conclusions can be found relating to the rights of third-country nationals:

> 'The European Union must ensure fair treatment of third country nationals who reside legally on the territory of its Member States. A more vigorous integration policy should aim at granting them rights and obligations comparable to those of EU citizens.

It should also enhance non-discrimination in economic, social and cultural life and develop measures against racism and xenophobia.'

The granting of freedom of movement to third-country nationals legally resident in one of the EU Member States has proven to be one of the most difficult measures to reach consensus on. However, the references cited above seem to indicate that nowadays this issue is considered to be a priority matter. Even so, I expect that it will prove to be difficult to make real progress in this area and thus it can be seen as a real additional challenge.

5. CONCLUSION

It is simply impossible in the context of this article to deal with all of the individual aspects of the development of a European asylum and immigration policy. But even the rather sketchy survey of the challenges ahead presented above shows that the next four years will be vital. When there is the political will to get things done, they normally will be done. I fear, however, that the enormous time pressures will make it difficult to agree on a logical package of legally binding instruments: it will depend very much on the role of the Commission, the European Parliament, public opinion and the position of individual Member States, whether the outcome of the negotiations will reflect the humanitarian approach as generally advocated in the Tampere Milestones.[6]

It is by no means easy for the European Commission to submit all the necessary proposals in time. However, I hope that the Commission will live up to its responsibility and will not lose sight of the need for a comprehensive approach as laid down in its own 1994 Communication. Even if it was felt unrealistic to invite the Council to agree on a comprehensive document outlining a real migration strategy, it would already be a step forward if the Commission clarified in each of its proposals how it relates to an overall strategy.

The European Parliament has of course limited powers, but since it will have to be consulted on each of the proposals for EC instruments, it can show that it has quality to offer. If its opinions contain consistent comments, it will become ever more difficult for the Council to ignore them. In the past, the EP has taken a vivid interest in defending Europe's humanitarian tradition: it would be extremely helpful and important if the EP continued this line of thinking.

Public opinion is not very consistent in respect of asylum and immigration policies. On the one hand, people tend to worry about immigration in general; on the other hand, there are many examples of people coming to the rescue of immigrants, even illegal immigrants, once they know them personally or when they

---

[6] For the involvement of the candidate Countries in this process, see Oliver Seiffarth's contribution elsewhere in this Chapter (1.6).

have been given a large amount of publicity. It is therefore difficult to see the public opinion per se as a key player in this respect. However, there are many influential NGOs which have specialised in parts of asylum and immigration policies. They could usefully contribute to the discussions by tabling concrete proposals and delivering comments on the proposals under discussion.

Finally, individual Member States could either use their right of initiative or their power of veto to exert influence. It would be a major step forward when Member States with a strong humanitarian tradition would join forces to steer the developments at the European level.

1.3

DECISION-MAKING IN JUSTICE AND HOME AFFAIRS

Helen Staples[1]

1. INTRODUCTION

The Treaty, signed by the Heads of States and Government in Maastricht in 1992 (the Treaty of Maastricht), established the Treaty on European Union (TEU). The pillar structure that was established by this Treaty has been compared with a Greek temple. The general provisions being the foundation and the roof. The pillars carrying the roof are the Treaty establishing the European Community, the Euratom and the European Coal and Steel Treaty (First Pillar), the provisions on Common Foreign and Security Policy in Title V of the TEU (Second Pillar) and the provisions in Title VI TEU on Co-operation in the Field of Justice and Home Affairs (Third Pillar). Measures to be adopted within the framework for Co-operation in Justice and Home affairs included, amongst others, asylum policy, rules governing the crossing by persons of external borders of the Member States and the exercise of controls thereon, as well as immigration policy and policy regarding nationals of third countries (Article K.1 TEU).

The entry into force of the Treaty of Amsterdam, on May 1, 1999, brought a significant change to European asylum and immigration policy. The Treaty of Amsterdam transferred asylum and immigration policies from the intergovernmental Third Pillar to a new Title, Title IV entitled Visas, Asylum, Immigration and other Policies related to Free Movement of Persons, in the Treaty establishing the European Community. This operation has left Police and Judicial Co-operation in Criminal Matters in Title VI TEU. Besides placing asylum and immigration policies in the Community Treaty, The Treaty of Amsterdam has also meant a renumbering of both the Community Treaty and the Treaty on European Union. Thus, the 'letter' numbering in the Union Treaty in the Maastricht version has been replaced by numbered provisions. For the Community Treaty this has

---

[1] Dr. Helen Staples is currently employed by the Faculty of Law of the University of Utrecht (the Netherlands). She is the author of *The Legal Status of Third Country Nationals Resident in the European Union* (Published by: Kluwer Law International, The Hague, 1999) defended on October 13, 1999 at the University of Utrecht.

P.J. van Krieken (Ed.), The Asylum Acquis Handbook
© 2000, T.M.C.Asser Press, The Hague, the Röling Foundation and the authors

meant that obsolete provisions were deleted and new provisions were inserted into this Treaty before the entire Treaty was renumbered. Unless otherwise indicated, references to Treaty provisions, be it the Treaty on European Union or the Community Treaty, will concern the provision as worded by the Maastricht Treaty.

Within the institutional framework for Co-operation in Justice and Home Affairs, the Council was to adopt measures in these fields by unanimous vote, acting upon an initiative of either one or more Member States or the Commission (Article K.3(2) TEU). The role assigned to the European Parliament in the legislative procedure was limited. This institution was informed regularly by both the Presidency and the Commission of discussions on matters concerning Justice and Home Affairs. In addition, the Presidency was required to consult the European Parliament on the principal aspects of activities and to ensure that the views of the European Parliament were duly taken into consideration (Article K.6 TEU). The European Parliament could ask questions of the Council and make recommendations to the latter institution. There was no guarantee that its views were actually taken into account on the adoption of a measure by the Council. As far as the European Court of Justice was concerned, the picture was the following. With the exception of the possibility to grant this Court jurisdiction in cases to interpret a provision in a Convention and to rule on any disputes regarding the application of a provision in a Convention, the European Court of Justice lacked the power to adjudicate in this policy area (Article L(b) TEU). Judicial control was thus left to the national judicial authorities in accordance with national rules of procedure.

Title VI TEU provided the Council with a set of new legal instruments for the adoption of measures in these fields. The legal instruments listed in Article K.2 TEU were:
– joint positions;
– joint actions; and
– conventions.

Title VI TEU also provided for the adoption of measures implementing joint actions or conventions. These measures are to be adopted by qualified majority vote. In addition, in order to promote co-operation so as to attain the objectives of Justice and Home Affairs, the Council could use any appropriate form and procedure.

There was no Treaty obligation to publish the measures adopted in the field of Justice and Home Affairs in the Official Journal of the European Community. A decision to publish legislative acts adopted within the framework for co-operation in Justice and Home Affairs was adopted by the Council in November 1995. This decision was published in the C-series of the Official Journal of the European Communities of September 19, 1996 along with a number of other measures adopted up to that date which had not already been published in that Journal.

In the following sections the legal instruments which can be used to adopt legislative measures in this policy area will be considered. Section 2 contains an analysis of these legal instruments. This section will be followed by an elaboration of the nature of these legal instruments (section 3). A final point that will be considered is the position of the candidate Member States vis-à-vis the acquis that has been developed in Justice and Home Affairs (section 4).

2. THE LEGAL INSTRUMENTS USED FOR JUSTICE AND HOME AFFAIRS

2.1 Legal Instruments with a Treaty Basis

Sui Generis Decisions
The Treaty on European Union provided the Council with new legal instruments for the adoption of measures concerning asylum and immigration. These instruments are joint positions, joint actions and conventions. If required, the Council could adopt measures implementing either a joint action or a convention. No specification as to the legal form of implementing measures was found in Title VI of the TEU. Besides these legal instruments, Article K.3(2)(a) TEU enabled the Council to use the appropriate form and procedures "to promote co-operation contributing to the pursuit of the objectives of the Union". Here again, Title VI TEU remained vague. It did not specify the circumstances dictating the use of a specific legal instrument. Neither was it established which legal instruments could be used by the Council to promote such co-operation. De facto this institution was thus given a monopoly in its choice of legal instrument and, consequently, the legal effects entailed by the act that would be eventually adopted (see further section 3). On more than one occasion, the Council has used this provision as a legal basis for Decisions. An example of a decision thus adopted is the Council Decision of 23 November 1995 on Publication in the Official Journal of the European Communities of acts and other Texts adopted by the Council in the Field of Asylum and Immigration (Official Journal of the European Communities 1996, C 274/1).

Joint positions
The first legal instrument listed in Article K.3(2) TEU is the joint position (sub. a). This Treaty provision does not specify what a joint position is. It also left in the dark the procedure to be followed by the Council when it adopted a joint position. Joint positions have been compared with common positions, which were introduced as legal instruments in Title V TEU, entitled Provisions on a Common Foreign and Security Policy. According to Article J.2 TEU, Member States had to ensure that their national policies conformed with a common position adopted within the framework of Title V TEU. This provision also required the Member States to uphold a common position in international organisations and at international conferences. Common positions in Title V thus served as guidelines

for action by Member States on the international playing field. An example of a joint position concerning asylum is the Joint Position (96/196/JHA) of 4 March 1996 defined by the Council on the basis of Article K.3 of the Treaty on European Union on the Harmonized Application of the Definition of the Term 'Refugee' in Article 1 of the Geneva Convention of 28 July 1951 relating to the Status of Refugees (Official Journal of the European Communities 1996, L 63/2). A second joint position that deserves to be mentioned here is Joint Position (96/622/JHA) of 25 October 1996 defined by the Council on the Basis of Article K.3(2)(a) of the Treaty on European Union, on Pre-Frontier Assistance and Training Assignments (Official Journal of the European Communities 1996, L 281/1).

Joint actions
The second instrument at the disposal of the Council acting within the framework of Title VI TEU was the joint action. From the wording of Article K.3(2)(b) TEU it followed that the Council could adopt a joint action if "the objectives of the Union can be attained better by joint action than by the Member States acting individually on account of the scale or effects of the action envisaged". Like Article K.3(2)(a) TEU, introducing the joint position, sub-paragraph (b), introducing the joint action, remained silent on what a joint action actually was. It merely stated the conditions under which the Council could adopt joint action. This was the case if the Member States acting collectively were considered to be better equipped to realise the objective sought. Two indications were given as to when this might be the case: the scale or effects of the envisaged action. In practice the discretionary power given to the Council gave those who were opposed to the Council's choice either to refrain from or to opt for joint action a hard time in contesting this decision. The joint action has not been used as a legal instrument to regulate questions related to asylum. Examples of joint action in other policy areas are:
– Joint Action (96/197/JHA) of 4 March 1996 adopted by the Council on the Basis of Article K.3 of the Treaty on European Union on Airport Transit Arrangements (Official Journal of the European Communities 1996, L 63/8); and
– Joint Action (98/700/JHA) of 3 December 1998 adopted by the Council on the Basis of Article K.3 of the Treaty on European Union concerning the setting up of a European Image Archiving System (FADO) (Official Journal of the European Communities 1998, L 333/4).

Conventions
The final legal instrument available to the Council acting as a legislator in the fields of asylum and immigration is the Convention. Conventions, so Article K.3(2)(c) TEU provided, were drawn up by the Council which subsequently recommended their adoption to the Member States. It was then for the Member States to adopt a Convention in accordance with their respective Constitutional

requirements. The Convention is an international agreement, a legal instrument long known in public international law.

Like most international agreements, the drawing up of Justice and Home Affairs Conventions has proven a slow, cumbersome means of realising the aims of co-operation in Justice and Home Affairs, especially since they required the approval of all of the Member States in accordance with their respective national procedures. An advantage of adopting a Convention rather than a joint action or a joint position is that the Member States could choose to grant the European Court of Justice jurisdiction to adjudicate on matters concerning the interpretation and application of provisions included in the Convention. Thus adjudication was possible on a non-ad hoc basis.

2.2 Legal Instruments without a Treaty Basis

Although the only instruments provided for, joint positions, joint actions and conventions have not been the only legal instruments used by the Council operating within the framework of Title VI TEU. Especially during the first years following the entry into force of the Treaty of Maastricht, the Council exhibited a clear preference for other legal instruments. Measures adopted in this period were adopted as resolutions, recommendations, decisions, declarations and conclusions. The explanation given for the Council's preference for these classic legal instruments, already at its disposal prior to the entry into force of the Treaty on European Union over the legal instruments listed in Article K.3(2) TEU are: a lack of political will and disagreement on the nature and binding force of the legal instruments found in Title VI TEU. In addition, they were considered to have the advantage of flexibility and of being capable of speedy adoption. A few examples of measures adopted in the form of a legal instrument not provided for in Title VI TEU are:
– Council Conclusions of 20 June 1994 concerning the Possible Application of Article K.9 of the Treaty on European Union to Asylum Procedures (Official Journal of the European Communities 1996, C 274/34);
– Guidelines for Joint Reports on Third Countries (adopted on June 20, 1994 and published in Official Journal of the European Communities 1996, C 274/52);
– Council Resolution of 20 June 1995 on Minimum Guarantees for Asylum Procedures (Official Journal of the European Communities 1996, C 274/13); and
– Joint principles for the Exchange of Data in CIREFI (Doc. 8927 CIREFI 35).

3. BINDING FORCE: THE CASE OF THE EUROPEAN UNION'S MEMBER STATES

3.1 Legal Instruments with a Treaty Basis

Conventions
The provisions in Title VI TEU were not clear as to the legal nature of the instruments which were at the disposal of the Council operating within this framework for co-operation. Conventions were considered to be legally binding instruments once they had been ratified by the Member States in accordance with their respective Constitutional procedures. The fact that the Member States had to approve of the text of a Convention in accordance with national law made these legal acts, acts of public international law. Thus it was the general principles of public international law that determined the binding force of the Conventions drawn up within the framework of Title VI TEU. Public international law leaves it for the States to determine the legal effects entailed by an act of public international law within their national legal order. Where a State party to an international agreement infringes an obligation flowing from that agreement, the other States party to that agreement can require compliance from the infringing State. Whether or not a measure of national law is required to give effect to an act of public international law depends on the view adhered to by a State concerning the effects of international law within its national legal order. Thus the effects of an act of public international law within the national legal order are determined by national law.

Joint positions, sui generis decisions and joint actions
Much has been said as to the legal nature of both joint positions and joint actions in Justice and Home Affairs. The reason why these two legal instruments gave rise to a debate as to their legal nature is the fact that the Treaty provision introducing joint positions and joint actions did not provide any insight into the nature of either of these legal instruments. The views adopted ranged from non-binding legislative acts to binding legislative acts. The general consensus can be summarised as follows. Both joint positions and joint actions may contain legally binding provisions. This however, is not necessarily the view advocated by the Member States. In the procedure leading to the ratification of the Treaty of Amsterdam the Dutch Government, for example, explicitly stated that joint positions adopted either prior to or after the entry into force of the Treaty of Amsterdam were in its opinion not capable of entailing legally binding effects.

In order to ascertain whether a provision in either a joint action or a joint position is binding, it will have to be assessed whether according to its objective and wording a joint position or joint action should be considered to be legally binding by nature. Additional criteria which have been put forward as an indication of the binding legal nature of a provision in a joint position or a joint action are:

- publication in either the L-series or the C-series of the European Communities Official Journal;
- the legal basis, if mentioned, given to a joint position or joint action; and
- the name that has been given to the act.

The same criteria may be used to establish whether a decision adopted with a view to promote co-operation in Justice and Home Affairs entails legal effect. The Council's Joint Position (96/196/JHA) of March 4, 1996 defined by the Council on the Basis of Article K.3 of the Treaty on European Union on the Harmonized Application of the Definition of the Term 'Refugee' in Article 1 of the Geneva Convention of 28 July 1951 relating to the Status of Refugees (OJ 1996, L 63/2) is used as an example of a joint position that entails legally binding effect.

Direct effect

Still a different question is whether an individual could successfully invoke a provision in a measure adopted within the framework for co-operation in Justice and Home Affairs in proceedings pending before a national judicial authority. The mere fact that a Member State could be held to comply with an obligation included in a measure adopted within the framework of Title VI TEU, does not mean that an individual may successfully rely on a provision in that measure that establishes a right for him. The Court of Justice had little to no powers to adjudicate on matters concerning measures adopted by the Council in the policy areas brought together in Title VI TEU. Therefore, it was the national judicial authorities adjudicating under their national rules of procedure which determined whether a provision in a binding legal measure could be invoked successfully in judicial proceedings by an individual. In other words, whether that provision could be considered to have direct effect within the national legal order of a Member State. A disadvantage is that this could lead to differences between the Member States which could not be corrected by an international judicial authority.

2.2 Legal Instruments without a Treaty Basis

The Council has not limited itself to adopting measures concerning co-operation in Justice and Home Affairs in the form of the legal instruments provided for in Article K.3(2) TEU. Thus there are numerous Justice and Home Affairs measures which have been adopted in the form of other legal instruments. These legal acts share with the joint actions and joint positions which have been adopted by the Council in Justice and Home Affairs the fact that their legal nature has not been provided for.

As a rule the measures which have been adopted in the form of legislative instruments not provided for in Title VI TEU are considered to be measures of soft law. As such it can be assumed that they are non-binding legal acts. This point of view was confirmed by the Council and the Commission in their Action Plan of December 3, 1998 in which they established the action to be adopted and the timetable for the adoption of measures ensuring the realisation of the Area of Freedom, Security and Justice, introduced by the Treaty of Amsterdam (Official Journal of the European Communities 1999, C 19/1). The fact that these measures were classed as soft Union law, however, did not necessarily mean that a Member State could disregard an obligation imposed on it by such a measure. The consequences of behaviour infringing an obligation found in an act of soft law could have been considerable. Like any act of public international law, the principle of good faith compelled the Member States to comply with the obligations imposed on them by a measure of soft Union law adopted within the framework for co-operation in Justice and Home Affairs.

4. CANDIDATE MEMBER STATES AND THE UNION ACQUIS

No explicit provision, comparable with the obligation found in Article 8 of the Schengen Protocol, is made concerning the obligations of the candidate Member States vis-à-vis adherence to the Justice and Home Affairs acquis. As part and parcel of the Union acquis, candidate Member States will be obliged to abide by the measures adopted by the Council co-operating in Justice and Home Affairs when they become full Members of the Union. Unless otherwise provided for in the Act of Accession, at this point, the measures adopted within the framework for co-operation in Justice and Home Affairs will entail the same legal effects for the new Member States as they do for the 'old' Member States.

This, however, does not explain the position of these States vis-à-vis this acquis during the period preceding their accession to the European Union. As legal acts of the Member States, candidate Member States are, in principle, isolated from the effects entailed by measures of Justice and Home Affairs. No rule of public international law can compel them to abide by the rules adopted amongst other States to which they are not a party. However, in the negotiation procedures preparing the candidate Member States for their accession to the European Union, the Member States may choose to impose an obligation regarding the Justice and Home Affairs acquis on the candidate Member States. One of the obligations actually imposed on these States is to adopt a national programme for the adoption of the acquis (NPAA). In principle this covers the Justice and Home Affairs acquis. Before full membership of the European Union is granted, a candidate Member State will have to have convinced the European Union that it has not only incorporated the acquis into its national legislation, but also applies this acquis within its legal order in accordance with the standards of the Union. As the Justice and Home Affairs acquis is part of the overall Union acquis, candidates for accession to the Member States will have to ensure compliance with the Justice and Home Affairs acquis in order to become full members of the European Union (See Official Journal of the European Communities 1998, L 191/8). A complicating factor for the candidate Member States in ensuring compliance with the Justice and Home Affairs acquis will be that this acquis is still in the process of being developed. Moreover, the Justice and Home Affairs acquis in the policy areas which were transferred to Title IV of the Treaty establishing the European Community by the Treaty of Amsterdam will have to be reconsidered by the Member States in the light of the framework established in this Title. Defining the acquis in Justice and Home Affairs, in particular that regarding movement of persons, will not prove an easy task. Close co-operation between all parties involved will therefore be required in establishing the legal effects entailed by individual measures which together form this acquis.

5. FUTURE DEVELOPMENTS

The already mentioned Treaty of Amsterdam saw an overhaul in Co-operation in Justice and Home Affairs. The transferral of asylum, immigration and visa policies to the Community Treaty is not without consequences. Although part of the Community Treaty, the procedure for decision making in these policy areas is not the same as the decision making procedure that applies to the other policy areas found in this Treaty. For instance, the Member States retain their right of initiative to table legislative drafts during the first five years after the entry into force of the Treaty of Amsterdam. The role of the European Parliament is consultative, as opposed to co-legislator and decisions are to be adopted by unanimity vote by the Council. The legal instruments available to the Community institutions in these policy areas are those found in Article 249 (new) TEC. Measures to be adopted within the framework of Title IV (new) TEC will therefore have to be adopted as:
– regulation;
– directive; or
– decision.

The legal effects of these instruments are determined by Article 249 (new) TEC itself. Regulations have general application, are binding in their entirety and are directly applicable in every Member State. A directive is binding as to the result to be achieved upon each Member State to which it is addressed, leaving the choice of form and methods to the national authorities. Decisions are binding in their entirety upon those to whom they are addressed. Two legal instruments without binding force, also listed in Article 249 (new) TEC, are recommendations and opinions.

The first of many more Title IV measure was tabled in the form of a directive on December 1, 1999. This draft directive was presented by the Commission and is a proposal for a Council Directive on the Right to Family Reunification

(COM(1999) 638 final, 1999/0258 CNS). Before this draft-text enters into force, it will have to pass through the decision-making channels established by Title IV (new) TEC. Candidate Member States are allowed to take part in the deliberations which take place before a Title IV (new) TEC measure enters into force. They are excluded from the final vote in the Council.

1.4

AMSTERDAM AND THE INSTITUTIONS

Georg Wirtz[1]

A. INTRODUCTION

This Essay considers some of the changes regarding the Third Pillar brought about by the Amsterdam Treaty which came into force on May 1st 1999. Although the Third Pillar is brought closer to the First Pillar, important differences between the two remain – especially in relation to the institutions' role and their range of possible measures.

B. THE THIRD PILLAR BEFORE AND AFTER THE AMSTERDAM TREATY

The organizational structure of the Third Pillar represents a convergence of the previously existing working groups and structures at European Union level. It has a legal nature different from that of the first pillar. Whereas the legal nature of the first pillar is that of amendments to the Treaties establishing the three European Communities – and thus Community law – the third pillar does not have this quality. Its provisions are not amendments to any of the three Treaties establishing the European Communities, hence they are not part of European Community law and its principles, such as the supremacy of Community law. The general legal acts of the EC – regulation, directive and decision – cannot be used to enforce a policy in the framework of the third pillar. Consequently, the relevant provisions do not automatically fall within the jurisdiction of the Court of Justice because Third Pillar measures are merely subject to public international law. Al-

---

[1] Based on: The legislative and judicial provisions of the new title of the EC Treaty on immigration, civil cooperation and asylum and of the revised 'Third Pillar' of the EU (criminal and police cooperation), as amended by the Amsterdam Treaty, a paper for a LLM European Community Law, May 1999; supervisors: Nicolas Bernard, Steve Peers [for this Handbook abridged by the editor].

though there may be hardly any effective legal enforceability of the provisions on the co-operation in internal matters, these provisions were nevertheless to exert the primary function of international treaties, namely persuasive and political authority in practical political life. However, the normal rule of international law still applies namely that parties are bound by their obligations (pacta sunt servanda) but are free to determine how to enforce these obligations through their national law.

The old Article K.1 TEU enumerated nine areas regarded as matters of common interest by the Member States: (1) asylum policy; (2) rules governing the crossing by persons of the external borders or the Member States and exercise of controls thereon; (3) immigration policy and policy regarding nationals of third countries, (4) combating drug addiction; (5) combating fraud on an international scale; (6) judicial co-operation in civil matters; (7) judicial co-operation in criminal matters; (8) customs co-operation; and finally (9) police co-operation. It can easily be seen that this catalogue does not contain all the fields usually considered as 'justice' or 'home affairs'. Nevertheless, a broad range of relevant matters is mentioned, and those that are not mentioned can be dealt with on an intergovernmental basis.

The Third Pillar covered a lot of the same ground like the Schengen Convention of 1990, a co-operative agreement on external immigration control with free internal borders. It provides for open frontiers with closer customs and police co-operation, allowing European citizens to come and go, while monitoring tightly the movement of non-European nationals. Among other measures on criminality and drug trafficking, it also confirms the rule established in the Dublin Convention that asylum seekers, once rejected from one member state, are rejected from all and sent back to the country from which they came. Up to now, all Member States of the European Union – except the United Kingdom and Ireland – have signed Accession Protocols to the Schengen Agreements. Like the third pillar, the Schengen Convention only consists of public international law.

I. Matters transferred to the first Pillar

Many of the objections which had been raised against the third pillar on Justice and Home Affairs under the Maastricht Treaty were addressed by the incorporation of a substantial part of its subject matter into the new Title IV of the EC Treaty on Visas, asylum, immigration and other policies related to free movement of persons. This holds for all aspects of asylum, immigration, external border controls, judicial co-operation in civil matters as well as the necessary closer administrative co-operation in areas covered by this Title. 'The essence of the criticism had been that many of the policies being decided under the JHA pillar called for institutional provisions and legal controls which were quite different from the intergovernmental processes established under its terms'.[2] These issues

---
[2] Craig and de Búrca, EU Law, 2nd edition, Oxford University Press 1998, p. 43.

touched on fundamental human rights and called for greater openness and accountability in this policy field, with a proper role for the European Parliament, and review jurisdiction for the Court of Justice 'in keeping with the high ideals of those who founded the European Community'.[3] After the debate with arguments ranging from improving the institutional provisions under JHA as it stood to absorbing the third pillar entirely into the Community pillar, the Intergovernmental Conference reviewing these provisions came up with a compromise with parts of what was JHA being incorporated into the new EC title, and the remaining provisions of the third pillar, to be renamed 'Police and Judicial Co-operation in criminal matters' (PJCC), being expanded and subjected to a range of institutional controls more like those under the Community pillar.

Two other issues have also been transferred from the third pillar to the EC Treaty, although not to the new Title. They concern actions against fraud affecting the financial interest of the EC (new Article 280 EC[4]) and measures to strengthen customs co-operation (Article 135 EC) both in so far as they do not affect the application of criminal law (which remains in Title VI TEU) – the exact meaning of this derogation might actually in practice prove hard to delineate. In these cases all normal EC procedures apply: qualified majority voting, co-decision by the European Parliament, right of initiative by the Commission and full jurisdiction of the European Court of Justice.

The Schengen Agreements are now incorporated into the Treaty in a Protocol[5] through which the 13 signatories are authorised to pursue closer co-operation in areas covered by these agreements. There is scope for partial judicial control by the Court of Justice. The Treaty provides that the legal basis in EU Law of each provision of the Schengen acquis that is absorbed is to be determined by the Council, acting by unanimity. Until this is done, the provisions or decisions that constitute the Schengen acquis shall be regarded as acts based on the third pillar. Therefore, the provisions and decisions with regard to police and judicial co-operation will presumably be assigned a legal basis in Title VI TEU and thus will remain within the sphere of public international law. The legal basis for the integration of the Schengen provisions and decisions concerning the external border controls, the entry and visa requirements and the Schengen/Dublin asylum concept will be found, however, in Articles 62 and 63 of the new Title IV EC Treaty on visas, asylum, immigration and other policies related to the free movement of persons. Thus, the Schengen provisions that will be attributed to the new Title in the EC Treaty ('communitarized') will be transformed to supranational Community law. 'The Schengen body of rules will be neither to be entirely communitari-

---

[3] Spencer, Human rights and the 'third pillar': an urgent case for reform, [1995] European Access 9.

[4] For the sake of simplicity this essay cites the renumbered Articles of the EC Treaty and the TEU except where stated otherwise.

[5] Protocol integrating the Schengen acquis into the framework of the European Union, OJ 1997 C340/93.

zed nor to be entirely left under Title VI, but to be divided and assigned, in Sclomon-like fashion, partly to the one system and partly to the other'.[6]

In a separate Protocol[7] the British and Irish are authorised to maintain identity checks at their external borders, whereas such controls should normally be abolished within the Schengen area. Another Protocol[8] referred to in Article 69 EC excludes the British and Irish from the new title on the free movement of people but allows them at any time to participate (opt in) in the Schengen 'acquis'. Each time they wish to act with their partners in the field of asylum and immigration, for example, they will be required to notify the European Commission of their interest within three months of the presentation of the proposal before the Council. Although Denmark was already a Contracting Party of the Schengen Implementation Agreement, the Danes have also been granted an opt out[9] from the Title on the Free Movement of Persons (except for visas) in order to facilitate the ratification of the new Treaty in Denmark. This opt out confirms the exemption secured following the failure of the first Danish referendum on the Maastricht Treaty in 1992. The current British government now plans an extensive opt-in to the Schengen Convention and the new Title IV EC Treaty. Ireland is likely to follow [...]. The broader participation alleviates to a certain extent the injustice that an EU Member State may choose to opt out but new applying States have to obey the acquis communautaire from their accession. [Another] positive side of the integration of Schengen into Title IV TEU is that there will be only one regulatory régime for internal security management in Europe instead of two.[...]

II. Third Pillar objectives

For the first time specific objectives have been set for action in the third pillar. The new Article 2, fourth indent, TEU describes as the overall aim the creation of 'an area of freedom, security, and justice in which the free movement of persons is assured'. To this end appropriate measures are to be taken to prevent and combat crime, in particular drug and arms trafficking, trafficking in persons and offences against children, corruption, and fraud (Article 29 TEU). The operational objectives of the subjects remaining in the third pillar under Title VI TEU – police and judicial co-operation in criminal matters, as well as the prevention and combating of racism and xenophobia – have been spelled out in Articles 31 and 32 TEU in much greater detail than before. There are three methods to achieve these aims: First through closer co-operation between police forces and customs

---

[6] Barrett, Justice and Home Affairs Cooperation – An Overview, in: Tonra (ed.) Amsterdam What the Treaty means, [1997] Institute of European Affairs, p. 128.

[7] Protocol on the application of certain aspects of Article 7a of the Treaty establishing the European Community to the United Kingdom and to Ireland, OJ 1997 C340/97.

[8] Article 1 Protocol on the position of the United Kingdom and Ireland, OJ 1997 C340/99.

[9] Protocol on the position of Denmark, OJ 1997 C340/101.

and other Member State authorities, with the help of the European Police Office (Europol), secondly through closer co-operation between judicial and other relevant Member State authorities, and thirdly through the approximation of criminal laws in the Member States.[...]

Bearing in mind that the Maastricht Treaty made no reference to any objective other than that of 'achieving the objectives of the Union, in particular the free movement of persons' (old Article K.1) the new provisions present a well defined clarification. This corresponds with the notion of the Third Pillar as a 'laboratory' for co-operation between the Member States. After Amsterdam it is much clearer which 'ingredients' are being experimented with. Articles 29 to 31 TEU mark a respectable step away from a mere 'top-layer programme for justice and home affairs matters, with little or no room for practical and operational initiatives at the bottom' (14) towards a homogeneous definition of the security in demand.

III. Legal instruments

The only legal instruments available for legislation in the Third Pillar were conventions, joint positions and joint actions. Due to their rather futile and uncertain character the Member States preferred to have recourse to more informal means not envisaged in the TEU by way of communications, opinions and recommendations.

After the Amsterdam Treaty the Council can still adopt common positions, which define the Union's approach to a given matter, and establish conventions, which are to be adopted by Member States in accordance with their constitutional requirements. But, in view of the experience of lengthy ratification procedures, future conventions will enter into force for all concerned as soon as they have been adopted by half the Member States (Article 34(2)(c) TEU). Furthermore the implementing decisions of such conventions can be adopted by the Council with a two-thirds majority. The Council can also adopt binding decisions addressed to Member States, but here the Treaty spells out explicitly that their purpose cannot be the harmonisation of Member States' legislation (Article 34(2)(d) TEU). A new category of acts has also been introduced in Article 34(2)(b) TEU, the 'framework decisions' whose legal features closely resemble those of EC Directives but which are expressly incapable of having direct effect. [...]

IV. Involved institutions

The old Article K.4 TEU provided for a Coordinating Committee, also known as the 'K.4 Committee' consisting of senior officials. This Committee occupied a key position co-ordinating the work of three steering groups and their preparatory Working Groups and was accountable to the Committee of Permanent Representatives (COREPER) and to the Council of Ministers of Justice and Home Affairs. Accordingly the Council acted under the Third Pillar on the initiative of the

Member States, the Commission and in fact the K.4 Committee. The old Title VI was partly modelled on a pre-existing intergovernmental co-operation system, which explains the charges directed against it that there were too many working levels within the third pillar and that it was over-complicated and not transparent enough. The new structure had established a central form of co-ordination, but the way the third pillar was structured gave the Community institutions only a small part to play and no real way of exercising any control over the Member States' decisions, thereby turning the rate of progress into a relatively slow one. Politicians had acknowledged this problem, and put the organizational structure of the Third Pillar on the agenda for the 1996 Intergovernmental Conferences. [...]

1. *Council*
With regard to those areas which the Treaty of Amsterdam has transferred to the EC Treaty, the role of the institutions is very different from the role they used to play under Title VI TEU. The Council was often paralysed by the requirement to take every decision by unanimous vote. It will continue to play the main role over the next five years so that it can take a number of decisions in the areas of Title IV EC. Over the first five years after the new treaty has come into force, the Council will take decisions unanimously, then the Council will have to decide by unanimous vote to apply the co-decision procedure and qualified majority voting when adopting measures under Title IV (Article 67(1) and (2) EC). Merely rules on visas for intended stay of no more than three months – already partially subject to qualified majority since Maastricht – shall be adopted by immediate qualified majority voting or automatic co-decision procedure after five years respectively according to Article 67(3) and (4) EC. In the event of stalemate among the 15, it will be possible to operate the Schengen Protocol. The German Länder with their major intake of asylum seekers seemed to fear that all immigration issues would be transferred to Community competence, and insisted successfully with their new-found influence that the unanimity rule will not automatically change into a qualified majority decision-making process once the five years have subsided. Therefore, the extension of Community competences appears quite impaired by 'one of the most-initiative paralysing features of the Third Pillar – the requirement that all Member States agree unanimously on a particular course of action'.[10]

Apart from its decision-making role, the Council's role as a co-ordinator between the relevant government departments in the member states and between them and the European Commission has been consolidated in Article 66 EC, which can be read as an official impetus for horizontal networking between national bureaucracies and as a reassertion of the already strong position of public

---

[10] Barrett, cited above, p. 123.

officials in the Member States. The many different levels of working groups that existed before have been abolished. All the working groups now stand on the same footing and report directly to COREPER. [...]

2. *Commission*

European co-operation on Third Pillar measures developed initially as a network of ad-hoc interior ministry networks, focusing on special state functions, such as border control and monitoring of illegal cross-border. These networks, as a straight transnational mirror of the existing national arrangements allowed no new openings to new actors. They were dominated by national state civil servants, and even closed in most cases to European politicians (the Parliament), European civil servants (the Commission), and European lawyers (the European courts). Given the great sensitivity of matters relating to public order, the Treaty has accorded very great weight to the Member States and to the bodies of the European Union in which they participate directly. The powers of the European Commission, the European Parliament and the Court of Justice have been limited for the same reason.

Under the old Third Pillar the Commission's right of initiative was limited by Article K.3(2) to only six out of the nine areas referred to in Article K.1 and was shared with the Member States. For example, it could exercise that right in the areas of asylum, immigration or combating international fraud, but it could not propose a text to the Council on judicial co-operation in criminal, police or customs matters. The Member States themselves had that right. The Commission, the European Parliament and some Member States were in favour of copying, to some degree, the Community decision-making process, which was considered more effective, in the field of justice and home affairs.

Those six areas where the Commission had a right of initiative have meanwhile been transferred to the new Title IV EC Treaty. After the Treaty of Amsterdam, two periods may be distinguished in this area from the institutional point of view: During the first five years the Council acts unanimously on a proposal by the Commission or on the initiative of a Member State, after consulting the European Parliament (Article 67(1) TEU). After that, the Commission may act on its own initiative, but must examine all requests from Member States to submit a proposal (Article 67(2) TEU).

This communitarization has been achieved at the price of a shared right of initiative between the Commission and Member States under the three areas remaining in the PJCC pillar. The solution chosen for the Third Pillar is and will be a policy-making process strongly dominated by the Council. However, Article 34(2) TEU equips the Commission with the right of general, and no longer limited, initiative. [...]

3. *European Parliament*

The European Parliament seems to have emerged as the institutional winner from the Inter-governmental conference that drafted the Amsterdam Treaty. Under the old JHA the European Parliament was unable to exercise efficient control over the measures taken in that context, owing to the very nature of the intergovernmental co-operation itself. Article K.6 of the Maastricht Treaty only called for regular information and consultation of the European Parliament by the Presidency and the Commission on principle developments in justice and home affairs and states that Parliament's views must be duly taken into consideration. The European Parliament was permitted to ask questions of the Council or make recommendations to it. Each year it was to hold a debate on the progress made in the areas of JHA.

The communitarization of immigration, asylum, external borders and legal cooperation in civil matters enhanced the role of the European Parliament in that it has to be consulted prior to the taking of initiatives (Article 67 EC). Should the optional Co-decision procedure be applied after the transitional period of five years, the European Parliament and the Council will be put on a even more powerful basis. The Co-decision procedure pursuant to Article 251 EC which the Amsterdam Treaty has simplified requires in essence the agreement of both the Council and the Parliament for a proposed law to pass. In other forms of European legislation, the balance is tipped in favour of the Council, which can ultimately overrule the Parliament. The result is that, under Co-decision, the veto formerly exercised by the Member States through the Council is instead transferred to the Parliament. Therefore, the European Parliament is able to exert a much stronger political direction over the Commission.

The rights of the European Parliament are still more restricted in the context of the remaining Third Pillar. Here, the significant new provision is that, with the exception of common positions, the European Parliament is given a slightly stronger consultative role in the decision-making process. The obligation to consult is now put on the Council instead of the Presidency and is to be effected in advance of any adoption. However, Article 39(1) TEU does not give the European Parliament an effective means of democratic control in PJCC matters, firstly because the intergovernmental nature of the Third Pillar means that the national parliaments have competence to exercise democratic control instead of the European Parliament, and secondly because the European Parliament cannot force the Commission or the Council to make information – which is an essential precondition for effective control – available in time. It shows a lack of trust in the institution that the European Parliament will have to give its opinion within a time limit of no less that three months and that in the absence of an opinion within that time limit Article 39 TEU allows to Council to act. The European Parliament has reasons to be disappointed since it requested co-decision for cases requiring qualified majority voting which is a far cry from the consultation right which it obtained. Amsterdam's failure to increase the European Parliament's powers in the third pillar is a major flaw. [...]

4. *European Court of Justice*

The normal judicial control of Community law by the Court of Justice applies to all measures under Title IV EC (For example Articles 226, 227, 230, 232 EC Treaty). However, a special procedure has been introduced under Article 68 EC concerning the request by national courts for preliminary rulings in a pending case pursuant to Article 234(3) EC which aim to secure uniform interpretation in all Member States. The Court does not have jurisdiction wherever the maintenance of law and order and the safeguarding of internal security is involved. Pursuant to Article 68(3) EC the Council, the Commission or a Member State may ask a ruling on the interpretation, but the ruling in response to such a request shall not apply to judgments which have become res judicata.

The revamped Third Pillar assigns a larger role to the European Court of Justice than before. Article 35(1) TEU widens the competence of the European Court of Justice to more legal instruments, as it can now also give preliminary rulings on the validity and interpretation of framework decisions and decisions, on the interpretation of conventions established under this Title and on the validity and interpretation of the measures implementing them. It is equivocal whether the word 'them' just refers to measures implementing conventions or also to measures implementing decisions or framework decisions. The European Court of Justice would likely decide the point on policy grounds, even though its competence to interpret Title VI TEU (as distinct from measures adopted pursuant to it) is not at all clear.

Such a preliminary ruling is similar though not identical to that of Article 234 EC except that it will only apply to the courts of a Member State where that State has expressly declared that it accepts such jurisdiction in relation to specified national courts. Spain has declared that such a request is possible only by that court or tribunal against whose decisions there is no judicial remedy under national law (Article 35(3)(a) TEU), whereas Belgium, Germany, Greece, Italy, Luxembourg, the Netherlands, Austria, Portugal, Finland and Sweden accept requests from any court or tribunal (Article 35(3)(b) TEU). Some States reserve the right to make provision in their national law that the court or tribunal against whose decision there is no remedy is obliged to bring the matter before the Court of Justice (21).

Further, the Court is given jurisdiction to review the legality of framework decisions and decisions at the suit of a Member State or the Commission, on the same grounds as those in Article 230 of the EC Treaty (Article 35(6) TEU). However, in a somewhat similar provision to that under Article 68(2) of the EC Treaty, Article 35(5) TEU restricts the Court's review jurisdiction, in that it cannot review the legality or proportionality of 'operations carried out by the police or other law enforcement services of a Member State or the exercise of the responsibilities incumbent upon Member States with regard to the maintenance of law and order and the safeguarding of internal security'. One could argue that hardly any measure or decision in the sector of police and judicial co-operation in criminal matters does not deal with 'law and order' and 'internal security'. But there is a declaration[11] clarifying that international criminal investigation activities are subject to appropriate[12] (23) judicial review by the competent national authorities in accordance with the rules applicable in each Member State, 'removing any inhibitions on the part of national courts to step in and vindicate the rights of the individual where appropriate'. Official judgments can also be obtained from the European Court of Human Rights.

Finally, the Court is given jurisdiction in disputes between Member States concerning the interpretation or application of a convention, if the Council cannot first resolve the dispute within six months (Article 35(7) TEU). Conventions may stipulate that the Court has more extensive jurisdiction to interpret the provisions of the convention, or to settle a dispute in applying the convention. However, in practice, not all the Member States are inclined to assign it that role. [...]

The European Court of Justice does not appear to be given general jurisdiction to rule on the actual provisions of this title of the Treaty, as opposed to the measures which are adopted under it. Nor does the Court of Justice have the authority that it wields under the First Pillar. Article 6(2) TEU raises additional questions on the safeguarding of human rights under the newly structured Third Pillar, in particular in relation to the operation of Europol. This provision reflects the Union's respect of the European Convention for the Protection of Human Rights and Fundamental Freedoms but the European Court of Justice is merely granted limited jurisdiction by Article 46(b) TEU over the operation of the Third Pillar. 'The role of the Court of Justice is thus to be focused on keeping the EU's own house in order rather than supervising the Member States themselves'[13] but it hopefully interprets the restrictions on its own jurisdiction in this regard very narrowly. Moreover, the rights of private citizens to have access to the Court's jurisdiction have been practically excluded. [...]

---

[11] Declaration on Article K.2 of the Treaty on European Union OJ 1997 C340/133.

[12] Collins, Freedom through security? The Third Pillar, [1998] Irish Journal of European Law p. 43.

[13] Barrett, cited above, p. 125.

THE DANISH EXCEPTION
Denmark's JHA Reservation and Amsterdam

Fabrice Liebaut[1]

THE DANISH RESERVATION

In the aftermath of the negative outcome of the referendum on the Treaty on European Union in June 1992, Denmark negotiated with its EU partners four reservations on various issues, including one on Justice and Home Affairs. These reservations were finalised in the Edinburgh Agreement of December 1992 and were approved by referendum in June 1992.

The reservation on Justice and Home Affairs states that 'Denmark will participate fully in co-operation on Justice and Home Affairs on the basis of the provision of Title VI of the Treaty on European Union. (...)'. In practice, this means that Denmark is participating in the co-operation on justice, internal and police affairs, which include asylum and migration issues, as long as it is inter-governmental, but steps down as soon as it becomes a supranational matter.

The wording of the reservation made it possible for Denmark to become a party to various inter-governmental agreements on asylum and migration, such as the Dublin Convention, in force since September 1997, or the Schengen agreements, which will enter into force in Denmark during the course of 2000.

However, with the Treaty of Amsterdam and the transfer of 'visas, asylum, immigration and other policies related to free movement of persons' from the 'Third Pillar' to the 'First Pillar', i.e., from inter-governmental to supranational co-operation, the Danish reservation became active. A Protocol on the position of Denmark was thus inserted in the Treaty, which reiterates the content of the reservation and details how it should be administrated.

---

[1] The author works with the Danish Refugee Council, Copenhagen as project co-ordinator and EU policy officer.

P.J. van Krieken (Ed.), The Asylum Acquis Handbook
© 2000, T.M.C.Asser Press, The Hague, the Röling Foundation and the authors

FOLLOWING THE TREATY OF AMSTERDAM

The position of Denmark after the entry into force of the Treaty of Amsterdam is as follows:

– Denmark participates fully in the European Council's discussions regarding the measures to be adopted under Article 63 of the Treaty on European Union, but does not take part in the voting.

– Denmark is not concerned with the measures adopted under Article 63 or any decisions made on the basis of Title IV of the Treaty on European Union or any interpretative decisions, which could be made by the European Court of Justice. Logically, Denmark is not required to participate in the financing of such measures.

– If Denmark wants to follow a measure adopted by the other Member States on the basis of the said Article 63, it must conclude a separate agreement with its EU partners. Such agreement will not be part of the First Pillar, but will fall under inter-governmental co-operation.

– The reservation does not apply to the rules regarding the establishment of a list of third countries, the nationals of which must have a visa to enter the EU, or to the rules on a uniform format for visas. Denmark participates fully in the European decisions taken on these visa issues.

– Denmark's obligations under the Schengen agreements still apply and will continue to do so, regardless of whether the respective Schengen provisions remain under the Third Pillar or are transferred to the First Pillar. Denmark will fully participate in any future changes or developments regarding the provisions still under the Third Pillar. Due to the reservation, it will not participate when the proposed measures concern those provisions that have become a matter of supranational co-operation under the First Pillar. However, it enjoys a 6-month delay to decide whether it wants to apply the measure adopted by the European Council and whether to introduce it in its own legislation or not. If it does, this decision will then create inter-governmental obligations between Denmark and its Schengen partners.

– Denmark can at any time lift its reservation or parts of it. However, according to the Danish constitutional provisions, this requires that such a decision be approved by referendum.

PRACTICAL CONSEQUENCES

Since the Treaty of Amsterdam entered into force, Denmark has been participating in the ongoing discussions on an equal footing with the other Member States. So far, its reservation on asylum and immigration issues has had very little effect, since no significant measure has yet been taken on the basis of Article 63 of the Treaty on European Union. When this happens, Denmark will have to decide, on a case-by-case basis, whether it wants to follow the new measure voted on the other Member States – and whether conclude a parallel agreement for that purpose – or not. For the same reason, the Danish reservation on asylum and migration has had very limited consequences up to now from the point of view of the other Member States and the EU.

Neither has the reservation had any impact on the situation of asylum seekers, refugees and aliens in Denmark. This may be the case in the future, depending on whether or not Denmark enters into parallel agreements with the EU on matters regarding which harmonised instruments are adopted by the other countries. It should be noted, however, that even if parallel agreements were concluded, such inter-governmental instruments would not automatically fall under the jurisdiction of the European Court of Justice.

1.6

THE ENLARGEMENT PROCESS AND JHA CO-OPERATION[1]

Oliver Seiffarth[2]

I. INTRODUCTION

The European Union is already 'familiar' with enlargement. In 1973 Denmark, Ireland and the United Kingdom joined the original six Member States (Belgium, France, Germany, Italy, Luxembourg and the Netherlands). In 1981 Greece, in 1987 Spain and Portugal and in 1995 Finland, Sweden and Austria also joined the European Union.

Nowadays the European Union is preparing for the largest expansion in its history. Once all the eleven candidate countries of Estonia, Latvia, Lithuania, Poland, the Czech Republic, Slovakia, Hungary, Slovenia, Romania, Bulgaria and Cyprus have joined the European Union, the area of the EU will increase by 34% and the population by 105 million people. Taking into account that the Helsinki European Council decided to accept also Malta and Turkey as applicant States, these figures will be even higher.

II THE CRITERIA FOR ACCESSION TO THE EUROPEAN UNION

With regard to the procedure for becoming a member of the European Union Article 49 TEU states that:

---

[1] This essay reflects only the personal views and experiences of the author and does not claim to give a complete overview of the enlargement process.

[2] Oliver Seiffarth studied law in Vienna and worked during his studies for different NGOs in the asylum and migration field. After having been employed with Caritas for one year, he worked for the International Centre for Migration Policy (ICMPD) in Vienna, for the General Secretariat of the Council of the European Union, DG Justice and Home Affairs, in Brussels and for the Austrian Federal Ministry of the Interior, EU Coordination Department, in Vienna. Since January 2000 he has been working as a pre-accession advisor (PAA) for a Twinning-project in the migration field in Slovenia.

P.J. van Krieken (Ed.), The Asylum Acquis Handbook
© 2000, T.M.C.Asser Press, The Hague, the Röling Foundation and the authors

'Any European State which respects the principles set out in Article 6(1)[3] may apply to become a member of the Union. It shall address its application to the Council, which shall act unanimously after consulting the Commission and after receiving the assent of the European Parliament, which shall act by an absolute majority of its component members.'

The conditions of admission and the adjustments to the Treaties on which the Union is founded which such admission entails shall be the subject of an agreement between the Member States and the applicant State in question. This agreement shall be submitted for ratification by all the contracting States in accordance with their respective 'constitutional requirements'.

The 1993 Copenhagen European Council set the criteria for accession known as the 'Copenhagen criteria'. According to these criteria, membership requires:
– Stability of institutions guaranteeing democracy, the rule of law, human rights and respect for and protection of minorities (political criteria);
– The existence of a functioning market economy as well as the capacity to cope with competitive pressures and market forces within the Union (economic criteria);
– The ability to take on the obligations of membership, including adherence to the aims of political, economic and monetary union.

The Helsinki European Council recalled that compliance with the political criteria is a prerequisite for the opening of accession negotiations and compliance with all the Copenhagen criteria is the basis for accession to the Union.[4]

III. THE OVERALL ENLARGEMENT PROCESS AS DEFINED BY THE 1997 LUXEMBOURG EUROPEAN COUNCIL

In July 1997, the European Commission published its 'Agenda 2000: For a stronger and wider Union', together with its Opinions on each candidate country's application for membership. The European Commission was favourable to opening negotiations with Hungary, Poland, Estonia, the Czech Republic and Slovenia.[5]

On the basis of the recommendations made by the Commission in Agenda 2000, in December 1997 the Luxembourg European Council defined the key elements of the 'overall enlargement process':

---

[3] 'The Union is founded on the principles of liberty, democracy, respect for human rights and fundamental freedoms, and the rule of law, principles which are common to the Member States.'

[4] Helsinki European Council, Presidency conclusion 4, 11 December 1999.

[5] The Opinion regarding Cyprus was presented in 1993.

1. European Conference

The European Conference met for the first time in London in March 1998 at the level of Heads of Governments. The European Conference is meant to be a multilateral forum for political consultation for the ten Central and Eastern European Countries (CEEC), Cyprus, Turkey and the Member States. It should address questions of general concern to the participants and 'broaden and deepen their co-operation on foreign and security policy, justice and home affairs, and other areas of common concern, particularly economic matters and regional co-operation'.[6]

The Conference met again in October 1998 and July 1999. Discussions took place on drug trafficking, organised crime, the environment etc. A report on organised crime prepared by the European Conference expert group on organised crime and drugs was presented to the Conference in July 1999. Also Switzerland, Norway and Iceland took part in this expert group.

Although the Conference was thought to be a discussion platform between the EU and Turkey, up to until that time Turkey had never attended. Therefore the future role and membership of the Conference was discussed at the Helsinki European Council in December 1999.

2. Accession Process

The accession process was launched in Brussels on 30 March 1998, by a meeting of the Ministers for Foreign Affairs of the fifteen EU Member States, the ten Central and Eastern European Countries (CEEC) and Cyprus. The Luxembourg European Council pointed out that all these States are 'destined to join the European Union on the basis of the same criteria and that they are participating in the accession process on an equal footing'.[7] At the same time each Candidate country will 'proceed at its own rate, depending on its degree of preparedness'.[8]

For these countries the Luxembourg European Council introduced the 'enhanced pre-accession strategy' which superseded the structured dialogue.

The Helsinki European Council decided that also Turkey 'is a candidate State destined to join the Union on the basis of the same criteria as applied to the other candidate States. Building on the existing European strategy, Turkey, like other candidate States, will benefit from a pre-accession strategy to stimulate and support its reforms.'[9]

The main elements of the enhanced pre-accession strategy are:

---

[6] Luxembourg European Council, Presidency conclusion 7, SN400/97, 12 December 1997.
[7] Luxembourg European Council, Presidency conclusion 10, SN400/97, 12 December 1997.
[8] Luxembourg European Council, Presidency conclusion 2, SN400/97, 12 December 1997.
[9] Helsinki European Council, Presidency conclusion 13, 11 December 1999.

2.1. Accession Partnerships[10]

In March 1998 the Council adopted the Accession Partnerships which set out the priorities for further work and are designed 'to mobilise all forms of assistance to the applicant countries in Central and Eastern Europe in a single framework'.[11] In these Accession partnerships 'the priorities to be observed in adopting the EU acquis and also the financial resources available for that purpose, in particular the PHARE programme' are covered in detail for each applicant country.[12] Short and medium-term objectives have been defined for a range of sectors including Justice and Home Affairs.

In that context financial assistance is linked to the applicant's progress. When an element essential to the continuation of pre-accession assistance is missing in an applicant State, the Council can take appropriate measures by unanimous decision.[13]

The Accession Partnerships for all applicant countries were agreed upon on 29 March 1998 by the Council.[14] They were updated by the end of 1999.

The monitoring of the Accession Partnerships is carried out through the mechanisms of the Europe Agreements.[15]

2.2. National Programmes for the Adoption of the Acquis (NPAA)

As a response to the Accession Partnerships, in 1998 each Candidate country prepared a National Programme for the Adoption of the Acquis (NPAA) which sets out the timetable and the human and financial resource allocations for the implementation of the priorities of the Accession Partnerships. All candidate countries have inserted in their NPAAs chapters dealing with Justice and Home Affairs.

The NPAAs were revised by the Candidate countries in 1999.

2.3. PHARE Programme

The PHARE Programme was set up in 1989 to support the economic and political transition of the ten Central and Eastern European Countries (CEEC).[16] For

---

[10] Council Regulation (EC) No. 622/98 of 16 March 1998 on assistance to the applicant States in the framework of the pre-accession strategy, and in particular on the establishment of Accession Partnerships, OJ No. 85, 20 March 1998, 1-2.

[11] Luxembourg European Council, Presidency conclusion 14, SN400/97, 12 December 1997.

[12] Luxembourg European Council, Presidency conclusion 15, SN400/97, 12 December 1997.

[13] Luxembourg European Council, Presidency conclusions 14 and 15, SN400/97, 12 December 1997.

[14] OJ No. L 121, 23 April 1998, 1-50; OJ No. C 202, 29 June 1998, 1-102.

[15] The Europe Agreements were signed with the ten CEEC between 1991 and 1996, and came into force between 1994 and 1999. Europe Agreements are mixed agreements and must be ratified by all Member States. For each country with which an Europe Agreement is in force, there has been a cycle of annual meetings of the Association Council and the Association Committee as well as frequent multidisciplinary sub-committee meetings.

[16] The original meaning of PHARE refers to: Pologne et Hongrie, Assiatance pour la Reconstruction Economique.

the 1990-1994 period Euro 4.2 billion were allocated. For the 1995-1999 period the PHARE allocation was increased to Euro 6.693 billion.

Following the decisions taken by the Berlin European Council in March 1999, for the 2000-2006 period the financial aid to the candidate countries will be more than doubled.[17] Pre-accession assistance for all countries together will amount to Euro 3.12 billion per year. PHARE, with Euro 1.56 billion per year, will remain at its old level. From 2000 onwards, there are two new programmes in addition to PHARE. SAPARD provides aid for agriculture and rural development with a yearly amount of Euro 520 million. ISPA helps finance investments in the fields of environment and transport with an annual amount of Euro 1.04 billion.

Financial support to the countries involved in the enlargement process is based on the principle of equal treatment, with particular attention being paid to countries with the greatest need.[18] As soon as the first accessions will take place, the same pre-accession funds will be reallocated to the remaining candidate countries, so that there will be more financial resources for fewer countries.

The PHARE Programme assists not only the ten CEEC who have applied for EU membership in their efforts to meet the accession criteria,[19] but also supports the transition of Albania, Bosnia and Herzegovina, and the former Yugoslav Republic of Macedonia to democracy and a market economy. In the near future the support for these three States shall be given under the OBNOVA Programme.

In 1998, new guidelines were adopted in order to redirect support towards the preparation of the candidate countries for accession in the key areas identified in the Accession Partnerships (from 'demand-driven' to 'accession-driven').[20] The first aim of the reorientation is to help the reinforcement of administrative and judicial capacity (institution building, about 30% of the overall amount). The second aim is to help the candidate countries to bring their industries and major infrastructure up to Community standards by mobilising the investment required in the fields of the environment, transport, working conditions etc. (about 70%).

For the field of Justice and Home Affairs the PHARE activities on institution building, in particular the Twinning projects between one or two (sometimes even more) Member States and a candidate country, but also the PHARE-Horizontal Programme are of particular interest.

Whenever more than one candidate State takes part in a PHARE project, the set-up of the project is handled by the PHARE Horizontal Programme (DG Enlargement) and the implementation by the Common Service for External Relations (SCR).

Under the 1996 PHARE National Programme one project started in April 1999 to support the ten CEEC in asylum matters (adaptation of legislation and

---

[17] Berlin European Council, Presidency conclusion 8, doc. 100/1/99 rev, 25 March 1999.
[18] Luxembourg European Council, Presidency conclusion 17, SN400/97, 12 December 1997.
[19] For the time being Malta and Cyprus are not covered by the PHARE-Programme.
[20] See in detail: European Commission, DG External Relations, What is Phare, May 1999, 6.

implementation), another project helps to align the standards in police co-operation.

Under the 1999 PHARE Horizontal Programme Euro 10 million are planned to be spent on projects concerning the rule of law, judicial co-operation in penal law, training of judges and visa, migration and border control.

The National PHARE Programme deals mainly with Twinning projects. Twinning, launched in May 1998, covers 4 priority sectors (Agriculture, the Environment, Finance and Justice and Home Affairs) and preparation for structural funds (Special Preparatory Programme). Under the 1998 PHARE National Programme 119 Twinning projects have been developed, based upon 470 proposals from Member States. Usually between Euro 0.3 to 1.5 million are spent on each Twinning project. Every Twinning project has at least one Pre-Accession Advisor, who is an individual seconded from a Member State's administration or another approved body to work full time in the candidate country for a minimum of 12 months to implement the project.

In November 1999 almost 30 Twinning projects were planned or had already started in the fields of asylum, migration, border management, police co-operation and judicial co-operation. The implementation of these Twinning projects is supervised by the Delegations of the European Commission in the candidate countries.

Furthermore, some Community programmes (e.g. education, training and research, but also Justice and Home Affairs) have been opened to applicant States to enable them to familiarise themselves with the Union´s policies and working methods. In the field of Justice and Home Affairs in particular the programmes ODYSSEUS, STOP, GROTIUS, DAPHNE and FALCONE are of interest for the candidate countries. Under certain conditions the applicant States are allowed to take part as observers and, for the parts which concern them, in the management committees responsible for monitoring the programmes.[21]

2.4. *Regular Reports of the European Commission on Progress towards Accession*

In November 1998, the European Commission presented its first annual reports to the Council on the progress achieved by each candidate country towards accession. These reports 'constitute a sound overall analysis of each applicant State´s situation in the light of the membership criteria set by the Copenhagen European Council'.[22] These regular reports serve as a basis for the Council to take the necessary decisions in conducting the accession negotiations or for extending them to other applicant countries.

In October 1999 the European Commission presented not only the progress report of each candidate country, but also a proposal to open accession negotia-

---

[21] Luxembourg European Council, Presidency conclusion 20, SN400/97, 12 December 1997.
[22] Luxembourg European Council, Presidency conclusion 23, SN400/97, 12 December 1997.

tions with all candidate countries except Turkey. Both the Vienna and the Helsinki European Council welcomed the Commission's Regular Reports and shared to a large extent the analysis and proposals made by the Commission.

3. Accession negotiations

Following the conclusions of the Luxembourg European Council, accession negotiations were formally opened on 31 March 1998 with six countries: Hungary, Poland, the Czech Republic, Estonia, Slovenia and Cyprus.

In December 1999 the Helsinki European Council decided to convene bilateral intergovernmental conferences in February 2000 to begin negotiations also with Romania, Slovakia, Latvia, Lithuania, Bulgaria and Malta.[23] These candidate States have the possibility to catch up within a reasonable period of time with those already in negotiations if they have made sufficient progress in their preparations.[24]

The decision to enter into negotiations does not imply that they will be successfully concluded at the same time. In the negotiations each candidate State will be judged on its own merits. This principle will apply both to the opening of the various negotiating chapters and to the conduct of the negotiations. Progress in the negotiations must go hand in hand with progress in incorporating the EU acquis into legislation and actually implementing and enforcing it. The conclusion and the subsequent accession of the different applicant States depends on the extent to which each applicant State complies with the Copenhagen criteria, but also on the ability of the EU to assimilate new members.[25]

With regard to Justice and Home Affairs the EU initial position for the opening of negotiations with the first six candidate countries – as agreed by Coreper on 5 March 1998 – reads as follows:

> 'With regard to Justice and Home Affairs, accession to the European Union will entail that you:
> a) accept in full on accession the justice and home affairs provisions, and the working practices designed to give them effect, of the Treaty on the European Union (in particular Title VI) and the EC Treaty, as amended in each case by the Treaty of Amsterdam when it enters into force;
> b) in respect of those conventions or instruments in the field of justice and home affairs which are inseparable from the attainment of the objectives of the Treaty on European Union and the EC Treaty, as amended in each case by the Treaty of Amsterdam, as well as those drawn up by the Council on the basis of Article K.3 TEU (or Article 34 following the coming into force of the Treaty of Amsterdam) including the creation of Europol:

---

[23] Helsinki European Council, Presidency conclusion 10, 11 December 1999.
[24] Helsinki European Council, Presidency conclusion 11, 11 December 1999.
[25] Luxembourg European Council, Presidency conclusion 26, SN400/97, 12 December 1997; Helsinki European Council, Presidency conclusion 11, 11 December 1999.

i) undertake to accede to those which have been drawn up by the Council or to those signed by, or which have been opened for signature to, the Member States by the date of your accession to the Union;

ii) accept, in relation to those still under negotiation, the points which have been agreed on by the Fifteen or by the Council at the date of your accession to the Union, participating in subsequent negotiations within the Union framework only on those points still to be resolved;

c) accept on accession the joint actions, joint positions adopted by the Council and resolutions, decisions and statements adopted by the Fifteen or by the Council in the field of justice and home affairs and accept, in relation to those still under examination, the points which have been agreed on by the Fifteen or by the Council at the date of your accession to the Union, participating in subsequent deliberations only on those points still to be resolved;

d) introduce administrative and other arrangements, such as those already adopted by the Fifteen or by the Council, so as to ensure close practical co-operation between Member States' institutions and organisations working in the field of justice and home affairs, as is necessary effectively to implement the "acquis";

e) (...) bring your institutions, management systems and administrative arrangements up to Union standards with a view to implementing effectively the "acquis" and in particular adopt and implement measures with respect to external border controls, asylum and immigration, and measures to prevent and combat organised crime, terrorism and illicit drug trafficking.

With the entry into force of the Amsterdam Treaty in prospect, the Schengen "acquis", including the safeguard clause and the implementation mechanisms provided for in the Schengen Agreement, will also be integrated into the framework of the European Union. You will need to provide the conditions and procedures applied in the Schengen co-operation before controls of persons at internal borders can be lifted.'[26]

3.1. *Acquis screening*

The Presidency conclusions of the Luxembourg European Council stated that the enhanced pre-accession strategy will be accompanied by 'an analytical study ('screening') of the acquis of the European Union for each applicant State taken individually'.[27]

As already mentioned above the EU acquis entails not only Treaties like the TEC and TEU, the EC legislation and the case law of the Court of Justice, but also all acts adopted by the Council under Title V TEU (Common Foreign and Security policy) and Title VI TEU (Provisions on Police and Judicial Co-operation in Criminal Matters) and finally international agreements concluded by the EC. For the acquis screening the EU acquis has been divided into 31 chapters.[28]

---

[26] Document 6473/3/98 REV 3 JAI 7 ELARG 51, 25 May 1998, point 4.

[27] Luxembourg European Council, Presidency conclusion 13, SN400/97, 12 December 1997.

[28] 1. Free movement of goods, 2. Freedom of movement for persons, 3. Freedom to provide services, 4. Free movement of capital, 5. Company law, 6. Competition policy, 7. Agriculture, 8. Fisheries, 9. Transport policy, 10. Taxation, 11. Economic and Monetary Union, 12. Statistics, 13. Social Policy and employment, 14. Energy, 15. Industrial policy, 16. Small and medium-sized undertak-

Chapter 24 deals with Justice and Home Affairs. On 27 May 1998, Coreper agreed to a list of the EU acquis in the field of Justice and Home Affairs proposed as set out in the document 6473/3/98 JAI 7 REV 3. This document has been made available to the applicant States. For the acquis screening the JHA acquis has again been listed again in the so-called 'TAIEX list'.

With the entry into force of the Treaty of Amsterdam on 1 May 1999, the Schengen acquis forms part of the EU acquis. The Schengen Acquis comprises the 1985 Schengen Agreement, the 1990 Schengen Convention, the Accession Protocols and Agreements and the declarations and decisions adopted by the Executive Committee as well as acts adopted by the organs upon which the Executive Committee has conferred decision-making powers, in particular the Central Group.[29]

For the implementation of the Protocol integrating the Schengen acquis into the framework of the European Union the Council adopted two decisions on 20 May 1999:
– Council Decision concerning the definition of the Schengen acquis for the purpose of determining, in conformity with the relevant provisions of the Treaty establishing the European Community and the Treaty on European Union, the legal basis for each of the provisions or decisions which constitute the acquis.
– Council Decision determining, in conformity with the relevant provisions of the Treaty establishing the European Community and the Treaty on European Union, the legal basis for each of the provisions or decisions which constitute the Schengen acquis.[30]

The acquis screening exercise consists of multilateral and bilateral sessions. In the multilateral session a presentation of the complete EU acquis is given to the candidate countries. The bilateral session serves the purpose of identifying problems of substance of which account will need to be taken in the pre-accession strategy and during the negotiations and to see how far each candidate country has come in transposing the EU-acquis into its national legislation. With regard to the practical implementation of the EU acquis the bilateral sessions were prepared by answering a questionnaire, whereas the adjustment of the legislation was made visible by an enumerative comparison of the TAIEX list and the relevant national laws and provisions.

For Cyprus, Hungary, Poland, the Czech Republic, Slovenia and Estonia the multilateral and bilateral acquis-screening took place in February/March 1999.

---

ings, 17. Science and research, 18. Education and training, 19. Telecommunication and information technologies, 20. Culture and audiovisual, 21. Regional policy and coordination of structural instruments, 22. Environment, 23. Consumer and health protection, 24. Cooperation in the fields of justice and home affairs, 25. Customs union, 26. External relations, 27. Common Foreign and Security Policy, 28. Financial Control, 29. Financial and budgetary provisions, 30. Institutions, 31. Other.

[29] Annex to the Protocol integrating the Schengen acquis into the framework of the European Union.

[30] OJ No. L 176, 10 July 1999, 17-30.

For Bulgaria, Romania, Latvia, Lithuania and Slovakia the multilateral acquis screening took place in October 1998, the bilateral acquis screening in June 1999 and the Schengen-acquis screening in November 1999.

For Malta, the acquis screening took place in December 1999.

The screening in Justice and Home Affairs differed from the other chapters in the sense that the Presidency and the EU Member States could participate in the screening process as observers.

3.2. *Negotiation procedure*

In October 1999 the European Commission presented its reports on the acquis screening of Chapter 24 (Justice and Home Affairs) for Cyprus, Hungary, Poland, the Czech Republic, Slovenia and Estonia. These reports are expected to be discussed in the Enlargement Group in January 2000. In February/March 2000 the European Commission will present its drafts for the Common Position of the European Union on Chapter 24. These drafts will be discussed, among others things, in the Enlargement Group and in Coreper up until May 2000 with the aim of being adopted by the General Affairs Council in June 2000.

By the end of 1999 Estonia, Poland, Hungary, the Czech Republic and Slovenia had prepared Position Papers on Chapter 24 of the EU acquis. Therefore the opening of bilateral negotiations at a ministerial level can be expected to take place as planned in June 2000.

III. SPECIAL ARRANGEMENTS FOR THE CO-OPERATION IN JUSTICE AND HOME AFFAIRS IN THE ENLARGEMENT PROCESS

1. Collective Evaluation Group

On 10 June 1998, Coreper set up the expert group 'Collective Evaluation'[31] which has the task of preparing and maintaining up to date collective evaluations of the situation in the applicant countries on the enactment, application and effective implementation of the acquis of the European Union in the field of Justice and Home Affairs. This group was initiated by the French Minister for the Interior, Chevènement, to guarantee that also the Council, in particular the Ministries of the Interior and Justice, have a say in the negotiations on Chapter 24 of the EU acquis.

This group of experts reports, through Coreper and in close cooperation with the Strategic Committee on Immigration, Frontiers and Asylum and the Article 36 Committee, to the Council on the progress and results of the evaluations. The

---

[31] Joint Action of 10 June 1998 establishing a mechanism for collective evaluation of the enactment, application and effective implementation by the applicant countries of the acquis of the European Union in the field of Justice and Home Affairs, OJ No. L 191, 7 July 1998, 8.

European Commission is invited to take account of the collective evaluations in its proposals for significant adjustments of the priorities and objectives of the Accession Partnerships.

At the same time the preamble and Article 1 of the Joint Action insist on the need that the evaluation exercise remains consistent with the enlargement process and does not prejudice the competence of the established structures for determining the position of the Member States in accession negotiations, in particular of the Council Working Group on Enlargement.

The first objective for the group is to produce for each candidate country a 'country report'. For this purpose the Presidency invited all Member States and international organisations like UNHCR to send in all their material to the General Secretariat of the Council. Four national experts have been seconded to the General Secretariat to process all this material and to draft the country reports.

At the end of 1999 country reports for Poland and Estonia had been submitted to the Justice and Home Affairs Council and the General Affairs Council. The draft country report for the Czech Republic was planned to be finalised under the Finnish Presidency and the draft country reports for Hungary and Slovenia should be completed in the spring of 2000. Each of the country reports which is confidential has been divided into five parts (external borders, migration, asylum, police co-operation, judicial co-operation).

2. **Pre-accession Pact on Organised Crime**

On 29 May 1998 the EU Member States and the ten CEEC and Cyprus agreed on the Pre-accession Pact on Organised Crime which enables existing co-operation to be intensified during the pre-accession period.[32] Whereas the text of the pact has been prepared by the Multidisciplinary Group on Organised Crime, implementation has been forwarded to an expert group composed of both the Member States and the candidate countries (Pre-accession Pact Experts Group – PAPEG).

3. **Ongoing co-operation in the field of visa policy and visa practice, as well as at the level of CIREFI exchange of statistics**

In November 1998 the Council Working Group on Visa and CIREFI met with experts from the candidate countries on a working document with the title 'Ongoing co-operation in the field of visa policy and visa practice, as well as at the level of CIREFI exchange of statistics'.[33]

This document entails an enforced co-operation in the following fields: visa policy, processing of and decisions on visa applications, consular co-operation,

---

[32] OJ No. C 202, 15 July 1998.
[33] Document 12477/98 ASIM 225 VISA 26.

management and organisation of visa-issuing offices, document security, inclusion of the applicant States in the CIREFI statistical exchange by 1 January 2000, training and equipment. In the spring of 1999 country partnerships between the Member States and the candidate countries were set up.

IV. DEEPENING AND ENLARGING THE EUROPEAN UNION – A CONTRADICTION?

Article 1 of the Protocol on the institutions with the prospect of enlargement of the European Union states that on the date of entry into force of the first enlargement of the Union, the Commission 'shall comprise one national of each of the Member States, provided that, by that date, the weighting of the votes in the Council has been modified, whether by re-weighting of the votes or by dual majority, in a manner acceptable to all Member States, taking into account all relevant elements, notably compensating those Member States which give up the possibility of nominating a second Member of the Commission'.

Article 2 of the Protocol reads as follows:

> 'At least one year before the membership of the European Union exceeds twenty, a conference of representatives of the governments of the Member States shall be convened in order to carry out a comprehensive review of the provisions of the Treaties on the composition and functioning of the institutions.'

In its Composite Paper on the 1999 Regular Reports the European Commission points out that there are two potentially conflicting objectives in the enlargement process: speed and quality – or in other words – deepening and enlarging the European Union.

A great deal has already been attained in the Union: the Common Market, the Monetary Union, and in Tampere progress has been made towards an area of freedom, security and justice. Nevertheless there is more than ever a need for institutional reform.

The Helsinki European Council has made a firm political commitment 'to make every effort to complete the Intergovernmental Conference on institutional reform by December 2000, to be followed by ratification. After ratification of the results of that Conference the Union should be in a position to welcome new Member States from the end of 2002 as soon as they have demonstrated their ability to assume the obligations of membership and once the negotiating process has been successfully completed'.[34]

---

[34] Helsinki European Council, Presidency conclusion 5, see also conclusions 14-24, 11 December 1999.

1.7

ACTORS AND SOURCES
(on external actors: the UN Family and others as a source of information gathering)

Peter van Krieken

In the Acquis instruments attention has been paid to UNHCR. Often reference is made to UNHCR as a source of information. Indeed, UNHCR can be considered a reliable source, although it should be underlined that being a source of information is not among UNHCR's core activities. It has sometimes been argued that being a source of information may have a negative impact on its actual task, namely to protect refugees in the country on which UNHCR negatively reports.

It is therefore of the utmost importance to rely, whenever and wherever relevant, on any possible alternative source, but also preferably from within the UN family, as the UN should be looked upon as the establisher of pertinent criteria, both as regards issues relating to peace and security, and e.g. where it concerns human rights. The main sources would appear to be: (reports and comments of) Human Rights Committees and (reports and resolutions of the) Commission on Human Rights.

1. INTRODUCTION

In a 1998 UNHCR letter on Angolan child soldiers[1] the issue of conscription was raised and it was stated that children under 18 should not be returned to their country of origin, as they might run the risk of being drafted into the army. This statement resulted in some misunderstanding, as a reference to the relevant Article of the Convention on the Rights of the Child (Art. 38) would have shown that the minimum age agreed upon in that Convention has been set at 15, regrettable as this may be. This shows that UNHCR as an 'actor' may not necessarily stick to internationally recognized criteria, although, most fortunately, CRC's Art. 38 is

---

[1] Included in Van Krieken (ed.), *Refugee Law in Context: The Exclusion Clause* (1999), pp. 43-45

now bound to be amended, vide the draft optional protocol of January 2000.[2] This development nevertheless reinforces the need to pay due attention to human rights in a general UN setting, rather than to rely on unilateral statements by a single UN organization

2. HUMAN RIGHTS

This example stresses the need to place the information obtained in the context of human rights violations, namely those violations which are relevant to the law of asylum (as not all violations are relevant). For this purpose information needs to be obtained from reliable sources, particularly those sources to which the receiving countries have legal obligations. It concerns
(a) Treaty obligations;
(b) Charter obligations.

As far as Treaties and Treaty bodies are concerned, mention should be made of the 1966 Covenants as well as Human Rights Treaties on Torture, Children, Discrimination and the like.

Charter-based obligations and organs could be subdivided into:
(b.1) the UN Commission on Human Rights;
(b.2) the United Nations High Commissioner of Human Rights and
(b.3) relevant Resolutions of the General Assembly, and in particular of the Security Council.

a) **Treaty Obligations**

a1) *Reports, recommendations and comments*
Most countries have ratified/acceded to the main human rights conventions (Covenants of 1966, CAT 1984, CRC 1989, etc.). Under these Conventions Committees have been set up, the main one being the Human Rights Committee. These committees have been established to monitor the implementation of the principal international human rights treaties (also referred to as 'treaty monitoring bodies' or 'treaty bodies'):
– the Human Rights Committee, which monitors the implementation of the International Covenant on Civil and Political Rights (CCPR);

---

[2] On 21 January 2000 a Working Group adopted by consensus a draft optional protocol to the Convention on the Rights of the Child on the involvement of children in armed conflicts. It has been laid down that 'State Parties shall take all feasible measures to ensure that members of their armed forces who have not attained the age of 18 years do not take a direct part in hostilities [and] shall ensure that persons who have not attained the age of 18 years are not compulsorily recruited into their armed forces' (Artt. 1 and 2). Moreover agreement was also reached on ensuring the voluntariness of voluntary recruitment. Of utmost importance is that the draft optional protocol also addresses 'armed groups, distinct from the armed forces of a State' (without affecting the legal status of any party to an armed conflict) (Art. 4).

– the Committee on Economic, Social and Cultural Rights, which monitors the implementation of the International Covenant on Economic, Social and Cultural Rights (CESCR);
– the Committee against Torture, which monitors the Convention against Torture and Other Cruel, Inhuman or Degrading Treatment or Punishment (CAT);
– the Committee on the Elimination of Racial Discrimination, which monitors the International Convention on the Elimination of All Forms of Racial Discrimination (CERD);
– the Committee on the Elimination of Discrimination against Women, which monitors the Convention on the Elimination of All Forms of Discrimination against Women (CEDAW); and
– the Committee on the Rights of the Child, which monitors the Convention on the Rights of the Child (CRC).

By adhering to one of these treaties, States parties agree to engage in a dialogue with the relevant treaty body. They assume a legal obligation to submit periodic 'State reports' outlining the legislative, judicial, administrative and other measures they have taken to ensure the enjoyment of the rights contained in the treaty. Treaty bodies normally examine State reports in the presence of representatives of the Government and conclude with the adoption of 'concluding observations' or 'concluding comments'. They also issue General Comments. These reports and comments are to be considered as the main sources by which to evaluate the information obtained, in particular because the Committees are independent, enjoy a clearly defined status, and have been able over the years to gather the necessary status and respect, so that their reports can indeed be considered fairly authoritative.[3]

The Committee reports have been drawn up in a relatively legal environment and more often than not lack political statements. This renders the Committees and their respective reports valuable. A disadvantage is to be found in the fact that the reports are relatively outdated, as most countries need to report only once every four to five years. Yet another handicap can be seen in the as yet inconclusive course the CRC and CAT Committees appear to take: it is herewith submitted that these Committees are still involved in some soul-searching, i.e., efforts to find the desired balance, a balance between *de lege lata* and *de lege ferenda*.[4] This is in particular true for individual cases ('communications').

---

[3] Recent reports include: CCPR/C/79/Add.99 *Belgium* Concluding observations of the Human Rights Committee 19/11/98; CCPR/C/79/Add.98 *Iceland* Concluding observations of the Human Rights Committee 11/11/98; CCPR/C/79/Add.97 *United Republic of Tanzania* Concluding observations of the Human Rights Committee 18/08/98; CCPR/C/79/Add.96 *The Former Yugoslav Republic of Macedonia* Concluding Observations of the Human Rights Committee 18/08/98; CCPR/C/79/Add.95 *Algeria* Concluding Observations of the Human Rights Committee 18/08/98; CCPR/C/79/Add.94 *Italy* Concluding observations of the Human Rights Committee 18/08/98; CCPR/C/79/Add.93 *Israel* Concluding Observations of the Human Rights Committee 18/08/98.

[4] Probably the best site to search for available information is the following: http://ww.unhchr.ch/tbs/doc.nsf.

a2) *Case-law and communications*
The same Treaty bodies also often have the possibility to deal with individual cases. This is true in Europe for the European Convention on Human Rights and Fundamental Freedoms (ECHR), under which the individual enjoys the possibility to submit cases to the Strasbourg Court. Article 3 of the ECHR gives individual rejectees, i.e., those whose application for asylum or a related residence permit has been rejected, the possibility to appeal to the Strasbourg-based Court on the basis of the claim that a return would expose the returnee to degrading or inhuman treatment. Case-law is now emerging and needs to be followed and scrutinized closely as the importance of this Strasbourg-based mechanism should not be underestimated as it forces the authorities to follow suit. On the other hand, however, it enables the authorities to dismiss claims of acting in violation of international human rights principles by the very fact that the individual could have submitted the case to Strasbourg or, upon having done so, by the fact that the case has been declared inadmissible (which happens much more often than would appear from the literature, which tends to focus on the cases which have been declared admissible)[5], or has been rejected following full procedures.

Similarly, the Committee under the Convention against Torture is entitled to deal with individual cases as well. The Geneva-based CAT Committee has thus far issued a number of communications which are worth being studied in detail.[6] Of interest may be the fact that among lawyers the CAT procedure appears to be preferred to the Strasbourg one, as the CAT Committee seems to be somewhat more generous in its findings. In an interesting case of two Peruvian brothers, CAT sided with the asylum seeker whereas 'Strasbourg' had dismissed the very similar claim. This trend, however, will surely be reversed or amended in the not too distant future.

The Raoul Wallenberg Institute (Lund, Sweden) has initiated a series on General Comments or Recommendations adopted by United Nations Human Rights Treaty Bodies, of which Volume 1: The Human Rights Committee (2nd edition, 1998) is most useful (Box 1155 SE-221 05 Lund).

[5] An interesting compilation of Strasbourg cases can be found in: Lawson & Schermers, *Leading Cases of the European Court of Human Rights* (1997). For a more exhaustive survey, which includes relevant cases which have been declared inadmissible: Steenbergen & Van den Broek: *Jurisprudentieoverzicht* 1989-1999 (The Hague 1999).

[6] Recent decisions include: CAT/C/22/D/62/1996 *Hungary* Communication No. 62/1996 11/06/99; CAT/C/22/D/120/1998 *Australia* Communication No. 120/1998 25/05/99; CAT/C/22/D/112/1998 *Switzerland* Communication No. 112/1998 03/06/99; CAT/C/22/D/106/1998 *Australia* Communication No. 106/1998 03/06/99; CAT/C/22/D/104/1998 *Sweden* Communication No. 104/1998 21/06/99; CAT/C/22/D/103/1998 *Sweden* Communication No. 103/1998 11/06/99; CAT/C/21/D/97/1997 *Sweden* Communication No. 97/1997 12/11/98; CAT/C/21/D/91/1997 *Netherlands* Communication No. 91/1997 13/11/98; CAT/C/21/D/88/1997 *Sweden* Communication No. 88/1997 16/11/98; CAT/C/21/D/66/1997 *Canada* Communication No. 66/1997 13/11/98; CAT/C/21/D/110/1998 *Venezuela* Communication No. 110/1998 16/12/98; CAT/C/21/D/101/1997 *Sweden* Communication No. 101/1997 16/12/98; CAT/C/21/D/100/1997 *Switzerland* Communication No. 100/1997 16/12/98; CAT/C/20/D/94/1997 *Switzerland* Communication No. 94/1997 19/05/98; CAT/C/20/D/90/1997 *Switzerland* Communication No. 90/1997 19/05/98; CAT/C/20/D/89/1997 *Sweden* Communication No. 89/1997 08/05/98; CAT/C/20/D/83/1997 *Sweden* Communication No. 83/1997 15/05/98; CAT/C/20/D/65/1997 *Sweden* Communication No. 65/1997 06/05/98 (Source e.g. www.unhchr.ch/tbs/doc.nsf).

b) Charter-Based Bodies

Often the Commission of Human Rights is confused with the Human Rights Committee. The latter, as we saw above, is a Treaty body, i.e., based and initiated by a specific Treaty from which it draws its existence and authority. Charter-based bodies are different as they are the result of a more administrative approach of the UN system. The Charter-based bodies fall within the UN.

The following bodies are in this respect worth focusing upon: the Commission on Human Rights and its Sub-Commission on the Promotion and Protection of Human Rights. Although these bodies claim to be fairly independent, they are nevertheless somewhat influenced by political considerations. This is quite logical, as discussions take place in a political, rather than legal setting. Resolutions[7] therefore do not necessarily carry the weight which one would have hoped, as the final texts are often the result of political deliberations. The reports, however, although not of any binding nature, are normally extremely informative as well as normative. These reports focus, on the one hand, on themes (like: disappearances, religious tolerance, the death penalty) and, on the other, on countries (like: Iraq, Iran, Afghanistan, Sudan).[8,9] These Commission (and Sub-Commission) reports and resolutions should be considered as a very important source of information

---

[7] The symbol of Commission Resolutions is: E/CN.4/Res/year/1 et seq. The Resolutions of the Sub-Committee have as symbol: E/CN.4/Sub.2/Res/year/1 et seq.

[8] Among the reports submitted to the Sub-Commission in 1999 were: (E/CN.4/Sub.2/1999/4) a note by the Secretariat on the Violations of the rights of human rights defenders in all countries; (E/CN.4/Sub.2/1999/7) a working paper on the rights of non-citizens; (E/CN.4/Sub.2/1999/10) a working paper on the content of the right to education; (E/CN.4/Sub.2/1999/11) a working paper on human rights as the primary objective of international trade, investment and finance policy and practice; (E/CN.4/Sub.2/1999/12) an updated study on the right to food; (E/CN.4/Sub.2/1999/13) a report of the Secretary-General on the situation of women and girls in Afghanistan; (E/CN.4/Sub.2/1999/14) the third report by the Special Rapporteur on the situation regarding the elimination of traditional practices affecting the health of women and the girl child; (E/CN.4/Sub.2/1999/15) a report of the Secretary-General on the implementation of the Programme of Action for the Prevention of the Sale of Children, Child Prostitution and Child Pornography; (E/CN.4/Sub.2/1999/16) a note by the Secretariat on systematic rape, sexual slavery and slavery-like practices during armed conflict, including internal armed conflict; (E/CN.4/Sub.2/1999/17) a report of the Working Group on Contemporary Forms of Slavery; (E/CN.4/Sub.2/1999/18) on indigenous people and their relationship to land; (E/CN.4/Sub.2/1999/20) the final report by the Special Rapporteur concerned: a study on treaties, agreements and other constructive arrangements between States and indigenous populations; (E/CN.4/Sub.2/1999/21) a report of the Working Group on Minorities; (E/CN.4/Sub.2/1999/26) a note by the Secretariat on adverse consequences of the transfer of arms and illicit trafficking in arms on the enjoyment of human rights; (E/CN.4/Sub.2/1999/27) a report by the Special Rapporteur on terrorism and human rights; (E/CN.4/Sub.2/1999/29) a working paper on the observance of human rights by States which are not parties to United Nations human rights conventions; (E/CN.4/Sub.2/1999/31) a list of States which have proclaimed or continued a state of emergency [ed: of great importance for fully appreciating the (non-)enforcement, relevance and violation of human rights provisions]; etcetera.

[9] Among the reports submitted to the Commission in 1999 were: (E/CN.4/1999/10) a report of the Secretary-General on the situation in occupied Palestine; (E/CN.4/1999/101) a report of the Special Representative of the Secretary-General for Human Rights in Cambodia; (E/CN.4/1999/102) a note by the Secretariat on the situation of human rights in Haiti; (E/CN.4/1999/103) a report of the Independent expert on the situation of human rights in Somalia; (E/CN.4/1999/105) a note by the

[nt. 9 continued]
Secretary-General on the programme of action for the elimination of the exploitation of child labour; (E/CN.4/1999/11) a report of the Special Rapporteur on the use of mercenaries; (E/CN.4/1999/111) a draft international convention on the protection of all persons from enforced disappearance; (E/CN.4/1999/113) a report of the Secretary-General on the rights of persons belonging to national or ethnic, religious and linguistic minorities; (E/CN.4/1999/12) a report of the High Commissioner for human rights on racism; (E/CN.4/1999/15) a report of the Special Rapporteur on contemporary forms of racism, racial discrimination, xenophobia and related intolerance; (E/CN.4/1999/25) a report of the Secretary-General on the situation of human rights in Cyprus; (E/CN.4/1999/26) a report of the Secretary-General on the human rights situation in Southern Lebanon and Western Bekaa; (E/CN.4/1999/28) a report of the Secretary-General on the situation in East Timor; (E/CN.4/1999/29) a report of the Secretary-General on the situation of human rights in Myanmar; (E/CN.4/1999/30) a note by the Secretariat on the work of the Secretary-General's Investigative Team in the Democratic Republic of the Congo; [and: (31)] a report of the Special Rapporteur on the situation of human rights in the Democratic Republic of the Congo; (E/CN.4/1999/32 report of the Special Representative on the situation of human rights in the Islamic Republic of Iran; (E/CN.4/1999/33 report of the Special Representative on the situation of human rights in Rwanda [and: 33] a note by the Secretariat on the situation of human rights in Rwanda; (E/CN.4/1999/35) a report of the Special Rapporteur on the situation of human rights in Myanmar; (E/CN.4/1999/36) a report of the Special Rapporteur on the situation of human rights in Nigeria; (E/CN.4/1999/37) a report of the Special Rapporteur on the situation of human rights in Iraq; (E/CN.4/1999/38) a report of the Special Rapporteur on the situation of human rights in the Sudan; (E/CN.4/1999/39) a report of the Special Rapporteur on extrajudicial, summary or arbitrary executions; (E/CN.4/1999/40) a report of the Special Rapporteur on the situation of human rights in Afghanistan; (E/CN.4/1999/41) a report of the Special Rapporteur on the human rights situation in the Republic of Equatorial Guinea; (E/CN.4/1999/42) a report of the Special Rapporteur on the situation of human rights in the former Yugoslavia; (E/CN.4/1999/43) a note by the Secretariat on the situation of human rights in Burundi; (E/CN.4/1999/52) a report on the question of the death penalty; (E/CN.4/1999/53) on the right to restitution, compensation and rehabilitation for victims of grave violations of human rights and fundamental freedoms; (E/CN 4/1999/54) a report of the Secretary-General on the Convention against Torture and Other Cruel, Inhuman or Degrading Treatment or Punishment; (E/CN.4/1999/56) a report of the Secretary-General on human rights and arbitrary deprivation of nationality; (E/CN.4/1999/57) a report of the Secretary-General on civil and political rights, including questions of: independence of the judiciary, administration of justice, impunity; (E/CN.4/1999/58) a report of the Special Rapporteur on religious intolerance; (E/CN.4/1999/60) a report of the Special Rapporteur on the independence of judges and lawyers; (E/CN.4/1999/61) a report of the Special Rapporteur on torture; (E/CN.4/1999/62) a report of the Working Group on enforced or involuntary disappearances; (E/CN.4/1999/63) a report of the Working Group on arbitrary detention; (E/CN.4/1999/64) a report of the Special Rapporteur on the protection and promotion of the right to freedom of opinion and expression; (E/CN.4/1999/65) a report of the independent expert on the right to restitution, compensation and rehabilitation for victims of grave violations of human rights and fundamental freedoms; (E/CN.4/1999/66) a note by the Secretary-General on the report on trafficking in women and girls; (E/CN.4/1999/68) a report of the Special Rapporteur on violence against women, its causes and consequences; (E/CN.4/1999/69) a report of the Secretary-General on abduction of children from Northern Uganda; (E/CN.4/1999/70) a report on the status of the Convention on the Rights of the Child; (E/CN.4/1999/71) a report of the Special Rapporteur on the sale of children, child prostitution and child pornography; (E/CN.4/1999/72) a note by the Secretary-General on the report of the Special Representative of the Secretary-General for children and armed conflict; (E/CN.4/1999/79) a report of the Representative of the Secretary-General on internally displaced persons; (E/CN.4/1999/81) a report of the High Commissioner for Human Rights on the implementation of the programme of activities for the International Decade of the World's Indigenous People; (E/CN.4/1999/9) the yearly report of the High Commissioner for Human Rights; (E/CN.4/1999/90) a report of the Secretary-General on human rights and bioethics; (E/CN.4/1999/91) a report of the Secretary-General on status of the international covenants on human rights; (E/CN.4/1999/96) on human rights and thematic procedures; etcetera.

for asylum determination officers/offices, albeit that it should be underlined that the Commission operates in a political context, which gives the reports/resolutions a somewhat political flavour.

c) Other Charter-Based Bodies

It is normally assumed that ECOSOC, the General Assembly and the Security Council are also of relevance for the appreciation of human rights situations as part of an asylum procedure. Indeed, both ECOSOC and the General Assembly can and do adopt resolutions on e.g. a) the activities of the UNHCR, and b) the human rights situation in a given country. These resolutions, although soft law, are of relevance and importance.

Resolutions of the Security Council are of the utmost relevance. They concern, after all, hard law, and may, more often than not, have an impact on the asylum procedure. Two examples may suffice. The question regarding, e.g., a draft evader from Armenia who expresses the fear to becoming involved in military activities in/around the Nagorno Karabach enclave, should be seen against the background of relevant SC Resolutions. The same is true for military activities towards the liberation of Kuwait, as well as the campaign concerning Kosovo: does it concern acts in violation of the *ius ad bellum* and/or *ius in bello*? Similarly, due attention should be paid to, e.g., SC Res. 1269 (1999)[10] on the issue of terrorism in which States have been called upon to take appropriate steps 'to deny those who plan, finance or commit terrorist acts safe havens by ensuring their apprehension and prosecution or extradition' and to ensure, before granting refugee status 'that the asylum-seeker has not participated in terrorist acts.' This being hard law, it has an immediate and direct impact on individual asylum procedures.

d) UNHCR

The Acquis refers on a number of occasions to the UNHCR, the United Nations High Commissioner for Refugees. This is, e.g., the case in the 1996 Joint Position, and in particular in the 1999 Tampere Milestones. In the latter document (para. 14) it can be read that '... the European Council stresses the importance of consulting UNHCR and other international organizations ...' The principle of consultation has also been laid down in the Schengen acquis. The Treaty of Amsterdam, like may of the Acquis documents, refers in art. 63 specifically to the 1951 Refugee Convention and the 1967 Protocol, and hence to the undertaking to cooperate with the UNHCR, as has been laid down in art. 35 of the 1951 Convention.

Of relevance in this respect is to fully appreciate the status of the UNHCR, but not so much its fitting as a subsidiary organization within the UN as a whole, re-

---

[10] Adopted at the SC's 4053rd meeting on 19 October 1999.

porting to ECOSOC, and through ECOSOC to the General Assembly, but rather as the basis of its statements, reports and guidelines.

As is the case with most international organizations, UNHCR is triple-faced:
aa) it functions as an arena, forum, that is for meetings, discussions, and exchange of views;
bb) it is an instrument, an implementor of programmes which individual states cannot possibly implement themselves; and
cc) it has over the years become an 'actor' in itself, wherby it issues statements which are not necessarily supported or screened by its constitutionary.

UNHCR is bound by the Statute (1950), but is not a member under the 1951 Convention. Yet, it has under the Convention been given the task (duty) to supervise the implementation of the Convention (Art. 35). Although the General Assembly, virtually every year, subscribes to UNHCR's activities, the more regular job of the supervision of UNHCR itself is carried out by the Executive Committee (ExCom), assisted by a Standing Committee (SC). The ExCom meets every year, in early October, whereas the Standing Committee tends to meet in January and June. The reports and conclusions of ExCom (and to a lesser extent SC) serve as fairly authoritative material: the Member States themselves adopt these Conclusions (e.g., the ones on international protection), and although it concerns soft law, the Conclusions are a useful tool in interpreting the Convention and solving outstanding legal questions.

The Acquis itself does not refer to the ExCom Conclusions, but on the basis of the Joint Position referring to The Handbook (*The Handbook on Procedures and Criteria for Determining Refugee Status*), which itself was the result of a request by ExCom at its 28th session, 1977), it could be concluded that ExCom itself, after all an inter-governmental body with virtually all 15 EU Member States on board, deserves the necessary attention.[11]

Of course, in interpreting refugee law, the 1951 Convention stands as the primary source, and the ExCom conclusions and the UNHCR Handbook are subsidiary sources at most. Yet, both the UNHCR Handbook and ExCom Conclusions should be considered part and parcel of the Acquis, albeit, let it be emphasized once again, soft law at most.

UNHCR is a major source at the very moment it bases itself on Art. 35 of the Convention (the duty to supervise the implementation of the Convention). However, many letters, positions, guidelines are based on the (cc) role, the role of actor, and seem to lack any hard legal standing. Those documents should be dealt with whilst keeping the above in mind.

UNHCR Background papers on countries of origin are sometimes of excellent quality, sometimes rather poor. It is herewith submitted that although the background papers are based on material in the public domain, every now and then

---

[11] An up-dated list of ExCom Conclusions as well as the introduction and conclusion of UNHCR's Handbook has been reproduced in the Chapter 'Additional Texts'.

they fall victim to cognitive dissonance. The background papers should therefore not be relied upon as the ultimate source, but rather in conjunction with sources such as The Economist, Keesing's Contemporary Archives (KCA), Reuters, etc.

As far as guidelines and letters to individual Governments are concerned, it needs to be stressed that divergencies do exist between those guidelines and letters, on the one hand, and, e.g., ExCom or Standing Committee documents on the other (for example, on the issue of the preliminary use of the exclusion clause).[12] Guidelines and letters, if no explicit reference is made to UNHCR acting in its capacity as supervisor ex Art. 35 of the 1951 Convention, might lack the authority which has often been presumed. This is of great importance in the case, if any, of (presumed) divergencies between the Acquis and the 1951 Convention.

3. OTHER ACTORS AND SOURCES

a) Embassies

As Embassies are part and parcel of the Executive, they should be fully relied upon as a source. Probably better use can be made of this source, particularly in combination with the public reports submitted by some member states.[13]

b) Amnesty International

AI is a NGO. No country is a member, no country is bound to follow suit. Yet the information is often useful, but has no official standing, no official status, particularly compared to the information available through the above mentioned Committees and Commissions. Moreover, AI represents only part of the human rights spectrum, and serves as a lobby, rather than a truly independent source.

The same could be submitted for Human Rights Watch, Helsinki Groups, etc.

c) Others

One of the most knowledgeable organizations almost by definition does not share the information it obtains: the ICRC. Different from the various national Red Cross Branches/Organizations, the ICRC is most often not available for informative purposes. The information which can be obtained through the national societies is often tainted, as its independence can not always be assured.

OSCE should also be considered as a reliable source. The High Commissioner

---

[12] Compare the significant absence in the Standing Committee Note dated 30 May 1997 of the requirement contained in the December 1995 Guidelines on the issue of applying 1A ahead of 1F.

[13] And for example the U.S. Congress yearly report on the status of human rights worldwide: Country Reports on Human Rights Practices 1999 (to be published in March 2000 and prepared by the Department of State).

for ethnic minorities has as an institution reached a level of authority which should not be neglected.

4. CONCLUSION

Any exchange of information and indeed any status determination is bound to be imperfect, if not matched by relevant human rights information on the subject/country concerned. It may therefore be submitted that there is a need to look into the possibility to obtain the necessary relevant human rights information on the various countries from where the asylum seekers originate. The context should always be established to the greatest extent possible. The standing of the source is of the utmost importance: Treaty-bodies should be given priority; Charter-based bodies should be consulted; UNHCR should be valued, but should not be considered the one and only reliable source; NGOs often provide useful information and can act as a trigger.

Countries should increasingly become aware of the contractual obligations they have entered into and the consequences these may yield. Similarly, they may also wish to appreciate the impact of soft law, information provided by lobbies and the like. It is the context which counts.

The following priority is therefore proposed, which could serve as a useful working tool:
– Resolutions by the Security Council
– observations and comments as submitted by Treaty bodies (such as the Human Rights Committee)
– general comments by Treaty bodies
– decisions in individual cases (Strasbourg case-law; communications under CAT)
– reports submitted by special rapporteurs to the (Sub-)Commission on Human Rights
– Resolutions adopted by Charter-based bodies (other than the Security Council)
– reports and judgments for/by International Tribunals
– UNHCR background papers, guidelines
– reports produced by or for bodies belonging to the executive (U.S. Congress; Danish or Dutch situation reports; HLWG– and CIREA reports, etc.)
– reports by/for ICRC, OSCE,
– Keesing's, the Economist, Reuters, etc.[14]
– reports produced by NGOs (Amnesty International, Human Rights Watch, Helsinki Federation, etc.).

This priority tool should enable all parties involved to strive for a harmonized use of sources and to ensure an economic and effective use.

---

[14] Regard should also be had to the BBC Worldservice, which is also available on internet: www.bbb.co.uk/worldservice.

2. LISTS

The official acquis list dates from May 1998, and has been updated late 1998: hence the 1 January 1999 date. Hereinbelow the original acquis list as per that date has been reproduced, indicating, however, which instruments had been added between May and December of that year. During 1999 no instruments have been added, which enables us to state that this list represents the 1 January 2000 picture.

The titles of some of the documents originally appeared in French, in fact the acquis document depicts a dual-language image, but have for the sake of accessibility everything has been duly translated into the English.

Those documents which have been **reprinted in this Handbook carry an asterisk**. Numbers (I.A.a.1, etcetera) have been added in improve transparency. Another number has been added (e.g. T.1) which refers to the TAIEX list, which we consider the most useful and authoritative one.

The original acquis list should also be seen in conjunction with the chronological list and the topical list. The chronological list gives insight in the process over time, and reflects at which moment which issue was on the agenda, and on which topic agreements could be reached. It represents the growing awareness that asylum and migration were to become truly European matters which deserve to be put on the main agenda, an awareness which found confirmation in Art. 63 of the Consolidated Treaty Establishing the European Community under which asylum and migration are gradually moved from the Third to the First Pillar, from matters to be exclusively dealt with in the respective Capitals to Community matters: the asylum acquis is only becoming part of the acquis communautaire.

The topical list aims at putting the various documents in a topical order (entry, determination, sojourn, return) in order to provide the user of this Handbook with some tools to improve accessibility.

The TAIEX list, finally is part for the screening exercise and is quite exhaustive, as it contains instruments which also indirectly have an impact on asylum in the broader context. It is therefore that the *complete* TAIEX list has been included, whereas the asylum acquis list as well as the chronological and topical ones have been limited to the issue of asylum and asylum-related migration.

The Commission has, as part of various training tools produced some Commentaries, which we consider extremely useful for the sake of understanding and appreciating the acquis. The general commentary on the acquis has been included in this Chapter.

2.1	Original list	85
2.2	Chronological list	95
2.3	Topical list	99
2.4	TAIEX list	104
2.5	What is the acquis (Brussels' Commentary)	115

2.1

ORIGINAL LIST

The original draft list of the 'acquis' of the Union and its Members States in the field of Justice and Home Affairs was presented by the Presidency to Coreper with a note, dated 25 May 1998, entailing the following background information. The list was annexed as per hereinbelow.

BACKGROUND

1. At its meeting of 6 March [1998] the K4 Committee examined a note of the Presidency containing a first draft of the JHA acquis. This note was largely based on a room document circulated by the Commission at the meeting of the K4 Committee on 24 February 1998.
2. At its meeting of 26/27 March, the K4 Committee examined a version of this note amended according to the comments made at the meeting of the K4 Committee on 6 march and those received in writing.

The present document takes into consideration all the comments made at the meeting of Coreper on 22 April 1998.

GENERAL CONSIDERATIONS

3. The K4 Committee agreed on the following:
(1) The JHA acquis is constantly evolving. Any list of the acquis presented to the candidate countries now will require regular updating. Each new instrument should be forwarded to the candidate countries immediately after its adoption by the Council.
(2) The fact that the Union is prepared to open negotiations means that each applicant State has accepted the 'Copenhagen criteria' and commits itself to their full implementation.
(3) Implementation is no less important than acceptance and ratification. This, together with the process of institution building and administrative support, will require assistance, monitoring and evaluation.
(4) The applicant States must complement and modernise their criminal and procedural legislation as well as their civil law and commercial law up to a minimum level which must be attained to ensure that their legal systems are capable of a proper functioning at national level as well as in relation to the legal systems of other countries.
(5) The Schengen acquis represents a new and significant element. It is not yet part of the Union acquis but can be expected to be so well before the completion of the enlargement negotiations. Implementation of the Schengen acquis will impose particular demands on the candidate countries.

P.J. van Krieken (Ed.), The Asylum Acquis Handbook
© 2000, T.M.C.Asser Press, The Hague, the Röling Foundation and the authors

THE ELEMENTS OF THE ACQUIS

4. The K4 Committee took as a starting point for drawing the list of the acquis the draft EU opening position for the opening of negotiations with the candidate countries. The text agreed in Coreper on 5 March reads as follows:

'With regard to Justice and Home Affairs, accession to the European Union will entail that you:
a) accept in full on accession the justice and home affairs provisions, and the working practices designed to give them effect, of the Treaty of the European Union and the EC Treaty, as amended in each case by the Treaty of Amsterdam when it enters into force;
b) in respect of those conventions or instruments in the JHA field which are inseparable from the attainment of the TEU and the EC Treaty, as amended in each case by the ToA, as well as drawn up by the Council on the basis of Art. K.3 (TEU) (or Art. 34 following the coming into force of the ToA) including the creation of Europol:
i) undertake to accede to those which have been drawn up by the Council or to those signed by it, or which have been opened for signature to, the Member States by the date of your accession to the Union;
ii) accept, in relation to those still under negotiation, the points which have been agreed on by the Fifteen or by the Council at the date of your accession to the Union, participating in subsequent negotiations within the Union framework only on those points still to be resolved;
c) accept on accession the joint actions, joint positions adopted by the Council and resolutions, decisions and statements adopted by the Fifteen or by the Council in the JHA field and accept, in relation to those still under examination, the points which have been agreed on by the Fifteen or by the Council at the date of your accession, participating in subsequent deliberations only on those points still to be resolved;
d) introduce administrative and other arrangements, such as those already adopted by the Fifteen or by the Council, so as to ensure close practical co-operation between Member States' institutions and organisations working in the JHA field, as is necessary effectively to implement the 'acquis';
e) bring your institutions, management systems and administrative arrangements up to Union standards with a view to implementing the 'acquis' and in particular adopt and implement measures with respect to external border controls, asylum and immigration, and measures to prevent and combat organized crime, terrorism and illicit drug trafficking (...)'

5. For the EU acquis this means
– conventions or instruments established by the Council on the basis of Article K3 TEU, including the creation of Europol;
– resolutions and decisions adopted by the Fifteen or by the Council and, as appropriate, statements agreed upon within the framework of JHA
– points agreed upon by the Fifteen or the Council at the date of accession in respect of conventions or instruments under negotiation.

6. The K4 Committee agreed to include, in line with para (b) of the draft EU opening position, a category of conventions in the JHA field which are inseparable from the attainment of the objectives of the TEU and the ToA.

7. Finally, the K4 Committee decided, in line with the approach adopted in the case of the last accessions, to include the relevant conventions which were concluded in the context of European political co-operation or which have been drawn up in other fora and are relevant to the areas covered by Title VI of the TEU, taking into account the state of signature and ratification of these Conventions by Member States.

8. Following the K4 discussion, the Presidency has not included at this stage draft instruments under negotiation since many of these will be adopted by the time of accession. candidate countries will be informed of the programme in HA as defined in the Resolution laying down the priorities in the JHA field for the period from 1 January 1998 to the date of the entry into force of the ToA. They will also be kept informed during the screening process of the areas covered by instruments under negotiation.

9. A list of the explanatory reports of the EU Conventions will also be forwarded to them.

10 The K4 Committee agreed in principle to hand over to the candidate countries the acquis in the area of police co-operation classified confidential, presented to the previous candidate countries, subject to a further study as to what is still relevant.

11. The Schengen acquis [not reproduced]

The Nature Of The Obligation

12. The various elements of the acquis do not all have the same legal status. Resolutions and declarations, for example, are not legally binding in the same way as conventions or joint actions. The K4 Committee took the view, however, that in the list itself there should not be a specific indication as to the extent to which particular instruments are legally binding. This might be dealt with in explaining the acquis to the candidate countries during the screening process.

13. In respect of the conventions referred to in para 7 above the K4 Committee agreed that the nature of the commitment on the part of the accessing countries should be qualified in the same way as for the last accessions. In the introduction to this category it was stated: 'These instruments are relevant to co-operation among the Twelve and applicant States should endeavour to become party to them in the same way as the Member States.'

Proposal Of Decision

14. [not reproduced]

ANNEX

'ACQUIS' OF THE EUROPEAN UNION IN THE FIELD OF JUSTICE AND HOME AFFAIRS, LISTED BY TOPIC

INTRODUCTION

I. ASYLUM
II. EXTERNAL BORDERS
III. MIGRATION
IV. ORGANIZED CRIME, FRAUD AND CORRUPTION
V. DRUGS
VI. TERRORISM
VII. POLICE COOPERATION
VIII. CUSTOMS COOPERATION
IX. JUDICIAL COOPERATION IN CIVIL MATTERS
X. JUDICIAL COOPERATION IN CRIMINAL MATTERS
XI. FUNDING OF ACTIVITIES UNDER TEU TITLE VI
XII. HUMAN RIGHTS RELATED ISSUES

INTRODUCTION

In the presentation of the 'acquis' of the European Union concerning cooperation in the field of justice and home affairs, the list of relevant instruments is given in the following order:[1]

A. Conventions to which the applicant States must accede
(a) Conventions established by the Council under Article K.3(2)(c) of the TEU;
(b) Other Conventions to be regarded as inseparable from the achievement of the objectives of the Union to which the States applying to join the European Union will be required to accede as the 'acquis' of the Community or the Union.

B. Joint actions and joint positions adopted by the Council under points (b) and (a) of Article K.3(2) of the TEU.

---

[1] The following six instruments were added to the original acquis list in the period May-December 1998:
– [T.1.d] (1.A.a.4) Decision 1/98 of 30 June 1998 of the Committee set up under Art. 18 of the Dublin Convention;
– [T.17/1/A]] (II.B.3) Joint Action of 3 December 1998 on FADO, the Image Archiving System;
– [T.19/1/A] (II.C.a.3) Recommendation of 28 May 1998 on forgery detection equipment;
– [T.32/1/A] (III.1.C.12) Conclusions on exchange of information on asylum and migration dd 19 March 1998
– [T.32/1/B] (III.1.C.13) Joint principles for the exchange of data in Cirefi
– [T.32/1/C] (III.1.C.14) decision on common standards re residence permits dd 3 December 1998.

C. Other instruments of the European Union
The other instruments adopted by the Council or by the representatives of the Member States (resolutions, recommendations, declarations and other decisions).

D. Other Conventions
Other Conventions established under EPC (European Political Cooperation) or in other fora and regarded as instruments affecting cooperation between the Fifteen. These are instruments which have not all been signed and/or ratified by all Member States, and the Member States are not mutually bound to ratify them, although in the case of some of them there is a political commitment by their Governments to initiate the internal process of ratification. States applying to join the European Union should endeavour to become parties to these Conventions on the same basis as the Member States.

I. **Asylum**[2]

I.A. *Conventions to which the candidate States must accede*

I.A.a) Convention adopted by the Member States of the European Communities prior to the entry into force of the Treaty on European Union:

I.A.a.1) [T.1.a] CONVENTION determining the State responsible for examining applications for asylum lodged in one of the Member States of the European Communities (DUBLIN Convention) (97/C254/01) Official Journal C 254, 19/08/1997 p. 0001 – 0012.(*)
I.A.a.2) [T.1.b] DECISION No 1/97 of 9 September 1997 of the Committee set up by Article 18 of the Dublin Convention of 15 June 1990, concerning provisions for the implementation of the Convention (97/662/CMS) Official Journal L 281, 14/10/1997 p. 0001 – 0025.(*)
I.A.a.3) [T.1.c] DECISION No 2/97 of 9 September 1997 of the Committee set up by Article 18 of the Dublin Convention of 15 June 1990, establishing the Committee's Rules of Procedure (97/663/CMS) Official Journal L 281, 14/10/1997 p. 0026–0026.
I.A.a.4) [T.1.d] DECISION No 1/98 of 30 June 1998 of the Committee set up by Article 18 of the Dublin Convention of 15 June 1990, concerning provisions for the implementation of the Convention (98/451/CMS) Official Journal L 196, 14/07/1998 p. 0049–0050. (*)

I.A.b) Other conventions to be regarded inseparable from the achievement of the objectives of the Union:

I.A.b.1) [T.2] Convention relating to the Status of Refugees (Geneva, 28 July 1951)
I.A.b.2) [T.3] Protocol relating to the Status of Refugees (New York, 31 January 1967)

---

[2] Ed.: The instruments which have been included in this Handbook have been indicated with an asterisk (*)

I.B. *Joint actions and joint positions*

I.B.1) [T.4] JOINT POSITION of 4 March 1996 defined by the Council on the basis of Article K.3 of the Treaty on European Union on the harmonized application of the definition of the term 'refugee' in Article 1 of the Geneva Convention of 28 July 1951 relating to the status of refugees (96/196/JHA) Official Journal L 063, 13/03/1996 p. 0002 – 0007.(*)

I.C. *Other instruments of the European Union*

I.C.1) [T.5] Decision of 11 June 1992 setting up the CIREA (Centre for Information, Discussion and Exchange on Asylum (document WG1 1107)(*)

I.C.2) [T.6] Resolution adopted 30 November 1992 on a harmonized approach to questions concerning host third countries (document WG1 1283)(*)

I.C.3) [T.7] Resolution adopted 30 November 1992 on manifestly unfounded applications for asylum (document WG1 1282 rev 1)(*)

I.C.4) [T.8] Conclusions adopted 30 November 1992 concerning countries in which there is generally no serious risk of persecution (document WG1 1281)(*)

I.C.5) [T.9] Circulation and confidentiality of joint reports on the situation in certain third countries (Text adopted by the Council on 20 June 1994) Official Journal C 274, 19/09/1996 p. 43.(*)

I.C.6) [T.10] Guidelines for joint reports on third countries (Text adopted by the Council on 20 June 1994) Official Journal C 274, 19/09/1996 p. 0052 – 0054.(*)

I.C.7) [T.11] Procedure for drawing up reports in connection with joint assessments of the situation in third countries (7472/92 CIREA 17, adopted by the Council on 20 June 1994)

I.C.8) [T.12] Council Resolution of 20 June 1995 on minimum guarantees for asylum procedures. Official Journal C 274, 19/09/1996 p. 0013 – 0017. (*)

I.C.9) [T.13] COUNCIL RESOLUTION of 25 September 1995 on burden-sharing with regard to the admission and residence of displaced persons on a temporary basis (95/C 262/01) Official Journal C 262, 07/10/1995 p. 0001 – 0003. (*)

I.C.10) [T.14] COUNCIL DECISION of 4 March 1996 on an alert and emergency procedure for burden-sharing with regard to the admission and residence of displaced persons on a temporary basis (96/198/JHA) Official Journal L 063, 13/03/1996 p. 0010 – 0011. (*)

I.C.11) [T.15] COUNCIL DECISION of 26 June 1997 on monitoring the implementation of instruments adopted concerning asylum (97/420/JHA) Official Journal L 178, 07/07/1997 p. 0006 – 0007. (*)

ORIGINAL LIST 91

I.D. *Other Conventions*

--

II. **External Borders**

II.A. *Conventions to which the Candidate States must accede*

--

II.B. *Actions and joint programmes*

II.B.1) [T.16] JOINT ACTION of 4 March 1996 adopted by the Council on the basis of Article K.3 of the Treaty on European Union on airport transit arrangements (96/197/JHA) Official Journal L 063, 13/03/1996 p. 0008 – 0009. (*)

II.B.2) [T.17] JOINT POSITION of 25 October 1996 defined by the Council on the basis of Article K.3 (2) (a) of the Treaty on European Union, on pre-frontier assistance and training assignments (96/622/JHA) Official Journal L 281, 31/10/1996 p. 0001 – 0002.

II.B.3) [T.17/1/A] JOINT ACTION of 3 December 1998 adopted by the Council on the basis of Article K.3 of the Treaty on European Union concerning the setting up of a European Image Archiving System (FADO) (98/700/JHA) Official Journal L 333, 09/12/1998 p. 0004 – 0007.

II.C. *Other instruments of the Union*

II.C.a Regulations adopted by the Council under Article 100 TEC

II.C.a.1) [T.18] COUNCIL REGULATION (EC) No 1683/95 of 29 May 1995 laying down a uniform format for visas Official Journal L 164, 14/07/1995 p. 0001 – 0004.
II.C.a.2) [T.19] COUNCIL REGULATION (EC) No 2317/95 of 25 September 1995 determining the third countries whose nationals must be in possession of visas when crossing the external borders of the Member States Official Journal L 234, 03/10/1995 p. 0001 – 0003. (*)
II.C.a.3) [[T.19/1/A] COUNCIL RECOMMENDATION of 28 May 1998 on the provision of forgery detection equipment at ports of entry to the European Union (98/C 189/02) Official Journal C 189, 17/06/1998 p. 0019 – 0020.

II.D. *Other Conventions*

III. **Migration**

III.1 *Admission*

III.1.A. Conventions to which the candidate States must accede

--

III.1.B. Actions and joint programmes

III.1.B.1) [T.20] COUNCIL DECISION of 30 November 1994 on a joint action adopted by the Council on the basis of Article K.3(2)(b) of the Treaty on European Union concerning travel facilities for school pupils from third countries resident in a Member State (94/795/JHA) Official Journal L 327, 19/12/1994 p. 0001 – 0003.

III.1.B.2) [T.21] JOINT ACTION of 16 December 1996 adopted by the Council on the basis of Article K.3 of the Treaty on European Union concerning a uniform format for residence permits (97/11/JHA) Official Journal L 007, 10/01/1997 p. 0001 – 0004.

III.1.C. Other instruments of the European Union

III.1.C.1) [T.22] Text adopted by Ministers on 11 June 1992 on acceptable/unacceptable travel documents (document WG1 1506 rev 1)

III.1.C.2) [T.23] Resolution of 1 June 1993 on harmonisation of family reunion (document WG 1497 rev 1) (*)

III.1.C.3) [T.24] COUNCIL RESOLUTION of 20 June 1994 on limitations on admission of third-country nationals to the territory of the Member States for employment. Official Journal C 274, 19/09/1996 p. 0003 – 0006.

III.1.C.4) [T.25] Council Resolution of 30 November 1994 relating to the limitations on the admission of third-country nationals to the territory of the Member States for the purpose of pursuing activities as self-employed persons. Official Journal C 274, 19/09/1996 p. 0007 – 0009.

III.1.C.5) [T.26] Council Resolution of 30 November 1994 on the admission of third-country nationals to the territory of the Member States for study purposes. Official Journal C 274, 19/09/1996 p. 0010 – 0012.

III.1.C.6) [T.27] Council Conclusions of 30 November 1994 on the organization and development of the Centre for Information, Discussion and Exchange on the Crossing of Frontiers and Immigration (Cirefi). Official Journal C 274, 19/09/1996 p. 0050 – 0051.

III.1.C.7) [T.28] Council Decision of 22 December 1995 on monitoring the implementation of instruments already adopted concerning admission of third-country nationals . Official Journal C 011, 16/01/1996 p. 0001 – 0001. (*)

III.1.C.8) [T.29] Council Resolution of 4 March 1996 on the status of third-country nationals residing on a long-term basis in the territory of the Member States. Official Journal C 080, 18/03/1996 p. 0002 – 0004.

III.1.C.9) [T.30] COUNCIL RECOMMENDATION of 4 March 1996 relating to local consular cooperation regarding visas (96/C 80/01) Official Journal C 080, 18/03/1996 p. 0001 – 0001.

III.1.C.10) [T.31] COUNCIL RESOLUTION of 26 June 1997 on unaccompanied minors who are nationals of third countries (97/C 221/03 Official Journal C 221, 19/07/1997 p. 0023 – 0027. (*)

III.1.C.11) [T.32] COUNCIL RESOLUTION of 4 December 1997 on measures to be adopted on the combating of marriages of convenience (97/C 382/01) Official Journal C 382, 16/12/1997 p. 0001 – 0002.

III.1.C.12) [T.32/1/A] Conclusions of the Council of 19 March 1998 on the exchange of information in the area of asylum and immigration, docs: ASIM 162 rev 2 and ASIM

73 rev 6

III.1.C.13) [T.32/1/B] Joint principles for the exchange of data in Cirefi doc 8927 CIREFI 35

III.1.C.14) [T.32/1/C] COUNCIL DECISION of 3 December 1998 on common standards relating to filling in the uniform format for residence permits (98/701/JHA) Official Journal L 333, 09/12/1998 p. 0008 – 0016.

III 1.D. Other conventions

--

III 2 *Expulsion*

III 2.A. Conventions to which the candidate States must accede

--

III 2.B. Actions and joint programmes

--

III 2.C. Other instruments of the European Union

III.2.C.1) [T.33] Recommendation of 30 November 1992 regarding practices followed by Member States on expulsion (document WG1 1266)

III.2.C.2) [T.34] Recommendation of 30 November 1882 concerning transit for the purpose of expulsion (document WG1 1266)

III.2.C.3) [T.35] Recommendation of the 1st June 1993 concerning checks on and expulsion of third country nationals residing or working without authorisation (document WG1 1516)

III.2.C.4) [T.36] Council Recommendation of 30 November 1994 concerning the adoption of a standard travel document for the expulsion of third-country nationals, Official Journal C 274, 19/09/1996 p. 0018 – 0019. (*)

III.2.C.5) [T.37] COUNCIL RECOMMENDATION of 22 December 1995 on harmonizing means of combating illegal immigration and illegal employment and improving the relevant means of control (96/C 5/01) Official Journal C 005, 10/01/1996 p. 0001 – 0003. (*)

III.2.C.6) [T.38] COUNCIL RECOMMENDATION of 22 December 1995 on concerted action and cooperation in carrying out expulsion measures (96/C 5/02) Official Journal C 005, 10/01/1996 p. 0003 – 0007. (*)

III.2.C.7) [T.39] COUNCIL RECOMMENDATION of 27 September 1996 on combating the illegal employment of third-country nationals (96/C 304/01) Official Journal C 304, 14/10/1996 p. 0001 – 0002.

III.2.C.8) [T.40] COUNCIL DECISION of 16 December 1996 on monitoring the implementation of instruments adopted by the Council concerning illegal immigration, readmission, the unlawful employment of third country nationals and cooperation in the implementation of expulsion orders (96/749/JHA) Official Journal L 342, 31/12/1996 p. 0005 – 0005. (*)

III.2.C.9) [T.41] COUNCIL DECISION of 26 May 1997 on the exchange of information concerning assistance for the voluntary repatriation of third-country nationals (97/340/JHA) Official Journal L 147, 05/06/1997 p. 0003 – 0004. (*)

III.2.D. Other Conventions
--

III.3 *Readmission*

III.3.A. Conventions to which the candidate States must accede
--

III.3.B. Actions and joint programmes
--

III.3.C. Other instruments of the European Union

   III.3.C.1) [T.42] Council Recommendation of 30 November 1994 concerning a specimen bilateral readmission agreement between a Member State and a third country, Official Journal C 274, 19/09/1996 p. 0020 – 0024. (*)
   III.3.C.2) [T.43] Council Recommendation of 24 July 1995 on the guiding principles to be followed in drawing up protocols on the implementation of readmission agreements, Official Journal C 274, 19/09/1996 p. 0025 – 0033. (*)
   III.3.C.3) [T.44] Council Conclusions of 4 March 1996 on readmission clauses to be inserted in future mixed agreements; not published in the OJ; see documents 4272/96 ASIM 6 et 5457/96 ASIM 37

III.3.D. Other Conventions
--[3]

---

[3] The instruments covering the acquis chapters IV thru XII, covering organized crime thru human rights related issues has not been included, but, see hereinbelow under TAIEX list.

CHRONOLOGICAL LIST
List of documents of the acquis in chronological order[1]

1951

[T 2] I.A.b.1) Convention relating to the Status of Refugees (Geneva, 28 July 1951)

1967

[T 3] I.A.b.2) Protocol relating to the Status of Refugees (New York, 31 January 1967)

1992

[T 5] I.C.1) Decision of 11 June establishing the clearing house on asylum (CIREA) (document WG1 1107) (*)
[T 22] III.1.C.1) Text adopted by Ministers on 11 June 1992 on acceptable/unacceptable travel documents (document WG1 1506 rev 1
[T 6] I.C.2) Resolution adopted 30 November 1992 on a harmonised approach to questions concerning host third countries (document WG1 1283 (*)
[T 7] I.C.3) Resolution adopted 30 November 1992 on manifestly unfounded applications for asylum (document WG1 1282 rev 1 (*)
[T 8] I.C.4) Conclusions adopted 30 November 1992 concerning countries in which there is generally no serious risk of persecutions (document WG1 1281 (*)
[T 33] III.2.C.1) Recommendation of 30 November 1992 regarding practices followed by Member States on expulsion (document WG1 1266
[T 34] III.2.C.2) Recommendation of 30 November 1982 concerning transit for the purpose of expulsion (document WG1 1266

1993

[T 23] III.1.C.2) Resolution of 1 June 1993 on harmonisation of family reunion (document WG 1497 rev 1 (*)
[T 35] III.2.C.3) Recommendation of the 1st June 1993 concerning checks on and expulsion of third country nationals residing or working without authorisation (document WG1 1516

---

[1] Asterisks (*) refer to inclusion of this document in full in the present Handbook.

P.J van Krieken (Ed.), *The Asylum Acquis Handbook*
© 2000, T.M.C.Asser Press, The Hague, the Röling Foundation and the authors

1994

[T.9] I.C.5) Circulation and confidentiality of joint reports on the situation in certain third countries (Text adopted by the Council on 20 June 1994) Official Journal C 274, 19/09/1996 p. 0043–0043. (*)

[T.10] I.C.6) Guidelines for joint reports on third countries (Text adopted by the Council on 20 June 1994) Official Journal C 274, 19/09/1996 p. 0052–0054. (*)

[T.11] I.C.7) Procedure for drawing up reports in connection with joint assessments of the situation in third countries (7472/92 CIREA 17, adopted by the Council on 20 June 1994

[T.24] III.1.C.3) Council Resolution of 20 June 1994 on limitations on admission of third-country nationals to the territory of the Member States for employment. Official Journal C 274, 19/09/1996 p. 0003–0006.

[T.25] III.1.C.4) Council Resolution of 30 November 1994 relating to the limitations on the admission of third-country nationals to the territory of the Member States for the purpose of pursuing activities as self-employed persons. Official Journal C 274, 19/09/1996 p. 0007–0009.

[T.26] III.1.C.5) Council Resolution of 30 November 1994 on the admission of third-country nationals to the territory of the Member States for study purposes. Official Journal C 274, 19/09/1996 p. 0010–0012.

[T.27] III.1.C.6) Council Conclusions of 30 November 1994 on the organization and development of the Centre for Information, Discussion and Exchange on the Crossing of Frontiers and Immigration (Cirefi). Official Journal C 274, 19/09/1996 p. 0050–0051.

[T.20] III.1.B.1) Council Decision of 30 November 1994 on a joint action adopted by the Council on the basis of Article K.3 (2) (b) of the Treaty on European Union concerning travel facilities for school pupils from third countries resident in a Member State (94/795/JHA) Official Journal L 327, 19/12/1994 p. 0001–0003.

[T.36] III.2.C.4) Council Recommendation of 30 November 1994 concerning the adoption of a standard travel document for the expulsion of third-country nationals Official Journal C 274, 19/09/1996 p. 0018–0019. (*)

[T.42] III.3.C.1) Council Recommendation of 30 November 1994 concerning a specimen bilateral readmission agreement between a Member State and a third country Official Journal C 274, 19/09/1996 p. 0020–0024. (*)

1995

[T.18] II.C.a.1) Council Regulation (EC) No 1683/95 of 29 May 1995 laying down a uniform format for visas Official Journal L 164, 14/07/1995 p. 0001–0004.

[T.12] I.C.8) Council Resolution of 20 June 1995 on minimum guarantees for asylum procedures. Official Journal C 274, 19/09/1996 p. 0013–0017. (*)

[T.43] III.3.C.2) Council Recommendation of 24 July 1995 on the guiding principles to be followed in drawing up protocols on the implementation of readmission agreements Official Journal C 274, 19/09/1996 p. 0025–0033. (*)

[T.13] I.C.9) Council Resolution of 25 September 1995 on burden-sharing with regard to the admission and residence of displaced persons on a temporary basis (95/C 262/01) Official Journal C 262, 07/10/1995 p. 0001–0003. (*)

[T.19] II.C.a.2) Council Regulation (EC) No 2317/95 of 25 September 1995 determining the third countries whose nationals must be in possession of visas when crossing the ex-

ternal borders of the Member States Official Journal L 234, 03/10/1995 p. 0001–0003. (*)
[T.28] III.1.C.7) Council Decision of 22 December 1995 on monitoring the implementaticn of instruments already adopted concerning admission of third-country nationals . Official Journal C 011, 16/01/1996 p. 0001–0001. (*)
[T.37] III.2.C.5) Council Recommendation of 22 December 1995 on harmonizing means of combating illegal immigration and illegal employment and improving the relevant means of control (96/C 5/01) Official Journal C 005, 10/01/1996 p. 0001–0003. (*)
[T.38] III.2.C.6) Council Recommendation of 22 December 1995 on concerted action and cooperation in carrying out expulsion measures (96/C 5/02) Official Journal C 005, 10/01/1996 p. 0003–0007. (*)

1996

[T.4] I.B.1) Joint Position of 4 March 1996 defined by the Council on the basis of Article K.3 of the Treaty on European Union on the harmonized application of the definition of the term 'refugee` in Article 1 of the Geneva Convention of 28 July 1951 relating to the status of refugees (96/196/JHA) Official Journal L 063, 13/03/1996 p. 0002–0007. (*)
[T.14] I.C.10) Council Decision of 4 March 1996 on an alert and emergency procedure for burden-sharing with regard to the admission and residence of displaced persons on a temporary basis (96/198/JHA) Official Journal L 063, 13/03/1996 p. 0010–0011. (*)
[T.16] II.B.1) Joint Action of 4 March 1996 adopted by the Council on the basis of Article K.3 of the Treaty on European Union on airport transit arrangements (96/197/JHA) Official Journal L 063, 13/03/1996 p. 0008–0009. (*)
[T.29] III.1.C.8) Council Resolution of 4 March 1996 on the status of third-country nationals residing on a long-term basis in the territory of the Member States. Official Journal C 080, 18/03/1996 p. 0002–0004.
[T.30] III.1.C.9) Council Recommendation of 4 March 1996 relating to local consular ccoperation regarding visas (96/C 80/01) Official Journal C 080, 18/03/1996 p. 0001–0001.
[T.44] III.3.C.3) Council Conclusions of 4 March 1996 on readmission clauses to be inserted in future mixed agreements; not published in the OJ; see documents 4272/96 ASIM 6 and 5457/96 ASIM 37
[T.39] III.2.C.7) Council Recommendation of 27 September 1996 on combating the illegal employment of third-country nationals (96/C 304/01) Official Journal C 304, 14/10/1996 p. 0001–0002.
[T.17] II.B.2) Joint Position of 25 October 1996 defined by the Council on the basis of Article K.3 (2) (a) of the Treaty on European Union, on pre-frontier assistance and training assignments (96/622/JHA) Official Journal L 281, 31/10/1996 p. 0001–0002.
[T.21] III.1.B.2) Joint Action of 16 December 1996 adopted by the Council on the basis of Article K.3 of the Treaty on European Union concerning a uniform format for residence permits (97/11/JHA) Official Journal L 007, 10/01/1997 p. 0001–0004.
[T.40] III.2.C.8) Council Decision of 16 December 1996 on monitoring the implementation of instruments adopted by the Council concerning illegal immigration, readmission, the unlawful employment of third country nationals and cooperation in the implementation of expulsion orders (96/749/JHA) Official Journal L 342, 31/12/1996 p. 0005–0005. (*)

1997

[T.41] III.2.C.9) Council Decision of 26 May 1997 on the exchange of information concerning assistance for the voluntary repatriation of third-country nationals (97/340/ JHA) Official Journal L 147, 05/06/1997 p. 0003–0004. (*)

[T.15] I.C.11) Council Decision of 26 June 1997 on monitoring the implementation of instruments adopted concerning asylum (97/420/JHA) Official Journal L 178, 07/07/1997 p. 0006–0007. (*)

[T.31] III.1.C.10) Council Resolution of 26 June 1997 on unaccompanied minors who are nationals of third countries (97/C 221/03 Official Journal C 221, 19/07/1997 p. 0023–0027. (*)

[T.1.a] I.A.a.1) Convention determining the State responsible for examining applications for asylum lodged in one of the Member States of the European Communities (Dublin Convention) (*) (97/C254/01) Official Journal C 254, 19/08/1997 p. 0001–0012.

[T.1.b] I.A.a.2) Decision No 1/97 of 9 September 1997 of the Committee set up by Article 18 of the Dublin Convention of 15 June 1990, concerning provisions for the implementation of the Convention (97/662/CMS) Official Journal L 281, 14/10/1997 p. 0001–0025. (*)

[T.1.c] I.A.a.3) Decision No 2/97 of 9 September 1997 of the Committee set up by Article 18 of the Dublin Convention of 15 June 1990, establishing the Committee's Rules of Procedure (97/663/CMS) Official Journal L 281, 14/10/1997 p. 0026–0026. (*)

[T.32] III.1.C.11) Council Resolution of 4 December 1997 on measures to be adopted on the combating of marriages of convenience (97/C 382/01) Official Journal C 382, 16/12/1997 p. 0001–0002.

1998

[T.32/1/A] III.1.C.12) Conclusions of the Council of 19 March 1998 on the exchange of information in the area of asylum and immigration docs: ASIM 162 rev 2 and ASIM 73 rev 6

[T.19/1/A] II.C.a.3) Council Recommendation of 28 May 1998 on the provision of forgery detection equipment at ports of entry to the European Union (98/C 189/02) Official Journal C 189, 17/06/1998 p. 0019–0020. (*)

[T.32/1/B] III.1.C.13) Joint principles for the exchange of data in Cirefi doc 8927 CIREFI 35

[T.1.d] I.A.a.4) Decision No 1/98 of 30 June 1998 of the Committee set up by Article 18 of the Dublin Convention of 15 June 1990, concerning provisions for the implementation of the Convention (98/451/CMS) Official Journal L 196, 14/07/1998 p. 0049–0050.

[T.32/1/C] III.1.C.14) Council Decision of 3 December 1998 on common standards relating to filling in the uniform format for residence permits (98/701/JHA) Official Journal L 333, 09/12/1998 p. 0008–0016.

[T.17/1/A] II.B.3) Joint Action of 3 December 1998 adopted by the Council on the basis of Article K.3 of the Treaty on European Union concerning the setting up of a European Image Archiving System (FADO) (98/700/JHA) Official Journal L 333, 09/12/1998 p. 0004–0007.

2.3

TOPICAL LIST
List of documents of the acquis in topical order[1]:
ENTRY / DETERMINATION / SOJOURN / RETURN[2]

1. ENTRY

– [T.22] III.1.C.1) Text adopted by Ministers on 11 June 1992 on acceptable/unacceptable travel documents (document WG1 1506 rev 1)
– [T.18] II.C.a.1) Council Regulation (EC) No 1683/95 of 29 May 1995 laying down a uniform format for visas Official Journal L 164, 14/07/1995 p. 0001–0004.
– [T.30] III.1.C.9) Council Recommendation of 4 March 1996 relating to local consular cooperation regarding visas (96/C 80/01) Official Journal C 080, 18/03/1996 p. 0001–0001.
– [T.19] II.C.a.2) Council Regulation (EC) No 2317/95 of 25 September 1995 determining the third countries whose nationals must be in possession of visas when crossing the external borders of the Member States Official Journal L 234, 03/10/1995 p. 0001–0003. (*)
– [T.28] III.1.C.7) Council Decision of 22 December 1995 on monitoring the implementation of instruments already adopted concerning admission of third-country nationals Official Journal C 011, 16/01/1996 p. 0001–0001. (*)
– [T.31] III.1.C.10) Council Resolution of 26 June 1997 on unaccompanied minors who are nationals of third countries (97/C 221/03 Official Journal C 221, 19/07/1997 p. 0023–0027. (*)
– [T.16] II.B.1) Joint Action of 4 March 1996 adopted by the Council on the basis of Article K.3 of the Treaty on European Union on airport transit arrangements (96/197/JHA) Official Journal L 063, 13/03/1996 p. 0008–0009. (*)
– [T.20] III.1.B.1) Council Decision of 30 November 1994 on a joint action adopted by the Council on the basis of Article K.3 (2) (b) of the Treaty on European Union concerning travel facilities for school pupils from third countries resident in a Member State (94/795/JHA) Official Journal L 327, 19/12/1994 p. 0001–0003.
– [T.13] I.C.9) Council Resolution of 25 September 1995 on burden-sharing with regard to the admission and residence of displaced persons on a temporary basis (95/C 262/01) Official Journal C 262, 07/10/1995 p. 0001–0003. (*)
– [T.14] I.C.10) Council Decision of 4 March 1996 on an alert and emergency procedure for burden-sharing with regard to the admission and residence of displaced persons on a

---

[1] Instruments to which an asterisk (*) has been added have been reproduced in full in this Handbook.
[2] Some other documents could also have been included which fall under the last part of the acquis such as the ECHR, Euro's CAT, CRC, etcetera [T.151 thru T.158].

F.J. van Krieken (Ed.), The Asylum Acquis Handbook
© 2000, T.M.C.Asser Press, The Hague, the Röling Foundation and the authors

temporary basis (96/198/JHA) Official Journal L 063, 13/03/1996 p. 0010–0011. (*)
– [T.37] III.2.C.5) Council Recommendation of 22 December 1995 on harmonizing means of combating illegal immigration and illegal employment and improving the relevant means of control (96/C 5/01) Official Journal C 005, 10/01/1996 p. 0001–0003. (*)
– [T.19/1/A] II.C.a.3) Council Recommendation of 28 May 1998 on the provision of forgery detection equipment at ports of entry to the European Union (98/C 189/02) Official Journal C 189, 17/06/1998 p. 0019–0020.
– [T.40] III.2.C.8) Council Decision of 16 December 1996 on monitoring the implementation of instruments adopted by the Council concerning illegal immigration, readmission, the unlawful employment of third country nationals and cooperation in the implementation of expulsion orders (96/749/JHA) Official Journal L 342, 31/12/1996 p. 0005–0005. (*)
– [T.7] I.C.3) Resolution adopted 30 November 1992 on manifestly unfounded applications for asylum (document WG1 1282 rev 1 (*)
– [T.12] I.C.8) Council Resolution of 20 June 1995 on minimum guarantees for asylum procedures. Official Journal C 274, 19/09/1996 p. 0013–0017. (*)
– [T.6] I.C.2) Resolution adopted 30 November 1992 on a harmonised approach to questions concerning host third countries (document WG1 1283 (*)
– [T.8] I.C.4) Conclusions adopted 30 November 1992 concerning countries in which there is generally no serious risk of persecutions (document WG1 1281 (*)
– [T.24] III.1.C.3) Council Resolution of 20 June 1994 on limitations on admission of third-country nationals to the territory of the Member States for employment. Official Journal C 274, 19/09/1996 p. 0003–0006.
– [T.25] III.1.C.4) Council Resolution of 30 November 1994 relating to the limitations on the admission of third-country nationals to the territory of the Member States for the purpose of pursuing activities as self-employed persons. Official Journal C 274, 19/09/1996 p. 0007–0009.
– [T.26] III.1.C.5) Council Resolution of 30 November 1994 on the admission of third-country nationals to the territory of the Member States for study purposes. Official Journal C 274, 19/09/1996 p. 0010–0012.
– [T.17] II.B.2) Joint Position of 25 October 1996 defined by the Council on the basis of Article K.3 (2) (a) of the Treaty on European Union, on pre-frontier assistance and training assignments (96/622/JHA) Official Journal L 281, 31/10/1996 p. 0001–0002.

2. DETERMINATION PROCESS

– [T.2] I.A.b.1) Convention relating to the Status of Refugees (Geneva, 28 July 1951)
– [T.3] I.A.b.2) Protocol relating to the Status of Refugees (New York, 31 January 1967)
– [T.4] I.B.1) Joint Position of 4 March 1996 defined by the Council on the basis of Article K.3 of the Treaty on European Union on the harmonized application of the definition of the term 'refugee` in Article 1 of the Geneva Convention of 28 July 1951 relating to the status of refugees (96/196/JHA) Official Journal L 063, 13/03/1996 p. 0002–0007. (*)
– [T.12] I.C.8) Council Resolution of 20 June 1995 on minimum guarantees for asylum procedures. Official Journal C 274, 19/09/1996 p. 0013–0017. (*)
– [T.15] I.C.11) Council Decision of 26 June 1997 on monitoring the implementation of instruments adopted concerning asylum (97/420/JHA) Official Journal L 178, 07/07/1997 p. 0006–0007. (*)

TOPICAL LIST 101

– [T.1.a] I.A.a.1) Convention determining the State responsible for examining applications for asylum lodged in one of the Member States of the European Communities (Dublin Convention) (97/C254/01) Official Journal C 254, 19/08/1997 p. 0001–0012. (*)
– [T.1.b] I.A.a.2) Decision No 1/97 of 9 September 1997 of the Committee set up by Article 18 of the Dublin Convention of 15 June 1990, concerning provisions for the implementation of the Convention (97/662/CMS) Official Journal L 281, 14/10/1997 p. 0001–0025. (*)
– [T.1.c] I.A.a.3) Decision No 2/97 of 9 September 1997 of the Committee set up by Article 18 of the Dublin Convention of 15 June 1990, establishing the Committee's Rules of Procedure (97/663/CMS) Official Journal L 281, 14/10/1997 p. 0026–0026. (*)
– [T.1.d] I.A.a.4) Decision No 1/98 of 30 June 1998 of the Committee set up by Article 18 of the Dublin Convention of 15 June 1990, concerning provisions for the implementation of the Convention (98/451/CMS) Official Journal L 196, 14/07/1998 p. 0049–0050.
– [T.5] I.C.1) Decision of 11 June 1992 setting up a Centre for Information, Discussion and Exchange on Asylum (Cirea) document WG1 1107 (*)
– [T.27] III.1.C.6) Council Conclusions of 30 November 1994 on the organization and development of the Centre for Information, Discussion and Exchange on the Crossing of Frontiers and Immigration (Cirefi). Official Journal C 274, 19/09/1996 p. 0050–0051.
– [T.32/1/A] III.1.C.12) Conclusions of the Council of 19 March 1998 on the exchange of information in the area of asylum and immigration docs: ASIM 162 rev 2 and ASIM 73 rev 6 – former nr. 49
– [T.32/1/B] III.1.C.13) Joint principles for the exchange of data in Cirefi doc 8927 CIREFI 35 – former nr. 50
– [T.9] I.C.5) Circulation and confidentiality of joint reports on the situation in certain third countries (Text adopted by the Council on 20 June 1994) Official Journal C 274, 19/09/1996 p. 0043–0043. (*)
– [T.10] I.C.6) Guidelines for joint reports on third countries (Text adopted by the Council on 20 June 1994) Official Journal C 274, 19/09/1996 p. 0052–0054. (*)
– [T.11] I.C.7) Procedure for drawing up reports in connection with joint assessments of the situation in third countries (7472/92 CIREA 17, adopted by the Council on 20 June 1994 – former nr. 14)
– [T.7] I.C.3) Resolution adopted 30 November 1992 on manifestly unfounded applications for asylum (document WG1 1282 rev 1 (*)
– [T.6] I.C.2) Resolution adopted 30 November 1992 on a harmonised approach to questions concerning host third countries (document WG1 1283 (*)
– [T.8] I.C.4) Conclusions adopted 30 November 1992 concerning countries in which there is generally no serious risk of persecutions (document WG1 1281 (*)

3. SOJOURN

– [T.23] III.1.C.2) Resolution of 1 june 1993 on harmonisation of family reunion (document WG 1497 rev 1 (*)
– [T.32] III.1.C.11) Council Resolution of 4 December 1997 on measures to be adopted on the combating of marriages of convenience (97/C 382/01) Official Journal C 382, 16/12/1997 p. 0001–0002.
– [T.35] III.2.C.3) Recommendation of the 1st June 1993 concerning checks on and expulsion of third country nationals residing or working without authorisation (document WG1 1516 – former nr. 34)

– [T.29] III.1.C.8) Council Resolution of 4 March 1996 on the status of third-country nationals residing on a long-term basis in the territory of the Member States. Official Journal C 080, 18/03/1996 p. 0002–0004.
– [T.20] III.1.B.2) Joint Action of 16 December 1996 adopted by the Council on the basis of Article K.3 of the Treaty on European Union concerning a uniform format for residence permits (97/11/JHA) Official Journal L 007, 10/01/1997 p. 0001–0004.
– [T.17/1/A] II.B.3) Joint Action of 3 December 1998 adopted by the Council on the basis of Article K.3 of the Treaty on European Union concerning the setting up of a European Image Archiving System (FADO) (98/700/JHA) Official Journal L 333, 09/12/1998 p. 0004–0007.
– [T.32/1/C] III.1.C.14) Council Decision of 3 December 1998 on common standards relating to filling in the uniform format for residence permits (98/701/JHA) Official Journal L 333, 09/12/1998 p. 0008–0016.
– [T.13] I.C.9) Council Resolution of 25 September 1995 on burden-sharing with regard to the admission and residence of displaced persons on a temporary basis (95/C 262/01) Official Journal C 262, 07/10/1995 p. 0001–0003. (*)
– [T.14] I.C.10) Council Decision of 4 March 1996 on an alert and emergency procedure for burden-sharing with regard to the admission and residence of displaced persons on a temporary basis (96/198/JHA) Official Journal L 063, 13/03/1996 p. 0010–0011. (*)
– [T.31] III.1.C.10) Council Resolution of 26 June 1997 on unaccompanied minors who are nationals of third countries (97/C 221/03 Official Journal C 221, 19/07/1997 p. 0023–0027. (*)
– [T.37] III.2.C.5) Council Recommendation of 22 December 1995 on harmonizing means of combating illegal immigration and illegal employment and improving the relevant means of control (96/C 5/01) Official Journal C 005, 10/01/1996 p. 0001–0003. (*)
– [T.40] III.2.C.8) Council Decision of 16 December 1996 on monitoring the implementation of instruments adopted by the Council concerning illegal immigration, readmission, the unlawful employment of third country nationals and cooperation in the implementation of expulsion orders (96/749/JHA) Official Journal L 342, 31/12/1996 p. 0005–0005. (*)
– [T.39] III.2.C.7) Council Recommendation of 27 September 1996 on combating the illegal employment of third-country nationals (96/C 304/01) Official Journal C 304, 14/10/1996 p. 0001–0002.

4. RETURN

– [T.33] III.2.C.1) Recommendation of 30 November 1992 regarding practices followed by Member States on expulsion (document WG1 1266 – former nr. 32)
– [T.34] III.2.C.2) Recommendation of 30 November 1882 concerning transit for the purpose of expulsion (document WG1 1266 – former nr. 33)
– [T.36] III.2.C.4) Council Recommendation of 30 November 1994 concerning the adoption of a standard travel document for the expulsion of third-country nationals Official Journal C 274, 19/09/1996 p. 0018–0019. (*)
– [T.42] III.3.C.1) Council Recommendation of 30 November 1994 concerning a specimen bilateral readmission agreement between a Member State and a third country Official Journal C 274, 19/09/1996 p. 0020–0024. (*)

– [T.43] III.3.C.2) Council Recommendation of 24 July 1995 on the guiding principles to be followed in drawing up protocols on the implementation of readmission agreements Official Journal C 274, 19/09/1996 p. 0025–0033. (*)
– [T.38] III.2.C.6) Council Recommendation of 22 December 1995 on concerted action and cooperation in carrying out expulsion measures (96/C 5/02) Official Journal C 005, 10/01/1996 p. 0003–0007. (*)
– [T.44] III.3.C.3) Council Conclusions of 4 March 1996 on readmission clauses to be inserted in future mixed agreements; not published in the OJ; see documents 4272/96 ASIM 6 et 5457/96 ASIM 37
– [T.40] III.2.C.8) Council Decision of 16 December 1996 on monitoring the implementation of instruments adopted by the Council concerning illegal immigration, readmission, the unlawful employment of third country nationals and cooperation in the implementation of expulsion orders (96/749/JHA) Official Journal L 342, 31/12/1996 p. 0005–0005. (*)
– [T.41] III.2.C.9) Council Decision of 26 May 1997 on the exchange of information concerning assistance for the voluntary repatriation of third-country nationals (97/340/JHA) Official Journal L 147, 05/06/1997 p. 0003–0004. (*)

2.4

TAIEX LIST
(Screening: Chapter 24)[1]

CO-OPERATION IN THE FIELDS OF JUSTICE AND HOME AFFAIRS (JHA)

[T.1.a][2]
Convention signed on 15 June 1990 in Dublin determining the State responsible for examining applications for asylum lodged in one of the Member States of the European Communities, which entered into force on 1 September 1997: OJ No C 254 of 19 August 1997 (297A0819(01))[3]

Implementing measures adopted:
[T.1.b] – Decision No 1/97 of 9 September 1997 concerning provisions for the implementation of the Dublin Convention: OJ No L 281 of 14 October 1997, pages 1 to 25 (497D0662)
[T.1.c] – Decision No 2/97 of 9 September 1997 establishing the Rules of Procedure of the Committee set up by Article 18 of the Dublin Convention: OJ No L 281 of 14 October 1997, page 26; (497 D 0663)
[T.1.d] – Decision No 1/98 of 30 June 1998 of the Committee set up by Article 18 of the Dublin Convention of 15 June 1990, concerning provisions for the implementation of the Convention
Official Journal L 196, 14/07/1998 p. 0049–0050 *(498D0451)

[T.2]
Convention relating to the Status of Refugees (Geneva, 28 July 1951)

[T.3]
Protocol relating to the Status of Refugees (New York, 31 January 1967)

---

[1] Ed.: This list, the so-called TAIEX list refers to the enlargement process, accession in particular. The TAIEX list – originally subdivided – names all the conventions, positions, rules, regulations etc. to which the candidate countries must accede, introduce and/or live up to in the JHA field. For details, see the Seiffarth contribution elsewhere in this Handbook. For the purpose of transparency and accessibility the instruments not directly dealing with the subject of this Handbook have been included as a footnote only. The other footnoted are the original ones.

[2] The numbers follow the TAIEX list. Some numbers, originally included, have meanwhile been deleted, and are hence missing in this text (i.e. 53, 56, 63, 65-69, 71-72).

[3] For the purpose of this list, the Dublin Convention has been treated on the same footing as conventions drawn up on the basis of Article K 3 of the TEU.

P.J. van Krieken (Ed.), *The Asylum Acquis Handbook*
© 2000, T.M.C.Asser Press, The Hague, the Röling Foundation and the authors

[T.4]
Joint Position of 4 March 1996 on the harmonized application of the definition of the term 'refugee' in Article 1 of the Geneva Convention: OJ No L 63 of 13 March 1996; (496X0196)

[T.5]
Decision of 11 June 1992 setting up the CIREA (Centre for Information, Discussion and Exchange on Asylum): WGI 1107;

[T.6]
Resolution adopted 30 November 1992 on a harmonized approach to questions concerning host third countries: WGI 1283;

[T.7]
Resolution adopted 30 November 1992 on manifestly unfounded applications for asylum: WGI 1282 REV 1;

[T.8]
Conclusions adopted on 30 November 1992 concerning countries in which there is generally no serious risk of persecutions: WGI 1281;

[T.9]
Text adopted on 20 June 1994 on the circulation and confidentiality of joint reports prepared by CIREA on the situation in certain third countries: OJ No C 274 of 19 September 1996, page 43; (396Y0919(12))

[T.10]
Guidelines of 20 June 1994 for joint reports on third countries: OJ No C 274 of 19 September 1996, pages 52 to 54; (396Y0919(16))

[T.11]
Procedure for drawing up reports in connection with joint assessments of the situation in third countries (7472/92 CIREA 17, adopted by the Council on 20 June 1994);

[T.12]
Resolution of 20 June 1995 on minimum guarantees for asylum procedures: OJ No C 274 of 19 September 1996, page 13; (396Y0919(05))

[T.13]
Resolution of 25 September 1995 on burden-sharing with regard to the admission and residence of displaced persons on a temporary basis: OJ No C 262 of 7 October 1995, page 1; (395Y1007(01))

[T.14]
Decision of 4 March 1996 on an alert and emergency procedure for burden-sharing with regard to the admission and residence of displaced persons on a temporary basis: OJ No L 63 of 13 March 1996, page 10; (396D0198)

[T.15]
Decision of 26 June 1997 on monitoring the implementation of instruments adopted concerning asylum: OJ No L 178 of 7 July 1997, page 6; (397D0420)

[T.16]
Joint Action of 4 March 1996 on airport transit arrangements: OJ No L 63 of 13 March 1996, page 8 (496X0197)[4]

[T.17]
Joint Position of 25 October 1996 on pre-frontier assistance and training assignments: OJ No L 281 of 31 October 1996, page 1; (496X0622)

[T.17/1/A]
Joint Action of 3 December 1998 adopted by the Council on the basis of Article K.3 of the Treaty on European Union concerning the setting up of a European Image Archiving System (FADO); Official Journal L 333, 09/12/1998 p. 0004–0007 (498X0700)

[T.18]
Council Regulation (EC) No 1683/95 of 29 May 1995, laying down a uniform format for visas; OJ L164, p. 1, 04/07/1995 (395R1683)

[T.19]
Council Regulation (EC) No 2317/95 of 25 September 1995 determining the third countries whose nationals must be in possession of visas when crossing the external borders of the Member States;[5] OJ L234, p. 1, 03/10/1995 (395R2317)

[T.19/1/A]
Council Recommendation of 28 May 1998 on the provision of forgery detection equipment at ports of entry to the European Union Official Journal C 189, 17/06/1998 p. 0019–0020; (398Y0617(01))

[T.20]
Joint Action of 30 November 1994 concerning travel facilities for school pupils from third countries resident in a Member State: OJ No L 327 of 19 December 1994, page 1 (494D0795)

[T.21]
Joint Action of 16 December 1996 concerning a uniform format for residence permits: OJ No L 7 of 10 January 1997; (497X0011)

[T.22]
Text adopted by Ministers on 11 June 1992 on acceptable/unacceptable travel documents: WGI 1506 REV 1

---

[4] This Joint Action is the subject of proceedings before the Court of Justice.
[5] This regulation was annulled by the Court of Justice, while retaining its effect. A revised draft Regulation is currently before the European Parliament.

[T.23]
Resolution of 1 June 1993 on harmonization of family reunification: WGI 1497 REV 1

[T.24]
Resolution of 20 June 1994 on limitation on admission of third-country nationals to the territory of the Member States for employment: OJ No C 274 of 19 September 1996, page 3; (396Y0919(02))

[T.25]
Resolution of 30 November 1994 relating to the limitations on the admission of third-country nationals to the territory of the Member States for the purpose of pursuing activities as self-employed persons: OJ No C 274 of 19 September 1996, page 7; (396Y0919(03))

[T.26]
Resolution of 30 November 1994 on the admission of third-country nationals to the territory of the Member States of the European Union for study purposes: OJ No C 274 of 19 September 1996, page 10; (396Y0919(04))

[T.27]
Conclusions of 30 November 1994 on the organisation and development of the Centre for Information, Discussion and Exchange on the Crossing of Frontiers and Immigration (CIREFI): OJ No C 274 of 19 September 1996, pages 50 and 51 (this instrument is also relevant for expulsion); (396Y0919(15))

[T.28]
Decision of 22 December 1995 on monitoring the implementation of instruments already adopted concerning admission of third-country nationals: OJ No C 11 of 16 January 1996, page 1; (396Y0116(01))

[T.29]
Resolution of 4 March 1996 on the status of third-country nationals residing on a long-term basis in the territory of the Member States: OJ No C 80 of 18 March 1996, page 2; (396Y0318(02))

[T.30]
Recommendation of 4 March 1996 relating to local consular cooperation regarding visas: OJ No C 80 of 18 March 1996, page 1; (396Y0318(01))

[T.31]
Resolution of 26 June 1997 on unaccompanied minors who are nationals of third countries: OJ No C 221 of 19 July 1997, pages 23 to 27; (397Y0719(02))

[T.32]
Resolution of 4 December 1997 on marriages of convenience: OJ No C 328 of 16 December 1997; (397Y1216(01))

[T.32/1/A]
Conclusions of the Council of 19 March 1998 on the exchange of information in the area of asylum and immigration. Docs ASIM 162 Rev 2, ASIM 73 Rev 6

[T.32/1/B]
Joint principles for the exchange of data in CIREFI. Doc 8927 CIREFI 35

[T.32/1/C]
Council Decision of 3 December 1998 on common standards relating to filling in the uniform format for residence permits. Official Journal L 333, 09/12/1998 p. 0008–0016; (398D0701)

[T.33]
Recommendation of 30 November 1992 regarding practices followed by Member States on expulsion: WGI 1266

[T.34]
Recommendation of 30 November 1992 concerning transit for the purpose of expulsion: WGI 1266

[T.35]
Recommendation of 1 June 1993 concerning checks on and expulsion of third-country nationals residing or working without authorisation: WGI 1516

[T.36]
Recommendation of 30 November 1994 concerning the adoption of a standard travel document for the removal/expulsion of third-country nationals: OJ No C 274 of 19 September 1996, page 18; (396Y0919(06))

[T.37]
Recommendation of 22 December 1995 on harmonizing means of combating illegal immigration and illegal employment and improving the relevant means of control: OJ No C 5 of 10 January 1996, page 1 (396Y0110(01))

[T.38]
Recommendation of 22 December 1995 on concerted action and cooperation in carrying out expulsion measures: OJ No C 5 of 10 January 1996, pages 3 to 7; (396Y0110(02))

[T.39]
Recommendation of 27 September 1996 on combating the illegal employment of third-country nationals: OJ No C 304 of 14 October 1996, page 1; (496Y1014(01))

[T.40]
Decision of 16 December 1996 on monitoring the implementation of instruments adopted by the Council concerning illegal immigration, readmission, the unlawful employment of third-country nationals and cooperation in the implementation of expulsion orders: OJ No L 342 of 31 December 1996, page 5; (396D0749)

TAREX LIST 109

[T.141]
Decision of 26 May 1997 on the exchange of information concerning assistance for the voluntary repatriation of third-country nationals: OJ No L 147 of 5 June 1997, page 3; (397D0340)

[T.142]
Recommendation of 30 November 1994 concerning a specimen bilateral readmission agreement between a Member State of the European Union and a third country: OJ No C 274 of 19 September 1996, pages 20 to 24; (396Y0919(07));

[T.143]
Recommendation of 24 July 1995 on the principles for the drafting of protocols on the implementation of readmission agreements: OJ No C 274 of 19 September 1996, page 25; (396Y0919(08))

[T.144]
Council conclusions of 4 March 1996 on clauses to be inserted in future mixed agreements: not published in the OJ; see 4272/96 ASIM 6 and 5457/96 ASIM 37

[T.137]
Joint Action of 15 July 1996 concerning Action to Combat Racism and Xenophobia: OJ No L 185 of 24 July 1996; (496X0443)

[T.149]
Joint Action of 19 March 1998 introducing a programme of training, exchanges and cooperation in the field of asylum, immigration and crossing of external borders (ODYSSEUS programme): OJ No L 99 of 31 March 1998, page 2; (498X0244)

[T.151]
European Convention for the Protection of Human Rights and Fundamental Freedoms (Rome, 4 November 1950) and its Protocol of 1952

[T.152]
UN Convention on the elimination of all forms of racial discrimination (New York, 7 March 1966);

[T.153]
Convention for the Protection of Individuals with regard to Automatic Processing of Personal Data (Strasbourg, 28 January 1981)

[T.154]
European Convention against Torture and Other Cruel, Inhuman or Degrading Treatment or Punishment (Strasbourg, 26 November 1987)

[T.155]
UN Convention on the rights of the child (New York, 20 November 1989).

Editor's Note

The other instruments are not directly related to asylum and/or asylum-related migration. They are nevertheless included in this note:
[T.45] Convention of 26 July 1995 on the establishment of a European Police Office: OJ No C 316 of 27 November 1995; (495A1127(01))
[T.45/1/A] Act of the Management Board of Europol laying down its rules of procedures; adopted by the Management Board 1 October 1998. Doc EUROPOL 91.
[T.45/1/B] Act of the Management Board of Europol concerning the rights and duties of Europol liaison officers; adopted by Management Board 1 October 1998. Doc EUROPOL 86
[T.45/1/C] Act of the Management Board of Europol concerning the rules on external relations of Europol with bodies linked to the EU; adopted by the Management Board 1 October 1998. Doc EUROPOL 95
[T.45/1/D] Council Act laying down rules governing Europol's external relations with third states and non European Union related bodies; adopted 3 November 1998. Doc EUROPOL 94
[T.45/1/E] Council Act laying down rules concerning the receipt of information by Europol from third parties; adopted 3 November 1998. Doc EUROPOL 92
[T.45/1/F] Council Act adopting rules on the confidentiality of Europol; adopted 3 November 1998. Doc EUROPOL 89
[T.45/1/G] Council Act adopting rules applicable to Europol analysis files; adopted 3 November 1998. Doc EUROPOL 87
[T.45/1/H] Council Act laying down the staff regulations applicable to Europol employees; adopted 3 December 1998. Doc EUROPOL 88
[T.45/1/I] Council Decision instructing Europol to deal with crimes committed or likely to be committed in the course of terrorist activities against life, limb, personal freedom or property; adopted 3 December 1998. Doc EUROPOL 118
[T.45/1/J] Council Decision supplementing the definition of the form of crime "traffic in human beings" in the Annex to the Europol Convention; adopted 3 December 1998. Doc EUROPOL 117
[T.46] Convention of 26 July 1995 on the protection of the European Communities' Financial Interests: OJ No C 316 of 27 November 1995 (also relevant for judicial cooperation in penal matters (495A1127(03))
[T.47] Protocol of 23 July 1996 on the interpretation, by way of preliminary rulings, by the Court of Justice of the EC of the Convention on the establishment of a European Police Office: OJ No C 299 of 9 October 1996; (496Y1009(01))
[T.48] Protocol of 27 September 1996 to the Convention on the Protection of Community Financial Interests: OJ No C 313 of 23 October 1996 (also relevant for judicial cooperation in penal matters); (496Y1023(01))
[T.49] Protocol of 29 November 1996 on the interpretation by the Court of Justice of the Convention on the protection of the Communities' financial interests (also relevant for judicial cooperation in penal matters)
[T.50] Convention of 26 May 1997 on the fight against corruption involving officials of the European Communities or officials of Member States of the European Union: OJ No C 195 of 25 June 1997 (also relevant for judicial cooperation in penal matters); (497A0625(01))
[T.51] Protocol of 19 June 1997 on the privileges and immunities of Europol, the members of its organs, the Deputy Director and employees of Europol: OJ No C 221 of 19 July; (497A0719(01))
[T.52] Second Protocol of 19 June 1997 to the Convention on the protection of the European Communities' financial interests: OJ No C 221 of 19 July 1997 (also relevant for judicial cooperation in penal matters); 497Y0719(02)
[T.54] Joint Action of 14 October 1996 providing for a common framework of the initiatives of the Member States of the EU concerning liaison officers: OJ No L 268 of 19 October 1996; (496X0602)
[T.55] Joint Action of 29 November 1996 concerning the creation and maintenance of a directory of specialized competences, skills and expertise in the fight against international organized crime, in order to facilitate law enforcement cooperation between the Member States: OJ No L 342 of 31 December 1996; (496X0747)
[T.57] Joint Action of 24 February 1997 concerning action to combat trafficking in human beings and sexual exploitation of children: OJ No L 63 of 4 March 1997 (also relevant for judicial cooperation) (497X0154)
[T.58] Joint Action of 9 June 1997 for the refining of targeting criteria, selection methods and collection of customs and police information: OJ No L 159 of 17 June 1997; (497X0372)
[T.59] Joint Action of 24 February 1997 adopted by the Council on the basis of Article K.3 of the Treaty

on European Union concerning action to combat trafficking in human beings and sexual exploitation of children; OJ No L063 p. 2, 1997/03/04 (497X0154)

[T.60] Joint Position of 6 October 1997 on negotiations held in the Council of Europe and the OECD on the fight against corruption (also relevant for judicial cooperation in penal matters);

[T.61] Second Joint Position of 13 November 1997 on negotiations held in the Council of Europe and the OECD on the fight against corruption (also relevant for judicial cooperation in penal matters);

[T.62] Joint Action of 5 December 1997 establishing a mechanism for evaluating the application and implementation at national level of international undertakings in the fight against organized crime (also relevant for judicial cooperation

[T.62/1/A] Joint Action of 22 December 1998 adopted by the Council on the basis of Article K.3 of the Treaty on European Union, on corruption in the private sector; Official Journal L 358, 31/12/1998 p. 0002–0004; (498X0742)

[T.64] Europol: Financial Regulation (19-20 March 1996);

[T.70] Europol: Rules concerning the transmission of personal data by Europol to Third States and bodies (4-5 December 1997);

[T.73] Conclusion on car crime (29-30 November 1993);

[T.74] Joint declaration of Berlin of September 1994 on combating organized crime

[T.75] Resolution of 17 January 1995 on Lawful interception of telecommunications

[T.76] Action programme of the Member States of the European Union and the associated countries of Central and Eastern Europe, including the Baltic States, on judicial cooperation against international organized crime (25-26 September 1995)

[T.77] Resolution of 23 November 1995 on the Protection of Witnesses in the Fight Against International Organized Crime: OJ No C 327 of 7 December 1995 (also relevant for judicial cooperation in penal matters) (395Y1207(04))

[T.78] Declaration on organized crime (19-20 March 1996) (also relevant for judicial cooperation in penal matters);

[T.79] Measures to step up the fight against organized crime (12 December 1996);

[T.80] Resolution of 20 December 1996 on Individuals who cooperate with the judicial process in the fight against international organized crime: OJ No C 10 of 11 January 1997 (also relevant for judicial cooperation in criminal matters). (497Y0111(01)

[T.81] Action plan to combat organized crime (adopted by the Council on 28 April 1997): OJ No C 251 of 15 August 1997; (497Y0815(01))

[T.82] Project-based action against transnational organized crime – practical guidance (adopted by the Council on 4 December 1997);

[T.83] Conclusions of 19 March 1998 on G8 principles on high-tech crime, recommendations on organized crime and related matters;

[T.83/1/A] Pre-accession Pact on organised crime between the Member States of the European Union and the applicant countries of Central and Eastern Europe and (Text approved by the JHA Council on 28 May 1998); Official Journal C 220, 15/07/1998 p. 0001–0005; (498Y0715(01))

[T.83/1/B] Council Resolution on the Prevention of Organised Crime with Reference to the Establishment of a Comprehensive Strategy for Combating it. Official Reference OJ C408 of 29.12.98

[T.83/1/C] Recommendation on Arms Trafficking. Adopted 7.12.98. Doc ENFOPOL 101 REV2 and ENFOPOL 121

[T.84] European Convention of 8 November 1990 on money laundering, search, seizure and confiscation of the proceeds from crime (Council of Europe) (also relevant for judicial cooperation in penal matters)

[T.85] OECD Convention of 17 December 1997 on combating bribery of foreign public officials in international business transactions

[T.86] Single Convention on Narcotic Drugs, 1961 (New York, 30 March 1961)

[T.87] Protocol amending the Single Convention on Narcotic Drugs (Geneva, 25 March 1972

[T.88] Convention on Psychotropic Substances (Vienna, 21 February 1971)

[T.89] United Nations Convention against the Illicit Traffic in Narcotic Drugs and Psychotropic Substances (Vienna, 20 December 1988) (also relevant for judicial cooperation in penal matters);

[T.90] Joint Action of 29 November 1996 concerning the exchange of information on the chemical profiling of drugs to facilitate improved cooperation between Member States in combating illicit drug trafficking: OJ No L 322 of 12 December 1996; (496X0699)

[T.91] Joint Action of 17 December 1996 concerning the approximation of the laws and practices of the Member States of the EU to combat drug addiction and to prevent and combat illegal drug trafficking: OJ

No L 342 of 31 December 1996 (also relevant for judicial cooperation in penal matters); (496X0750)
[T.92] Joint Action of 16 June 1997 concerning the information exchange, risk assessment and the control of new synthetic drugs: OJ No L 167 of 25 June 1997; (497X0396)
[T.93] Resolution of 29 November 1996 on the drawing up of police/customs agreements in the fight against drugs: OJ No C 375 of 12 December 1996; (496Y1212(01))
[T.94] Resolution of 29 November 1996 on measures to address the drug tourism problem within the EU: OJ No C 375 of 12 December 1996; (496Y1212(02))
[T.95] Resolution of 16 December 1996 on measures to combat and dismantle the illicit cultivation and production of drugs within the EU: OJ No C 389 of 23 December 1996; (496Y1223(01))
[T.96] Resolution of 20 December 1996 on Sentencing for Serious Illicit Drug Trafficking: OJ No C 10 of 11 January 1997; (497Y0111(02))
[T.97] Agreement on illicit traffic by sea, implementing Article 17 of the United Nations Convention against illicit traffic in narcotic drugs and psychotropic substances (ETS No 156 – Strasbourg, 31 January 1995) (also relevant for judicial cooperation in criminal matters)
[T.98] European Convention on the Suppression of Terrorism (Strasbourg, 27 January 1977)
[T.99] Joint Action of 15 October 1996 concerning the creation and maintenance of a Directory of specialized counter-terrorist competences, skills and expertise to facilitate counter-terrorist cooperation between the Member States of the EU: OJ No L 273 of 25 October 1996; (496X0610)
[T.100] Declaration of 30 November 1993 on financing of terrorism
[T.101] Declaration on terrorism (La Gomera Declaration) of 14 October 1995 issued by the Ministers of Home Affairs and Justice
[T.102] Joint Action of 26 May 1997 with regard to cooperation on law and order and security: OJ No L 147 of 5 June 1997; (497X0339)
[T.103] Resolution on radio communications (29-30 November 1993, JHA Council)
[T.104] Declaration on motor cycle gangs (29-30 November 1993)
[T.105] Recommendation on the responsibility of organizers of sporting events (29-30 November 1993)
[T.106] Recommendation on Environmental Crime (29-30 November 1993)
[T.107] Recommendation of 6 May 1994 for a training module on the operational analysis of criminality
[T.108] Recommendation on guidelines for preventing and restraining disorder connected with football matches (22 April 1996): OJ No C 131 of 3 May 1996; (396Y0503(02))
[T.109] Resolution of 9 June 1997 on preventing and restraining football hooliganism through the exchange of experience, exclusion from stadiums and media policy: OJ No C 193 of 24 June 1997; (397Y0624(01))
[T.110] Resolution of 9 June 1997 on the exchange of DNA analysis results: OJ No C 193 of 24 June 1997; (397Y0624(02))
[T.110/1/A] Council Conclusions concerning encryption and law enforcement. Adopted by the Council of 28 May 1998. Doc ENFOPOL 69 Rev 1
[T.111] Convention of 26 July 1995 on the use of information technology for customs purposes: OJ No C 316 of 27 November 1995; (495A1127(02))
[T.111/1/A] Convention on the use of information technology for customs purposes and Council regulation 515/97 of 13 March 1997 – delimitation of information to be captured in the data banks. Doc ENFOCUSTOM 63
[T.112] Protocol of 29 November 1996 on the interpretation, by way of preliminary rulings, by the Court of Justice of the EC of the Convention on the use of information technology for customs purposes
[T.113] Convention of 18 December 1997 on Mutual Assistance and Cooperation between customs administrations: OJ No C 24 of 23 January 1998; (498A0123(01))
[T.114] Joint Action of 29 November 1996 on cooperation between customs authorities and business organizations on combating drugs trafficking: OJ No L 322 of 12 December 1996; (496X0698)
[T.115] Conclusions concerning a contribution to the development of a strategic Union plan to combat customs fraud in the internal market (30 November – 1 December 1994)
[T.116] Decision of 29 November 1996 on revised arrangements for future joint customs surveillance operations (10607/96 ENFOCUSTOM 42, Annex A)
[T.117] Resolution of 9 June 1997 concerning a handbook for joint customs surveillance operations: OJ No C 193 of 24 June 1997; (397Y0624(03))
[T.117/1/A] Customs Information System for the Third Pillar (CIS) – objectives for technical requirements. Adopted 22 December 1998. Doc ENFOCUSTOM 56
[T.118] Agreement of 26 July 1995 on provisional application between certain Member States of the EU of

the Convention on the use of information technology for customs purposes: OJ No C 316 of 27 November 1995; (495A1127(04))

[T.119] Convention of 26 May 1997 on the Service in the Member States of the European Union of judicial and extrajudicial documents in civil or commercial matters, including the protocol on the competence of the Court: OJ No C 261 of 27 August 1997; (497A0827(01))

[T.119/1/A] Convention drawn up on the basis of Article K.3 of the Treaty on European Union, on Jurisdiction and the Recognition and Enforcement of Judgments in Matrimonial Matters. Official Journal C 221, 16/07/1998 p. 0002–0018; (498A0716(01))

[T.120] Convention on Jurisdiction and Enforcement of Judgments in Civil and Commercial Matters (Brussels, 27 September 1968): OJ No L 299 of 31 December 1972; 468A0927(01); and Protocol on its Interpretation by the Court of Justice (Luxembourg, 3 June 1971): OJ L 204 of 2 August 1975; (471X0603(03)); – as amended by:
- Convention on the Accession of the United Kingdom of Denmark, Ireland and the United Kingdom of Great Britain and Northern Ireland to the Brussels Convention of 1968 (Brussels, 9 October 1978): OJ L 304 of 30 October 1978; (478A1009(01))
- Convention on the Accession of the Hellenic Republic to the Brussels Convention of 1968 (Brussels, 25 October 1982): OJ L 388 of 31 December 1982; (482A1025(01))
- Convention on the Accession of the Kingdom of Spain and the Portuguese Republic to the Brussels Convention of 1968 (San Sebastián, 26 May 1989): OJ L 285 of 3 October 1989; (489A0535)
- Convention on the Accession of the Republic of Austria, the Republic of Finland and the Kingdom of Sweden to the Brussels Convention of 1968 (Dublin, 29 November 1996): OJ C15 of 15 January 1997; (497Y0115(01))

[T.121] Convention on the Law applicable to Contractual Obligations (Rome, 19 June 1980); OJ L 266 of 9 October 1980; (480A0934); 1st Protocol to the Convention on the Law applicable to Contractual Obligations on Interpretation by the Court of Justice (Brussels, 19 December 1988) and 2nd Protocol to the Convention on the Law applicable to Contractual Obligations (Brussels, 19 December 1988); as amended by:
- Convention on the Accession of the Hellenic Republic to the Rome Convention of 1980 (Luxembourg, 10 April 1984): OJ L 146 of 31 May 1984; (484A0297);
- Convention on the Accession of the Kingdom of Spain and the Portuguese Republic to the Rome Convention of 1980 (Funchal, 18 May 1992): OJ L 333 of 18 November 1992; (492A0529)
- Convention on the Accession of the Republic of Austria, the Republic of Finland and the Kingdom of Sweden to the Rome Convention of 1980: OJ No C 15 of 15 January 1997 (Dublin, 29 November 1996): OJ C 015 of 15 January 1997; (497Y0115(02))

[T.122] Joint Action of 22 November 1996 concerning measures protecting against the effects of the extraterritorial application of legislation adopted by a third country, and actions based thereon or resulting therefrom: OJ No L 309 of 29 November 1996, p. 7); (496X0668)

[T.123] Convention on Civil Procedure (The Hague, 1 March 1954)

[T.124] Convention on the Service Abroad of Judicial and Extrajudicial Documents in Civil or Commercial Matters (The Hague, 15 November 1965)

[T.125] Convention on the Taking of Evidence Abroad in Civil or Commercial Matters (The Hague, 18 March 1970)

[T.126] European Convention on the Recognition and Enforcement of Decisions concerning Custody of Children and on Restoration of Custody of Children (Luxembourg, 20 May 1980)

[T.127] Convention on International Access to Justice (The Hague, 25 October 1980)

[T.128] Convention on the Civil Aspects of International Child Abduction (The Hague, 25 October 1980)

[T.129] Convention abolishing the Legalization of Documents in the Member States of the European Communities (Brussels, 25 May 1987); [T.130]Convention on Jurisdiction and Enforcement of Judgments in Civil and Commercial Matters (Lugano, 16 September 1988)/ OJ L 319 of 25 November 1988; (488A0592)

[T.130]Convention on Jurisdiction and Enforcement of Judgments in Civil and Commercial Matters (Lugano, 16 September 1988)/ OJ L 319 of 25 November 1988; (488A0592)

[T.131] Convention between the Member States of the European Communities on the Simplification of Procedures for the Recovery of Maintenance Payments (Rome, 6 November 1990)

[T.132] Convention of 10 March 1995 on Simplified Extradition Procedures between the Member States of the European Union: OJ No C 78 of 30 March 1995; (495A0330(01))

[T.133] Convention of 27 September 1996 relating to Extradition between the Member States of the European Union: OJ No C 313 of 23 October 1996; (496Y1023(02))

[T.133/1/A] Convention drawn up on the basis of Article K.3 of the Treaty on European Union on Driving Disqualifications.Official Journal C 216, 10/07/1998 p. 0002–0012; (498A0710(01))
[T.134] European Convention on Extradition (Paris, 13 December 1957)
[T.135] European Convention on Mutual Assistance in Criminal Matters (Strasbourg, 20 April 1959)
[T.136] Joint Action of 22 April 1996 concerning a framework for the exchange of liaison magistrates to improve judicial cooperation between the Member States of the European Union: OJ No L 105 of 27 April 1996; (496X0277)
[T.137/1/A] Joint Action of 29 June 1998 adopted by the Council on the basis of Article K.3 of the Treaty on European Union, on good practice in mutual legal assistance in criminal matters; Official Journal L 191, 07/07/1998 p. 0001–0003; (498X0427)
[T.137/1/B] Joint Action of 29 June 1998 adopted by the Council on the basis of Article K.3 of the Treaty on European Union, on the creation of a European Judicial Network. Official Journal L 191, 07/07/1998 p. 0004–0007; (498X0428)
[T.137/1/C] Joint Action of 3 December 1998 adopted by the Council on the basis of Article K.3 of the Treaty on European Union, on money laundering, the identification, tracing, freezing, seizing and confiscation of instrumentalities and the proceeds from crime. Official Journal L 333, 09/12/1998 p. 1–3; (498X0699)
[T.137/1/D] Joint Action to make it a criminal offence to participate in a criminal organisation in the Member States of the European Union. Official Reference OJ L351 of 29.12.98
[T.138] European Convention on the International Validity of Criminal Judgments (The Hague, 28 May 1970)
[T.139] European Convention on the Transfer of Proceedings in Criminal Matters (Strasbourg, 15 May 1972)
[T.140] First Additional Protocol to the European Convention on Extradition (Strasbourg 15 October 1975)
[T.141] Second Additional Protocol to the European Convention on Extradition (Strasbourg, 17 March 1978)
[T.142] Additional Protocol to the European Convention on Mutual Legal Assistance in Criminal Matters (Strasbourg, 17 March 1978);
[T.143] Convention on the Transfer of Sentenced Persons (Strasbourg, 21 March 1983)
[T.144] Convention between the Member States of the European Communities on the Transfer of Proceedings in Criminal Matters (Rome, 6 November 1990);
[T.145] Convention between the Member States of the European Communities on the Enforcement of Foreign Criminal Sentences (Brussels, 13 November 1991)
[T.146] Joint Action of 28 October 1996 on a programme of incentives and exchanges for legal practitioners (GROTIUS programme): OJ No L 287 of 8 November 1996, page 3; (496X0636)
[T.147] Joint Action of 29 November 1996 establishing an incentive and exchange programme for persons responsible for combating trade in human beings and sexual exploitation of children (STOP programme): OJ No L 322 of 12 December 1996, page 7; (496X0700)
[T.148] Joint Action of 20 December 1996 providing a common programme for the exchange and training and cooperation between law enforcement authorities (OISIN programme): OJ No L 7 of 10 January 1997, page 5; (497X0012)
[T.150] Joint Action of 19 March 1998 establishing a programme of exchange, training and cooperation for persons responsible for action to combat organized crime (FALCONE programme): OJ No L 99 of 31 March 1998, page 8; (498X0245)
[T.156-158] The following protocols to the European Convention for the Protection of Human Rights and Fundamental Freedoms:
156: Protocol No 4 of 1963
157: Protocol No 6 concerning the abolition of the death penalty of 1983
158: Protocol No 7 of 1984
[T.159] Joint Action of 29 June 1998 adopted by the Council on the basis of Article K.3 of the Treaty on European Union, establishing a mechanism for collective evaluation of the enactment, application and effective implementation by the applicant countries of the acquis of the European Union in the field of Justice and Home Affairs. Official Journal L 191, 07/07/1998 p. 0008–0009; (498X0429).

2.5

THE EU ACQUIS ON ASYLUM

WHAT IS THE 'ACQUIS'?

The term Acquis is normally reserved for the Acquis Communautaire; this is the sum of legislation, standards and practices which has been developed within the Community framework (First Pillar), which governs Member State actions in matters within the competence of the Community and which cannot be disassociated from the achievements of the objectives of the Community. The European Court of Justice (ECJ) has jurisdiction over the acquis communautaire.

Instruments, standards and practices have also been developed within the framework of the Union, i.e. in the Second and Third Pillars. Here, following the European Council formula, we should use the term 'acquis of the Union and its Member States'. With the entry into force of the Amsterdam Treaty the Third Pillar asylum instruments will be codified in EU law instruments.

For the purpose of this [commentary], we refer to this wider set of EU instruments and standards. The EU Acquis should be adopted and transposed into policy and practice by each Member State and it must be accepted by candidate countries as a condition for EU membership.[1]

THE EU ACQUIS ON ASYLUM

Prior to the TEU I (Maastricht) asylum policy had been handled as a matter for co-operation between Member States outside the European Community institutions, as asylum policy was not mentioned in the Treaty on the European Communities.[2]

In the TEU I, asylum policy became listed with other justice and home affairs areas in Title VI 'Provisions on co-operation in the fields of Justice and Home Affairs' as a 'matter of common interest' for the Member States (Article K.1).[3]

---

[1] Candidate countries for membership in the EU are required to begin the adoption process before accession.

[2] Treaty of Rome, 1957.

[3] As Title VI constitutes the Third Pillar, there is no acquis communautaire on asylum, instead, the measures on asylum adopted after the TEU I under Article K.3 form part of the 'Acquis of the Union and its Member States'.

P.J. van Krieken (Ed.), *The Asylum Acquis Handbook*
© 2000, T.M.C.Asser Press, The Hague, the Röling Foundation and the authors

WHAT IS COMMUNITARISATION?

In order for an instrument to be officially considered to be part of the EU acquis communautaire, the official decision taking mechanisms involving the main institutions[4] of the EU's First Pillar must be utilised to incorporate the instrument into the body of EC laws and legislation.[5]

TEU II (Amsterdam) allows for the 'communitarisation' of virtually all of the instruments, which make up today the EU acquis on asylum. Once the instruments have been taken into the First Pillar they will form part of the acquis communautaire.

In Article 63 of TEC a 'Five Year Window' (five year time limit after its ratification by all Member States) for the 'communitarisation' of specified asylum measures is formally set out. The 'communitarisation' of asylum measures will follow the procedure outlined in Article 67.

TEXTS OF THE EU ACQUIS ON ASYLUM

In May 1998 the Acquis of the Union and of its Member States on Justice and Home Affairs was listed and formally approved by the Committee of Permanent Representatives of the Council Members –Coreper and on December 1998 an addendum was issued.[6] The EU acquis on asylum contains the instruments relevant for the development of asylum systems in the CEEC's.[7]

The relevant documents which make up the EU acquis on asylum are taken from the parts dealing with Asylum (I), Migration (III) and Human Rights related issues (XII) of the Justice and Home Affairs Acquis which comprises twelve subsections.[8]

International conventions, which are regarded as indissociable from the achievements of the objectives of the EU, are considered to be part of the EU acquis. In asylum matters these include the 1951 Refugee Convention and its 1967 Protocol, and the European Convention on Human Rights and Fundamental Freedoms (ECHR). The EU acquis on asylum also includes the Dublin Convention and its implementing provisions, Joint Actions and Positions adopted by the Council, Resolutions, Decisions and Ministerial Conclusions which have been adopted.

---

[4] The EU Commission, Council of Ministers and European Parliament.

[5] The EU Commission and the EU Member States acting through the Council are responsible for drafting instruments and amending successive drafts. Theoretically, the European Court of Justice has jurisdiction over the interpretation of such instruments.

[6] A complete list of instruments which make up the EU acquis in the field of Justice and Home Affairs is included at the beginning of the compilation of the EU Acquis on Asylum text book.

[7] Central and Eastern European Countries with agreements to join the EU.

[8] The main documents are presented and explained in more detail in the following section.

For clarity these documents have been divided into three categories:
1) International conventions to be regarded as indissociable from the achievements of the objectives of the EU related to asylum;
2) Instruments adopted by Member States before the entry into force of the TEU I (Maastricht);
3) Instruments adopted by the Council after entry into force of the TEU I (Maastricht).

1. International conventions to be regarded as indissociable from the achievements of the objectives of the EU related to asylum

1.A. 1951 Convention Relating to the Status of Refugees (Geneva, 28 July 1951)[9]

The 1951 Refugee Convention is the most important international instrument for the protection of refugees. The definition of a refugee in Article 1A of the Convention serves as the basis for all national and regional instruments providing protection for refugees. The Convention lays down the rights and obligations for persons that have been recognised as refugees in the framework of the Convention. The Convention contains the most fundamental provision for international refugee protection: non-refoulement (Article 33).

However, under the Convention, only persons who had become displaced as a result of events occurring before 1st January 1951 could be recognised as refugees.

1.B. Protocol Relating to the Status of Refugees (New York, 31 January 1967)

The 1967 Protocol amends the 1951 Refugee Convention. The Protocol removes the deadline of 1st January 1951, and therefore covers any person who can be considered as a refugee according to the definition given in Article 1A of the Convention.

The Protocol is also to be applied without any geographical reservation, although States, which had already signed the Convention and had restricted its geographical scope to Europe could continue to apply this restriction.

1.C. European Convention for the Protection of Human Rights and Fundamental Freedoms (ECHR, Rome, 4 November 1950)

ECHR is a European-specific Convention for the protection of basic human rights.[10] The Convention was drafted outside the European Community/Union

---

[9] Referred to as the 1951 Refugee Convention.
[10] ECHR is supported by the European Court of Human Rights and Commission based in Strasbourg. The Protocols No.: 4 (1963, regarding the right to liberty), 6 (1983, regarding the death penalty) and 7 (1984, regarding expulsion of aliens) have also become part of the EU acquis (XII, D).

framework: indeed, the European Community did not exist at the time. However, although the EU is not a party in its own right to the Convention, every EU Member State and CEEC is a signatory.[11]

Art. 3 protects persons against expulsion to a country where they would be facing a real risk of exposure to torture, or to inhuman or degrading treatment or punishment.

ECHR includes several other provisions, which are directly applicable to refugees and asylum seekers. Article 5 relates to detention and states that everyone has the right to liberty and security of person. Article 6 guarantees the right of access to a fair and impartial tribunal, while Article 8 contains considerations for family unity and reunification. Furthermore, Article 13 provides everyone with the right to an effective remedy before a national authority. All these rights apply irrespective of nationality or legal status.

2. **Instruments adopted by Member States before the entry into force of the TEU I (Maastricht)**

2.1. Convention Determining the State Responsible for Examining Applications for Asylum Lodged in one of the Member States of the European Communities (Dublin, 15 June 1990)

The Dublin Convention was concluded between the (then) twelve Member States of the EC before the passage of TEU I. New Member States must accede to the Dublin Convention, which is binding, and is therefore considered part of the acquis on asylum, although not strictly a Community instrument.[12]

It sets up common criteria to determine the single Member State responsible for examining an asylum request based on a list of criteria. The stated aim of the Convention is that the responsible Member State has to conduct the full examination procedure to its conclusion. However, due to the application of the safe third country notion it is possible that the substance of an asylum seeker's claim will not be examined by one of the Member States.

2.2. Acts Implementing the Dublin Convention

A series of instruments have been agreed upon at Ministerial level in order to improve the implementation of the Dublin Convention. These instruments include a standard form for the examination and application of asylum requests, guidelines

---

[11] The ECHR is listed under section XII A of the abovementioned Council document (JAI 7) of May 1998. By virtue of Article F TEU I and Article 6 of TEU II it forms one of the cornerstones of the asylum acquis.

[12] It entered into force 1 September 1997 for 12 Member States, 1 October 1997 for Austria and Sweden, and 1 January 1998 for Finland.

for the means of proof, transfers, time periods, or the application of the family reunion criteria.

2.3. Decision of June 1992 Establishing a Centre for Information, Reflection and Exchange on Asylum (CIREA)

CIREA was established to operate as an informal forum for exchange of information and consultations without any decision making powers and, so doing, fulfill the obligation deriving of art. 15 of the Dublin Convention.

CIREA gathers documents and disseminates information and compiles documentation on matters relating to asylum. It is considered a 'clearing house' with no formal rules of accession but its guidelines do include Member State obligations.

2.4. Resolution on Manifestly Unfounded Applications for Asylum (London, 30 November and 1 December 1992): London Resolution I

This Resolution, adopted by the Ministers for Immigration, defines a manifestly unfounded application as a claim where there is clearly no substance to the applicant's claim to fear of persecution in his/her own country; where the claim is based on deliberate deception; or is an abuse of asylum procedures.

Manifestly unfounded applications can be handled through an accelerated procedure which should lead to a decision within one month.

2.5. Resolution on a Harmonised Approach to Questions of Host Third Country (London, 30 November and 1 December 1992): London Resolution II.

This Resolution, adopted by the Ministers for Immigration, defines host third countries as countries of transit or potential destination where:
– the applicant is not threatened with refoulement in the meaning of art.33 of the 1951 refugee Convention nor torture or inhuman or degrading treatment within the meaning of art.3 ECHR;
– the applicant either has already been granted protection or has had the opportunity to seek protection there, or there is evidence of his admissibility into that country:
– the applicant can be afforded effective protection against refoulement

The principles for a procedural basis for applying the concept where an applicant can be sent back are established according to the first paragraph of the Resolution, whereby in principle the formal identification of a host third country precedes the substantive examination of the asylum application. Therefore each case is not necessarily examined on its merits.

Furthermore, the Resolution sets out the relationship between the application of the concept of the Host Third Country and the procedures of the Dublin Convention. A Member State may make a decision to return an asylum seeker to a host third country before it makes a decision to return the applicant to another Member State under the Dublin Convention.

2.6. Conclusion on Countries in which there is Generally No Serious Risk of Persecution (London, 30 November and 1 December 1992): London Resolution III

This Resolution, adopted by the Ministers for Immigration, provides basic elements, which determine whether a country is safe, which could create a presumption that an application for asylum is manifestly unfounded.

These elements include the observance of human rights by the country of origin, the existence of democratic institutions and stability, and a low number of previous asylum seekers as well as low recognition rates.

3. Instruments adopted by the Council after entry into force of the TEU I (Maastricht)

3.1. Council Recommendations concerning readmission agreements (Brussels, 30 November 1994 and 24 July 1995)

The Council Recommendations concerning readmission agreements are listed under the EU acquis on migration – rather than asylum. However, they are an important reality as readmission agreements are designed to facilitate the return of asylum applicants rejected on the basis of safe third country grounds or because their claim has been determined to be manifestly unfounded.

Two Council Recommendations have been produced, one concerning a specimen bilateral readmission agreement, and the second which sets out the guiding principles to be followed in the drawing up of readmission agreements.

3.2. Council Resolution on Minimum Guarantees for Asylum Procedures (Brussels, 20 June 1995)[13]

This Council Resolution, adopted according to the procedures laid down in Articles K.3 and 4 of TEU I[14], draws up the minimum guarantees for the asylum procedures in the Member States.

The Resolution includes a list of minimum rights for asylum seekers during all examination, appeal and review procedures. The general principle is that the asylum seeker may remain in the territory of the Member State for the full asylum

---

[13] OJ No. C 274, 19.09.1996, p.13.

[14] As is the case with all other instruments listed below, except for those which are still in draft form.

application procedure, up to and including the appeal. There are additional safeguards for women and unaccompanied minors.

However, there are also special provisions for processing manifestly unfounded asylum applications and for applications that are made at the border which limit the application of the guarantees applicable in the normal procedure by allowing for exceptions and derogations, under certain conditions.[15]

3.3. Council Resolution on Burden Sharing with Regard to the Admission and Residence of Displaced Persons on a Temporary Basis (Brussels, 25 September 1995)[16] (Temporary Protection and Burden Sharing)

This Resolution emphasises the need for Member States to admit persons fleeing armed conflicts, civil wars or similar situations that have resulted in mass population movements and requires prompt action.

This is to be done on a temporary basis and if necessary in lieu of the normal asylum procedure. The Resolution includes a list of situations, which must be taken into account by the Member States when admitting displaced persons into their territory.

The Resolution also provides for solidarity measures and burden sharing in such situations, based on the contributions each Member State makes in regard to the prevention or resolution of the conflict, with economic, social and political factors being taken into account. The allocation of persons from the crisis region is considered as a matter of priority.

3.4. Council Decision on an Alert and Emergency Procedure for Burden Sharing with Regard to the Admission and Residence of Displaced Persons on a Temporary Basis (Brussels, 4 March 1996)[17] (Burden Sharing Decision)

This Decision, a supplement to the Council Resolution on Burden Sharing, establishes a swift alert and emergency procedure, giving the Presidency, Member State or the Commission the possibility to call the Coordinating Committee (established by TEU I, Title VI Article K.4) to an urgent meeting in order to examine whether a situation exists that requires concerted action by the EU for the ad-

---

[15] Each Member State must create their own provisions concerning access to the asylum procedure including its basic features and competent authorities. This must be done within the frame work of the ECHR, 1951 Refugee Convention and 1967 Protocol.

[16] OJ No. L 63, 13.03.1996, p. 10. The Resolution is not examined in detail in the Manual as there is currently a draft Joint Action on Temporary Protection and Burden Sharing which will supersede this Resolution.

[17] OJ No. L 63, 13.03.1996, p. 10. The Resolution is not examined in detail in the Manual as there is currently a draft Joint Action on Temporary Protection and Burden Sharing which will supersede this Resolution.

mission and residence of displaced persons on a temporary basis within its territory.

3.5. Joint Position Defined by the Council on the Basis of Article K.3 of the Treaty on European Union on the Harmonised Application of the Definition of the Term of Refugee in Article 1 of the Geneva Convention of 28 July 1951 Relating to the Status of Refugees (Brussels, 4 March 1996)[18] (Joint Position)

The Joint Position is an instrument[19] which requests Member States to consider its guidelines for the application of criteria for recognition and admissions as a refugee. It gives the definition generally agreed upon of 'persecution' within the meaning of Article 1A of the 1951 Refugee Convention as the Convention does not define this term. The Joint Position also gives examples on the origins and grounds of persecution (especially agents of persecution), that the Member States should bear in mind when examining an application for asylum.

3.6. Council Resolution on Unaccompanied Minors who are Nationals of Third Countries (Brussels, 26 June 1997)[20] Council Resolution

This Council Resolution concerns third-country nationals below the age of eighteen who arrive on the territory of a Member State unaccompanied or not awaited on arrival by an adult responsible for them. It also applies to minors who are left after being brought into the territory of the Member States.

The Resolution establishes guidelines for the treatment for unaccompanied minors (UAM) with regard to reception, stay and return conditions and the handling of their applications for asylum, taking into consideration the particular needs of minors and their vulnerable situation. The Resolution also recognises especially the need to provide, as soon as possible, the assistance of a legal guardian, either a specifically appointed adult representative or an institution.

The resolution also stresses the importance of making efforts to trace the minor's relatives in order to, whenever possible and in the best interest of the child, reunite him/her with them.

---

[18] OJ No. L 63, 13.03.1996, p. 2.

[19] However, the Joint Position was adopted within the limits of the Constitutional powers of the Governments of the Member States, and does not bind the legislative authorities or affect the decisions of judicial authorities of the Member States.

[20] OJ No. C 221, 19.07.97, p. 23.[T.2]. Convention relating to the Status of Refugees (Geneva, 28 July 1951)

3. TEXTS

The following instruments have been reproduced in this Handbook. For the sake of transparency and accessibility it has been decided not to reproduce all the relevant texts. The Handbook strives for consumer-friendliness, rather than completeness. Any choice is arbitrary and this one is no exception to this rule. An effort has nevertheless been made to include the instruments which are most useful for understanding and appreciating the present level of awareness-building, level-setting, and harmonization of implementation.

Included, therefore, have been primarily the instruments dealing with minimum guarantees, host third countries, countries of origin, Dublin, unaccompanied minors, family reunification, burden sharing, the gathering and exchange of information, the interpretation of the 1951 Convention, and return:

T.1 (a-c), T.4-10, T.12-16, T.19, T.23, T.28, T.31, T.36-38, and T.40-43, in total 26 documents, it being understood that although some of the documents prima facie focus on migration in general they all are related one way or another to the issue of asylum.

We followed a topical order, i.e. entry, determination and return. Included, therefore are:[1]

1. ENTRY

a) **Visa and airports**

3.1 [T.19] II.C.a.2) Council Regulation (EC) No 2317/95 of 25 September 1995 determining the third countries whose nationals must be in possession of visas when crossing the external borders of the Member States Official Journal L 234, 03/10/1995 p. 0001–0003   127

3.2 [T.16] II.B.1) Joint Action of 4 March 1996 adopted by the Council on the basis of Article K.3 of the Treaty on European Union on airport transit arrangements (96/197/JHA) Official Journal L 063, 13/03/1996 p. 0008–0009   130

b) **Children and family**

3.3 [T.31] III.1.C.10) Council Resolution of 26 June 1997 on unaccompanied minors who are nationals of third countries (97/C 221/03 Official Journal C 221, 19/07/1997 p. 0023–0027
     132

3.4 [T.23] III.1.C.2) Resolution of 1 June 1993 on harmonisation of family reunion (document WG 1497 rev 1   137

---

[1] Instruments which have been commented upon by the Brussels' Commission have been provided with a double asterisk (**).

c) **Temporary protection / burden sharing**

3.5 [T.13] I.C.9) Council Resolution of 25 September 1995 on burden-sharing with regard to the admission and residence of displaced persons on a temporary basis (95/C 262/01) Official Journal C 262, 07/10/1995 p. 0001–0003   140

3.6 [T.14] I.C.10) Council Decision of 4 March 1996 on an alert and emergency procedure for burden-sharing with regard to the admission and residence of displaced persons on a temporary basis (96/198/JHA) Official Journal L 063, 13/03/1996 p. 0010–0011   143

d) **Illegal entry**

3.7 [T.37] III.2.C.5) Council Recommendation of 22 December 1995 on harmonizing means of combating illegal immigration and illegal employment and improving the relevant means of control (96/C 5/01) Official Journal C 005, 10/01/1996 p. 0001–0003   144

e) **Supervision / co-operation**

3.8 [T.28] III.1.C.7) Council Decision of 22 December 1995 on monitoring the implementation of instruments already adopted concerning admission of third-country nationals. Official Journal C 011, 16/01/1996 p. 0001–0001   147

3.9 [T.40] III.2.C.8) Council Decision of 16 December 1996 on monitoring the implementation of instruments adopted by the Council concerning illegal immigration, readmission, the unlawful employment of third country nationals and cooperation in the implementation of expulsion orders (96/749/JHA) Official Journal L 342, 31/12/1996 p. 0005–0005   148

2. DETERMINATION PROCESS

a) **Interpretation**

3.10 [T.4] I.B.1) Joint Position of 4 March 1996 defined by the Council on the basis of Article K.3 of the Treaty on European Union on the harmonized application of the definition of the term 'refugee' in Article 1 of the Geneva Convention of 28 July 1951 relating to the status of refugees (96/196/JHA) Official Journal L 063, 13/03/1996 p. 0002–0007. (**)   149

b) **Procedures and background**

3.11 [T.12] I.C.8) Council Resolution of 20 June 1995 on minimum guarantees for asylum procedures. Official Journal C 274, 19/09/1996 p. 0013–0017. (**)   157

3.12a [T.1.a] I.A.a.1) Convention determining the State responsible for examining applications for asylum lodged in one of the Member States of the European Communities (Dublin Convention) (97/C254/01) Official Journal C 254, 19/08/1997 p. 0001–0012. (**)   162

3.12b [T.1.b] I.A.a.2) Decision No 1/97 of 9 September 1997 of the Committee set up by Article 18 of the Dublin Convention of 15 June 1990, concerning provisions for the implementation of the Convention (97/662/CMS) Official Journal L 281, 14/10/1997 p. 0001–0025. (**)
171

3.12c [T.1.d] I.A.a.4) Decision No 1/98 of of 30 June 1998 of the Committee set up by Article 18 of the Dublin Convention of 15 June 1990, concerning provisions for the implementation of the Convention (98/451/CSM) Official Journal L 196, 14/07/1998 p. 0049–0050. (**)   178

3.13 [T.7] I.C.3) Resolution adopted 30 November 1992 on manifestly unfounded applications for asylum (document WG1 1282 rev 1 (**)   179

3.14 [T.6] I.C.2) Resolution adopted 30 November 1992 on a harmonised approach to questions concerning host third countries (document WG1 1283 (**)   183

3.15 [T.8] I.C.4) Conclusions adopted 30 November 1992 concerning countries in which there is generally no serious risk of persecutions (document WG1 1281 (**)   185

c) **Information gathering**

3.16 [T.5] I.C.1) Decision of 11 June 1992 setting up a Centre for Information, Discussion and Exchange on Asylum (Cirea) document WG1 1107   186

3.17 [T.10] I.C.6) Guidelines for joint reports on third countries (Text adopted by the Council on 20 June 1994) Official Journal C 274, 19/09/1996 p. 0052–0054   188

3.18 [T.9] I.C.5) Circulation and confidentiality of joint reports on the situation in certain third countries (Text adopted by the Council on 20 June 1994) Official Journal C 274, 19/09/1996 p. 0043–0043   191

d) **Supervision / co-operation**

3.19 [T.15] I.C.11) Council Decision of 26 June 1997 on monitoring the implementation of instruments adopted concerning asylum (97/420/JHA) Official Journal L 178, 07/07/1997 p. 0006–0007   191

3. RETURN

a) **Voluntary repatriation**

3.20 [T.41] III.2.C.9) Council Decision of 26 May 1997 on the exchange of information concerning assistance for the voluntary repatriation of third-country nationals (97/340/JHA) Official Journal L 147, 05/06/1997 p. 0003–0004   193

b) **Readmission**

3.21 [T.42] III.3.C.1) Council Recommendation of 30 November 1994 concerning a specimen bilateral readmission agreement between a Member State and a third country Official Journal C 274, 19/09/1996 p. 0020–0024. (**)   194

3.22 [T.43] III.3.C.2) Council Recommendation of 24 July 1995 on the guiding principles to be followed in drawing up protocols on the implementation of readmission agreements Official Journal C 274, 19/09/1996 p. 0025–0033. (**)   199

c) **Expulsion**

3.23 [T.38] III.2.C.6) Council Recommendation of 22 December 1995 on concerted action and cooperation in carrying out expulsion measures (96/C 5/02) Official Journal C 005, 10/01/1996 p. 0003–0007   202

3.24 [T.36] III.2.C.4) Council Recommendation of 30 November 1994 concerning the adoption of a standard travel document for the expulsion of third-country nationals Official Journal C 274, 19/09/1996 p. 0018–0019   207

3.1

Council Regulation (EC) No 2317/95 of 25 September 1995 determining the third countries whose nationals must be in possession of visas when crossing the external borders of the Member States[2]

THE COUNCIL OF THE EUROPEAN UNION,
Having regard to the Treaty establishing the European Community,
Having regard to the proposal from the Commission,[3]
Having regard to the opinion of the European Parliament,[4]
Whereas Article 100c of the Treaty requires the Council to determine the third countries whose nationals must be in possession of a visa when crossing the external borders of the Member States;

Whereas the drawing up of the common list annexed to this Regulation represents an important step towards the harmonization of visa policy; whereas the second paragraph of Article 7a of the Treaty stipulates in particular that the internal market shall comprise an area without internal frontiers in which the free movement of persons is ensured in accordance with the Treaty; whereas other aspects of the harmonization of visa policy, including the conditions for the issue of visas, are matters to be determined under Title VI of the Treaty on European Union;

Whereas risks relating to security and illegal immigration should be given priority consideration when the said common list annexed hereto is drawn up; whereas, in addition, Member States' international relations with third countries also play a role;

Whereas the principle that a Member State may not require a visa from a person wishing to cross its external borders if that person holds a visa issued by another Member State which meets the harmonized conditions governing the issue of visas and is valid throughout the Community or if that person holds an appropriate permit issued by a Member State is a matter that should be determined under Title VI of the Treaty on European Union;

Whereas this Regulation shall not prevent a Member State from deciding under what conditions nationals of third countries lawfully resident within its territory may re-enter it after having left the territory of the Member States of the Union during the period of validity of their permits;

Whereas, in special cases justifying an exemption where visa requirements would in principle exist, Member States may exempt certain categories of person in keeping with international law or custom;

Whereas since national rules differ on stateless persons, recognized refugees and persons who produce passports or travel documents issued by a territorial entity or authority which is not recognized as a State by all Member States, Member States may decide on visa requirements for that group of persons, where that territorial entity or authority is not on the said common list;

---

[2] Official Journal L 234, 03/10/1995 p. 0001–0003; 395R2317.
[3] OJ C11, 15 January 1994, p. 15.
[4] OJ C128, 9 May 1994, p. 350.

P.J. van Krieken (Ed.), The Asylum Acquis Handbook
© 2000, T.M.C.Asser Press, The Hague, the Röling Foundation and the authors

Whereas when adding new entities to the list it is necessary to take account of diplomatic implications and guidelines adopted on the matter by the European Union; whereas, at all events the inclusion of a third country on the common list is entirely without prejudice to its international status;

Whereas the determination of third countries whose nationals must be in possession of visas when crossing the external borders of the Member States should be achieved gradually; whereas Member States will constantly endeavour to harmonize their visa policies with regard to third countries not on the common list; whereas the present provisions must not prejudice the achievement of free movement for persons as provided for in Article 7a of the Treaty; whereas the Commission should draw up a progress report on harmonization after five years;

Whereas, with a view to ensuring that the system is administered openly and that the persons concerned are informed, Member States must communicate to the other Member States and to the Commission the measures which they take pursuant to this Regulation; whereas for the same reasons that information must also be published in the Official Journal of the European Communities;

Whereas the information provided for in Articles 2(4) and 4(2) must be published before the other provisions of this Regulation come into force; whereas Articles 2(4) and 4(2) must therefore become applicable one month before the other provisions of the Regulation,

HAS ADOPTED THIS REGULATION:

Article 1
1. Nationals of third countries on the common list in the Annex shall be required to be in possession of visas when crossing the external borders of the Member States.[5]
2. Nationals of countries formerly part of countries on the common list shall be subject to the requirements of paragraph 1 unless and until the Council decides otherwise under the procedure laid down in Article 100c of the Treaty.

Article 2
1. The Member States shall determine the visa requirements for nationals of third countries not on the common list.
2. The Member States shall determine the visa requirements for stateless persons and recognized refugees.

---

[5] Ed: The Common List referred to in this Article contained the following States: Afghanistan, Albania, Algeria, Angola, Armenia, Azerbaijan, Bahrain, Bangladesh, Belarus, Benin, Bhutan, Bulgaria, Burkina Faso, Burundi, Cambodia, Cameroon, Cape Verde, Central African Republic, Chad, China, Comorros, Congo, Côte d'Ivoire, Cuba, Djibouti, Dominican Republic, Egypt, Equatorial Guinea, Eritrea, Ethiopia, Fiji, Gabon, the Gambia, Georgia, Ghana, Guinea, Guinea Bissau, Guyana, Haiti, India, Indonesia, Iran, Iraq, Jordan, Kazakstan, Kyrgyzstan, Kuwait, Laos, Lebanon, Liberia, Libya, Madagascar, Maldives, Mali, Mauritania, Mauritius, Moldova, Mongolia, Morocco, Mozambique, Myanmar, Nepal, Niger, Nigeria, North Korea, Oman, Pakistan, Papua New Guinea, Peru, Philippines, Quatar, Romania, Russia, Rwanda, Sao Tomé and Principe, Saudi Arabia, Senegal, Sierra Leone, Somalia, Sri Lanka, Sudan, Suriname, Syria, Tajikistan, Tanzania, Thailand, Togo, Tunisia, Turkey, Turkmenistan, Uganda, United Arab Emirates, Uzbekistan, Vietnam, Yemen, Zaire, Zambia; and the following Entities and Territorial Authorities not recognized as States by all the Member States: Taiwan, Former Yugoslav Republic of Macedonia, and Federal Republic of Yugoslavia (Serbia and Montenegro).

3. The Member States shall determine the visa requirements for persons who produce passports or travel documents issued by a territorial entity or authority which is not recognized as a State by all Member States if that entity or territorial authority is not on the common list.

4. Within ten working days of the entry into force of this paragraph, Member States shall communicate to the other Member States and the Commission the measures they have taken pursuant to paragraphs 1, 2 and 3. Any further measures taken pursuant to paragraph 1 shall be similarly communicated within five working days. The Commission shall publish the measures communicated pursuant to this paragraph and updates thereof in the Official Journal of the European Communities for information.

Article 3

Five years after the entry into force of this Regulation the Commission shall draw up a progress report of the harmonization of Member States' visa policies with regard to third countries not on the common list and, if necessary, submit to the Council proposals for further measures required to achieve the objective of harmonization laid down in Article 100c.

Article 4

1. A Member State may exempt nationals of third countries subject to visa requirements under Article 1(1) and (2) from those requirements. This shall apply in particular to civilian air and sea crew, flight crew and attendants on emergency or rescue flights and other helpers in the event of disaster or accident and holders of diplomatic passports, official duty passports and other official passports.

2. Article 2(4) shall apply mutatis mutandis.

Article 5

For the purposes of this Regulation, 'visa' shall mean an authorization given or a decision taken by a Member State which is required for entry into its territory with a view to:
– an intended stay in that Member State or in several Member States of no more than three months in all,
– transit through the territory of that Member State or several Member States, except for transit through the international zones of airports and transfers between airports in a Member State.

Article 6

This Regulation shall be without prejudice to any further harmonization between individual Member States, going beyond the common list, determining the third countries whose nationals must be in possession of a visa when crossing their external borders.

Article 7

This Regulation shall enter into force six months after its publication in the Official Journal of the European Communities except for Articles 2(4) and 4(2) which shall enter into force on the day following publication. This Regulation shall be binding in its entirety and directly applicable in all Member States.

3.2

Joint Action of 4 March 1996 adopted by the Council on the basis of Article K.3 of the Treaty on European Union on airport transit arrangements (96/197/JHA)[6]

THE COUNCIL OF THE EUROPEAN UNION,
Having regard to the Treaty on European Union, and in particular Article K.3(2)(b) thereof,
Having regard to the initiative of 23 February 1995 from the French Republic,
Whereas the determination of the conditions of entry and movement by nationals of third countries into and within the territory of Member States, and combating unauthorized immigration by nationals of third countries, are matters of common interest under Article K.1(3)(a) and (c) respectively of the Treaty;
Whereas the air route, particularly when it involves applications for entry or de facto entry, in the course of airport transit, represents a significant way in with a view in particular to illegally taking up residence within the territory of the Member States; whereas improvements should be sought in controlling that route;
Whereas Annex 9 to the Chicago Convention on International Civil Aviation establishes the principle of free transit passage through the international areas of airports; whereas States may nevertheless make exceptions to this general principle by notifying the International Civil Aviation Organization (ICAO) and requiring an airport transit visa; whereas this possibility should be limited as far as possible to avoid any unnecessary constraint on the development of air transport;
Whereas the harmonization of Member States' policies in this field is an accordance with the objectives of security and control of illegal immigration of the Treaty, while contributing to harmonizing the conditions of competition between airlines and airports in the Member States;
Whereas this matter does not concern visas required when crossing the external borders of the Member States and is therefore not covered by Article 100c(1) of the Treaty establishing the European Community; whereas it is nevertheless of common interest and could be more effectively dealt with by means of joint action;
Whereas the Member States that do not have airport visa arrangements should be allowed sufficient time to draw up such arrangements,

HAS ADOPTED THIS JOINT ACTION:

Article 1
For the purposes of this joint action, 'airport transit visa (ATV)' shall mean the authorization to which nationals of certain third countries are subject, as an exception to the principle of free transit laid down in Annex 9 to the Chicago Convention on International Civil Aviation, for transit through the international areas of the airports of Member States.

Article 2
1. The airport transit visa shall be issued by the consular services of the Member States.
2. The conditions of issue of airport transit visas shall be determined by each Member

---

[6] Official Journal L 063, 13/03/1996 p. 0008–0009 [EUDOR] 496X0197.

State subject to adoption by the Council of criteria to the preliminaries for and issue of visas. In all cases, the consular services must ascertain that there is no security risk or risk of illegal immigration. They must above all be satisfied that the application for an airport transit visa is justified on the basis of the documents submitted by the applicant, and that as far as possible these documents guarantee entry into the country of final destination, in particular by presentation of a visa where so required.

3. With effect from the entry into force of the provisions contained in Council Regulation (EC) No 1683/95 of 29 May 1995 laying down a uniform format for visas,[7] Member States shall issue airport transit visas using the uniform visa format laid down in that Regulation.

Article 3
Each Member State shall require and airport transit visa of nationals of third countries included on the joint list annexed hereto who do not already hold an entry or transit visa for the Member State in question when passing through the international areas of airports situated within its territory.

Article 4
A Member State may provide for exceptions to the requirement for an airport transit visa in respect of nationals of third countries included on the joint list annexed hereto, in particular for:
– crew member of aircraft and ships,
– holders of diplomatic, official or service passports,
– holders of residence permits or equivalent documents issued by a Member State,
– holders of visas issued by a Member State, or by a State which is a party to the Agreement on the European Economic Area.

Article 5
Each Member State shall decide whether an airport transit visa should be required of nationals of countries not included on the joint list annexed hereto.

Article 6
Each Member State shall determine the airport transit arrangements applicable to statutory stateless persons and refugees.

Article 7
Within 10 working days of the entry into force of this joint action, Member States shall notify the other Member States and the General Secretariat of the Council of the measures taken pursuant to Articles 4, 5 and 6. Those measures shall be published, for information, in the Official Journal.

Article 8
Each year the Council Presidency shall draw up a report on progress in the harmonization of airport transit arrangements within the Union. The Council shall examine any proposal for amending the list annexed hereto.

---

[7] OJ No L 164, 14.7.1995, p. 1.

Article 9
This joint action shall not prevent closer airport-transit harmonization between some Member States, extending in scope beyond the joint list annexed hereto.

Article 10
This joint action shall enter into force on the first day of the sixth month following its publication in the Official Journal. However, in the case of Denmark, Finland and Sweden, it shall enter into force on the first day of the 18th month following its publication in the Official Journal.

3.3

Council Resolution of 26 June 1997 on unaccompanied minors who are nationals of third countries (97/C 221/03)[8]

THE COUNCIL OF THE EUROPEAN UNION,
Having regard to the Treaty on European Union, and in particular Article K.1 thereof,
Whereas, pursuant to Article K.1(3)(a), (b) and (c) of the Treaty, the conditions of entry of, and residence by, nationals of third countries on the territory of Member States and measures to combat unauthorized immigration and residence by nationals of third countries on the territory of Member States constitute matters of common interest;
Whereas Article K.1(1) of the Treaty provides that asylum policy is to be regarded as a matter of common interest for the Member States;
Whereas third-country minors sometimes enter and stay in the territory of member States without being accompanied by a responsible person and without obtaining the necessary authorization;
Whereas unaccompanied minors who are nationals of third countries can be the victims of facilitators, and it is important for Member States to cooperate in combating such form of facilitating;
Whereas unaccompanied minors who are nationals of third countries generally are in a vulnerable situation requiring special safeguards and care;
Whereas recognition of the vulnerable situation of unaccompanied minors in the territory of Member States justifies the laying down of common principles for dealing with such situations;
Whereas, in accordance with Article K.2(1) of the Treaty, this Resolution is without prejudice to the international commitments entered into by the Member States pursuant to the European Convention for the Protection of Human Rights and Fundamental Freedoms of 4 November 1950;
Whereas this Resolution is without prejudice to the international commitments entered into by the Member States pursuant to the United Nations Convention on the Rights of the Child, 1989;
Whereas, pursuant to Article 2 of that Convention, States Parties shall respect the rights set forth in the Convention without discrimination;

---

[8] Official Journal C 221, 19/07/1997 p. 0023–0027 [EUDOR] 397Y0719(02).

Whereas, pursuant to Article 3 of that Convention, in all actions concerning children, the best interests of the child shall be a primary consideration;

Whereas Article 22 of that Convention aims to protect and assist minors who seek refugee status or who are regarded as refugees;

Whereas it is of great importance for the Member States, true to their common humanitarian tradition and in accordance with the provisions of the Geneva Convention of 28 July 1951 relating to the Status of Refugees, as amended by the New York Protocol of 31 January 1967, to grant refugees appropriate protection;

Whereas on 20 June 1995 the Council adopted a Resolution on minimum guarantees for asylum procedures;

Whereas this Resolution is without prejudice to the Strasbourg Convention of 28 January 1981 of the Council of Europe for the Protection of Individuals with regard to Automatic Processing of Personal Data;

Whereas the unauthorized presence in the territory of Member States of unaccompanied minors who are not regarded as refugees must be temporary, with Member States endeavouring to cooperate among themselves and with the third countries of origin to return the minor to his country of origin or to a third country prepared to accept him, without jeopardizing his safety, in order to find, whenever possible, the persons responsible for the minor, and to reunite him with such persons;

Whereas the application of such principles should not interfere with the application of national laws on public policy, public health or public security,

HEREBY ADOPTS THIS RESOLUTION:

Article 1 Scope and purpose

1. This Resolution concerns third-country nationals below the age of eighteen, who arrive on the territory of the Member States unaccompanied by an adult responsible for them whether by law or custom, and for as long as they are not effectively in the care of such a person. This Resolution can also be applied to minors who are nationals of third countries and who are left unaccompanied after they have entered the territory of the Member States. The persons covered by the previous two sentences shall be referred to herein as 'unaccompanied minors'.

2. This Resolution shall not apply to third-country nationals who are members of the family of nationals of a Member State of the European Union, nor to nationals of a Member State of the European Free Trade Association party to the Agreement on the European Economic Area and the members of their family, whatever the latter's nationality may be, where, pursuant to the Treaty establishing the European Community or the Agreement on the European Economic Area respectively, rights to freedom of movement are being exercised.

3. The purpose of this Resolution is to establish guidelines for the treatment for unaccompanied minors, with regard to matters such as the conditions for their reception, stay and return and, in the case of asylum seekers, the handling of applicable procedures.

4. This Resolution shall be without prejudice to more favourable provisions of national law.

5. The following guidelines are to be notified to the competent authorities responsible for

matters covered by this Resolution, and such authorities shall take them into consideration in their action. Implementation of these guidelines is not to be subject to any form of discrimination.

Article 2 Admission
1. Member States may, in accordance with their national legislation and practice, refuse admission at the frontier to unaccompanied minors in particular if they are without the required documentation and authorizations. However, in case of unaccompanied minors who apply for asylum, the Resolution on Minimum Guarantees for Asylum Procedures is applicable, in particular the principles set out in paragraphs 23 to 25 thereof.
2. In this connection, Member States should take appropriate measures, in accordance with their national legislation, to prevent the unauthorized entry of unaccompanied minors and should cooperate to prevent illegal entry and illegal residence of unaccompanied minors on their territory.
3. Unaccompanied minors who, pursuant to national provisions, must remain at the border until a decision has been taken on their admission to the territory or on their return, should receive all necessary material support and care to satisfy their basic needs, such as food, accommodation suitable for their age, sanitary facilities and medical care.

Article 3 Minimum guarantees for all unaccompanied minors
1. Member States should endeavour to establish a minor's identity as soon as possible after arrival, and also the fact that he or she is unaccompanied. Information on the minor's identity and situation can be obtained by various means, in particular by means of an appropriate interview, which should be conducted as soon as possible and in a manner in keeping with his age. The information obtained should be effectively documented. In requesting, receiving, forwarding and storing information obtained, particular care and confidentiality should be exercised, in particular in the case of asylum seekers in order to protect both the minor and the members of his family. This early information may in particular enhance the prospects of reunification of the minor with his family in the country of origin or a third country.
2. Irrespective of their legal status, unaccompanied minors should be entitled to the necessary protection and basic care in accordance with the provisions of national law.
3. Member States should, with a view to reunification, endeavour to trace the members of the family of an unaccompanied minor as soon as possible, or to identify the place of residence of the members of the family, regardless of their legal status and without prejudging the merits of any application for residence.
Unaccompanied minors may also be encouraged and assisted in contacting the International Committee of the Red Cross, national Red Cross organizations, or other organizations for the purpose of tracing their family members. Particularly, in the case of asylum seekers, whenever contracts are made in the context of tracing family members, confidentiality should be duly respected in order to protect both the minor and the members of his family.
4. For the purposes of applying this Resolution, Member States should provide as soon as possible for the necessary representation of the minor by:
(a) legal guardianship, or

(b) representation by a (national) organization which is responsible for the care and well-being of the minor, or
(c) other appropriate representation.
5. Where a guardian is appointed for an unaccompanied minor, the guardian should ensure, in accordance with national law, that the minor's needs (for example, legal, social, medical or psychological) are duly met.
6. When it can be assumed that an unaccompanied minor of school age will be staying in a Member State for a prolonged period, the minor should have access to general education facilities on the same basis as nationals of the host Member State or alternatively, appropriate special facilities should be offered to him.
7. Unaccompanied minors should receive appropriate medical treatment to meet immediate needs. Special medical or other assistance should be provided for minors who have suffered any form of neglect, exploitation, or abuse, torture or any other form of cruel, inhuman or degrading treatment or punishment, or armed conflicts.

Article 4 Asylum procedure
1. Every unaccompanied minor should have the right to apply for asylum. However, Member States may reserve the right to require that a minor under a certain age, to be determined by the Member State concerned, cannot apply for asylum until he has the assistance of a legal guardian, a specifically appointed adult representative or institution.
2. Having regard to the particular needs of minors and their vulnerable situation, Member States should treat the processing of asylum applications by unaccompanied minors as a matter of urgency.
3. (a) In principle, an unaccompanied asylum-seeker claiming to be a minor must produce evidence of his age.
(b) If such evidence is not available or serious doubt persists, Member States may carry out an assessment of the age of an asylum-seeker. Age assessment should be carried out objectively. For such purposes, Member States may have a medical age-test carried out by qualified medical personnel, with the consent of the minor, a specially appointed adult representative or institution.
4. Member States should normally place unaccompanied minors during the asylum procedure:
(a) with adult relatives,
(b) with a foster-family,
(c) in reception centres with special provisions for minors, or
(d) in other accommodation with suitable provisions for minors, for example such as to enable them to live independently but with appropriate support.
Member States may place unaccompanied minors aged 16 or above in reception centres for adult asylum seekers.
5. (a) During any interview on their asylum application, unaccompanied minor asylum-seekers may be accompanied by a legal guardian, specially appointed adult representative or institution, adult relative or legal assistant.
(b) The interview should be conducted by officers who have the necessary experience or training. The importance of appropriate training for officers interviewing unaccompanied minor asylum-seekers should be duly recognized.
6. When an application for asylum from an unaccompanied minor is examined, allowance should be made, in addition to objective facts and circumstances, for a minor's age,

maturity and mental development, and for the fact that he may have limited knowledge of conditions in the country of origin.

7. As soon as an unaccompanied minor is granted refugee status or any other permanent right of residence, he should be provided with long-term arrangements for accommodation.

Article 5 Return of unaccompanied minors

1. Where a minor is not allowed to prolong his stay in a Member State, the Member State concerned may only return the minor to his country of origin or a third country prepared to accept him, if on arrival therein – depending on his needs in the light of age and degree of independence – adequate reception and care are available. This can be provided by parents or other adults who take care of the child, or by governmental or non-governmental bodies.

2. As long as return under these conditions is not possible, Member States should in principle make it possible for the minor to remain in their territory.

3. The competent authorities of the Member States should, with a view to a minor's return, cooperate:

(a) in re-uniting unaccompanied minors with other members of their family, either in the minor's country of origin or in the country where those family members are staying;

(b) with the authorities of the minor's country of origin or with those of another country, with a view to finding an appropriate durable solution;

(c) with international organizations such as UNHCR or UNICEF, which already take an active part in advising governments on guidelines for dealing with unaccompanied minors, in particular asylum-seekers;

(d) where appropriate, with non-governmental organizations in order to ascertain the availability of reception and care facilities in the country to which the minor will be returned.

4. In any case, a minor may not be returned to a third country where this return would be contrary to the Convention relating to the status of refugees, the European Convention on Human Rights and Fundamental Freedoms or the Convention against Torture and other Cruel, Inhuman or Degrading treatment or Punishment or the Convention on the Rights of the Child, without prejudice to any reservations which Member States may have tabled when ratifying it, or the Protocols to these Conventions.

Article 6 Final provisions

1. Member States should take account of these guidelines in the case of all proposals for changes to their national legislations. In addition, Member States should strive to bring their national legislations into line with these guidelines before 1 January 1999.

2. Member States shall remain free to allow for more favourable conditions for unaccompanied minors.

3. The Council, in conjunction with the Commission and in consultation with UNHCR in the framework of its competences, shall review the application of the above guidelines once a year, commencing on 1 January 1999, and if appropriate adapt them to developments in asylum and migration policy.

ANNEX

MEASURES TO COMBAT TRAFFICKING IN MINORS
Member States, mindful of the particular vulnerability of minors, should take all measures to prevent and combat the trafficking and exploitation of minors, and cooperate in this regard.

MEASURES TO PREVENT ILLEGAL ENTRY
Measures which Member States may take to prevent the unauthorized arrival in the territory of the Member States of unaccompanied minors who are nationals of third countries may include:
(i) collaboration with competent authorities and bodies including airline companies in the countries of departure, in particular through the use of liaison officers;
(ii) observation at airports of arrival of flights from sensitive countries;
(iii) consequent application of international obligations including carriers' liability legislation where unaccompanied minors who are nationals of third countries arrive without the appropriate documentation.

3.4

Council Resolution of 1 June 1993 on the Harmonization of national Policies on Family Reunification.[9]

Ministers (...) responsible for Immigration adopted the following Resolution (...)
The question of family reunification is already to some extent governed by international Conventions (...)
On the other hand, there is also a need to control migration flows into the territories of the Member States [MS]. This is considered to be one of the factors for the successful integration of immigrants who are lawfully resident within the territories of [MS].
With these considerations in mind, [the] Ministers resolved that the national policies (...) should be governed by the principles set out below. (...) The principles are not legally binding on the [MS] and do not afford a ground of action by individuals.

---

[9] Copenhagen, 1 June 1993, SN 2828/1/93 WGI 1497. Rec 1.
December 1999, a draft Directive cum Explanatory Memorandum was presented with the purpose to establish a right to family reunification for the benefit of third-country nationals residing lawfully in the territory of the Member States and Union citizens who do not exercise their right to free movement; this right is to be exercised in a manner prescribed by that Directive. The Directive focuses also on refugees, (pursuant to the 1951 Convention) irrespective of the duration of the residence permit, and persons enjoying subsidiary protection (provided for by international law, national legislation or the practice of MS). Asylum-seekers ('applicants') have been expressly excluded from this right during the whole procedure. In general, MS *shall* authorize the entry and residence of an explicitly defined group of family members, under explicit, practical conditions (accommodation, stable and sufficient resources, sickness insurance, etc). MS applicants for FR must have resided lawfully in their territory for a period not exceeding one year, prior to having family members joining the applicant, but this condition shall not apply if the applicant is a refugee or a person enjoying subsidiary protection. In the case of a refugee being an unaccompanied minor, MS *may* be more flexible. See for comments: *Migration News Sheet*, Brussels, November and December 1999.

The harmonization efforts are confined at this stage (...) to persons who are not nationals of a [MS] but who are lawfully resident (...) on a basis which affords them an expectation of permanent or long-term residence. (...)
This Resolution does [not] cover family reunification in respect of persons who have been granted refugee status, for whom some [MS] have more favourable policies.
The harmonization of policy in respect of the families of persons in [this category] will be further examined in the course of considering admission policies in respect of them.

Principles Governing Member States' Policies on Family Reunification

(1. Non-Community nationals to whom the Principles relate)

2. The [MS] will normally grant admission, under the conditions set out in the remainder of this Resolution, to
– the resident's spouse (that is, a person bound to him or her in a marriage recognized by the host [MS])
– the children, other than adopted children, of the resident and his or her spouse,
– children adopted by both the resident and his or her spouse while they were resident together in a third country, in accordance with a decision taken by the competent administrative authority or court of that state and which is recognized and accepted by the Member State of residence, and where the adopted children have the same rights and obligations as the other children and there has been a definitive break with the family of origin.
The spouse and the children may be admitted only for the purpose of living together with the resident.

3. [MS] reserve the right to require non-EC nationals to be lawfully present in their territory for certain periods of time before family members may be reunited with them under the terms of these principles.

4. [MS] reserve the right to determine whether a marriage was contracted solely or principally for the purpose of enabling the spouse to enter and take up residence in a [MS], and to refuse permission to enter and stay accordingly.

5. A wife and her children will not be admitted for the purpose of family reunification if the marriage is polygamous and the resident already has a wife resident in the territory of a [MS].

6. [MS] reserve the option of admitting a child (including an adopted child) where the child is the offspring of the resident or of his/her spouse, but not of the couple involved (... parental authority ... custody ... effectively in their charge).

7. [MS] reserve the possibility of admitting a child adopted by both the resident and his or her spouse while one or both were resident in a [MS] (...)

8. In order to qualify for admission for the purpose of family reunification children must be below a maximum age, which the [MS] agree should be between 16 and 18 years, and must not have married or have formed an independent family unit or be leading an inde-

pendent life.

9. [MS] will consider whether and adoption has been arranged solely or principally for the purpose of enabling the child to enter and take up residence in a [MS], and whether to refuse permission to enter and stay accordingly.

10. [MS] reserve the possibility of permitting the entry and stay of family members, other than those envisaged in paragraphs 2, 6 and 7 of this Resolution, for compelling reasons which justify the presence of the person concerned.

11. An authorization to stay on the basis of family reunification may, for such a period as the [MS] concerned determines, be conditional upon the continued fulfilment of the criteria for admission.

12. Within a reasonable period of time following their admission, family members, in accordance with the national legislation in each [MS], may be authorized to stay on a personal basis independently from the person whom they joined on the basis of family reunification, and, if appropriate, be authorized to work.

13. The authorization to stay granted to a family member may be terminated at any time if there are grounds for presuming that it was obtained by means of fraud or forgery.

14. A person will normally not be admitted to the territory of a [MS] for the purpose of family reunification without a visa or other prior written authorization for that purpose, issued by the [MS] in which the family intends to reside. The application must normally be made whilst the family member concerned is outside the territory of the [MS] concerned. A visa or prior written authorization will not be issued unless the applicant meets all the criteria for entry and stay in the territory of the [MS] concerned as set out in these principles.

15. Family members must also, in principle, be in possession of valid travel documents which are recognized by the [MS] in which the family intends to reside.

16. [MS] reserve the right to make the entry and stay of family members conditional upon the availability of adequate accommodation and of sufficient resources to avoid a burden being placed on the public funds of the [MS] concerned, and on the existence of sickness insurance.

17. [MS] will normally refuse entry and stay to a family member if his presence would constitute a threat to national security or public policy ('ordre publique'). They reserve the right to refuse entry and stay on grounds of public health.

2.5

Council Resolution of 25 September 1995 on burden-sharing with regard to the admission and residence of displaced persons on a temporary basis (95/C 262/01)[10]

THE COUNCIL OF THE EUROPEAN UNION,
Having regard to the Treaty on European Union, and in particular Article K.1. thereof,
Having regard to the priority work programme adopted by the Council on 30 November 1993, which makes provision for a detailed examination of the question of burden-sharing with respect to the admission and residence of refugees in western Europe,
Having regard to the resolution on people displaced by the conflict in the former Yugoslavia, adopted by the ministers with responsibility for immigration at their meeting in London on 30 November and 1 December 1992,
Having regard to the resolution on certain common guidelines as regards the admission of particularly vulnerable groups of distressed persons from the former Yugoslavia, adopted by the ministers with responsibility for immigration at their meeting in Copenhagen on 1 and 2 June 1993,
Having regard to the resolution adopted by the European Parliament on 19 January 1994 on the general principles of a European refugee policy, which emphasized the need for refugees to be distributed evenly among the various countries of the Union,
Having regard to the communication on immigration and asylum policies submitted by the Commission on 23 February 1994,
Whereas the European Council meeting in Essen on 9 and 10 December 1994 paid tribute to the readiness shown by individual Member States to admit temporarily a large number of refugees of war or civil war and called upon the Council (Justice and Home Affairs) to study the problems caused by an influx of refugees with a view to finding as soon as possible an effective arrangement for future sharing of the burden of humanitarian assistance;
Whereas the top priority in conflict situations where people are being displaced is for measures to restore peace; whereas aid to the civilian population caught up in these situations should mainly be provided on the spot, in particular by creating safe areas and security corridors and by providing humanitarian aid;
Whereas, however, the Council agrees that the Member States should, where possible, continue to give temporary refuge to people whose lives or health are under threat as a result of armed conflict or civil war in future, if there is no other way of averting danger, bearing in mind the United Nations High Commissioner for Refugees principle of regionalization;
Whereas, when such a situation arises, it is desirable that the conditions for admission and residence of such persons should be arranged in a concerted fashion and in a spirit of solidarity between the Member States;

---

[10] Official Journal C 262, 07/10/1995 p. 0001–0003 [EUDOR] 395Y1007(01).
Ed.: Regard should also be had to a Resolution agreed upon by the Ministers Responsible for Immigration at their Copenhagen meeting of 1 and 2 June 1995. The Resolution is officially not part of the acquis, but is nevertheless of relevance: Resolution on Certain Common Guidelines as Regards the Admission of Particularly Vulnerable Groups of Persons from the Former Yugoslavia. The Resolution covers above all persons who had been held in a PoW camp, victims of rape, the injured and seriously ill and for whom medical treatment cannot be obtained locally, and those who have come directly from combat zones and who cannot return to their homes because of the conflict and human rights abuses.

Whereas, in this regard, the Member States express their desire to share responsibility as best they can regarding the admission and residence of displaced persons on a temporary basis;

Whereas the Member States are wedded to the principle that the reaction to emergencies in countries close to the European Union should, where circumstances so permit, be as far as possible the same;

Whereas the effect which differences between Member States' arrangements for displaced persons have on the destination of migratory flows should be kept to a minimum;

Whereas it is also necessary to agree on a sufficiently precise framework which would regulate operational initiatives but be flexible enough to authorize the admission – if necessary outside the normal procedures for applying for refugee status – of persons forced to leave their countries;

Whereas Member States must ensure that the use in such cases of the emergency procedure provided for in the Council's rules of procedure[11] makes it possible to arrive rapidly at a balanced sharing of the burden in a spirit of solidarity;

Whereas Member States could also envisage the possible implementation of forms of financial compensation;

Whereas, in the case of persons who have applied to a Member State for protection under the Geneva Convention on the Status of Refugees of 28 July 1951, this resolution must not stand in the way of the rules laid down by the Dublin Convention of 15 June 1990;

Whereas, moreover, situations of great urgency, particularly as a result of armed conflict or civil war in third countries, which confront Member States with sudden major population movements, require prompt action and the development beforehand of principles governing the admission of displaced persons; whereas it is therefore necessary to enable the Council to adopt decisions which need to be taken urgently in certain situations requiring prompt action without their being delayed in complicated procedures which have to be initiated beforehand,

HEREBY ADOPTS THIS RESOLUTION:

1. (a) Without prejudice to paragraph 7, this resolution applies to persons whom Member States are prepared to admit on a temporary basis under appropriate conditions in the event of armed conflict or civil war, including where such persons have already left their region of origin to go to one of the Member States. The persons concerned are in particular:

– those who have been held in a prisoner-of-war or internment camp and who cannot otherwise be saved from a threat to life or limb,

– those who are injured or seriously ill and for whom medical treatment cannot be obtained locally,

– those who are, or have been, under a direct threat to life or limb and whose protection in their region of origin cannot otherwise be secured,

– those who have been subjected to sexual assault provided that there is no suitable means for assisting them in safe areas situated as close as possible to their homes,

---

[11] OJ No L 304, 10.12.1993, p. 1.

– those who, having come directly from combat zones, are within the borders of their countries and cannot return to their homes because of the conflict and human rights abuses.

(b) This resolution does not apply to any person with respect to whom there are serious reasons for considering that he has:
– committed a crime against peace, a war crime or a crime against humanity, as defined in the international instruments drawn up to make provision in respect of such crimes,
– committed a serious non-political crime prior to being admitted by one of the Member States on a temporary basis.

2. A given situation may require harmonized action to help displaced persons when, for instance, there is a mass influx of displaced persons into the territory of the Member States or a strong probability that the Member States may soon have to cope with such an influx. An action of this kind will be envisaged in particular, after obtaining the opinion of the United Nations High Commissioner for Refugees, if help and adequate protection are not available in the region of origin or if the European Union is so close to the region concerned that it could itself be considered as belonging to the region of origin.

3. Some situations may require prompt action to avert a serious threat to human life. In such situations the relevant provisions laid down by the Council's Rules of Procedure for urgent cases will apply.[12]

4. The Council agrees that the burden in connection with the admission and residence of displaced persons on a temporary basis in a crisis could be shared on a balanced basis in a spirit of solidarity, taking into account the following criteria:[13]
– the contribution which each Member State is making to prevention or resolution of the crisis, in particular by the supply of military resources in operations and missions ordered by the United Nations Security Council or the Organization for Security and Cooperation in Europe and by the measures taken by each Member State to afford local protection to people under threat or to provide humanitarian assistance,
– all economic, social and political factors which may affect the capacity of a Member State to admit an increased number of displaced persons under satisfactory conditions.

5. It is understood that the allocation of persons from the crisis regions is a matter of priority which will enable fairness to be best achieved in the interests of the persons concerned.

6. This resolution does not affect practices relating to admission on humanitarian grounds followed by individual Member States or by all Member States under bilateral or multilateral agreements.

7. The abovementioned procedure does not apply to displaced persons who were admitted to the various Member States before adoption of this resolution.

---

[12] Articles 1(1), 8(1), 10(1) and 19(1) of the Rules of Procedure.

[13] These criteria are norms of reference that may be supplemented by further criteria in the light of specific situations.

3.6

Council Decision of 4 March 1996 on an alert and emergency procedure for burden-sharing with regard to the admission and residence of displaced persons on a temporary basis (96/198/JHA)[14]

THE COUNCIL OF THE EUROPEAN UNION,

Having regard to the Treaty on European Union, and in particular Article K.3(2)(a) thereof,

Having regard to the Council resolution of 25 September 1995 on burden-sharing with regard to the admission and residence of displaced persons on a temporary basis,[15]

Whereas the aforementioned resolution must be supplemented if the principles set out therein are to be applied effectively when crisis situations arise requiring swift action;

Whereas it is necessary to this end to introduce an alert and emergency procedure,

HAS DECIDED AS FOLLOWS:

1. Initiation of the procedure

On the initiative of the Presidency, a Member State or the Commission, an urgent meeting of the Coordinating Committee referred to in Article K.4 may be convened, the members of which shall be advised by those responsible in the Member States for asylum and immigration affairs, to note whether a situation exists which requires concerted action by the European Union for the admission and residence of displaced persons on a temporary basis. When an action of this type is envisaged, the conditions laid down in paragraphs 1 and 2 of the Council resolution of 25 September 1995 must be fulfilled. Periodically and in any event prior to the meeting, the Presidency shall, in collaboration with the Commission, in the light of the opinion of the United Nations High Commissioner for Refugees and with the assistance of the General Secretariat of the Council, prepare a report on the situation. That report shall be forwarded to the Member States.

2. Agenda for the meeting

The agenda for the meeting may in particular cover the following:

– a study of the situation and an assessment of the extent of population movement,

– an appraisal of the expediency of urgent intervention at European Union level,

– a study of other possibilities, including any local action,

– the drawing up of a timetable and a progressive plan for anticipated admission requirements,

– an indication by each Member State of the number of persons who will be admitted and when they will be admitted, pursuant to paragraph 4 of the Council resolution of 25 September 1995,

– coordination with the Commission's actions in the area of humanitarian aid,

– exchange of information with the United Nations High Commissioner for Refugees and coordination of the admission plan,

– coordination with third countries.

---

[14] [T.14] Official Journal L 063, 13/03/1996 p. 0010–0011 [EUDOR] 396D0198.
[15] OJ No C 262, 7.10.1995, p. 1.

3. Decision on burden-sharing

In the light of the outcome of the proceedings of the meeting of the abovementioned Co-ordinating Committee, a proposal shall be prepared for submission to the Council for approval. If it is judged necessary, in accordance with paragraph 3 of the Council resolution of 25 September 1995 and if a month has elapsed without agreement being reached within the Coordinating Committee, the provisions laid down by the Council's Rules of Procedure for urgent cases may be applied.

4. Monitoring of the situation

The detailed arrangements for admitting displaced persons shall be decided on by each Member State. While the crisis lasts, the abovementioned Coordinating Committee may hold frequent meetings at intervals to be decided on by the Committee itself and on the basis of paragraph 2 of this Decision.

3.7

Council Recommendation of 22 December 1995 on harmonizing means of combating illegal immigration and illegal employment and improving the relevant means of control (96/C 5/01)[16]

THE COUNCIL OF THE EUROPEAN UNION,
Having regard to the Treaty on European Union, and in particular K.3(2) thereof,
Having regard to the initiative submitted by the French Republic on 22 December 1994,
Having regard to the recommendation of the Ministers of the Member States of the European Communities with responsibility for immigration of 1 June 1993 concerning checks on, and expulsion of, third-country nationals residing or working without authorization,
Having regard to the recommendation of the Ministers of the Member States of the European Communities with responsibility for immigration of 30 November 1992 regarding practices followed by Member States on expulsion,
Whereas, pursuant to Article K.1(2) and (3) of the EC Treaty, policy regarding nationals of third countries and in particular combating unauthorized immigration, residence and work are matters of common interest and therefore fall within the areas for cooperation between Member States referred to in Title VI of the Treaty;
Whereas the Member States, faced with an increase in illegal immigration, have already adopted specific measures to ensure better control of population flows and to avoid the continued unlawful presence in their territories of foreign nationals who have entered or are residing without authorization;
Whereas, however, the efficiency of that action implies the implementation of coordinated and consistent measures;
Whereas, although recommendations laying down guiding principles for practice with regard to expulsion have already been adopted, that effort at alignment needs to be reinforced by recommending Member States to comply with a number of principles designed

---

[16] Official Journal C 005, 10/01/1996 p. 0001–0003 [EUDOR] 396Y0110(01).

to ensure a better check on the situation of foreign nationals present within their territories;

Whereas this recommendation is in keeping with Community legislation, the Convention for the Protection of Human Rights and Fundamental Freedoms of 4 November 1950, and in particular Articles 3 and 14 thereof, and the Geneva Convention of 28 July 1951 relating to the Status of Refugees, as amended by the New York Protocol of 31 January 1967,

HEREBY RECOMMENDS Member States to harmonize further the means for checking on foreign nationals to verify that they fulfil the conditions laid down by the rules applicable to entry, residence and employment on the basis of the following guidelines:

1. This recommendation does not extend to citizens of the European Union or to nationals of EFTA member countries party to the Agreement on the European Economic Area, or to members of their families entitled under Community law.

2. Where an identity check is carried out on a foreigner in accordance with national law, at least where a person appears to be residing in the country unlawfully, his residence situation should be verified. This may apply in particular in the following cases:
– identity checks in connection with the investigation or prosecution of offences,
– identity checks to ward off threats to public order or security,
– identity checks in order to combat illegal entry or residence in certain areas (e.g. frontier areas and ports, airports and railways stations handling international traffic), without prejudice to border controls.

3. Third-country nationals should be in a position, according to national law, to present to the competent authorities confirmation, for example by way of papers or documents by virtue of which they are so authorized, of their authority to reside within the territory of the Member State where they are.

4. Where national law regards the residence or employment situation as a prerequisite for foreign nationals to qualify for benefits provided by a public service of a Member State in particular in the area of health, retirement, family or work, that condition cannot be met until it has been verified that the residence and employment situation of the person concerned and his or her family does not disqualify them from the benefit.

Verification of residence or employment status is not required where intervention by a public authority is necessary on overriding humanitarian grounds.

Such verifications are carried out by the services providing the benefits, with the assistance, if necessary, of the authorities responsible in particular for issuing residence or work permits, in accordance with national law relating, in particular, to data protection.

Member States should inform the central or local authorities responsible for dispensing benefits to foreign nationals of the importance of combating illegal immigration in order to encourage them to report to the competent authorities, in accordance with national law, such cases of breaches of the residence rules as they may detect in the course of their work.

The attention of the authorities responsible for issuing residence permits should also be drawn to the risk of marriages of convenience.

5. Employers wishing to recruit foreign nationals should be encouraged to verify that their residence or employment situations are in order by requiring them to present the document(s) by virtue of which they are authorized to reside and work in the Member State concerned. Member States could stipulate that employers may, if necessary, under

the conditions laid down by national law relating, in particular, to data protection, check with the authorities responsible in particular for issuing residence and work permits; the said authorities may communicate the relevant information under procedures which guarantee confidentiality in the transmission of individual data.

6. Any person who is considered, under the national law of the Member State concerned, to be employing a foreign national who does not have authorization should be made subject to appropriate penalties.

7. The authorities competent to authorize residence should be empowered to take measures to check that persons who have been refused authorization to reside within the territory of the Member State have left that territory of their own accord.

8. Each Member State should consider setting up a central file of foreign nationals containing information on the administrative situation of foreign nationals with regard to residence, including any refusal of authorization to reside and any expulsion measures. Any file thus set up will operate in compliance with the standards laid down in Council of Europe Convention 108 of 28 January 1981 for the Protection of Individuals with regard to Automatic Processing of Personal Data.

9. Member States should satisfy themselves that residence documents issued to foreign nationals are adequately secured against forgery and fraudulent use – particularly by colour photocopying – and, should, if necessary, amend them accordingly.

10. Member States should take the measures necessary to reinforce and improve means of identifying foreign nationals who are not in a lawful position and who have no travel documents or other documents by which they can be identified. Where a foreign national who is not in a lawful position is, or is likely to be, detained under the circumstances provided for in Chapter II of the recommendation of 30 November 1992 of the Ministers of the Member States of the European Communities with responsibility for immigration regarding practices followed by Member States on expulsion, the period of detention should be used in particular to obtain the necessary travel documents for expelling foreign nationals who have no documents. The consular authorities of the country of origin or the country of the nationality of the foreign national concerned should be encouraged to make additional identification efforts to obtain travel documents. Foreign nationals who have deliberately brought about their illegal position, particularly by refusing to supply travel documents, should be subject to penalties. In appropriate cases, such penalties may fall under criminal law. Member States will review the follow-up to Chapter III.2 of the recommendation of 30 November 1992 of the Ministers of the Member States of the European Communities with responsibility for immigration regarding practices followed by Member States on expulsion.

The Council will review regularly, for example once a year, the progress made on harmonization in the fields covered by this recommendation.

3.8

Council Decision of 22 December 1995 on monitoring the implementation of instruments already adopted concerning admission of third-country nationals (96/C 11/01; T.28)[17]

THE COUNCIL OF THE EUROPEAN UNION,
Having regard to Article K.3(2)(a) of the Treaty on European Union,
Having regard to the priority work programme adopted by the Council on 30 November 1993 in Brussels, calling in particular for the preparation of an annual report on achievements in the field of justice and home affairs,
Whereas Article K.1(3)(a) of the Treaty on European Union states that Member States shall regard conditions of entry by nationals of third countries on the territory of Member States as a matter of common interest;
Whereas the instruments adopted by the Council concerning the admission of third-country nationals express a common political will;
Whereas monitoring of the implementation of the provisions contained in these instruments will reveal the practical effect of the Council's work in this matter and provide useful lessons for its future work;
Whereas Member States consequently intend to agree on practical arrangements for such monitoring,

HAS DECIDED AS FOLLOWS:

Article 1
Preparation of a questionnaire
Each year, the Presidency shall forward to the Member States a questionnaire designed to show how they have implemented the resolutions and acts already adopted by the Council concerning the admission of third-country nationals.

Article 2
Content of the questionnaire
The questionnaire shall refer to the following:
– provisions adopted during the preceding year by the Member States in any of the areas referred to by the instruments already adopted,
– difficulties in adopting those provisions,
– the possibility of any provision on those areas being adopted in the near future,
– application in practice of the instruments, irrespective of the adoption of internal provisions where appropriate.

Article 3
Evaluation of the replies
A report on the application of the instruments referred to in Article 1 shall be drawn up on the basis of the replies from the Member States and shall be submitted to the Council.

---

[17] Ed.: T.28: Official Journal C 011, 16/01/1996 p. 0001–0001; see also T.15 on monitoring the implementation of instruments adopted concerning asylum.

Article 4
Implementation
The first questionnaire shall be sent to the Member States in the first half of 1996.

3.9

Council Decision of 16 December 1996 on monitoring the implementation of instruments adopted by the Council concerning illegal immigration, readmission, the unlawful employment of third country nationals and cooperation in the implementation of expulsion orders (96/749/JHA)[18]

THE COUNCIL OF THE EUROPEAN UNION,
Having regard to the Treaty on European Union and in particular Article K.3(2)(a) thereof,
Having regard to the priority work programme adopted by the Council on 30 November 1993 in Brussels, calling in particular for the preparation of an annual report on achievements in the field of justice and home affairs and to the Council resolution on 14 October 1996, laying down the priorities for cooperation in the field of justice and home affairs for the period from 1 July 1996 to 30 June 1998.
Whereas Article K.1(3)(c) of the Treaty states that Member States shall regard the combating of unauthorized immigration, residence and work by nationals of third countries on the territory of Member States as a matter of common interest;
Whereas monitoring the implementation by Member States of the instruments adopted by the Council in this area will reveal the practical effect of the Council's work in this matter and provide useful lessons for its future work,

HAS DECIDED AS FOLLOWS:

Article 1
Preparation of a questionnaire
Each year, the Presidency shall forward to the Member States a questionnaire designed to show how they have implemented the instruments adopted by the Council concerning illegal immigration, readmission, the unlawful employment of third country nationals and cooperation in the implementation of expulsion orders.

Article 2
Content of the questionnaire
The questionnaire shall refer to the following matters:
– provisions adopted during the preceding year by the Member States in any of the areas covered by the instruments referred to in Article 1,
– any difficulties encountered in adopting such provisions,
– the likelihood of provisions in the areas referred to in the first indent being adopted in the near future,
– practical application of the aforementioned instruments and provisions.

---

[18] Official Journal L 342, 31/12/1996 p. 0005–0005 [EUDOR] 396D0749.

Article 3
Evaluation of the replies
A report shall be drawn up by the General Secretariat of the Council on the basis of the replies received from the Member States and shall be submitted to the Council.

Article 4
Implementation for the first time
The first questionnaire shall be sent to the Member States no later than 30 June 1997 and shall cover the period since the entry into force of the Treaty on European Union.

3.10

Joint Position of 4 March 1996 defined by the Council on the basis of Article K.3 of the Treaty on European Union on the harmonized application of the definition of the term 'refugee' in Article 1 of the Geneva Convention of 28 July 1951 relating to the status of refugees (96/196/JHA)[19]

THE COUNCIL OF THE EUROPEAN UNION,
Having regard to the Treaty on European Union, and in particular Article K.3(2)(a) thereof,
Whereas under Article K.1 of the Treaty, asylum policy is regarded as a matter of common interest;
Whereas the European Council, meeting in Strasbourg on 8 and 9 December 1990, set the objective of harmonizing Member States' asylum policies, which was further developed by the European Council in Maastricht on 9 and 10 December 1991 and in Brussels on 10 and 11 December 1993, and in the Commission communication on immigration and asylum policies of 23 February 1994;
Emphasizing, in keeping with the Member States' common humanitarian tradition, the importance of guaranteeing appropriate protection for refugees in accordance with the provisions of the Geneva Convention of 28 July 1951 relating to the Status of Refugees, as amended by the New York Protocol of 31 January 1967, hereafter referred to as the 'Geneva Convention';
Having established that the Handbook of the United Nations High Commissioner for Refugees (UNHCR) is a valuable aid to Member States in determining refugee status;
Whereas harmonized application of the criteria for determining refugee status is essential for the harmonization of asylum policies in the Member States,

HAS ADOPTED THIS JOINT POSITION:
− The guidelines set out below for the application of criteria for recognition and admission as a refugee are hereby approved.
− These guidelines shall be notified to the administrative bodies responsible for recognition of refugee status, which are hereby requested to take them as a basis, without prejudice to Member States' caselaw on asylum matters and their relevant constitutional positions.

[9] Official Journal L 063, 13/03/1996 p. 0002–0007 [EUDOR] 496X0196.

– This joint position is adopted within the limits of the constitutional powers of the Governments of the Member States; it shall not bind the legislative authorities or affect decisions of the judicial authorities of the Member States.
– The Council shall review the application of these guidelines once a year and, if appropriate, adapt them to developments in asylum applications.

1. Recognition as a refugee

Determination of the status of refugee is based on criteria according to which the competent national bodies decide to grant an asylum-seeker the protection provided for in the Geneva Convention. This document relates to implementation of the criteria as defined in Article 1 of that Convention.
It in no way affects the conditions under which a Member State may, according to its domestic law, permit a person to remain in its territory if his safety or physical integrity would be endangered if he were to return to his country because of circumstances which are not covered by the Geneva Convention but which constitute a reason for not returning him to his country of origin.

2. Individual or collective determination of refugee status

Each application for asylum is examined on the basis of the facts and circumstances put forward in each individual case and taking account of the objective situation prevailing in the country of origin.
In practice it may be that a whole group of people are exposed to persecution. In such cases, too, applications will be examined individually, although in specific cases this examination may be limited to determining whether the individual belongs to the group in question.

3. Establishment of the evidence required for granting refugee status

The determining factor for granting refugee status in accordance with the Geneva Convention is the existence of a well-founded fear of persecution on grounds of race, religion, nationality, political opinions or membership of a particular social group. The question of whether fear of persecution is well-founded must be appreciated in the light of the circumstances of each case. It is for the asylum-seeker to submit the evidence needed to assess the veracity of the facts and circumstances put forward. It should be understood that once the credibility of the asylum-seeker's statements has been sufficiently established, it will not be necessary to seek detailed confirmation of the facts put forward and the asylum-seeker should, unless there are good reasons to the contrary, be given the benefit of the doubt. The fact that an individual has already been subject to persecution or to direct threats of persecution is a serious indication of the risk of persecution, unless a radical change of conditions has taken place since then in his country of origin or in his relations with his country of origin. The fact that an individual, prior to his departure from his country of origin, was not subject to persecution or directly threatened with persecution does not per se mean that he cannot in asylum proceedings claim a well-founded fear of persecution.

4. 'Persecution' within the meaning of Article 1A of the Geneva Convention

The term 'persecution' as it is used in this document is taken from Article 1A of the Geneva Convention. The term is not defined in the Convention. Nor is a universally accepted definition to be found either in the conclusions of the UNHCR Executive Committee or in legal literature on the subject. The guidelines in this document do not constitute a definition. However, it is generally agreed that, in order to constitute 'persecution' within the meaning of Article 1A, acts suffered or feared must:

– be sufficiently serious, by their nature or their repetition: they must either constitute a basic attack on human rights, for example, life, freedom or physical integrity, or, in the light of all the facts of the case, manifestly preclude the person who has suffered them from continuing to live in his country of origin (1), and

– be based on one of the grounds mentioned in Article 1A: race, religion, nationality, membership of a particular social group or political opinions.

Grounds of persecution may overlap and several will often be applicable to the same person. The fact that these grounds are genuine or simply attributed to the person concerned by the persecutor is immaterial.

Several types of persecution may occur together and the combination of events each of which, taken separately, does not constitute persecution may, depending on the circumstances, amount to actual persecution or be regarded as a serious ground for fear of persecution.

In the following guiding principles, the term 'persecution' is to be understood with reference to this section.

5. Origins of persecution

5.1. Persecution by the State

Persecution is generally the act of a State organ (central State or federal States, regional and local authorities) whatever its status in international law, or of parties or organizations controlling the State.

In addition to cases in which persecution takes the form of the use of brute force, it may also take the form of administrative and/or judicial measures which either have the appearance of legality and are misused for the purposes of persecution, or are carried out in breach of the law.

5.1.1. Legal, administrative and police measures

(a) General measures

The official authorities of a country are sometimes moved to take general measures to maintain public order, safeguard State security, preserve public health, etc. As required, such measures may include restrictions on the exercise of certain freedoms. They may also be accompanied by the use of force, but such restrictions or use of force do not in themselves constitute sufficient grounds for granting refugee status to the individuals against whom the measures are directed. However, if it emerges that such measures are being implemented in a discriminatory manner on one or more of the grounds mentioned in Article 1A of the Geneva Convention and may have sufficiently serious consequences, they may give rise to a well-founded fear of persecution on the part of individuals who are victims of their improper application. Such is the case, in particular, where general measures are used to camouflage individual measures taken against persons who, for the reasons mentioned in Article 1A, are likely to be threatened by their authorities.

(b) Measures directed against certain categories

Measures directed against one or more specific categories of the population may be legitimate in a society, even when they impose particular constraints or restrictions on certain freedoms. However, they may be considered as justifying fears of persecution, in particular where the aim which they pursue has been condemned by the international community, or where they are manifestly disproportionate to the end sought, or where their implementation leads to serious abuses aimed at treating a certain group differently and less favourably than the population as a whole.

(c) Individual measures

Any administrative measure taken against an individual, leaving aside any consideration of general interest referred to above, on one of the grounds mentioned in Article 1A, which is sufficiently severe in the light of the criteria referred to in section 4 of this Joint Position, may be regarded as persecution, in particular where it is intentional, systematic and lasting. It is important, therefore, to take account of all the circumstances surrounding the individual measure reported by the asylum-seeker, in order to assess whether his fears of persecution are well-founded. In all the cases referred to above, consideration must be given to whether there is an effective remedy or remedies which would put an end to the situation of abuse. As a general rule, persecution will be indicated by the fact that no redress exists or, if there are means of redress, that the individual or individuals concerned are deprived of the opportunity of having access to them or by the fact that the decisions of the competent authority are not impartial (see 5.1.2) or have no effect.

5.1.2. Prosecution

Whilst appearing to be lawful, prosecution or court sentences may amount to persecution where they include a discriminatory element and where they are sufficiently severe in the light of the criteria referred to in section 4 of this Joint Position. This is particularly true in the event of:

(a) Discriminatory prosecution.

This concerns a situation in which the criminal law provision is applicable to all but where only certain persons are prosecuted on grounds of characteristics likely to lead to the award of refugee status. It is therefore the discriminatory element in the implementation of prosecution policy which is essential for recognizing a person as a refugee.

(b) Discriminatory punishment.

Punishment or the threat thereof on the basis of a universally applicable criminal law provision will be discriminatory if persons who breach the law are punished but certain persons are subject to more severe punishment on account of characteristics likely to lead to the award of refugee status. The discriminatory element in the punishment imposed is essential. Persecution may be deemed to exist in the event of a disproportionate sentence, provided that there is a link with one of the grounds of persecution referred to in Article 1A.

(c) Breach of a criminal law provision on account of the grounds of persecution

Intentional breach of a criminal law provision – whether applicable universally or to certain categories of persons – on account of the grounds of persecution must be clearly the result of pronouncements or participation in certain activities in the country of origin or be the objective consequence of characteristics of the asylum-seeker liable to lead to the grant of refugee status. The deciding factors are the nature of the punishment, the severity of the punishment in relation to the offence committed, the legal system and the human rights situation in the country of origin. Consideration should be given to whether the intentional breach of the criminal law provision can be deemed unavoidable in the light of the individual circumstances of the person involved and the situation in the country of origin.

5.2. Persecution by third parties
Persecution by third parties will be considered to fall within the scope of the Geneva Convention where it is based on one of the grounds in Article 1A of that Convention, is individual in nature and is encouraged or permitted by the authorities. Where the official authorities fail to act, such persecution should give rise to individual examination of each application for refugee status, in accordance with national judicial practice, in the light in particular of whether or not the failure to act was deliberate. The persons concerned may be eligible in any event for appropriate forms of protection under national law.

6. Civil war and other internal or generalized armed conflicts

Reference to a civil war or internal or generalized armed conflict and the dangers which it entails is not in itself sufficient to warrant the grant of refugee status. Fear of persecution must in all cases be based on one of the grounds in Article 1A of the Geneva Convention and be individual in nature. In such situations, persecution may stem either from the legal authorities or third parties encouraged or tolerated by them, or from de facto authorities in control of part of the territory within which the State cannot afford its nationals protection. In principle, use of the armed forces does not constitute persecution where it is in accordance with international rules of war and internationally recognized practice; however, it becomes persecution where, for instance, authority is established over a particular area and its attacks on opponents or on the population fulfil the criteria in section 4. In other cases, other forms of protection may be provided under national legislation.

7. Grounds of persecution

7.1 Race
The concept of race should be understood in the broad sense and include membership of different ethnic groups. As a general rule, persecution should be deemed to be founded on racial grounds where the persecutor regards the victim of his persecution as belonging to a racial group other than his own, by reason of a real or supposed difference, and this forms the grounds for his action.

7.2 Religion
The concept of religion may be understood in the broad sense and include theistic, non-theistic and atheistic beliefs. Persecution on religious grounds may take various forms, such as a total ban on worship and religious instruction, or severe discriminatory measures against persons belonging to a particular religious group. For persecution to occur, the interference and impairment suffered must be sufficiently severe in the light of the criteria referred to in section 4 of this Joint Position. This may apply where, over and above measures essential to maintain public order, the State also prohibits or penalizes religious activity even in private life. Persecution on religious grounds may also occur where such

interference targets a person who does not wish to profess any religion, refuses to take up a particular religion or does not wish to comply with all or part of the rites and customs relating to a religion.

7.3. Nationality
This should not be confined exclusively to the idea of citizenship but should also include membership of a group determined by its cultural or linguistic identity or its relationship with the population of another State.

7.4. Political opinions
Holding political opinions different from those of the government is not in itself a sufficient ground for securing refugee status; the applicant must show that:
– the authorities know about his political opinions or attribute them to him,
– those opinions are not tolerated by the authorities,
– given the situation in his country he would be likely to be persecuted for holding such opinions.

7.5. Social group
A specific social group normally comprises persons from the same background, with the same customs or the same social status, etc. Fear of persecution cited under this heading may frequently overlap with fear of persecution on other grounds, for example race, religion or nationality. Membership of a social group may simply be attributed to the victimized person or group by the persecutor. In some cases, the social group may not have existed previously but may be determined by the common characteristics of the victimized persons because the persecutor sees them as an obstacle to achieving his aims.

8. Relocation within the country of origin

Where it appears that persecution is clearly confined to a specific part of a country's territory, it may be necessary, in order to check that the condition laid down in Article 1A of the Geneva Convention has been fulfilled, namely that the person concerned 'is unable or, owing to such fear (of persecution), is unwilling to avail himself of the protection of that country', to ascertain whether the person concerned cannot find effective protection in another part of his own country, to which he may reasonably be expected to move.

9. Refugee sur place

The fear of persecution need not necessarily have existed at the time of an asylum-seeker's departure from his country of origin. An individual who had no reason to fear persecution on leaving his country of origin may subsequently become a refugee sur place. A well-founded fear of persecution may be based on the fact that the situation in his country of origin has changed since his departure, with serious consequences for him, or on his own actions. In any event the asylum-related characteristics of the individual should be such that the authorities in the country of origin know or could come to know of them before the individual's fear of persecution can be justified.

9.1. Fear arising from a new situation in the country of origin after departure
Political changes in the country of origin may justify fear of persecution, but only if the

asylum-seeker can demonstrate that as a result of those changes he would personally have grounds to fear persecution if he returned.

9.2. Fear on account of activities outside the country of origin

Refugee status may be granted if the activities which gave rise to the asylum-seeker's fear of persecution constitute the expression and continuation of convictions which he had held in his country of origin or can objectively be regarded as the consequence of the asylum-related characteristics of the individual. However, such continuity must not be a requirement where the person concerned was not yet able to establish convictions because of age. On the other hand, if it is clear that he expresses his convictions mainly for the purpose of creating the necessary conditions for being admitted as a refugee, his activities cannot in principle furnish grounds for admission as a refugee; this does not prejudice his right not to be returned to a country where his life, physical integrity or freedom would be in danger.

10. Conscientious objection, absence without leave and desertion

The fear of punishment for conscientious objection, absence without leave or desertion is investigated on an individual basis. It should in itself be insufficient to justify recognition of refugee status. The penalty must be assessed in particular in accordance with the principles set out in point 5. In cases of absence without leave or desertion, the person concerned must be accorded refugee status if the conditions under which military duties are performed themselves constitute persecution. Similarly, refugee status may be granted, in the light of all the other requirements of the definition, in cases of punishment of conscientious objection or deliberate absence without leave and desertion on grounds of conscience if the performance of his military duties were to have the effect of leading the person concerned to participate in acts falling under the exclusion clauses in Article 1F of the Geneva Convention.

11. Cessation of refugee status (Article 1C)

Whether or not refugee status may be withdrawn on the basis of Article 1C of the Geneva Convention is always investigated on an individual basis. The Member States should make every effort, by exchanging information, to harmonize their practice with regard to the application of the cessation clauses of Article 1C wherever possible. The circumstances in which the cessation clause in Article 1C may be applied should be of a fundamental nature and should be determined in an objective an verifiable manner. Information provided by the Centre for Information, Discussion and Exchange on Asylum (Cirea) and the UNHCR may be of considerable relevance here.

12. Article 1D of the Geneva Convention

Any person who deliberately removes himself from the protection and assistance referred to in Article 1D of the Geneva Convention is no longer automatically covered by that Convention. In such cases, refugee status is in principle to be determined in accordance with Article 1A.

13. Article 1F of the Geneva Convention

The clauses in Article 1F of the Geneva Convention are designed to exclude from protection under that Convention persons who cannot enjoy international protection because of the seriousness of the crimes which they have committed. The may also be applied where the acts become known after the grant of refugee status (see point 11). In view of the serious consequences of such a decision for the asylum-seeker, Article 1F must be used with care and after thorough consideration, and in accordance with the procedures laid down in national law.

13.1. Article 1F(a)
The crimes referred to in Article 1F(a) are those defined in international instruments to which the Member States have acceded, and in resolutions adopted by the United Nations or other international or regional organizations to the extent that they have been accepted by the Member States.

13.2. Article 1F(b)
The severity of the expected persecution is to be weighed against the nature of the criminal offence of which the person concerned is suspected. Particularly cruel actions, even if committed with an allegedly political objective, may be classified as serious non-political crimes. This applies both to the participants in the crime and to its instigators.

13.3. Article 1F(c)
The purposes and principles referred to in Article 1F(c) are in the first instance those laid down in the Charter of the United Nations, which determines the obligations of the States party to it in their mutual relations, particularly for the purpose of maintaining peace, and with regard to human rights and fundamental freedoms. Article 1F(c) applies to cases in which those principles have been breached and is directed notably at persons in senior positions in the State who, by virtue of their responsibilities, have ordered or lent their authority to action at variance with those purposes and principles as well as at persons who, as members of the security forces, have been prompted to assume personal responsibility for the performance of such action. In order to determine whether an action may be deemed contrary to the purposes and principles of the United Nations, Member States should take account of the conventions and resolutions adopted in this connection under the auspices of the United Nations.

3.11

Council Resolution of 20 June 1995 on minimum guarantees for asylum procedures[20]

THE COUNCIL OF THE EUROPEAN UNION,
Having regard to the Treaty on European Union, and in particular Article K.1 thereof,
Determined, in keeping with the common humanitarian tradition of the Member States, to guarantee adequate protection to refugees in need of such protection in accordance with the Geneva Convention of 28 July 1951 relating to the Status of Refugees, as amended by the New York Protocol of 31 January 1967,
Recalling the Member States' commitments under the European Convention for the Protection of Human Rights and Fundamental Freedoms of 4 November 1950,
Noting that, under national legislation, Member States may exceptionally allow aliens to stay for compelling reasons other than those covered by the 1951 Geneva Convention,
Affirming the intention of Member States to apply the Dublin Convention of 15 June 1990 determining the State responsible for examining applications for asylum lodged in one of the Member States of the European Communities,
Convinced that this requires decisions on asylum applications to be taken on the basis of equivalent procedures in all Member States and common procedural guarantees to be adopted for asylum-seekers to that end, taking into account the conclusions of the Executive Committee of the United Nations High Commissioner for Refugees (UNHCR) and Recommendation R (81) 16 of the Committee of Ministers of the Council of Europe,

HEREBY ADOPTS THIS RESOLUTION:

I. The guarantees provided for in this resolution will apply to the examination of asylum applications within the meaning of Article 3 of the Dublin Convention, with the exception of procedures to determine the Member State responsible under the said Convention. The specific guarantees applicable to those procedures will be determined by the Executive Committee set up by the Dublin Convention.

II. Universal principles concerning fair and effective asylum procedure
1. Asylum procedures will be applied in full compliance with the 1951 Geneva Convention, and the 1967 New York Protocol relating to the Status of Refugees and other obligations under international law in respect of refugees and human rights. In particular, the procedures will comply fully with Article 1 of the 1951 Convention concerning the definition of a refugee, Article 33 relating to the principle of 'non-refoulement' and Article 35 concerning cooperation with the Office of the UNHCR, including the facilitation of its duty of supervising the application of the Convention.
2. In order to ensure effectively the principle of 'non-refoulement', no expulsion measure will be carried out as long as no decision has been taken on the asylum application.

---

[20] T.12. Official Journal C 274, 19/09/1996 p. 0013–0017 [EUDOR] 396Y0919(05). [Ed.: See the Brussels Commentary elsewhere in this Handbook as well as T.7, the London Resolution on Manifestly Applications.

III. Guarantees concerning the examination of asylum applications

3. The regulations on access to the asylum procedure, the basic features of the asylum procedure itself and the designation of the authorities responsible for examination of asylum applications are to be laid down in the individual Member State's legislation.

4. Asylum applications will be examined by an authority fully qualified in the field of asylum and refugee matters. Decisions will be taken independently in the sense that all asylum applications will be examined and decided upon individually, objectively and impartially.

5. When examining an application for asylum the competent authority must, of its own initiative take into consideration and seek to establish all the relevant facts and give the applicant the opportunity to present a substantial description of the circumstances of the case and to prove them. For his part the applicant must present all the facts and circumstances known to him and give access to all the available evidence. Recognition of refugee status is not dependent on the production of any particular formal evidence.

6. The authorities responsible for the examination of the asylum application must be fully qualified in the field of asylum and refugee matters. To this effect, they must:
 - have at their disposal specialized personnel with the necessary knowledge and experience in the field of asylum and refugee matters, who have an understanding of an applicant's particular situation,
 - have access to precise and up-to-date information from various sources, including information from the UNHCR, concerning the situation prevailing in the countries of origin of asylum-seekers and in transit countries,
 - have the right to ask advice, whenever necessary, from experts on particular issues, e.g. a medical issue or an issue of a cultural nature.

7. The authorities responsible for border controls and the local authorities with which asylum applications are lodged must receive clear and detailed instructions so that the applications, together with all other information available, can be forwarded without delay to the competent authority for examination.

8. In the case of a negative decision, provision must be made for an appeal to a court or a review authority which gives an independent ruling on individual cases under the conditions laid down in paragraph 4.

9. Member States must ensure that the competent authorities are adequately provided with staff and equipment so that they can discharge their duties promptly and under the best possible conditions.

IV. Rights of asylum-seekers during examination, appeal and review procedures

10. An asylum-seeker must have an effective opportunity to lodge his asylum application as early as possible.

11. Declarations made by the asylum-seeker and other details of his application are very sensitive data, requiring protection. National law must therefore provide adequate data protection guarantees, particularly as against the authorities of the asylum-seeker's country of origin.

12. As long as the asylum application has not been decided on, the general principle applies that the applicant is allowed to remain in the territory of the State in which his application has been lodged or is being examined.

13. Asylum-seekers must be informed of the procedure to be followed and of their rights and obligations during the procedure, in a language which they can understand. In particular:

— they must be given the services of an interpreter, whenever necessary, for submitting their case to the authorities concerned. These services must be paid for out of public funds, if the interpreter is called upon by the competent authorities,
— in accordance with the rules of the Member State concerned, they may call in a legal adviser or other counsellor to assist them during the procedure,
— they must be given the opportunity, at all stages of the procedure, to communicate with the Office of the UNHCR or with other refugee organizations which may be working on behalf of the UNHCR in the Member State concerned, and vice versa. In addition, asylum-seekers may enter into contact with other refugee organizations under procedures laid down by the Member States. The opportunity for an asylum-seeker to communicate with the UNHCR and other refugee organizations need not necessarily prevent implementation of a decision,
— the representative of the Office of the UNHCR must be given the opportunity to be informed of the course of the procedure, to learn about the decisions of the competent authorities and to submit his observations.

14 Before a final decision is taken on the asylum application, the asylum-seeker must be given the opportunity of a personal interview with an official qualified under national law.

15 The decision on the asylum application must be communicated to the asylum-seeker in writing. If the application is rejected, the asylum-seeker must be informed of the reasons and of any possibility of having the decision reviewed. The asylum-seeker must have the opportunity, inasmuch as national law so provides, to acquaint himself with or be informed of the main purport of the decision and any possibility of appeal, in a language which he understands.

16 The asylum-seeker must be given an adequate period of time within which to appeal and to prepare his case when requesting review of the decision. These time limits must be communicated to the asylum-seeker in good time.

17 Until a decision has been taken on the appeal, the general principle will apply that the asylum-seeker may remain in the territory of the Member State concerned. Where the national law of a Member State permits a derogation from this principle in certain cases, the asylum-seeker should at least be able to apply to the bodies referred to in paragraph 8 (court or independent review authority) for leave to remain in the territory of the Member State temporarily during procedures before those bodies, on the grounds of the particular circumstances of his case; no expulsion may take place until a decision has been taken on this application.

Manifestly unfounded asylum applications

18. Manifestly unfounded asylum applications within the meaning of the resolution adopted by the Ministers responsible for immigration at their meeting on 30 November and 1 December 1992 will be dealt with in accordance with that resolution. Subject to the principles laid down therein, the guarantees laid down in the present resolution will apply.

19. By way of derogation from paragraph 8, Member States may exclude the possibility of lodging an appeal against a decision to reject an application if, instead, an independent body which is distinct from the examining authority has already confirmed the decision.

20. The Member States observe that, with due regard for the 1951 Geneva Refugee Convention, there should be no de facto or de jure grounds for granting refugee status to an asylum applicant who is a national of another Member State. On this basis, a particularly

rapid or simplified procedure will be applied to the application for asylum lodged by a national of another Member State, in accordance with each Member State's rules and practice, it being specified that the Member States continue to be obliged to examine individually every application for asylum, as provided by the Geneva Convention to which the Treaty on European Union refers.

21. Member States may provide for exceptions to the principle in paragraph 17 in limited cases, under national law, when, in consideration of objective criteria extraneous to the application itself, an application is manifestly unfounded in accordance with points 9 and 10 of the resolution adopted by the Ministers responsible for immigration on 30 November and 1 December 1992. However, in such cases it should at least be guaranteed that the decision on the application is taken at a high level and that additional sufficient safeguards (e.g. the same assessment, before the execution of the decision, by another authority which must be of a central nature and have the necessary knowledge and experience in the field of asylum and refugee law) ensure the correctness of the decision.

22. Member States may provide for exceptions to the principle in paragraph 17 with respect to asylum applications where, under national law, the host third-country concept is applicable in accordance with the resolution adopted by the Ministers responsible for immigration at their meeting on 30 November and 1 December 1992. In such cases Member States may also provide, by way of derogation from paragraph 15, that the decision rejecting the application, its underlying reasons and the asylum-seeker's rights may be communicated to him orally instead of in writing. Upon request, the decision will be confirmed in writing. The third-country authorities must, where necessary, be informed that the asylum application was not examined as to substance.

Asylum applications at the border

23. Member States will adopt administrative measures ensuring that any asylum-seeker arriving at their frontiers is afforded an opportunity to lodge an asylum application.

24. Member States may, inasmuch as national law so provides, apply special procedures to establish, prior to the decision on admission, whether or not the application for asylum is manifestly unfounded. No expulsion measure will be carried out during this procedure. Where an application for asylum is manifestly unfounded, the asylum-seeker may be refused admission. In such cases, the national law of a Member State may permit an exception to the general principle of the suspensive effect of the appeal (paragraph 17). However, it must at least be ensured that the decision on the refusal of admission is taken by a ministry or comparable central authority and that additional sufficient safeguards (for example, prior examination by another central authority) ensure the correctness of the decision. Such authorities must be fully qualified in asylum and refugee matters.

25. In addition, where, under national law, the host third country concept is applicable in accordance with the resolution adopted by the Ministers responsible for immigration at their meeting on 30 November and 1 December 1992, Member States may provide for exceptions to the principles in paragraphs 7 and 17. Member States may also provide, by way of derogation from paragraph 15, that the decision rejecting the application, its underlying reasons and any possibility of appeal may be communicated to the asylum-seeker orally instead of in writing. Upon request, the decision will be confirmed in writing. The procedure in the cases referred to in the first sentence of the preceding subparagraph may be carried out before the decision on admission has been taken. In such cases, admission may be refused.

V. Additional safeguards for unaccompanied minors and women

– Unaccompanied minors

26. Provision must be made for unaccompanied minors seeking asylum to be represented by a specifically appointed adult or institution if they do not have capacity under national law. During the interview, unaccompanied minors may be accompanied by that adult or representatives of that institution. These persons are to protect the child's interests.
27. When an application for asylum from an unaccompanied minor is examined, his mental development and maturity will be taken into account.

– Women

28. Member States must endeavour to involve skilled female employees and female interpreters in the asylum procedure where necessary, particularly where female asylum-seekers find it difficult to present the grounds for their application in a comprehensive manner owing to the experiences they have undergone or to their cultural origin.

VI. Residence where the criteria for classification as a refugee are met

29. A Member State which, notwithstanding national provisions on application of the host third-country concept, has examined an asylum application must grant refugee status to an asylum-seeker fulfilling the criteria of Article 1 of the Geneva Convention. Member States may provide, in accordance with their national law, that they will not make full use of the exclusion clauses contained in the Geneva Convention. The refugee should in principle be granted the right of residence in the Member State concerned.

VII. Other cases

30. This resolution does not affect the laws and regulations of the various Member States regarding the cases covered in point 11 of the resolution on manifestly unfounded asylum applications adopted by the Ministers responsible for immigration at their meeting on 30 November and 1 December 1992.

VIII. Further action

31. Member States will take account of these principles in the case of all proposals for changes to their national legislation. In addition, Member States will strive to bring their national legislation into line with these principles by 1 January 1996. In conjunction with the Commission and in consultation with the UNHCR, they will periodically review the operation of these principles and consider whether any additional measures are necessary.

IX. More favourable provisions

32. Member States have the right to enact national provisions on guarantees provided by procedures applicable to asylum-seekers which are more favourable than those contained in the common minimum guarantees.

3.12a

Convention determining the State responsible for examining applications for asylum lodged in one of the Member States of the European Communities – Dublin Convention 15/06/1990[21]

HAVING REGARD to the objective, fixed by the European Council meeting in Strasbourg on 8 and 9 December 1989, of the harmonization of their asylum policies;
DETERMINED, in keeping with their common humanitarian tradition, to guarantee adequate protection to refugees in accordance with the terms of the Geneva Convention of 28 July 1951, as amended by the New York Protocol of 31 January 1967 relating to the Status of Refugees, hereinafter referred to as the 'Geneva Convention' and the 'New York Protocol' respectively;
CONSIDERING the joint objective of an area without internal frontiers in which the free movement of persons shall, in particular, be ensured, in accordance with the provisions of the Treaty establishing the European Economic Community, as amended by the Single European Act:
AWARE of the need, in pursuit of this objective, to take measures to avoid any situations arising, with the result that applicants for asylum are left in doubt for too long as regards the likely outcome of their applications and concerned to provide all applicants for asylum with a guarantee that their applications will be examined by one of the Member States and to ensure that applicants for asylum are not referred successively from one Member State to another without any of these States acknowledging itself to be competent to examine the application for asylum;
DESIRING to continue the dialogue with the United Nations High Commissioner for Refugees in order to achieve the above objectives;
DETERMINED to co-operate closely in the application of this Convention through various means, including exchanges of information,
HAVE DECIDED TO CONCLUDE THIS CONVENTION AND TO THIS END HAVE DESIGNATED AS THEIR PLENIPOTENTIARIES:
(...)
HAVE AGREED AS FOLLOWS:

Article 1
1. For the purposes of this Convention:
(a) 'Alien' means: any person other than a national of a Member State;
(b) 'Application for asylum' means: a request whereby an alien seeks from a Member State protection under the Geneva Convention by claiming refugee status within the meaning of Article 1 of the Geneva Convention, as amended by the New York Protocol;
(c) 'Applicant for asylum' means: an alien who has made an application for asylum in respect of which a final decision has not yet been taken;
(d) 'Examination of an application for asylum' means: all the measures for examination, decisions or rulings given by the competent authorities on an application for asylum, except for procedures to determine the State responsible for examining the application for asylum pursuant to this Convention;

---

[21] Official Journal C 254, 19/08/1997 p. 0001–0012 [EUDOR] 497A0819(01).

(e) 'Residence permit' means: any authorization issued by the authorities of a Member State authorizing an alien to stay in its territory, with the exception of visas and 'stay permits' issued during examination of an application for a residence permit or for asylum;

(f) 'Entry visa' means: authorization or decision by a Member State to enable an alien to enter its territory, subject to the other entry conditions being fulfilled;

(g) 'Transit visa' means: authorization or decision by a Member State to enable an alien to transit through its territory or pass through the transit zone of a port or airport, subject to the other transit conditions being fulfilled.

2. The nature of the visa shall be assessed in the light of the definitions set out in paragraph 1 (f) and (g).

Article 2

The Member States reaffirm their obligations under the Geneva Convention, as amended by the New York Protocol, with no geographic restriction of the scope of these instruments, and their commitment to co-operating with the services of the United Nations High Commissioner for Refugees in applying these instruments.

Article 3

1. Member States undertake to examine the application of any alien who applies at the border or in their territory to any one of them for asylum.

2. That application shall be examined by a single Member State, which shall be determined in accordance with the criteria defined in this Convention. The criteria set out in Articles 4 to 8 shall apply in the order in which they appear.

3. That application shall be examined by that State in accordance with its national laws and its international obligations.

4. Each Member State shall have the right to examine an application for asylum submitted to it by an alien, even if such examination is not its responsibility under the criteria defined in this Convention, provided that the applicant for asylum agrees thereto. The Member State responsible under the above criteria is then relieved of its obligations, which are transferred to the Member State which expressed the wish to examine the application. The latter State shall inform the Member State responsible under the said criteria if the application has been referred to it.

5. Any Member State shall retain the right, pursuant to its national laws, to send an applicant for asylum to a third State, in compliance with the provisions of the Geneva Convention, as amended by the New York Protocol.

6. The process of determining the Member State responsible for examining the application for asylum under this Convention shall start as soon as an application for asylum is first lodged with a Member State.

7. An applicant for asylum who is present in another Member State and there lodges an application for asylum after withdrawing his or her application during the process of determining the State responsible shall be taken back, under the conditions laid down in Article 13, by the Member State with which that application for asylum was lodged, with a view to completing the process of determining the State responsible for examining the application for asylum. This obligation shall cease to apply if the applicant for asylum has since left the territory of the Member States for a period of at least three months or has obtained from a Member State a residence permit valid for more than three months.

Article 4
Where the applicant for asylum has a member of his family who has been recognized as having refugee status within the meaning of the Geneva Convention, as amended by the New York Protocol, in a Member State and is legally resident there, that State shall be responsible for examining the application, provided that the persons concerned so desire. The family member in question may not be other than the spouse of the applicant for asylum or his or her unmarried child who is a minor of under eighteen years, or his or her father or mother where the applicant for asylum is himself or herself an unmarried child who is a minor of under eighteen years.

Article 5
1. Where the applicant for asylum is in possession of a valid residence permit, the Member State which issued the permit shall be responsible for examining the application for asylum.
2. Where the applicant for asylum is in possession of a valid visa, the Member State which issued the visa shall be responsible for examining the application for asylum, except in the following situations:
(a) if the visa was issued on the written authorization of another Member State, that State shall be responsible for examining the application for asylum. Where a Member State first consults the central authority of another Member State, inter alia for security reasons, the agreement of the latter shall not constitute written authorization within the meaning of this provision.
(b) where the applicant for asylum is in possession of a transit visa and lodges his application in another Member State in which he is not subject to a visa requirement, that State shall be responsible for examining the application for asylum.
(c) where the applicant for asylum is in possession of a transit visa and lodges his application in the State which issued him or her with the visa and which has received written confirmation from the diplomatic or consular authorities of the Member State of destination that the alien for whom the visa requirement was waived fulfilled the conditions for entry into that State, the latter shall be responsible for examining the application for asylum.
3. Where the applicant for asylum is in possession of more than one valid residence permit or visa issued by different Member States, the responsibility for examining the application for asylum shall be assumed by the Member States in the following order:
(a) the State which issued the residence permit conferring the right to the longest period of residency or, where the periods of validity of all the permits are identical, the State which issued the residence permit having the latest expiry date;
(b) the State which issued the visa having the latest expiry date where the various visas are of the same type;
(c) where visas are of different kinds, the State which issued the visa having the longest period of validity, or, where the periods of validity are identical, the State which issued the visa having the latest expiry date. This provision shall not apply where the applicant is in possession of one or more transit visas, issued on presentation of an entry visa for another Member State. In that case, that Member State shall be responsible.
4. Where the applicant for asylum is in possession only of one or more residence permits which have expired less than two years previously or one or more visas which have expired less than six months previously and enabled him or her actually to enter the territory

of a Member State, the provisions of paragraphs 1, 2 and 3 of this Article shall apply for such time as the alien has not left the territory of the Member States. Where the applicant for asylum is in possession of one or more residence permits which have expired more than two years previously or one or more visas which have expired more than six months previously and enabled him or her to enter the territory of a Member State and where an alien has not left Community territory, the Member State in which the application is lodged shall be responsible.

Article 6
When it can be proved that an applicant for asylum has irregularly crossed the border into a Member State by land, sea or air, having come from a non-member State of the European Communities, the Member State this entered shall be responsible for examining the application for asylum. That State shall cease to be responsible, however, if it is proved that the applicant has been living in the Member State where the application for asylum was made at least six months before making his application for asylum. In that case it is the latter Member State which is responsible for examining the application for asylum.

Article 7
1 The responsibility for examining an application for asylum shall be incumbent upon the Member State responsible for controlling the entry of the alien into the territory of the Member States, except where, after legally entering a Member State in which the need for him or her to have a visa is waived, the alien lodges his or her application for asylum in another Member State in which the need for him or her to have a visa for entry into the territory is also waived. In this case, the latter State shall be responsible for examining the application for asylum.
2. Pending the entry into force of an agreement between Member States on arrangements for crossing external borders, the Member State which authorizes transit without a visa through the transit zone of its airports shall not be regarded as responsible for control on entry, in respect of travellers who do not leave the transit zone.
3. Where the application for asylum is made in transit in an airport of a Member State, that State shall be responsible for examination.

Article 8
Where no Member State responsible for examining the application for asylum can be designated on the basis of the other criteria listed in this Convention, the first Member State with which the application for asylum is lodged shall be responsible for examining it.

Article 9
Any Member State, even when it is not responsible under the criteria laid out in this Convention, may, for humanitarian reasons, based in particular on family or cultural grounds, examine an application for asylum at the request of another Member State, provided that the applicant so desires. If the Member State thus approached accedes to the request, responsibility for examining the application shall be transferred to it.

Article 10
1. The Member State responsible for examining an application for asylum according to the criteria set out in this Convention shall be obliged to:

(a) Take charge under the conditions laid down in Article 11 of an applicant who has lodged an application for asylum in a different Member State,
(b) Complete the examination of the application for asylum,
(c) Readmit or take back under the conditions laid down in Article 13 an applicant whose application is under examination and who is irregularly in another Member State,
(d) Take back, under the conditions laid down in Article 13, an applicant who has withdrawn the application under examination and lodged an application in another Member State,
(e) Take back, under the conditions laid down in Article 13, an alien whose application is has rejected and who is illegally in another Member State.
2. If a Member State issues to the applicant a residence permit valid for more than three months, the obligations specified in paragraph 1(a) to (e) shall be transferred to that Member State.
3. The obligations specified in paragraph 1(a) to (d) shall cease to apply if the alien concerned has left the territory of the Member States for a period of at least three months.
4. The obligations specified in paragraph 1(d) and (e) shall cease to apply if the State responsible for examining the application for asylum, following the withdrawal or rejection of the application, takes and enforces the necessary measures for the alien to return to his country of origin or to another country which he may lawfully enter.

Article 11
1. If a Member State with which an application for asylum has been lodged considers that another Member State is responsible for examining the application, it may, as quickly as possible and in any case within the six months following the date on which the application was lodged, call upon the other Member State to take charge of the applicant. If the request that charge be taken is not made within the six-month time limit, responsibility for examining the application for asylum shall rest with the State in which the application was lodged.
2. The request that charge be taken shall contain indications enabling the authorities of that other State to ascertain whether it is responsible on the basis of the criteria laid down in this Convention.
3. The State responsible in accordance with those criteria shall be determined on the basis of the situation obtaining when the applicant for asylum first lodged his application with a Member State.
4. The Member State shall pronounce judgment on the request within three months of receipt of the claim. Failure to act within that period shall be tantamount to accepting the claim.
5. Transfer of the applicant for asylum from the Member State where the application was lodged to the Member State responsible must take place not later than one month after acceptance of the request to take charge or one month after the conclusion of any proceedings initiated by the alien challenging the transfer decision if the proceedings are suspensory.
6. Measures taken under Article 18 may subsequently determine the details of the process by which applicants shall be taken in charge.

Article 12
Where an application for asylum is lodged with the competent authorities of a Member State by an applicant who is on the territory of another Member State, the determination

of the Member State responsible for examining the application for asylum shall be made by the Member State on whose territory the applicant is. The latter Member State shall be informed without delay by the Member State which received the application and shall then, for the purpose of applying this Convention, be regarded as the Member State with which the application for asylum was lodged.

Article 13
1. An applicant for asylum shall be taken back in the cases provided for in Article 3(7) and in Article 10 as follows:
(a) the request for the applicant to be taken back must provide indications enabling the State with which the request is lodged to ascertain that it is responsible in accordance with Article 3(7) and with Article 10;
(b) the State called upon to take back the applicant shall give an answer to the request within eight days of the matter being referred to it. Should it acknowledge responsibility, it shall then take back the applicant for asylum as quickly as possible and at the latest one month after it agrees to do so.
2 Measures taken under Article 18 may at a later date set out the details of the procedure for taking the applicant back.

Article 14
1 Member States shall conduct mutual exchanges with regard to:
– national legislative or regulatory measures or practices applicable in the field of asylum,
– statistical data on monthly arrivals of applicants for asylum, and their breakdown by nationality. Such information shall be forwarded quarterly through the General Secretariat of the Council of the European Communities, which shall see that it is circulated to the Member States and the Commission of the European Communities and to the United Nations High Commissioner for Refugees.
2. The Member States may conduct mutual exchanges with regard to:
– general information on new trends in applications for asylum,
– general information on the situation in the countries of origin or of provenance of applicants for asylum.
3. If the Member State providing the information referred to in paragraph 2 wants it to be kept confidential, the other Member States shall comply with this wish.

Article 15
1. Each Member State shall communicate to any Member State that so requests such information on individual cases as is necessary for:
– determining the Member State which is responsible for examining the application for asylum,
– examining the application for asylum,
– implementing any obligation arising under this Convention.
2. This information may only cover:
– personal details of the applicant, and, where appropriate, the members of his family (full name and where appropriate, former name; nicknames or pseudonyms; nationality, present and former; date and place of birth),
– identity and travel papers (references, validity, date of issue, issuing authority, place of issue, etc.),

– other information necessary for establishing the identity of the applicant,
– places of residence and routes travelled,
– residence permits or visas issued by a Member State,
– the place where the application was lodged,
– the date any previous application for asylum was lodged, the date the present application was lodged, the stage reached in the proceedings and the decision taken, if any.

3. Furthermore, one Member State may request another Member State to let it know on what grounds the applicant for asylum bases his or her application and, where applicable, the grounds for any decisions taken concerning the applicant. It is for the Member State from which the information is requested to decide whether or not to impart it. In any event, communication of the information requested shall be subject to the approval of the applicant for asylum.

4. This exchange of information shall be effected at the request of a Member State and may only take place between authorities the designation of which by each Member State has been communicated to the Committee provided for under Article 18.

5. The information exchanged may only be used for the purposes set out in paragraph 1. In each Member State such information may only be communicated to the authorities and courts and tribunals entrusted with:
– determining the Member State which is responsible for examining the application for asylum,
– examining the application for asylum,
– implementing any obligation arising under this Convention.

6. The Member State that forwards the information shall ensure that it is accurate and up-to-date. If it appears that this Member State has supplied information which is inaccurate or which should not have been forwarded, the recipient Member State shall be immediately informed thereof. They shall be obliged to correct such information or to have it erased.

7. An applicant for asylum shall have the right to receive, on request, the information exchanged concerning him or her, for such time as it remains available. If he or she establishes that such information is inaccurate or should not have been forwarded, he or she shall have the right to have it corrected or erased. This right shall be exercised in accordance with the conditions laid down in paragraph 6.

8. In each Member State concerned, the forwarding and receipt of exchanged information shall be recorded.

9. Such information shall be kept for a period not exceeding that necessary for the ends for which it was exchanged. The need to keep it shall be examined at the appropriate moment by the Member State concerned.

10. In any event, the information thus communicated shall enjoy at least the same protection as is given to similar information in the Member State which receives it.

11. If data are not processed automatically but are handled in some other form, every Member State shall take the appropriate measures to ensure compliance with this Article by means of effective controls. If a Member State has a monitoring body of the type mentioned in paragraph 12, it may assign the control task to it.

12. If one or more Member States wish to computerize all or part of the information mentioned in paragraphs 2 and 3, such computerization is only possible if the countries concerned have adopted laws applicable to such processing which implement the principles of the Strasbourg Convention of 28 January 1981 for the Protection of Individuals, with

regard to automatic processing of personal data and if they have entrusted an appropriate national body with the independent monitoring of the processing and use of data forwarded pursuant to this Convention.

Article 16
1. Any Member State may submit to the Committee referred to in Article 18 proposals for revision of this Convention in order to eliminate difficulties in the application thereof.
2. If it proves necessary to revise or amend this Convention pursuant to the achievement of the objectives set out in Article 8a of the Treaty establishing the European Economic Community, such achievement being linked in particular to the establishment of a harmonized asylum and a common visa policy, the Member State holding the Presidency of the Council of the European Communities shall organize a meeting of the Committee referred to in Article 18.
3. Any revision of this Convention or amendment hereto shall be adopted by the Committee referred to in Article 18. It shall enter into force in accordance with the provisions of Article 22.

Article 17
1 If a Member State experiences major difficulties as a result of a substantial change in the circumstances obtaining on conclusion of this Convention, the State in question may bring the matter before the Committee referred to in Article 18 so that the latter may put to the Member States measures to deal with the situation or adopt such revisions or amendments to this Convention as appear necessary, which shall enter into force as provided for in Article 16(3).
2. If, after six months, the situation mentioned in paragraph 1 still obtains, the Committee, acting in accordance with Article 18(2), may authorize the Member State affected by that change to suspend temporarily the application of the provisions of this Convention, without such suspension being allowed to impede the achievement of the objectives mentioned in Article 8a of the Treaty establishing the European Economic Community or contravene other international obligations of the Member States.
3. During the period of suspension, the Committee shall continue its discussions with a view to revising the provisions of this Convention, unless it has already reached an agreement.

Article 18
1. A Committee shall be set up comprising one representative of the Government of each Member State. The Committee shall be chaired by the Member State holding the Presidency of the Council of the European Communities. The Commission of the European Communities may participate in the discussions of the Committee and the working parties referred to in paragraph 4.
2. The Committee shall examine, at the request of one or more Member States, any question of a general nature concerning the application or interpretation of this Convention. The Committee shall determine the measures referred to in Article 11(6) and Article 13(2) and shall give the authorization referred to in Article 17(2). The Committee shall adopt decisions revising or amending the Convention pursuant to Articles 16 and 17.
3. The Committee shall take its decisions unanimously, except where it is acting pursuant to Article 17(2), in which case it shall take its decisions by a majority of two-thirds of the votes of its members.

4. The Committee shall determine its rules of procedure and may set up working parties. The Secretariat of the Committee and of the working parties shall be provided by the General Secretariat of the Council of the European Communities.

Article 19
As regards the Kingdom of Denmark, the provisions of this Convention shall not apply to the Faroe Islands nor to Greenland unless a declaration to the contrary is made by the Kingdom of Denmark. Such a declaration may be made at any time by a communication to the Government of Ireland which shall inform the Governments of the other Member States thereof.As regards the French Republic, the provisions of this Convention shall apply only to the European territory of the French Republic. As regards the Kingdom of the Netherlands, the provisions of this Convention shall apply only to the territory of the Kingdom of the Netherlands in Europe. As regards the United Kingdom the provisions of this Convention shall apply only to the United Kingdom of Great Britain and Northern Ireland. They shall not apply to the European territories for whose external relations the United Kingdom is responsible unless a declaration to the contrary is made by the United Kingdom. Such a declaration may be made at any time by a communication to the Government of Ireland, which shall inform the Governments of the other Member States thereof.

Article 20
This Convention shall not be the subject of any reservations.

Article 21
1. This Convention shall be open for the accession of any State which becomes a member of the European Communities. The instruments of accession will be deposited with the Government of Ireland.
2. It shall enter into force in respect of any State which accedes thereto on the first day of the third month following the deposit of its instrument of accession.

Article 22
1. This Convention shall be subject to ratification, acceptance or approval. The instruments of ratification, acceptance or approval shall be deposited with the Government of Ireland.
2. The Government of Ireland shall notify the Governments of the other Member States of the deposit of the instruments of ratification, acceptance or approval.
3. This Convention shall enter into force on the first day of the third month following the deposit of the instrument of ratification, acceptance or approval by the last signatory State to take this step. The State with which the instruments of ratification, acceptance or approval are deposited shall notify the Member States of the date of entry into force of this Convention.

3.12b

Decision No 1/97 of 9 September 1997 of the Committee set up by Article 18 of the Dublin Convention of 15 June 1990, concerning provisions for the implementation of the Convention (97/662/CMS)[22]

THE COMMITTEE set up by Article 18 of the Convention determining the State responsible for examining applications for asylum lodged in one of the Member States of the European Communities, signed in Dublin of 15 June 1990,
HAVING REGARD to Articles 11(6), 13(2) and 18(1) and (2) of that Convention,
WHEREAS it is necessary to adopt provisions to ensure the effective implementation of the Convention following its entry into force on 1 September 1997,
HEREBY DECIDES AND CONFIRMS:

Article 1
(...)

CHAPTER I
GENERAL GUIDELINES FOR IMPLEMENTATION OF THE CONVENTION

Article 2
Lodging an application for asylum
1. An application for asylum is regarded as having been lodged from the moment the authorities of the Member State concerned have something in writing to that effect (...)
2. In the event of a non-written application, the period between the statement of intent and the drawing up of the official statement must be as short as possible.

Article 3
Reaction to a request that an applicant be taken in charge
Any response to a request that charge be taken of an applicant with a view to staying the effect of the provision concerning the three-month deadline laid down in Article 11(4) to produce effect must take the form of a written communication.

Article 4
Time limit for replying to a request that an applicant be taken in charge (...) one month from the date on which the request was received. 2. In cases where particular difficulties arise, the requested Member State may also, before the time limit of one month is reached, produce a temporary reply (...) 3. If a negative reply is given within the time limit of one month, the requesting Member State still has the option, within a period of one month from the date on which it receives the negative reply, to contest that reply if, after the date on which the request was acknowledged, new and important facts have been brought to its attention which show that responsibility lies with the requested Member State. (...)

Article 5
Urgent procedure
When a request for asylum is submitted to a Member State following refusal to allow entry or residence, arrest as a result of illegal residence or service or execution of a removal

---

[22] Official Journal L 281, 14/10/1997 p. 0001–0025 497D0662.

measure, that Member State shall forthwith notify this to the Member State deemed to have responsibility; such notification shall give the reasons of fact and law why a swift reply is necessary and the deadline within which a reply is requested. The latter Member State shall endeavour to provide a reply within the specified periods. If this is not possible, it shall inform the requesting Member State thereof as quickly as possible.

Article 6
Exceeding the eight-day period for replying to a request for an applicant to be taken back
1. Article 13(1)(b) of the Convention makes it very clear that Member States are obliged to respond to the request to take back the applicant within eight days of its submission.
2. In exceptional cases Member States may, within this eight-day period, give a provisional reply (...)
3. If the requested Member State fails to react:
– within the eight-day period mentioned in paragraph 1,
– within the one-month period mentioned in paragraph 2,
it shall be considered to have agreed to take back the applicant for asylum.

Article 7
Measures to expel an alien
The Member State responsible for examining the application must provide proof that the alien has actually been expelled from the territory of the Member States. These are therefore concrete acts of expulsion, involving an obligation relating to the result rather than the intention, which in effect means that in such cases the Member State provide written proof.

Article 8
Departure from the territory of the Member States
1. Where the applicant for asylum himself produces proof that he has left the territory of the Member States for more than three months, the second Member State may examine the veracity of that information, (...).
2. In other cases the Member State in which the initial application was lodged has to provide proof,(...). In the context of cooperation between Member States, the Member State in which the second application was lodged is best able to give the date on which the applicant for asylum returned to his territory.

Article 9
Exceptions where the applicant for asylum is in possession of a visa
1. Article 5(2) provides for three separate cases where the responsibility of a Member State for examining the application for asylum ceases even if the applicant for asylum is in possession of a valid visa issued by that State.
2. The first exception (subparagraph (a)) concerns a visa issued on the authorization of another Member State; as a general rule, exceptional cases should be proved by the Member States which invoked them.
3. The second exception (subparagraph (b)) arises from a situation in which an application is lodged in a Member State in which the applicant is not subject to a visa requirement; there will be no need to seek proof since the problem is not relevant.
4. The third exception (subparagraph (c)) refers to the case of an applicant for asylum who is in possession of a transit visa issued on the written authorization of the diplomatic

or consular authorities of the Member State of final destination; the question of burden of proof is irrelevant here since there is prior written conformation that the transit visa was issued.

Article 10
Determination of the State responsible in the event of an applicant possessing several residence permits or visas
In the event of an applicant possessing several residence permits or visas issued by different Member States (in particular in the case of Article 5(3)(c)), proof for the purposes of determining the State responsible does not arise in that the relevant information appears in the entry document produced by the applicant for asylum.

Article 11
Determining the periods of time and actual entry into a State
1. As regards the determination of the periods of time, the date of expiry of residence permits or visas is calculated from the date on which the application for asylum is lodged.
2. In addition, checking the expiry date of residence permits and visas is not necessary if such information appears on the asylum applicant's papers.
3. As regards proof that the individual has actually entered a Member State, the following situations should be distinguished:
– if an applicant for asylum has actually entered a Member State, proof can be provided through information supplied by the Member State in which the application for asylum was lodged,
– if an applicant for asylum has not left the territory of the Member States, the Member State which issued the expired residence permit or visa has to provide the information required,- if an applicant for asylum himself supplies the information that he has left the territory of the Member States, the second Member State in which an application was lodged will check the truth of the statements. These rules apply in respect of actual entry in both subparagraphs of Article 5(4).

Article 12
Irregular crossing of the border into a Member State
1. Proof that an applicant for asylum has irregularly crossed the border into a Member State (first subparagraph of Article 6) must be examined after the list of means of proof has been drawn up.
2. Proof of a Member State ceasing to be responsible when the applicant for asylum lodges his application in the Member State where he has lived for six months (in accordance with the second subparagraph of Article 6) must be supplied in the first instance by the Member State invoking this exception in a spirit of collaboration between the two Member States concerned.
3. If the applicant for asylum claims that he has lived in a Member State for more than six months, it is for that Member State to check the truth of those statements. The initial information to the other Member State concerned will in any case have to include statements made by the applicant for asylum which may be used subsequently as counter-indications.

Article 13
Formal rules applying to approval by the applicant for asylum

1. Approval must be given in writing.
2. As a general rule an applicant must give his approval when the Member State claiming responsibility for examining the application has submitted a request for exchange of information.
3. The applicant for asylum must in any case know to what information he is giving his agreement.
4. The approval concerns the reasons given by the applicant for asylum and, where applicable, the reasons for the decisions taken with regard to the applicant.

Article 14
Notification procedures
1. The system of exchange of information must also include data on notification procedures. Accordingly, notification must be given:
– as quickly as possible in writing,
– using the technical means available,
– to the Member States claiming responsibility for examining an application for asylum.
2. Such notification, which will avoid the possibility of two procedures being initiated simultaneously in two Member States, applies in respect of Articles 3 (4) and 12.
3. Where implementation of a decision determining responsibility is suspended, such suspension is notified so that the Member States are kept fully informed. It is very useful for the Member State where the application was lodged to be informed that an applicant for asylum is not being transferred pending a decision in his case by the second Member State.

Article 15
Standard form for determining the State responsible
A specimen standard form for determining the State responsible for examining an application for asylum is given in Annex I hereto.

CHAPTER II
CALCULATION OF PERIODS OF TIME IN THE FRAMEWORK OF THE CONVENTION

Article 16
General rule
For the purposes of calculating the periods referred to in the Convention, Saturdays, Sundays and public holidays must be included.

Article 17
Supplementary rule
For the purposes of calculating the periods provided for in Articles 11 (4) and 13 (1) (b), the following rules shall also apply:
– the period begins on the day following receipt of the request,
– the final day of the period is the deadline for sending the reply.

CHAPTER III
TRANSFER OF ASYLUM APPLICANTS

Article 18
Introductory provisions
(...)

Article 19
Notification to the applicant for asylum
(...)

Article 20
Transfer of the applicant for asylum
(...)

Article 21
Deadlines for transfer of applicant for asylum
(...)

Article 22
Laissez-passer for transfer of applicants
A specimen laissez-passer for transfer of applicants for asylum is provided in Annex II hereto.

CHAPTER IV
MEANS OF PROOF IN THE FRAMEWORK OF THE CONVENTION

Article 23
Principles regarding the collection of evidence
1. The way in which evidence is used to determine the State responsible for examining an asylum application is fundamental to the implementation of the Convention.
2. Responsibility for processing an asylum application should in principle be determined on the basis of as few requirements of proof as possible.
3 If establishment of proof carried excessive requirements, the procedure for determining responsibility would ultimately take longer than examination of the actual application for asylum. In that case, the Convention would fail totally to have the desired effect and would even contradict one of its objectives since the delays would create a new category of 'refugees in orbit', asylum-seekers whose applications would not be examined until the procedure laid down under the Convention had been completed.
4 Under too rigid a system of proof the Member States would not accept responsibility and the Convention would be applied only in rare instances, while those Member States with more extensive national registers would be penalized since their responsibility could be proved more easily.
5. A Member State should also be prepared to assume responsibility on the basis of indicative evidence for examining an asylum application once it emerges from an overall examination of the asylum applicant's situation that, in all probability, responsibility lies with the Member State in question.
6. The Member States should jointly consider in a spirit of genuine cooperation on the basis of all the evidence available to them, including statements made by the asylum-seeker, whether the responsibility of one Member State can be consistently established.
7. Lists A and B referred to in Articles 24 and 25 of this Decision are drawn up on the basis of those considerations.

Article 24
General considerations regarding lists A and B
1. It was considered necessary to draw up two lists of means of proof: probative evidence as in list A and indicative evidence as in list B. These lists are to be found in Annex III to this Decision.
2. List A sets out the means of probative evidence which conclusively prove responsibility under the Convention, save where rebutted by evidence to the contrary (e. g. showing documents not to be genuine).
3. List B is not exhaustive and contains means of proof consisting of indicative elements to be used within the framework of the Convention. These are means of proof having indicative value. Indicative evidence as in list B may be sufficient to determine responsibility, depending on the weighing-up of evidence in a particular case. It is by nature rebuttable.
4. These lists may be revised in the light of experience.
5. It seems useful to indicate that the weight of proof of these elements may vary according to the circumstances of each individual case. Items will be classified as probative evidence or indicative evidence according to the point to be proved. For instance, a fingerprint may provide probative evidence of an asylum-seeker's presence in a Member State, yet form only indicative evidence as to whether the asylum-seeker entered the Community at a particular external frontier.
6. This distinction made it necessary to draw up two separate lists of probative evidence (list A) and indicative evidence (list B) for each point to be proved under the Convention; Annex III hereto gives a breakdown of means of proof according to the point to be proved.
7. By the same token, the probative force of official documents is not always the same from one Member State to another. The same document can be drawn up for different purposes or by different authorities, depending on the Member State concerned.

Article 25
Probative force of elements in lists A and B
(...)

Article 26
Consequences a to determination of responsibility
(...)

Article 27
Acceptance of responsibility on the basis of a declaration by the asylum applicant
(...)

CHAPTER V
EXCHANGE OF INFORMATION

Article 28
Statistical and individual information
1. Member States will conduct three-monthly exchanges of statistical information concerning the practical implementation of the Convention using the tables given in Annex IV hereto.

2. The Member States to which a request within the meaning of Article 15 is addressed should make every effort to reply to the request if possible immediately and in any event within one month.

FINAL PROVISION

Article 29
Entry into force. This Decision shall come into force on today's date. It shall apply from 1 September 1997.

(...)

ANNEX I
STANDARD FORM FOR DETERMINING THE STATE RESPONSIBLE FOR EXAMINING AN APPLICATION FOR ASYLUM

ANNEX II
Specimen laissez-passer for transfer of applicants

ANNEX III
– LIST A
A. MEANS OF PROOF
I. Process of determining the State responsible for examining an application for asylum (...)
II. Obligation on the Member State responsible for examining the application for asylum to re-admit or take back the asylum seeker (...)
– LIST B
B. INDICATIVE EVIDENCE
I. Process of determining the State responsible for examining an application for asylum (...)
II. Obligation on the Member State responsible for examining the application for asylum to re-admit or take back the asylum seeker (...)

ANNEX IV
– TABLE 1
Requests for transfer (of persons) by [Member State] within (three-month period) to other Member States (...)
– TABLE 2
Requests for transfers of (persons) to [Member State] within (three-month period) by other Member States (...)
– TABLE 3
Average time limits for replies to transfer requests (three-month period) (...)
– TABLE 4
Total number of asylum applications (three-month period) (...)
Statistical data on the application of the Dublin Convention

3.12c

Decision No 1/98 of 30 June 1998 of the Committee set up by Article 18 of the Dublin Convention of 15 June 1990, concerning provisions for the implementation of the Convention (98/451/CMS)[23]

THE COMMITTEE set up by Article 18 of the Convention determining the State responsible for examining applications for asylum lodged in one of the Member States of the European Communities, signed in Dublin on 15 June 1990 (1) (hereinafter referred to as 'the committee' and 'the Convention' respectively),

HAVING REGARD to Article 18(1) and (2) of the Convention,

WHEREAS it is necessary to supplement Decision No 1/97 of the committee of 9 September 1997 concerning provisions for the implementation of the Convention (2), in order to ensure the effective implementation thereof;

WHEREAS, in particular, the use of information on the ways and means asylum seekers enter the European Union in determining the State responsible under the Convention should be clarified;

WHEREAS the exchange of fingerprint data between Member States, in accordance with their national law, is a useful mechanism for confirming identity and identifying the Member State of arrival in the European Union in support of the operation of the Convention;

WHEREAS the development of practical cooperation between the Member States would facilitate implementation of the Convention,

HAS DECIDED AS FOLLOWS:

Article 1
Information on ways and means asylum seekers enter the European Union
1. Subject to paragraph 2, when making and examining applications under Article 11 of the Convention, the Member States concerned should be prepared together to take account, in appropriate cases, of relevant information from reliable and verifiable sources on the ways and means asylum seekers enter the European Union.
2. It is understood that the information referred to in paragraph 1 is not in itself sufficient to determine the responsibility and the competence of a Member State under the Convention, but it may contribute to the evaluation of other indications relating to the individual asylum seeker.
3. Member States shall ensure that information obtained about the ways and means asylum seekers enter the European Union is made available promptly to officials responsible for making and examining applications under Article 11 of the Convention.

Article 2
Exchange of fingerprints under Article 15 of the Convention
1. Without prejudice to any provisions in the Convention or in other decisions of the committee, each Member State may request fingerprint information under Article 15(2) of

---
[23] Official Journal L 196, 14/07/1998 p. 0049–0050 [EUDOR] 498D0451.

the Convention from another Member State where there are reasons to do so in pursuance of the objectives stated in Article 15(1) thereof.
2. The provision of fingerprint information in response to requests made pursuant to paragraph 1 shall be subject to the national law of the requested Member State and to the principles of data protection applicable in the European Union.

Article 3
Applications to assume responsibility
Applications under Article 11 of the Convention shall contain all the information available to the Member State making the application which is necessary for determining responsibility for examining the asylum application.

Article 4
Liaison and cooperation
1. Each Member State shall take such steps as are necessary, in particular by means of visits, where practicable, to ensure that close working relationships are maintained between its own officials and officials in other Member States who are responsible for carrying out functions in relation to the Convention and with whom it has significant dealings.
2. Where possible and where mutually beneficial to do so, each Member State should exchange liaison officers with other Member States, with a view to improving communication links.
3. A handbook for practitioners of the Convention shall be prepared, distributed, updated and supplemented by the General Secretariat of the Council of the European Union. The handbook shall contain such information as would be helpful to practitioners. Its contents shall be kept under regular review.

Article 5
Entry into force
This Decision shall enter into force on the day of its publication in the Official Journal.[24]

3.13

Resolution on Manifestly Unfounded Applications for Asylum (London, 30 November and 1 December 1992)

MINISTERS OF THE MEMBER STATES OF THE EUROPEAN COMMUNITIES responsible for Immigration, meeting in London on 30 November and 1 December 1992,
HAVING REGARD to the objective, fixed by the European Council meeting in Strasbourg in December 1989, of the harmonization of their asylum policies and the work programme agreed at the meeting at Maastricht in December 1991;
DETERMINED, in keeping with their common humanitarian tradition, to guarantee adequate protection to refugees in accordance with the terms of the Geneva Convention of

---

[24] I.e. 14 July 1998.

28 July 1951, as amended by the New York Protocol of 31 January 1967, relating to the Status of Refugees;
NOTING that Member States may, in accordance with national legislation, allow the exceptional stay of aliens for other compelling reasons outside the terms of the 1951 Geneva Convention;
REAFFIRMING their commitment to the Dublin Convention of 15 June 1990, which guarantees that all asylum applicants at the border or in the territory of a Member State will have their claim for asylum examined and sets out rules for determining which Member State will be responsible for that examination;
AWARE that a rising number of applicants for asylum in the Member States are not in genuine need of protection within the Member States within the terms of the Geneva Convention, and concerned that such manifestly unfounded applications overload asylum determination procedures, delay the recognition of refugees in genuine need of protection and jeopardize the integrity of the institution of asylum;
INSPIRED by Conclusion No. 30 of the Executive Committee of the United Nations High Commissioner for Refugees;
CONVINCED that their asylum policies should give no encouragement to the misuse of asylum procedures;

HAVE ADOPTED THE FOLLOWING RESOLUTION:

Manifestly unfounded applications
1. (a) An application for asylum shall be regarded as manifestly unfounded if it is clear that it meets none of the substantive criteria under the Geneva Convention and New York Protocol for one of the following reasons:
– there is clearly no substance to the applicant's claim to fear persecution in his own country (paragraphs 6 to 8); or
– the claim is based on deliberate deception or is an abuse of asylum procedures (paragraphs 9 and 10).
(b) Furthermore, without prejudice to the Dublin Convention, an application for asylum may not be subject to determination by a Member State of refugee status under the terms of the Geneva Convention on the Status of Refugees when it falls within the provisions of the Resolution on host countries adopted by Immigration Ministers meeting in London on 30 November and 1 December 1992.

2. Member States may include within an accelerated procedure (where it exists or is introduced), which need not include full examination at every level of the procedure, those applications which fall within the terms of paragraph 1, although an application need not be included within such procedures if there are national policies providing for its acceptance on other grounds. Member States may also operate admissibility procedures under which applications may be rejected very quickly on objective grounds.

3. Member States will aim to reach initial decisions on applications which fall within the terms of paragraph 1 as soon as possible and at the latest within one month and to complete any appeal or review procedures as soon as possible. Appeal or review procedures may be more simplified than those generally available in the case of other rejected asylum applications.

4. A decision to refuse an asylum application which falls within the terms of paragraph 1 will be taken by a competent authority at the appropriate level fully qualified in asylum or refugee matters. Amongst other procedural guarantees the applicant should be given the opportunity for a personal interview with a qualified official empowered under national law before any final decision is taken.

5. Without prejudice to the provisions of the Dublin Convention, where an application is refused under the terms of paragraph 1 the Member State concerned will ensure that the applicant leaves Community territory, unless he is given permission to enter or remain on other grounds.

No substance to claim to fear persecution
6. Member States may consider under the provisions of paragraph 2 above all applications the terms of which raise no question of refugee status within the terms of the Geneva Convention. This may be because:
(a) the grounds of the application are outside the scope of the Geneva Convention: the applicant does not invoke fear of persecution based on his belonging to a race, a religion, a nationality, a social group, or on his political opinions, but reasons such as the search for a job or better living conditions;
(b) the application is totally lacking in substance: the applicant provides no indications that he would be exposed to fear of persecution or his story contains no circumstantial or personal details;
(c) the application is manifestly lacking in any credibility: his story is inconsistent, contradictory or fundamentally improbable.

7. Member States may consider under the provisions of paragraph 2 above an application for asylum from claimed persecution which is clearly limited to a specific geographical area where effective protection is readily available for that individual in another part of his own country to which it would be reasonable to expect him to go, in accordance with Article 33.1 of the Geneva Convention. When necessary, the Member States will consult each other in the appropriate framework, taking account of information received from UNHCR, on situations which might allow, subject to an individual examination, the application of this paragraph.

8. It is open to an individual Member State to decide in accordance with the conclusions of Immigration Ministers of 1 December 1992 that a country is one in which there is in general terms no serious risk of persecution. In deciding whether a country is one in which there is no serious risk of persecution, the Member State will take into account the elements which are set out in the aforementioned conclusions of Ministers. Member States have the goal to reach common assessment of certain countries that are of particular interest in this context. The Member State will nevertheless consider the individual claims of all applicants from such countries and any specific indications presented by the applicant which might outweigh a general presumption. In the absence of such indications, the application may be considered under the provisions of paragraph 2 above.

Deliberate deception or abuse of asylum procedures
9. Member States may consider under the provisions of paragraph 2 above all applica-

tions which are clearly based on deliberate deceit or are an abuse of asylum procedures. Member States may consider under accelerated procedures all cases in which the applicant has, without reasonable explanation:

(a) based his application on a false identity or on forged or counterfeit documents which he has maintained are genuine when questioned about them;
(b) deliberately made false representations about his claim, either orally or in writing, after applying for asylum;
(c) in bad faith destroyed, damaged or disposed of any passport, other document or ticket relevant to his claim, either in order to establish a false identity for the purpose of his asylum application or to make the consideration of his application more difficult;
(d) deliberately failed to reveal that he has previously lodged an application in one or more countries, particularly when false identities are used;
(e) having had ample earlier opportunity to submit an asylum application, submitted the application in order to forestall an impending expulsion measure;
(f) flagrantly failed to comply with substantive obligations imposed by national rules relating to asylum procedures;
(g) submitted an application in one of the Member States, having had his application previously rejected in another country following an examination comprising adequate procedural guarantees and in accordance with the Geneva Convention on the Status of Refugees. To this effect, contacts between Member States and third countries would, when necessary, be made through UNHCR.

Member States will consult in the appropriate framework when it seems that new situations occur which may justify the implementation of accelerated procedures.

10. The factors listed in paragraph 9 are clear indications of bad faith and justify consideration of a case under the procedures described in paragraph 2 above in the absence of a satisfactory explanation for the applicant's behaviour. But they cannot in themselves outweigh a well-founded fear of persecution under Article 1 of the Geneva Convention and none of them carries any greater weight than any other.

Other cases to which accelerated procedures may apply

11. This Resolution does not affect national provisions of Member States for considering under accelerated procedures, where they exist, other cases where an urgent resolution of the claim is necessary, in which it is established that the applicant has committed a serious offence in the territory of the Member States, if a case manifestly falls within the situations mentioned in Article 1.F of the 1951 Geneva Convention, or for serious reasons of public security, even where the cases are not manifestly unfounded in accordance with paragraph 1.

Further action

12. Ministers agreed to seek to ensure that their national laws are adapted, if need be, to incorporate the principles of this Resolution as soon as possible, at the latest by 1 January 1995. Member States will from time to time, in co-operation with the Commission and in consultation with UNHCR, review the operation of these procedures and consider whether any additional measures are necessary.

3.14

Resolution on a Harmonized Approach to Questions concerning Host Third Countries (London, 30 November and 1 December 1992)

THE MINISTERS OF THE MEMBER STATES OF THE EUROPEAN COMMUNITIES responsible for Immigration, meeting in London on 30 November and 1 December 1992;
DETERMINED to achieve the objective of harmonizing asylum policies as it was defined by the Luxembourg European Council in June 1991 and clarified by the Maastricht European Council in December 1991;
TRUE to the principles of the Geneva Convention of 28 July 1951, as amended by the New York Protocol of 31 January 1967, relating to the Status of Refugees, and in particular Articles 31 and 33 thereof;
CONCERNED especially at the problem of refugees and asylum seekers unlawfully leaving countries where they have already been granted protection or have had a genuine opportunity to seek such protection and CONVINCED that a concerted response should be made to it, as suggested in Conclusion No. 58 on Protection adopted by the UNHCR Executive Committee at its 40th session (1989);
CONSIDERING the Dublin Convention of 15 June 1990 determining the State responsible for examining applications for asylum lodged in one of the Member States of the European Communities, and in particular Article 3(5) thereof, and WISHING to harmonize the principles under which they will act under this provision;
ANXIOUS to ensure effective protection for asylum seekers and refugees who require it;

HAVE ADOPTED THE FOLLOWING RESOLUTION:

Procedure for application of the concept of host third country
1. The Resolution on manifestly unfounded applications for asylum, adopted by Ministers meeting in London of 30 November and 1 December 1992, refers in paragraph 1(b) to the concept of host third country. The following principles should form the procedural basis for applying the concept of host third country:
(a) The formal identification of a host third country in principle precedes the substantive examination of the application for asylum and its justification.
(b) The principle of the host third country is to be applied to all applicants for asylum, irrespective of whether or not they may be regarded as refugees.
(c) Thus, if there is a host third country, the application for refugee status may not be examined and the asylum applicant may be sent to that country.
(c) If the asylum applicant cannot in practice be sent to a host third country, the provisions of the Dublin Convention will apply.
(e) Any Member State retains the right, for humanitarian reasons, not to remove the asylum applicant to a host third country.
Cases falling within this concept may be considered under the accelerated procedures provided for in the aforementioned Resolution.

Substantive application: requirements and criteria for establishing whether a country is a host third country

2. Fulfilment of all the following fundamental requirements determines a host third country and should be assessed by the Member State in each individual case:

(a) In those third countries, the life or freedom of the asylum applicant must not be threatened, within the meaning of Article 33 of the Geneva Convention.

(b) The asylum applicant must not be exposed to torture or inhuman or degrading treatment in the third country.

(c) It must *either* be the case that the asylum applicant has already been granted protection in the third country or has had an opportunity, at the border or within the territory of the third country, to make contact with that country's authorities in order to seek their protection, before approaching the Member State in which he is applying for asylum, *or* that there is clear evidence of his admissibility to a third country.

(d) The asylum applicant must be afforded effective protection in the host third country against *refoulement*, within the meaning of the Geneva Convention.

If two or more countries fulfil the above conditions, the Member States may expel the asylum applicant to one of those third countries. Member States will take into account, on the basis in particular of the information available from the UNHCR, known practice in the third countries, especially with regard to the principle of *non-refoulement* before considering sending asylum applicants to them.

Dublin Convention

3. The following principles set out the relationship between the application of the concept of the third host country, in accordance with Article 3(5) of the Dublin Convention, and the procedures under the Convention for determining the Member State responsible for examining an asylum application:

(a) The Member State in which the application for asylum has been lodged will examine whether or not the principle of the host third country can be applied. If that State decides to apply the principle, it will set in train the procedures necessary for sending the asylum applicant to the host third country before considering whether or not to transfer responsibility for examining the application for asylum to another Member State pursuant to the Dublin Convention.

(b) A Member State may not decline responsibility for examining an application for asylum, pursuant to the Dublin Convention, by claiming that the requesting Member State should have returned the applicant to a host third country.

(c) Notwithstanding the above, the Member State responsible for examining the application will retain the right, pursuant to its national laws, to send an applicant for asylum to the host third country.

(d) The above provisions do not prejudice the application of Article 3(4) and Article 9 of the Dublin Convention by the Member State in which the application for asylum has been lodged.

Future action

4. Ministers agreed to seek to ensure that their national laws are adapted, if need be, and to incorporate the principles of this resolution as soon as possible, at the latest by the time of the entry into force of the Dublin Convention. Member States will from time to time, in co-operation with the Commission and in consultation with UNHCR, review the operation of these procedures and consider whether any additional measures are necessary.

3.15

Conclusions on Countries in Which There is Generally no Serious Risk of Persecution (London, 30 November and 1 December 1992)

1. The Resolution on manifestly unfounded applications for asylum (WGI 1282) includes at paragraph 1(a) a reference to the concept of countries in which there is in general terms *no serious risk of persecution*.

This concept means that it is a country which can be clearly shown, in an objective and verifiable way, normally not to generate refugees or where it can be clearly shown, in an objective and verifiable way, that circumstances which might in the past have justified recourse to the 1951 Geneva Convention have ceased to exist.[25]

Purpose
2. The aim of developing this concept is to assist in establishing a harmonized approach to applications from countries which give rise to a high proportion of clearly unfounded applications and to reduce pressure on asylum determination systems that are at present excessively burdened with such applications. This will help to ensure that refugees in genuine need of protection are not kept waiting unnecessarily long for their status to be recognized and to discourage misuse of asylum procedures. Member States have the goal of reaching common assessment of certain countries that are of particular interest in this context. To this end, Member States will exchange information within an appropriate framework on any national decisions to consider particular countries as ones in which there is generally no serious risk of persecution. In making such assessments, they will use, as a minimum, the elements of assessment laid down in this document.

3. An assessment by an individual Member State of a country as one in which there is generally no serious risk of persecution should not automatically result in the refusal of all asylum applications from its nationals or their exclusion from individualized determination procedures. A Member State may choose to use such an assessment in channelling cases into accelerated procedures as described in paragraph 2 of the Resolution on manifestly unfounded applications, agreed by Immigration Ministers at their meeting on 30 November and 1 December 1992. The Member State will nevertheless consider the individual claims of all applicants from such countries and any specific indications presented by the applicant which might outweigh a general presumption,

Elements in the assessment
4. The following elements should be taken into consideration in any assessment of the general risk of persecution in a particular country:
(a) *Previous numbers of refugees and recognition rates.* It is necessary to look at the recognition rates for asylum applicants from the country in question who have come to Member States in recent years. Obviously, a situation may change and historically low recognition rates need not continue following (for example) a violent coup. But in the absence of any significant change in the country it is reasonable to assume that low recognition rates will continue and that the country tends not to produce refugees.

---

[25] Report from Immigration Ministers to the European Council meeting in Maastricht (WGI 930, page 38).

(b) *Observance of human rights.* It is necessary to consider the *formal* obligations undertaken by a country in adhering to international human rights instruments and in its domestic law and how *in practice* it meets those obligations. The latter aspect is clearly more important: adherence or non-adherence to a particular instrument cannot in itself result in a country being considered as one in which there is generally no serious risk of persecution. It should be recognized that a pattern of breaches of human rights may be exclusively linked to a particular group within a country's population or to a particular area of the country. The readiness of the country concerned to allow monitoring by NGOs of their human rights observance is also relevant in judging how seriously a country takes its human rights obligations.

(c) *Democratic institutions.* The existence of one or more specific institutions cannot be a *sine qua non* but consideration should be given to democratic processes, elections, political pluralism and freedom of expression and thought. Particular attention should be paid to the availability and effectiveness of legal avenues of protection and redress.

(d) *Stability.* Taking into account the above-mentioned elements, an assessment must be made of the prospect for dramatic change in the immediate future. Any view formed must be reviewed over time in the light of events.

5. Assessments of the risk of persecution in individual countries should be based upon as wide a range of sources of information as possible, including advice and reports from diplomatic missions, international and non-governmental organizations and press reports.
Information from UNHCR has a specific place in this framework. UNHCR forms views of the relative safety of countries of origin both for their own operational purposes and in responding to requests for advice. They have access to sources of information within the UN system and non-governmental organizations.

6. Member States may take into consideration other elements of assessment than those previously mentioned, which will be reviewed from time to time.

3.16

Decision establishing the clearing house[26]

The Ministers responsible for Immigration, hereinafter referred to as 'The Ministers'
Whereas Art. 14 of [the Dublin Convention],
Whereas (...) they decided to establish a clearing house for information, discussion and exchange on asylum [CIREA];
Wishing (...)
Considering (...)

---

[26] London, 30 November, 1 December 1992 SN 2836/93 WG1 1505.
 Ed.: On the same day a decision was taken to set up a Centre for Information, Discussion and Exchange on the Crossing of Borders and Immigration (CIREFI). Although the Cirea document does not refer to CIREFI, para 8. of the CIREFI Decision indicates that the latter may work in conjunction with CIREA on matters which fall within the sphere of interest of both.

Have decided to:
- agree to provisions set out in the Annex for the establishment of [CIREA];
- ask the ad hoc group on Immigration to draw up in proper from the act which (...) will be submitted to the Council for approval under the procedures laid down for that purpose;
- ask the ad hoc Group on Immigration to:

supervise the provisional operation of [CIREA], until the abovementioned act is adopted; (and) to carry out further studies on the definitive structures and financing of [CIREA].

[CIREA], to operate within the framework of the GS of the Council of the European Communities, is hereby established.

The Member States shall designate to participate in [CIREA]:
- their delegates, who shall in principle be the persons dealing with asylum matters in the relevant Council body;
- officials responsible in the Member States for implementing laws and regulations on asylum and more specifically experts responsible for processing asylum applications.

The Commission shall be fully associated with the work of [CIREA].

The tasks and operating methods of [CIREA] shall be as follows:

I. Powers
[CIREA] shall
- for the time being operate provisionally within the framework of this Decision;
- act within the framework of the provisions of the act to be adopted (...) as soon as possible after [the act] comes into force
- be an informal forum for exchanges of information and consultations, without any decision-making power.

II. Objectives
[CIREA] shall gather, exchange and disseminate information and compile documentation on all matters relating to asylum.
The aim of this exchange of information shall be the development within [CIREA] of greater informal consultation, itself designed to facilitate, through competent bodies, coordination and harmonization of asylum practice and policies.
[CIREA] may draw the attention of national bodies and/or the Council to certain problems. Those bodies via the Ministers and/or the Ministers themselves may ask [CIREA] to conduct studies, which may be accompanies by proposals.

III. Gathering of Information
The following information shall be exchanged within [CIREA]:
- Member States' legislation and rules on the right of asylum;
- important policy documents (in their final form)
- important case-law and legal principles;
- statistics.

The Ministers recognize the usefulness to [CIREA] of exchanges of information concerning in particular:

– the situation in the countries of origin of applicants for asylum;
– indications available as an early warning;
– routes taken by asylum seekers and the involvement of intermediaries and/or transport operators;
– reception and accommodation conditions;
– matters already harmonized.

Data stored by [UNHCR] or by other bodies may be taken into account.
This information is to serve as a basis for documentation and discussion and is to be disseminated under the conditions described below.

IV. Dissemination of Information

The Ministers, national authorities participating in the work of [CIREA] and the Commission shall have access to the information held by [CIREA].
The Ministers shall determine the framework and conditions for [CIREA] to disseminate information to international organizations, [NGOs], universities and the media in particular.
When supplying information, Member States shall state how they wish it to be classified. A Member State may oppose the dissemination of information which it has supplied.[27]

3.17

Guidelines for joint reports on third countries (Text adopted by the Council on 20 June 1994)[28]

A. INTRODUCTION

1. The Ministers responsible for immigration have on several occasions spoken of the desirability of drawing up joint situation reports on certain third countries of origin of asylum-seekers. They believe this to be essential if a convergent and eventually harmonized analysis of asylum applications is to be obtained.
2. To achieve this aim fully, there are certain items of information which it is important that the reports should contain.
3. It is suggested that the reports drawn up by Member States' embassies on the spot should contain as far as possible the points set out below.
4. The reports ought to provide an accurate overall picture of the political, economic and

---

[27] Ed.: An activity report on the Centre for Information, Discussion and Exchange on Asylum (Cirea) for 1996 (Text approved by the Council on 26 May 1997) was published in OJ C 191 23.06.97 p. 21; 397Y0623(05); see also [T.32/1/A]: Conclusions of the Council of 19 March 1998 on the exchange of information in the area of asylum and immigration, docs ASIM 162 rev 2 and ASIM 73 rev 6. Moreover, regard could be had to [T.9] and [T.10] on respectively Circulation and confidentiality of joint reports on the situation in certain third countries (OJ C274, 19 September 1996, p. 43); and Guidelines for joint reports on third countries (OJ C274, pp. 52-54).

[28] Official Journal C 274, 19/09/1996 p. 0052–0054; [EUDOR] 396Y0919(16).
[Ed: see also T.9 on the confidentiality and circulation of joint reports, as well as Actors and Sources, as included in this Handbook].

social situation in the third country, without being over-detailed since it is vital that they be drawn up quickly.
5. It has been agreed that the following guidelines could be adjusted according to the country on which a joint report is requested. In some cases this would mean omitting certain points. In others, certain specific questions would be added, depending on the information needed.
6. This outline could be revised in the light of experience.

B. CONTENT OF JOINT REPORTS

I. General political situation
1. Recent political developments
2. Current actual situation in the country, and in particular:
(a) specify the following points if possible regarding its regime:
- free elections;
- multi-party system;
- freedom of opinion and assembly;
- religious freedom;
- independent judiciary;
- security service activity;
- situation of minorities;
(b) security situation in the country (including situations of war or civil war).
3. Prospects
(a) So far as one can tell, is the political situation stable?
(b) Are there any known political deadlines (election dates, etc.)?

II. General human rights situation
1. Has the country acceded to any instruments for the protection of human rights? Preferably state which. How does it comply in practice with the principles they contain?
2. Are international human rights organizations able to monitor whether human rights are respected?
3. Actual practice as regards human rights Are people exposed to acts contrary to human rights, in particular:
(a) torture, inhuman or degrading treatment and punishment (e.g. beating imposed by a court, legislation enshrining racial discrimination);
(b) frequent use of the death penalty (in countries where such sentences continue to be carried out);
(c) conditions of imprisonment which are contrary to human rights, arbitrary arrest, lack of freedom to travel, denial of recourse to the courts, or specific measures against political prisoners?

III. Specific information on persecution for reasons of race, religion, nationality, membership of a particular social group or political opinion
1. Persecution by the State
(a) Are there any forms of persecution by the State, such as repressive measures or arbitrary treatment by State bodies of certain groups of individuals?
(b) What is the extent of such persecution, especially as regards:
- Interference with life, health and freedom including religious freedom?

– Extreme conditions involved in military service, where relevant?
– Other types of social discrimination?
2. Are there other forms of indirect persecution by the State (acts of persecution not carried out by the public authorities but attributable to them), such as the situation where the national authorities are unwilling to give sufficient protection to members of a particular group in the population who are seriously threatened by their fellow citizens?

IV. Possibility of fleeing within the State (in the event of persecution)
1. Are there persecution situations confined to one part of the State's territory?
2. Is it possible to escape such persecution by going to another part of the territory?

V. Movement of nationals of the State
1. What sort of controls are carried out at these States' external frontiers (air, sea and land) as regards their own nationals? In particular, what formalities do the nationals of these States have to complete on entering or leaving? Are they discriminatory compared with the controls imposed on other nationals?
2. On the basis of the information available, are there any illegal networks facilitating the departure of nationals of the State?

VI. Authenticity of documents
1. What credence should be given to documents held by nationals and issued by the national authorities, especially travel documents?
2. Can nationals of the country easily get hold of false official documents or certificates?

VII. Return to country of origin
1. Does the fact of having lodged an asylum application in another country mean that a national risks being subjected to punishments, torture or inhuman or degrading treatment when he returns to his country of origin?
2. What attitude do the State's authorities take towards foreign nationals, especially asylum-seekers?

VIII. Economic and social situation
It is useful to indicate general features of the economic and social situation that might induce people to leave the country. For example:
1. What is the current general economic situation in the country and, where appropriate, in some of its regions, and what are the prospects for future development?
2. What is the current unemployment level and what are the expected trends?
3. Is there a welfare system?

IX. Preparation of reports on host third countries
The above guidelines concerning countries of origin should be used as far as possible when drawing up reports on host third countries.
Details on the following points would also be desirable:
1. Has the country acceded to the Geneva Convention of 28 July 1951 on the Status of Refugees, the European Convention for the Protection of Human Rights and Fundamental Freedoms or any other similar human rights convention? How does it comply in practice with the principles they contain (where this adds to the answers given under II.1)?

2. Can any national of a third country submit an application for asylum in the host State? Is it possible, at the frontier or in the territory, for him to request the protection of the authorities of that country before applying to the Member State where he is seeking asylum? If not, is this the case for persons of certain nationalities or origins?
3. Is it certain that he can be admitted to the host country? If not, is that the case for persons of certain nationalities or origins?
4. Does the asylum-seeker benefit or potentially benefit from effective protection against 'refoulement' as defined by the Geneva Convention?

X. Place and date of the drawing up of the report
It would be useful to state where and when the joint report was drawn up.

3.18

Circulation and confidentiality of joint reports on the situation in certain third countries (Text adopted by the Council on 20 June 1994)[29]

– The joint reports, possibly accompanied by an internal note from Cirea, addressed to Steering Group I (Asylum/Immigration) and containing its observations, will be sent to the heads of delegations in that Group and they will be responsible for deciding on national circulation of joint reports within the limits laid down in the two indents below.
– The national authorities responsible for matters concerning asylum and third country nationals will be able to use the reports together with the other items of information at their disposal.
– Depending on national procedures, these reports may be made available to the parties involved in a dispute when there is an appeal against a decision by the authorities responsible for matters concerning asylum or aliens.

3.19

Council Decision of 26 June 1997 on monitoring the implementation of instruments adopted concerning asylum (97/420/JHA)[30]

THE COUNCIL OF THE EUROPEAN UNION,
Having regard to the Treaty on European Union and in particular Article K.3(2)(a) thereof,
Having regard to the priority work programme adopted by the Council on 30 November 1993, calling in particular for the preparation of an annual report on achievements in the fields of justice and home affairs and to the Council Resolution on 14 October 1996, laying down the priorities for cooperation in the field of justice and home affairs for the period from 1 July 1996 to 30 June 1998,[31]

---

[29] Official Journal C 274, 19/09/1996 p. 0043–0043 [EUDOR] 396Y0919(12).
[30] Official Journal L 178, 07/07/1997 p. 0006–0007 [EUDOR] 397D0420.
[31] OJ No C 319, 26.10.1996, p. 1.

Having regard to the resolutions of the European Parliament adopted in the field of asylum,

Whereas Article K.1(1) of the Treaty states that Member States are to regard asylum policy as a matter of common interest;

Whereas monitoring of the implementation by Member States of the instruments adopted in this area will reveal the practical effect of the Council's work in this matter and provide useful lessons for its future work,

HAS DECIDED AS FOLLOWS:

Article 1

Each year, the Presidency shall forward to the Member States a questionnaire designed to show how they have implemented the instruments concerning asylum adopted by the Council and by the Ministers responsible for immigration. The questionnaire shall refer to the following matters:

– provisions, policies and practical measures adopted during the preceding year by the Member States in any of the areas covered by the instruments referred to in the first paragraph,

– any difficulties encountered in adopting such provisions, policies and practical measures,

– the likelihood of provisions, policies and practical measures in the areas referred to in the first indent being adopted in the near future,

– practical application of the aforementioned instruments, provisions, policies and practical measures and any difficulties encountered therewith.

Article 2

On the basis of the questionnaire referred to in Article 1, Member States shall prepare an information note in which they may refer to or include relevant parts of their regular submissions to the Centre for Information, Reflection and Exchange on Asylum (CIREA).

Article 3

The General Secretariat of the Council shall translate the information notes referred to in Article 2 and make them available to all Member States and to the Commission. It shall also prepare a summary report based on the information notes.

Article 4

On the basis of the summary report and any other relevant material, for example from UNHCR and, if appropriate, from non-governmental organizations, the Presidency, in conjunction with the Commission, and after consultation of the UNHCR shall draw up a report which shall contain an analysis suggesting inter alia whether there are issues requiring a further exchange of views between Member States and whether any additional measures are necessary. This report shall be examined within the framework of the Council with a view to its submission for consideration by the Council. The Presidency will seek the views of the UNHCR on the report and ensure that any comments are communicated to Member States.

Article 5
The questionnaire shall be sent to the Member States before 1 July each year and Member States shall submit their information notes before 1 October following. The first questionnaire shall cover implementation for the period up to 1 July 1997.

3.20

Council Decision of 26 May 1997 on the exchange of information concerning assistance for the voluntary repatriation of third-country nationals (97/340/JHA)[32]

THE COUNCIL OF THE EUROPEAN UNION,
Having regard to the Treaty on European Union, and in particular Article K.3(2) (a) thereof,
Whereas Article K.1(3) of the Treaty on European Union states that the Member States shall regard immigration policy and policy regarding nationals of third countries as matters of common interest;
Whereas point 111 of the Communication by the Commission dated 23 February 1994 on immigration and asylum policy suggests that Member States' policies on the voluntary return of third-country nationals be approximated;
Whereas a number of Member States have established programmes to support the voluntary return of legally as well as illegally resident third-country nationals;
Whereas, in the case of legally resident third-country nationals, Member States' policies should aim at their integration into society and whereas assistance for voluntary return should not be interpreted as reflecting a policy of actively encouraging such return, but is purely designed to facilitate return of those who have taken a decision of their own free will to this effect;
Whereas assistance for the voluntary return of illegally resident third-country nationals is in line with the European humanitarian tradition and may contribute to finding a dignified solution to reducing the number of illegally resident third-country nationals in the Member States; whereas it should be avoided that such assistance leads to undesired incentive effects;
Whereas this Decision is without prejudice to the provisions of the European Convention for the Protection of Human Rights and Fundamental Freedoms of 4 November 1950 and the Geneva Convention of 28 July 1951 relating to the Status of Refugees, as amended by the New York Protocol of 31 January 1967,

HAS DECIDED AS FOLLOWS:

Article 1 Information exchange
1. Those Member States which have taken steps to develop programmes to support the voluntary return of third-country nationals to their country of origin shall report annually on them to the General Secretariat of the Council. The General Secretariat shall circulate such information to all Member States and the Commission.

---

[32] Official Journal L 147, 05/06/1997 p. 0003–0004 [EUDOR] 397D0340.

2. Information on these national return programmes shall, in particular, include the following information:
– the authorities responsible for carrying out the programme, i.e. non-governmental and/or international organizations;
– the scope of the programme in terms of the persons covered;
– any further requirements to be met by individual returnees in order to be considered for assistance under the programme;
– any requirements to be met by the country of origin under the programme;
– the type and level of assistance granted (e.g. travel expenses for the returnee and his/her family, removal costs, repatriation allowance);
– estimate of the effects of the programme, including the number of beneficiaries and the occurrence of any incentive effects.

Article 2 Analysis
1. The General Secretariat of the Council shall make available annually to Member States and the Commission a draft report on the information received on the basis of Article 1. This report shall be exhaustive in nature and shall contain specific information on each of the points listed in Article 1(2).
2. The draft report referred to in paragraph 1 shall be examined by the Member States concerned and the Commission and adjusted if necessary.

Article 3 Coordination
1. On the basis of the draft report referred to in Article 2(1), Member States concerned and the Commission shall, within the Council, exchange their views on the programmes referred to in Article 1. In so doing, they shall, in particular, compare the scope, conditions and effects of those programmes with a view to their possible approximation.
2. The Member States concerned which have not introduced these programmes shall examine the results and usefulness thereof.

Article 4
1. This Decision shall be published in the Official Journal.
2. The Member States concerned shall draw up the report mentioned in Article 1 for the first time within six months of the publication of this Decision in the Official Journal.

3.21

Council Recommendation of 30 November 1994 concerning a specimen bilateral readmission agreement between a Member State and a third country[33]

THE COUNCIL OF THE EUROPEAN UNION,
Having regard to the Treaty on European Union, and in particular Article K.1(3) thereof,
Recalling that these policies are regarded as matters of common interest under the Treaty,
Determined to combat unauthorized immigration to the Member States,

---

[33] Official Journal C 274, 19/09/1996 p. 0020–0024 [EUDOR] 396Y0919(07).

Noting that the laying down of principles which must appear in bilateral and multilateral readmission agreements appears in the action plan in the field of justice and home affairs which was approved by the Council and endorsed by the European Council in December 1993,

Recalling that these principles were approved by the Council in May 1994 and that it was agreed to devise a specimen readmission agreement on the basis of these principles at a later date,

Whereas the specimen readmission agreement is to be used flexibly by the Member States and that it may be adapted to the particular needs of the Contracting Parties;

Hereby RECOMMENDS

that with effect from 1 January 1995 the specimen agreement attached should be used by the Member States as a basis for negotiation with third countries on the conclusion of readmission agreements.

ANNEX

SPECIMEN AGREEMENT
between the Government of (... Member State ...) and the Government of (... third country ..) on the readmission of persons residing without authorization
(Readmission Agreement)
THE GOVERNMENT OF (... MEMBER STATE ...) and THE GOVERNMENT OF (... THIRD COUNTRY ...),
hereinafter referred to as the 'Contracting Parties', desirous of facilitating the readmission of persons staying illegally on the territory of the other Contracting Party, i.e. persons who do not, or who no longer, fulfil the conditions in force for entry or residence, and of facilitating the transit of persons in a spirit of cooperation and on the basis of reciprocity, HAVE AGREED AS FOLLOWS:

Article 1
Readmission of own nationals
1. Each Contracting Party shall readmit at the request of the other Contracting Party and without any formality persons who do not, or who no longer, fulfil the conditions in force for entry or residence on the territory of the requesting Contracting Party provided that it is proved or may be validly assumed that they possess the nationality of the requested Contracting Party. The same shall apply to persons who have been deprived of the nationality of the requested Contracting Party since entering the territory of the requesting Contracting Party without at least having been promised naturalization by the requesting Contracting Party.
2. Upon application by the requesting Contracting Party, the requested Contracting Party shall without delay issue the persons to be readmitted with the travel documents required for their repatriation.
3. The requesting Contracting Party shall readmit such persons again under the same conditions if checks reveal that they where not in possession of the nationality of the requested Contracting Party when they departed from the territory of the requesting Contracting Party. This shall not apply if the readmission obligation is based on the fact that the requested Contracting Party deprived the person in question of its nationality after that person had entered the territory of the requesting Contracting Party without that person at least having been promised naturalization by the requesting Contracting Party.

Article 2
Readmission in the case of third-country nationals who entered via the external frontier
1. The Contracting Party via whose external frontier a person can be proved, or validly assumed, to have entered who does not meet, or who no longer meets, the conditions in force for entry or residence on the territory of the requesting Contracting Party shall readmit the person at the request of that Contracting Party and without any formality.
2. For the purposes of this Article, the external frontier shall be deemed to be the first frontier to have been crossed which is not a frontier common to the Contracting Parties.
3. The readmission obligation pursuant to paragraph 1 shall not apply in respect of a person who was in possession of a valid residence permit issued by the requesting Contracting Party when the person entered the territory of that Contracting Party or who was issued with a residence permit by that Contracting Party after entering its territory.
4. The Contracting Parties shall make every effort to give priority to deporting nationals of an adjacent State to their country of origin.

Article 3
Readmission of nationals of third countries by the Contracting Party responsible for the entry
1. If a person who has arrived in the territory of the requesting Contracting Party does not fulfil the conditions in force for entry or residence and if that person is in possession of a valid visa issued by the other Contracting Party or a valid residence permit issued by the requested party, that Contracting Party shall readmit the person without any formality upon application by the requesting Contracting Party.
2. If both Contracting Parties issued a visa or a residence permit, responsibility shall reside with the Contracting Party whose visa or residence permit expires last.
3. Paragraphs 1 and 2 shall not apply where a transit visa was issued.

Article 4
Residence permits
A residence permit pursuant to Article 2(3) and Article 3 means an authorization of any type issued by one Contracting Party, entitling the person to reside on the territory of that Contracting Party. This shall not include temporary permission to reside on the territory of one of the Contracting Parties in connection with the processing of an asylum application.

Article 5
Time limits
1. The requested Contracting Party shall reply to readmission requests addressed to it without delay, and in any event within a maximum of 15 days.
2. The requested Contracting Party shall take charge of persons whose readmission has been agreed to without delay, and in any event, within a maximum of one month. Upon application by the requesting Contracting Party, this time limit may be extended by the time taken to deal with legal or practical obstacles.

Article 6
Time limit after which the readmission obligation will lapse The application for readmission must be submitted within a maximum of one year of the Contracting Party noting the illegal entry and presence of the said national of a third country on its territory.

Article 7
Transit
1. Without prejudice to Article 11, the Contracting Parties shall allow third-country nationals to pass through their territory in transit if the other Contracting Party so requests and if admission to other possible States of transit and to the State of destination is assured.
2 It shall not be essential for the requested Contracting Party to issue a transit visa.
3 Notwithstanding any authorization issued, persons taken in charge for transit purposes may be returned to the other Contracting Party if circumstances within the meaning of Article 11 subsequently arise or come to light which stand in the way of a transit operation or if the onward journey or admission by the State of destination is no longer assured.
4. The Contracting Parties shall endeavour to restrict transit operations to aliens who cannot be returned to their States of origin directly.

Article 8
Data protection
In so far as personal data have to be communicated in order to implement this Agreement, such information may concern only the following:
1. the particulars of the person to be transferred and, where necessary, of the members of the person's family (surname, forename, any previous names, nicknames or pseudonyms, aliases, date and place of birth, sex, current and any previous nationality);
2. passport, identity card and other identity and travel documents and laissez-passer (number, period of validity, date of issue, issuing authority, place of issue, etc.);
3. other details needed to identify the persons to be transferred;
4. stopping places and itineraries;
5. residence permits or visas issued by one of the Contracting Parties;
6. in the cases covered by Article 7, the place where the asylum application was submitted and the date of submission of any previous asylum application, the date of submission of the present asylum application, the present stage of the procedure and the content of any decision taken.

Article 9
Costs
1. The costs of transporting persons taken in charge pursuant to Articles 1, 2 and 3 shall be borne by the requesting Contracting Party as far as the border of the requested party.
2. The costs of transit as far as the border of the State of destination, and, where necessary, the costs arising from return transport, shall be borne by the requesting Contracting Party in accordance with Article 7.

Article 10
Committee of Experts
1. The Contracting Parties shall provide each other with mutual assistance in the application and interpretation of this Agreement. To this end, they shall set up a Committee of

Experts to:

(a) monitor application of this Agreement;
(b) submit proposals for resolving problems associated with the application of this Agreement;
(c) propose amendments and additions to this Agreement;
(d) prepare and recommend appropriate measures for combating illegal immigration.

2. The Contracting Parties shall reserve the right to agree to the proposals and measures or not to do so.

3. The Committee shall be composed of three representatives of each Contracting Party. The Contracting Parties shall appoint the chairman and his deputies from among them, and shall also appoint alternate members. Additional experts may be associated with the consultations.

4. The Committee shall meet at the initiative of one of the chairmen and at least once a year.

Article 11

Clause stipulating that international agreements/conventions shall not be affected These agreements shall not affect the Contracting Parties' obligations arising from:

1. the Convention of 28 July 1951 on the Status of Refugees as amended by the Protocol of 31 January 1967 on the Status of Refugees;
2. international conventions on extradition and transit;
3. the Convention of 4 November 1950 for the Protection of Human Rights and Fundamental Freedoms;
4. international conventions on asylum, in particular under the Dublin Convention of 15 June 1990 determining the State responsible for examining applications for asylum lodged in a Member State of the European Community;
5. international conventions and agreements on the readmission of foreign nationals.

Article 12

Entry into force

This Agreement shall enter into force on the first day of the second month following its signature. It shall not be applied until the date agreed upon by the Contracting Parties in an exchange of notes.

Article 13

Suspension, termination

1. This Agreement is concluded for an indefinite period.
2. After informing the other Contracting Party each Contracting Party may suspend this Agreement by giving notification on important grounds, in particular on the grounds of the protection of State security, public order or public health. The Contracting Parties shall notify each other of the cancellation of any such measure without delay via diplomatic channels.
3. After informing the other Contracting Party, each Contracting Party may terminate this Agreement on important grounds by giving notification.
4. The suspension or termination of this Agreement shall become effective on the first day of the month following the month in which notification was received by the other Contracting Party.

Done at ... this ... day of ... 19.. in two originals, one in the ... language and one in the ... language, each text being equally authentic. On behalf of the Government of (... Member State ...) On behalf of the Government of (... third country ...)

3.22

Council Recommendation of 24 July 1995 on the Guiding Principles to be Followed in Drawing Up Protocols on the Implementation of Readmission Agreements[34]

THE COUNCIL OF THE EUROPEAN UNION,
Having regard to the Treaty on European Union, and in particular Article K.1(3) thereof,
Recalling that the Council has adopted a recommendation concerning a specimen bilateral readmission agreement between a Member State and a third Country,
Whereas such readmission agreements are often accompanied by protocols laying down certain technical details for their implementation; whereas a series of guiding principles should therefore be adopted for Member States to use as a basis when negotiating such protocols;

RECOMMENDS that, as from 1 July 1995, the Member States should use the following guiding principles as a basis for negotiations with third countries when drawing up protocols on implementing readmission agreements.

I. Readmission procedures

1. Common forms
For the return/readmission of persons residing without authorization, it is recommended that provision be made for the Contracting Parties to use common forms. The forms concerned are as follows:
– record of the return/readmission of a person under the simplified procedure,
– request for the readmission/transit of a person,
– record of the return/readmission of a person.
Member states could use the three documents annexed hereto as a basis for drawing up such forms, incorporating the relevant headings from them according to the specific nature of relations with the third country party to the agreement and the resulting information requirements. The need for simplicity and speed should be the prime concern.

2. Return/readmission under the simplified procedure
Persons apprehended in a border area are to be returned/readmitted under the simplified procedure. A provision allowing this should therefore be included in the protocol. The Contracting Parties will determine the total time taken by the simplified readmission procedure (comprising the submission and answering of all requests), which should in any event be very short. Member States may take as a basis agreements already signed by

---

[34] OJ C274, 19 September 1996, p. 25-33.

some of them in which that time does not exceed 48 hours. Formalities for the return of a person should be simplified in the case of this procedure. Notification of the return would be given in any form (by telephone, fax, telex or orally) and it would be carried out directly by the local border authorities. If necessary, a record (see I.1) may be drawn up.

3. Return/readmission under the normal procedure
This procedure is applicable where a person cannot be returned or readmitted under the simplified procedure. The readmission request should be made and the answer given in writing. The Parties could take as a basis the document annexed hereto. Answers should be compulsory and be given within a short time determined by the Parties. In accordance with the specimen draft bilateral agreement, the time in question must not exceed 15 days. However, it would be desirable for Member States to take as a basis agreements already signed in which this time is shorter.

II. Means of identifying persons to be readmitted

1. Effect of proof or a presumption
Proof produced of nationality and entry should have to be accepted by the Parties without further investigation. A presumption established of nationality and entry should be deemed accepted by the Parties unless the requested party proves otherwise.

2. Proof or a presumption of nationality or of entry via an external frontier
The protocol should clearly lay down the means of proving or establishing a presumption of nationality. Nationality may be proved by means of:
– nationality papers which can be definitely ascribed to a particular person,
– any type of passport (national, diplomatic or official duty passport or officially issued passport substitutes with a photograph) or any other travel document indicating nationality,
– consular registration cards,
– identity cards (even if provisional or temporary),
– a minor's travel document in lieu of passport,
– provisional identity papers,
– service record books and military passes.
A presumption of nationality may be established in particular by means of:
– specific information from the official authorities,
– an official service pass,
– a company pass,
– a driving license,
– an extract from register office records,
– a seaman's book,
– a bargeman's identity document,
– photocopies of any of the above documents,
– statements by witnesses,
– particulars supplied by the person concerned,
– the language of the person concerned.
The protocol should also clearly lay down the means of proving or establishing a presumption of entry via an external frontier, under Article 2 of the specimen readmission agreement.

Entry via an external frontier may be proved by means of:
- an entry stamp or equivalent entry in a travel document,
- an exit stamp of a State adjacent to a Member State, taking into account the travel route and the date of the frontier crossing,
- an entry stamp in a false or falsified passport,
- travel tickets which can formally establish entry across an external frontier,
- fingerprints taken by authorities at the time of crossing an external frontier.

A presumption of entry via an external frontier may be established in particular by means of:
- statements by the person to be transferred,
- statements by officials and other persons,
- fingerprints other than those taken by the authorities at the time of crossing an external frontier, travel tickets,
- hotel bills,
- cards for access to public or private amenities in the Member States,
- appointment cards for doctors, dentists etc.,
- data showing that the person to be transferred has used the services of a facilitator or travel agency.

II. Designation of the competent authorities

The protocol should stipulate that Ministers with responsibility for border controls are to designate the border posts which may be used for aliens' readmission and entry in transit and the central or local authorities competent to deal with readmission and transit requests. The choice should be geared to efficiency and speed.

IV. Conditions for transit of third-country nationals under escort

In their relations with third-country Contracting Parties, Member States could make provision for the use of a readmission/transit form for requests for transit under escort in accordance with Article 7 of the specimen readmission agreement. They could use the appropriate form annexed hereto as a basis. However, the parties could dispense with such formalities for the transit of a third-country national being repatriated by one of the Contracting Parties via an airport in the other Contracting Party. In that event, the competent authority of the requesting party would notify the competent authority of the other party in good time of the intended repatriation, informing it of the identity of the person concerned, the flight details and the particulars of any official escorts.

V. Data protection

An article on data protection could be inserted; its content will largely depend on the legislation in force within Member States. It should in any event be stipulated that information must be supplied only for the purposes for which the agreement has been concluded.

VI. Conditions of applicability of the protocol

It should be stipulated that the protocol is to enter into force at the same time as the readmission agreement, that its application is to be suspended upon suspension of the agreement's application and that it will cease to be applicable once the agreement is no longer applicable.[35]

3.23

Council Recommendation of 22 December 1995 on concerted action and cooperation in carrying out expulsion measures (96/C 5/02)[36]

THE COUNCIL OF THE EUROPEAN UNION,
Having regard to the recommendation of the Ministers of the Member States of the European Communities responsible for immigration of 30 November 1992 concerning transit for the purposes of expulsion and the addendum thereto of 1 and 2 June 1993,
Whereas Article K.1(3)(c) of the Treaty on European Union stipulates that combating unauthorized immigration, residence and work by nationals of third countries on the territory of Member States are matters of common interest;
Whereas the Council has already adopted specific measures to secure better control of migratory flows and to prevent third-country nationals entering Member States' territory unauthorized and remaining there illegally;
Whereas expulsion measures in respect of third-country nationals whose presence is unauthorized cannot be carried out owing to the absence of travel or identity documents;
Whereas, in order to achieve the effective carrying-out of expulsion measures, recommendations addressed to the Member States of the European Union and aimed at better coordination of those measures should be adopted at Council level;
Whereas the provisions of this recommendation are without prejudice to the European Convention for the Protection of Human Rights and Fundamental Freedoms of 4 November 1950 of to the Geneva Convention of 28 July 1951 relating to the Status of Refugees, as amended by the New York Protocol of 31 January 1967,

HEREBY RECOMMENDS MEMBER STATES' GOVERNMENTS:

to apply the principles set out below:

– with a view to cooperation in the procurement of the necessary documentation
1. to implement specific mechanisms to improve the procurement of the necessary documentation from the consular authorities of the third State to which third-country nationals are to be expelled when they lack travel or identity documents;

---

[35] Ed: the 'Record of the return/readmission of a person under the simplified procedure'; nor, 'the request for readmission / transit of a person'; nor 'the record of the return / readmission of a person' forms have been reproduced in this Handbook.

[36] Official Journal C 005, 10/01/1996 p. 0003–0007 [EUDOR] 396Y0110(02)/396Y0110(02)R(01).

2. where Member States experience repeated difficulties with certain third States in the matter of procuring documentation:
(a) to make a particular effort to arrange for persons to be expelled to be identified by the consular authorities;
(b) to issue repeated invitations to consular authorities to visit centres in which third-country nationals are being held, where appropriate, in order to identify them for the purpose of providing documentation;
(c) to urge the same authorities to issue travel documents with a period of validity sufficient for expulsion to be carried out;
3. in the first instance to make use of the provisions on presumption of nationality of the standard readmission agreement adopted by the Council on 30 November 1994;
4. to issue, where it is not possible to obtain the necessary travel documents by using the above means, the standard travel document adopted by the Council on 30 November 1994;

— with a view to cooperation in carrying out transit for expulsion purposes
5. to cooperate to facilitate transit for expulsion purposes when the decision has been adopted by another Member State on the basis of the principles set out herein:
(a) In accordance with the Ministers' recommendation of 30 November 1992 concerning transit for the purposes of expulsion and the addendum thereto of 1 and 2 June 1993, which are annexed hereto, any Member State may, at the request of another Member State, authorize the transit of a third-country national across its territory for expulsion purposes.
(b) The Member State requesting the transit shall notify the requested State whether it considers it essential for the person being expelled to have an escort.
(c) The requested State shall be free to decide on the transit procedures; whether the escort is to be provided by the Member State which decided on the expulsion, whether it will provide the escort itself during transit or whether escort during transit will be arranged jointly with the State which decided on the expulsion.
(d) In the case of unescorted transit, the Member State which adopted the expulsion measure may, giving sufficient notice, request the State which has authorized transit to take the necessary measures in order to ensure departure to the place of destination.
(e) In the event of a third-country national's refusal to embark in the transit Member State, the Member States concerned may consider, in accordance with their laws and lest expulsion prove impossible to carry out, the possibility of availing themselves of, or seeking to establish, the appropriate legal machinery for enforcing expulsion.
(f) The transit Member State may return the third-country national to the territory of the Member State which adopted the expulsion measure if, for any reason whatsoever, the expulsion measure cannot be carried out.
(g) Member States may determine bilaterally the circumstances in which it may be possible to forego the refunding of costs on a case-by-case basis and replace it with an annual settlement of expenses occasioned by expulsion operations at either party's request;

— with a view to concerted action in carrying out expulsions
6. to carry out expulsions, in appropriate instances, as a concerted effort with other Member States on the basis of the following principles:
(a) the Member State which adopts the expulsion measure shall assume responsibility for

carrying out measures for the expulsion of a third-country national it has itself adopted and shall use the resources available on the air transport market or, if necessary, resources it has organized itself.

(b) The Member State which adopts the expulsion measure may request cooperation from another Member State to locate seats available to carry out the expulsion by air.

(c) The Member State whose cooperation has been requested for carrying out an expulsion measure by air shall be entitled to refuse to allow expulsion to be carried out from its territory.

(d) With a view to coordinating the carrying-out of expulsion measures, each Member State shall inform other Member States which authority in its territory shall be responsible for:
— centralizing information on seats available on flights for expulsion purposes,
— contacting the competent authorities in the other Member States with a view to using seats available on flights,
— requesting authorization from other Member States to use seats available on flights departing from them,
— exchanging information with the authorities in other Member States in relation to carrying out expulsions by air,

— with a view to monitoring the implementation of this recommendation the Council shall regularly review the progress achieved in relation to the practical application of the cooperation and concerted action measures
covered by this recommendation.

Annex I

RECOMMENDATION concerning transit for the purposes of expulsion (approved by the Ministers on 30 November 1992)
The Ministers with responsibility for immigration,
CONSIDERING Member States' practices regarding transit for the purposes of expulsion;
WHEREAS it is appropriate to standardize such practices with a view to their harmonization;
WHEREAS the measures to be applied should meet the criteria of speed, efficiency and economy,
RECOMMEND that the following guidelines be applied:

I
For the purposes of this recommendation 'transit' means the transit of a person who is not a national of a Member State through the territory or the transit zone of a port or airport of a Member State.

II
A Member State which has decided to expel a third-country national
— to a third country should in principle do so without the person transiting through the territory of another Member State,
— to another Member State should in principle do so without the person transiting through the territory of a third Member State.

III

1. Where there are special reasons to justify this and, in particular, in the interests of efficiency, speed and economy, Member States may ask another Member State to authorize entry into its territory or transit through its territory of third-country nationals who are the subject of an expulsion measure.
2. The State which has adopted the expulsion measure shall prove, before such a request is made, that the expellee's right to continue his journey and to enter the country of destination are guaranteed in the normal way.
3. The State to which the request is made shall deal with it without prejudice to the cases referred to in section VI.

IV

The State taking the expulsion measure shall notify the transit State whether the person being expelled needs to be escorted. The transit State may:
- authorize the State which adopted the expulsion measure to provide the escort itself,
- decide to provide the escort itself, or
- decide to provide the escort in cooperation with the State which adopted the expulsion measure.

V

1 Requests for transit for purposes of expulsion must include information concerning:
- the identity of the third-country national being expelled,
- the State of final destination,
- the nature and date of the expulsion decision, and the authority which took the decision,
- factors enabling a judgment to be made as to whether the third-country national can be admitted to the country of final destination or the second transit country,
- the travel documents or other personal documents in the possession of the person concerned,
- the identification of the department making the request,
- the conditions of transit through the requested State (timetable, route, means of transport, etc.),
- whether an escort is required, and the details thereof.

2. Requests for transit for expulsion purposes must be submitted as soon as possible in accordance with the domestic legislation of the requested State to the authorities responsible for expulsion, who must reply to the request at the earliest opportunity.
3. The transit State may request information, particularly concerning the need for transit.

VI

Cases in which transit for expulsion purposes may be refused:
- where the third-country national who is the subject of a request for overland transit constitutes a threat to public order, national security or the international relations of the transit State,
- where the information referred to in Section V(3) is not considered satisfactory.

VII

If for some reason the expulsion measure cannot be carried out, the State through which transit is to take place may return the expellee, without any formalities, to the territory of the requesting State.

VIII

Where expulsion cannot be carried out at the expense of the third-country national or a third party, the requesting State shall be liable for:
– travel and other expenses, including escort costs, up until the departure from the territory of the Member State of transit of a third-country national whose transit has been authorized
– the costs involved in any return.

IX

These recommendations shall not preclude closer cooperation between two or more Member States.

X

Member States which propose to conduct negotiations with another Member State or with a third State on transit for purposes of expulsion shall inform the other Member States in due time.

XI

This recommendation shall not contravene the provisions of the European Convention for the Protection of Human Rights and Fundamental Freedoms of 4 November 1950, nor those of the Convention on the Status of Refugees of 28 July 1951. This recommendation shall not contravene the provisions of international conventions currently in force concerning extradition and extradition in transit. This recommendation shall not replace extradition and transit extradition procedures by the transit procedure for expulsion purposes.

Annex II

ADDENDUM to the recommendation concerning transit for the purposes of expulsion (approved by the Ministers on 1 and 2 June 1993)
1. With a view to meeting the criteria of efficiency, speed and economy in connection with transit for purposes of expulsion a distinction may be made between the different expulsion measures, by air, sea or land, applied by the Member States.
2. Expulsion by air accompanied by transit through the transit zone of an airport should be excluded from the provisions requiring an entry and transit authorization (see Section III of the recommendation), so that in such cases it will be sufficient to notify the country of transit.
3. Notification of transit for expulsion purposes by air should contain the information required for transit requests indicated in Section V of the recommendation.
4. In the case of expulsion by land or sea, requests for and notifications of entry into the territory of a State or transit through that State shall be addressed to a central contact body designated by the transit State, in accordance with the recommendations set out in the recommendation.

If, in the case of expulsion by air, the transit State does not grant permission, that information must be communicated to the requesting State within 24 hours of the notification of transit.

5. Member States shall draw up a joint list of contact bodies. In the case of expulsion by air, it would be desirable to contact directly the competent official(s) of the transit airport concerned or, in accordance with national procedures, any other competent official, provided that the 24-hour rule is observed (see point 4 above).

3.24

Council Recommendation of 30 November 1994 concerning the adoption of a standard travel document for the expulsion of third-country nationals[37]

THE COUNCIL OF THE EUROPEAN UNION,
Having regard to the Treaty on European Union, and in particular Article K.1(3)(c) thereof,
Whereas combating unauthorized immigration, residence and work by nationals of third countries on the territory of Member States is regarded as a matter of common interest;
Noting that consultation and cooperation on the execution of expulsion measures is considered a priority action in the 1994 work programme;
Acknowledging that a recent seminar on expulsion measures showed that the great majority of Member States experience difficulties in cases of third-country nationals possessing no travel documents who are required to be expelled from their territory;
Desirous of improving the efficiency with which expulsion measures are executed,

HEREBY RECOMMENDS THAT:

– with effect from 1 January 1995 the attached standard travel document valid for a single journey shall be used as appropriate by all Member States in the case of third-country nationals being expelled from the territory of the Union,
– the document shall be established in the language of the Member State executing the expulsion order,
– the document, where appropriate, shall be translated into both French and English.[38]

---

[37] Official Journal C 274, 19/09/1996 p. 0018–0019 [EUDOR] 396Y0919(06).

4. COMMENTARIES

Various efforts have been undertaken to provide commentaries which should be read in conjunction with the text of the various acquis documents. Some commentaries have been published and/or provided in training sessions, but they seem sometimes somehow somewhat value driven.

It was only November 1999 that the Commission made commentaries available which could be considered authoritative ones. They cover subjects like the Joint Position of March 1996, of great importance for a harmonized interpretation of the 1951 Refugee Convention, and the 30 November 1992 London Resolutions on issues like manifestly unfounded applications, host third countries, minimum guarantees etcetera.

This Chapter starts with a Working Document dated 3 March 1999 which contains a fairly detailed description of what may be ahead whilst Europe strives for a common asylum policy. The Commentary on the character of the acquis has been reproduced in the Chapter containing the various lists.

This Chapter, therefore, entails:

4.1	Commission Working Document dd 3 March 1999: Towards Common Standards on Asylum Procedures	211
4.2	Joint Position, 4 March 1996 [JP]	224
4.3	Minimum Guarantees for Asylum Procedures [MG]	233
4.4	Host Third Countries [HTC]	245
4.5	('Safe') Countries ('of Origin') [CoO]	250
4.6	Manifestly Unfounded Applications [MUA]	253
4.7	Unaccompanied Minors [UM]	260
4.8	Readmission Agreements	267
4.9	Dublin and Eurodac	272

4.1

COMMISSION WORKING DOCUMENT
Towards common standards on asylum procedures
(Brussels, 3 March 1999)

PREFACE

The Treaty establishing the European Community as amended by the Treaty of Amsterdam will require the Council to adopt measures on minimum standards on procedures in Member States for granting or withdrawing refugee status. The Commission intends to bring forward a proposal for a Community legal instrument on asylum procedures after the entry into force of the new treaty.

This working document is intended to launch a discussion on asylum procedures which will take place in the Council and the European Parliament. After this debate has taken place, the Commission will finalise a proposal for a Community legal instrument on asylum procedures. The paper will also serve as the basis for a dialogue with the United Nations High Commissioner for Refugees and with the non-governmental sector. This is consistent with declaration number 17 on the Treaty of Amsterdam, which states that consultations shall be established with the United Nations High Commissioner for Refugees and other relevant international organisations on matters relating to asylum policy.

A. INTRODUCTION

The European Union has already taken the first steps towards creating common standards for asylum procedures in the Member States. A number of non-binding 'soft law' instruments relating to asylum procedures have been adopted.

Prior to the entry into force of the Treaty on European Union, when European co-operation in the field of asylum operated on a purely intergovernmental basis outside the framework of the treaties, Ministers responsible for Immigration adopted conclusions on countries in which there is generally no serious risk of persecution, the resolution on manifestly unfounded applications for asylum, and the resolution on a harmonized approach to questions concerning host third countries (the so-called 'London Resolutions' of 30 November and 1 December 1992).

Since the entry into force of the Treaty on European Union, the Council has adopted the resolution of 20 June 1995 on minimum guarantees for asylum procedures. In addition, its resolution of 26 June 1997 on unaccompanied minors who are nationals of third countries contains specific provisions on asylum procedures. In its 1994 Communication to the Council and the European Parliament on immigration and asylum policies, the Commission identified the need for a legally binding instrument on asylum procedures.

The Commission originally intended to bring forward a proposal for a convention on asylum procedures under the Treaty on European Union. After the signing of the Treaty of Amsterdam, however, the Commission concluded that it is preferable for its proposal on asylum procedures to take the form of a binding Community legal instrument. Indeed the new treaty will require the Council to adopt, within five years of its entry into force, measures on minimum standards on procedures in Member States for granting or withdrawing refugee status. In its 1994 Communication, the Commission argued that a legally binding instrument was required in order to ensure legal certainty for both asylum applicants and the Member States. The Commission suggested that a general approach might be to define objective criteria for fairness and efficiency, which would set a certain general framework, while leaving it to each Member State to fill in the exact nature of the asylum procedure.

The importance of an approach focusing on criteria for fairness and efficiency has not diminished. Guarantees must be in place to ensure that persons in need of protection under the 1951 Geneva Convention relating to the status of refugees have access to asylum procedures and that all the circumstances of their claims are examined on an individual basis, in order to protect people who are refugees within the meaning of Article 1A of that Convention. At the same time, procedures must be efficient, so that refugees can be identified as quickly as possible, and applications from people who are not in need of international protection can be processed expeditiously.

B. THE TREATY OF AMSTERDAM: A WORK PROGRAMME ON ASYLUM AND PROTECTION ISSUES

In considering the possible scope of a Community legal instrument on asylum procedures, it is important to take account of the work programme on asylum contained in the Treaty of Amsterdam. The new treaty will require the Council to adopt measures in a number of specific areas of asylum and protection policy, mostly within five years of its entry into force. In its Communication of July 1998 entitled 'Towards an area of Freedom, Security and Justice', the Commission indicated a number of priorities in the field of asylum, including minimum standards for asylum procedures.

Further indications on priorities are contained in the 'Action Plan of the Council and the Commission on how best to implement the provisions of the Treaty of Amsterdam establishing an area of freedom security and justice' of December 1998 (hereafter referred to as the 'Action Plan'). In particular, the Action Plan identifies a number of measures in the field of asylum, including the adoption of minimum standards on procedures in Member States for granting or withdrawing refugee status, which should be taken within two years of the entry into force of the new treaty. The legislative programme on asylum and protection issues following the entry into force of the Treaty of Amsterdam can be divided into the following eight topics:

– Criteria and mechanisms for determining which Member State is responsible for considering an application for asylum submitted by a national of a third country in one of the Member States (Article 63(1)(a) TEC). This area is covered by the Dublin Convention, which will in due course need to be replaced by an instrument of Community law. In this context, it will be necessary to determine whether it will be sufficient simply to address certain weaknesses which have been identified in the Dublin system, or whether a fundamentally different approach is required.

– Eurodac (Article 63(1)(a) TEC). This is a fingerprint comparison system which will be established for the purpose of implementing the Dublin Convention. It has been under negotiation in the form of a draft Convention and Protocol, but in December 1998 the Council asked the Commission to bring forward a proposal for Eurodac in the form of a Community regulation shortly after the entry into force of the Treaty of Amsterdam.

– Minimum standards on the reception of asylum seekers in Member States (Article 63(1)(b) TEC). The scope of an instrument in this field will cover such matters as accommodation, means of subsistence, medical care, education, employment and access to the labour market for asylum seekers.

– Minimum standards with respect to the qualification of nationals of third countries as refugees (Article 63(1)(c) TEC). An instrument in this area will be concerned with interpretation of the refugee definition contained in Article 1 of the Geneva Convention i.e. with substantive questions of who is a refugee.

Issues such as persecution by non-state agents, which has been a controversial feature of the 1996 Joint Position on the harmonized application of the term 'refugee' in Article 1 of the Geneva Convention, will need to be revisited in the context of this instrument.

– Minimum standards on procedures in Member States for granting or withdrawing refugee status (Article 63(1)(d) TEC). The existing soft law is referred to in the introduction to this paper. The possible content of a future Community instrument is the subject of this Working Document.

– Minimum standards for complementary/subsidiary protection for persons in need of international protection (Article 63(2)(a) second part TEC). An instrument in this area will deal with the provision of protection on an individual basis to persons who are not refugees within the meaning of the Geneva Convention, but who are nevertheless in need of international protection in accordance with other international obligations or humanitarian reasons.

– Minimum standards for giving temporary protection to displaced person from third countries who cannot return to their countries of origin (Article 63(2)(a) first part TEC). The Commission has already made a proposal on this subject, on the basis of the Treaty on European Union. After the entry into force of the new Treaty, the Commission will revise and represent its proposal as a draft Community instrument, with appropriate modifications. Promoting a balance of effort between Member States in receiving and bearing the consequences of receiving refugees and displaced persons (Article 63(2)(b) TEC). This is also referred to as 'solidarity' or 'burden sharing'. The Commission has already made a proposal on this subject in relation to the beneficiaries of temporary protection. This proposal will also be revised and represented as a draft Community instrument after the entry into force of the new treaty. Since the European Union has, in drawing up the existing soft law, already made progress on minimum standards for asylum procedures, and the Treaty of Amsterdam will allow the use of binding Community legal instruments in this area for the first time, the Commission considers that it is appropriate to start work under the new treaty with a proposal on asylum procedures.

– The scope and content of an instrument on asylum procedures must be considered in the light of the overall work programme under the Treaty of Amsterdam. In some cases, it will be necessary to decide where the dividing line between asylum procedures and reception conditions lies. In other cases, it will similarly be necessary to draw a dividing line between asylum procedures and questions of interpreting the refugee definition.

Questions also arise on the relationship between guarantees for asylum procedures and the application of the Dublin Convention, and on the link between asylum procedures and procedures for examining claims for other forms of protection. These issues are addressed in section C of this Working Document.

The Treaty establishing the European Community as amended by the Treaty of Amsterdam specifically states that measures on asylum, including on asylum procedures, must be in accordance with the Geneva Convention of 28 July 1951 and the Protocol of 31 January 1967 relating to the status of refugees and other relevant treaties.

The Treaties thus enshrine the basic principle that Community legislation on asylum must be compatible with the key international refugee and human rights instruments.

Proposals under Title IV of the amended Treaty establishing the European Community will be treated at variable geometry, in accordance with the relevant protocols. In this context, it should be noted that a proposal for a Community instrument on minimum standards on procedures in Member States for granting or withdrawing refugee status would not constitute a proposal or initiative to build upon the Schengen acquis.

The new treaty talks in terms of 'minimum standards' in the field of asylum, in relation to procedures, to reception conditions, and to the refugee definition. Common minimum standards will support several objectives. In the first place, they are necessary in order to ensure that any individual asylum applicant would receive the same decision on his or her application, irrespective of the Member State in which he or she lodges the asylum claim. If the European Union is to maintain a system of determining which Member State is responsible for considering an asylum application and transferring asylum applicants from one Member State to another, it is important to ensure that this does not affect the individual's chances of receiving protection. In the second place, common minimum standards have a role to play in preventing secondary migration of asylum applicants between Member States.

C. SCOPE AND CONTENT OF A COMMUNITY LEGAL INSTRUMENT ON ASYLUM PROCEDURES

This section is intended to raise a number of issues which arise in the context of preparing a future Community legal instrument on asylum procedures. It is not in any way intended to be a comprehensive inventory of every procedural issue which will need to be addressed. It is recalled that the document's function is to provide a basis for discussion and debate.

C.1 Broad approach

General approach. Broadly, there are two possible approaches to a first pillar instrument on asylum procedures:
(a) to establish a certain level of procedural safeguards and guarantees which all Member States would have to provide, in the interests of procedural fairness, whilst allowing Member States some degree of flexibility to determine the details of the administrative arrangements necessary for implementing these guarantees and to decide whether they wished to apply all the measures available for speeding up procedures; or
(b) to adopt a more prescriptive approach, which would require all Member States to apply exactly the same procedure, so that full harmonisation would be achieved.

The Commission envisages that in the first instance it will bring forward a proposal in line with approach (a) above, in view of the structure of the Action Plan on how best to implement the provisions of the Treaty of Amsterdam establishing an area of freedom, security and justice. The Action Plan envisages an instrument on asylum procedures within two years of the entry into force of the new treaty. Separately, it makes provision for a study with a view to establishing the merits of a single European asylum procedure, also within the two year timetable. This seems to imply that the European Union should first aim to put in place a binding instrument on asylum procedures, and then in the slightly longer term, on the basis of the study which the Action Plan calls for, should consider the merits of a single asylum system (which would presumably also cover such issues as reception and the refugee definition).

Scope of the proposal: the existing soft law. As mentioned in the introduction to this paper, the existing soft law (principally the 1995 resolution on minimum guarantees for asylum procedures and the 1992 London resolutions) can be viewed as the first steps towards common minimum standards on asylum procedures. The Commission takes the view that it will be necessary to revisit some of the concepts and principles found in the soft law and to propose the removal of some of the exceptions and derogations which weaken these instruments. In general terms, however, the Commission regards these resolutions as the starting point in preparing a proposal for a Community legal instrument.

Scope of the proposal: subsidiary protection
Both the Council and the European Parliament have already begun to examine the issue of complementary or subsidiary forms of protection. As previously mentioned in this paper, the Treaty of Amsterdam will require the adoption of measures relating to complementary protection. There is a good case for using a single procedure to determine both whether a person qualifies for protection under the Geneva Convention and whether they qualify for protection under some other international instrument or are otherwise in need of protection. This would avoid having different procedures which might have to be applied consecutively, thus extending the time it takes to deal with an individual case. Moreover, an applicant's interests would appear to be best served by a single general review of all the circumstances and different aspects of their case. A single procedure would seem to imply a single set of procedural guarantees for asylum and for complementary forms of protection.

Whilst there is therefore a good case for establishing a single procedure for examining all the protection issues raised by an individual case, there are equally persuasive arguments for excluding procedures for granting complementary forms of protection from the scope of the forthcoming proposal.

The Action Plan places asylum procedures within the two year timetable, whilst complementary protection is within the five year timetable. This distinction is made for a good reason. A considerable amount of work still needs to be done on defining which types of cases should be covered by complementary protection arrangements. It therefore seems sensible to restrict the scope of a Community legal instrument on asylum procedures to claims for protection under the Geneva Convention. When at a later date a proposal on complementary forms of protection is drawn up, this instrument could make provision for a single procedure for asylum and subsidiary protection issues.

C 2 Responsibility for considering an asylum application

Issues related to the Dublin Convention. Although the area covered by the Dublin Convention will in due course be the subject of a Community regulation or directive, issues related to the Dublin system do not fall entirely outside the scope of a Community legal instrument on asylum procedures. For example, the 1992 resolution on a harmonized approach to questions concerning host third countries deals with the relationship between the Dublin system and the application of the safe third country concept. This relationship will also need to be addressed in a Community legal instrument on asylum procedures.

Another issue which will need to be addressed, either in a Community legal instrument on asylum procedures or in a future instrument replacing the Dublin Convention, is that of procedural guarantees in relation to determining which Member State is responsible considering an application for asylum. When the 1995 resolution on minimum guarantees for asylum procedures was negotiated, it was agreed that procedural guarantees relating to the application of the Dublin Convention would be drawn up by the Article 18 Committee, and this is reflected in section I of that resolution. The implementing measures which have been adopted by the Article 18 Committee since the Dublin Convention's entry into force do not, however, include specific procedural guarantees. The Commission attaches importance to the adoption of such guarantees, and believes that they should be contained in a binding legal instrument. It will be necessary to determine whether such procedural guarantees should be contained in the proposal for a Community legal instrument on asylum procedures, or in a Community instrument replacing the Dublin Convention. Whilst the former approach could be justified on the basis of the link between Dublin procedures, safe third country procedures, and substantive asylum procedures, the latter approach might be more appropriate if it became clear that there was a consensus in favour of a fundamental revision of the Dublin system.

The safe third country concept and refusing applications on objective grounds. Paragraph 2 of the resolution on manifestly unfounded applications for asylum states that Member States may operate admissibility procedures under which applications may be rejected very quickly on objective grounds. The resolution offers no further clarification of what is meant by 'objective grounds'. The Commission envisages that a Community legal instrument on asylum procedures would draw a clear distinction between a decision not to consider the substance of an asylum application because the applicant could be returned to a third country, and a decision to refuse an asylum application on the substance. The Commission envisages that the Community legal instrument would employ a concept of 'admissibility' which is restricted to determining whether the Member States in question should consider the substance of the asylum application, or whether the applicant should be sent to a third country under the safe or host third country concept or to another Member State under the Dublin Convention. Member

States would still retain the flexibility to refuse asylum claims rapidly on substantive grounds, provided that they applied the basic procedural safeguards which the Community legal instrument would prescribe for all cases where Member States examine the substance of the claim to fear persecution.

The safe third country concept: a common approach
The 1992 resolution on a harmonized approach to questions concerning host third countries lays down a procedure for examining whether an asylum applicant can be sent to a safe third country (outside the European Union). The application of the safe third country concept must be subject to stringent safeguards in order to ensure that the principle of non-refoulement contained in Article 33 of the Geneva Convention is given effect. Paragraph 2 of the resolution duly sets out four fundamental requirements for determining the safety of a third country. Paragraph 4 of the resolution states that these procedures should be reviewed from time to time, and that consideration should be given to whether any additional measures are necessary. A comparison of national practices has been undertaken in accordance with the Council decision on monitoring the implementation of instruments adopted concerning asylum, and this has revealed some areas where Member States' practices vary significantly. The Commission has identified the following issues which could usefully be reviewed with a view to adopting additional measures or clarifying existing measures: (i) the need for contacts with the third country and the provision of documentation to ensure that the asylum applicant will be readmitted and that the third country is aware that the substance of the applicant's asylum claim has not been examined; (ii), whether the requirement currently set out in paragraph 2(d) of the resolution that the applicant must be afforded effective protection in the host third country against refoulement should be amended to state that effective protection must include the availability of an effective remedy in the third country; (iii) clarification of the obligation to assess in each individual case that the fundamental requirements for the determination of a host third country are fulfilled; (iv) the scope for common assessments of third countries, for the purpose of assessing whether an applicant's life or freedom would be threatened in the third country (paragraph 2(a) of the resolution) and whether an applicant would be exposed to torture or inhuman or degrading treatment in the third country (paragraph 2(b) of the resolution), and the role of safe third country lists; (v) the application of the concept in situations of 'mere transit'.

C.3 Substantive asylum procedures

Speeding up asylum procedures
The Action Plan states that measures on asylum procedures should be adopted 'with a view, inter alia, to reducing the duration of asylum procedures'. The Commission agrees that it is important to ensure that asylum procedures should

not be so long and drawn out that people in need of protection have to go through a long period of uncertainty before their cases are decided, and people who have no need of protection but who wish to remain on the territory of the Member States see an asylum application as a means of prolonging their stay by several years. At the same time, it is essential that asylum procedures contain the necessary safeguards to ensure that all those in need of protection are correctly identified. The Commission does not consider that the level of guarantees envisaged in the resolution on minimum guarantees for asylum procedures in relation to such basic safeguards as appeal rights, legal advice and interpretation facilities can be reduced (indeed, as indicated in paragraph 10 above it will be necessary to revisit some of the derogations and exceptions). There is, however, certainly scope for reducing the duration of asylum procedures, although this issue should be approached from the starting point of increasing efficiency rather than weakening existing safeguards.

Speeding up procedures: a simple structure for the asylum system
The Commission proposes to adopt an approach which envisages a simple structure for the asylum system. The Community legal instrument would not, for instance, require Member States to introduce or maintain multi-tiered appeal systems. The extent to which Member States will be able to simplify appeal arrangements will of course be determined to a significant extent by their judicial systems and in some cases by constitutional requirements. The starting point of the proposal will, however, be that provided the necessary safeguards are in place to ensure a good standard of decision making by asylum determination bodies, a single appeal or review of the substance of the decision will normally be sufficient (without prejudice to the power of higher courts to rule on points of law).

Speeding up procedures: working practices
The Commission sees scope for a more detailed examination of some of the ideas which were presented at the end of 1997 by the Danish and UK delegations in Council papers on the swift processing of asylum applications. These papers focused, inter alia, on issues such as good practice in relation to management, training, the use of information technology etc. If the conclusion of a discussion on these issues was that changes were required in working practices, rather than in the basic legislative framework, there would be scope for following this up in the framework of the Odysseus programme. Speeding up procedures: time limits. The 1992 resolution on manifestly unfounded applications for asylum applied time limits to manifestly unfounded cases, setting 1 month as a target time for taking an initial decision in such cases. The one month time limit has apparently proved to be over ambitious and unrealistic in many cases. Nevertheless, in negotiations on the Action Plan, Member States have indicated that reducing the duration of asylum procedures is a priority. It is therefore worth considering whether prescribed time limits have a role to play in future minimum standards for asylum

procedures. Time limits could be used at each stage of the procedure. For example, at the admissibility stage, there could be a time limit after which the safe third country concept could not be applied. The imposition of a time limit does not in itself provide Member States with a tool to reduce the duration of the asylum procedure. In order to meet any time limits, Member States would have to ensure that their asylum determination authorities were adequately resourced (a requirement of the 1995 resolution on minimum guarantees for asylum procedures), and that their working practices were efficient. They would also be free to make use of the procedural devices which the instrument would permit for accelerating the handling of certain types of cases. In drawing up time limits, it would be necessary to examine whether an element of flexibility could be introduced to take account of increases in the number of new asylum applications which a Member State received.

Speeding up procedures: repeat asylum applications
The resolutions which have already been adopted on asylum procedures do not address the issue of repeat asylum applications. In principle, a refused asylum applicant who has no need of international protection should not be able to postpone the requirement for him or her to leave the territory of the Member State which has considered his asylum application by lodging a second asylum application. At the same time, it is necessary to ensure that there are appropriate safeguards to cover cases where a genuine change of circumstances has taken place or new evidence has come to light. The Council has recently taken steps to collate information on national practice in relation to repeat asylum applications. It will be appropriate to consider, in the light of this information, whether there is scope for introducing legislation at the European level on this point.

Standard of proof
The case for including a provision on the standard of proof which should be applied when determining asylum applications should be seriously considered. Whilst the issues of establishment of the evidence and benefit of the doubt have been addressed in the soft law which has been adopted on the basis of the Treaty on European Union, the specific standard of proof has not been. But arguably, it is one of the most important procedural issues. One of the main purposes of the package of measures on asylum envisaged by the Treaty of Amsterdam is to ensure that an applicant for asylum would receive the same decision irrespective of which Member State considered his or her application for asylum. Clearly, the attainment of this objective requires measures which are outside the scope of an instrument on asylum procedures, including a common interpretation of the refugee definition and a common approach to the situation in countries of origin. But in the procedural area, it is important to ensure that some Member States do not require a significantly higher standard of proof than others, with the consequence that the same claim would result in acceptance as a refugee in some Member

States but not in others. Disparities in national practices may have the consequence that a greater proportion of asylum applicants will seek asylum in the Member States which are regarded as less demanding in this respect, which has consequences for achieving the objective of promoting an equitable balance between the Member States. The Commission recognises, however that the standard of proof is a difficult issue related to Member States' individual legal systems, and it would be necessary to proceed with caution in this area.

The 'manifestly unfounded' concept
The 1992 resolution on manifestly unfounded applications for asylum makes provision for the consideration of asylum applications to be subject to accelerated procedures in certain circumstances. The Commission envisages that its proposal for a Community legal instrument will maintain this general concept, with certain modifications. First, a more appropriate name might be found for the concept, since it is arguably inaccurate to describe a case as manifestly unfounded whilst the procedures to determine precisely whether or not the case is well founded are still in operation. Second, there is a case for stating more specifically what procedural consequences the application of the 'manifestly unfounded' concept could have. Third, whilst the Commission envisages proposing the retention of the concept for most categories of cases currently covered by the 1992 resolution, it considers that the arguments for applying the concept on the grounds that the applicant lacks credibility, or that an internal flight alternative is available, or that the 'exclusion clauses' in Article 1F of the Geneva Convention apply deserve to be re-examined. Fourth, as indicated in paragraph 13 above, the Commission envisages spelling out more clearly the distinction between on the one hand cases which are 'manifestly unfounded' because the safe third country concept can be applied, and on the other 'manifestly unfounded' cases where the substance of the asylum claim is examined.

The safe country of origin concept
The use of the 'safe country of origin' concept also merits re-examination. This concept is set out in the 1992 resolution on manifestly unfounded applications for asylum, and in the conclusions on countries in which there is generally no serious risk of persecution. These conclusions indicate a number of elements of assessment which a Member State must as a minimum take into account when considering whether a particular country in one in which there is generally no serious risk of persecution. Nevertheless, the recent monitoring exercise has shown that Member States' practice in using this concept varies widely, in particular in relation to the countries which they treat as 'safe'. In addition, it is the only ground for applying an accelerated procedure to an asylum claim which does not depend on an individual rather than a general factor in the case. It is therefore appropriate to review the use of this concept. Broadly, there are three options for proceeding:
(a) To abandon the safe country of origin concept. In looking at this option, the

considerations might be: whether it is procedurally fair to apply a mechanism which does not take account of the individual circumstances of the case; whether, in the light of experience, the concept has genuinely been useful to Member States in enabling them to speed up the processing of individual cases; and whether the Member States have noted a sustained decrease in the number and proportion of unfounded claims which they have received from countries which they treat as 'safe'.

(b) to retain the concept, but to address the differences in national lists of 'safe countries of origin' by providing for a central determination of safe countries within the framework of the Council. Such an approach would be justified if there was a consensus that the safe country concept was useful and justifiable, but that it was procedurally unfair for one Member State to apply the safe country of origin concept in relation to a country which no other Member State regards as 'safe'.

(c) to retain the concept in its present form, and to allow for the adoption of implementing measures which would be broadly along the lines of the 1992 conclusions, so that each Member State would decide independently to which countries of origin it would apply the concept, if indeed it chose to make use of the concept at all.

C.4 Other issues

Vulnerable groups
The Action Plan on how best to implement the provisions of the Treaty of Amsterdam establishing an area of freedom, security and justice states that in the context of an instrument on asylum procedures special attention should be paid to the situation of children. The resolution on minimum guarantees for asylum procedures contains specific provisions on children and women, and the resolution on unaccompanied minors who are nationals of third countries contains specific provisions on asylum procedures in relation to unaccompanied minors. The Commission envisages that the Community legal instrument will contain specific procedural safeguards in relation to children and women, building on those already contained in the soft law. It will also be necessary to consider whether specific procedural safeguards are appropriate in relation to victims of torture and victims of persecution of a sexual nature.

Withdrawal of refugee status
The legal basis in the amended Treaty establishing the European Community (Article 63(1)(d)) refers to minimum standards on procedures in Member States for granting or withdrawing refugee status. Withdrawal of refugee status can be subdivided into (a) cancellation when it transpired that the grant had been made on the basis of false information and (b) application of the cessation clauses (Article 1C of the Geneva Convention) when the person concerned was no longer in need of international protection.

(a) Cancellation. Neither the Geneva Convention nor the soft law of the European Union address the issue of cancellation of refugee status, and the Commission is not persuaded that cancellation is a sufficiently common occurrence to merit the inclusion of provisions in a Community legal instrument.

(b) Cessation. The joint position on the harmonized application of the term 'refugee' in Article 1 of the Geneva Convention contains some provisions on cessation: that investigation should be on an individual basis; that Member States should make efforts to harmonise their practice through the exchange of information; and that the circumstance in which cessation is applied should be of a fundamental nature and should be determined in an objective and verifiable manner. It will be appropriate to consider whether the principle of investigating cessation on an individual basis should be incorporated in a Community legal instrument on asylum procedures. (In this context, it is worth noting that EXCOM conclusion no.69 makes provision for applying the cessation clauses on a group basis, provided that all refugees affected by a group or class decision have the possibility, on request, to have the application of the cessation clauses in their cases reconsidered on grounds relevant to their individual case.) It will also be appropriate to consider whether the Community legal instrument should provide that other safeguards which are available during the procedure for granting refugee status should also be available in any procedure conducted with a view to withdrawing refugee status.

4.2

JOINT POSITION ON THE HARMONISED APPLICATION OF THE DEFINITION OF THE TERM 'REFUGEE' IN ARTICLE 1 OF THE GENEVA CONVENTION OF 28 JULY 1951 RELATING TO THE STATUS OF REFUGEES[1]

(Brussels, 4 March 1996)

I. BACKGROUND

General

During its meeting on 4 March 1996 in Brussels the EU Council of Ministers responsible for Justice and Home Affairs adopted a 'Joint Position' on the Harmonised Application of the Definition of the Term 'Refugee'.[2]

Current relevance

The Joint position is meant to provide guidelines to the administrative bodies dealing with eligibility to refugee status and provides a set of answers to questions, which arise in interpreting the 1951 Refugee Convention's refugee definition. In this connection, the Joint position acknowledges the value of the UNHCR Handbook as a useful tool in answering questions relating to the determination of refugee status.

In accordance with Article 63 TEC, this resolution will be replaced by a binding EC law instrument (Action Plan of the European Council Vienna 1998).

Reservations

The Joint Position states that: '... it shall not bind the legislative authorities or effect decisions of the judicial authorities of Member States'.

---

[1] OJ No. L63, 13.03.1996, p. 2.

[2] According to TEU I (Maastricht) the Joint Position is one of the possible forms of action to achieve the Union's objectives in the second (CFSP) and third Pillar (JHA).

II. PURPOSE

Outline of a common ground

The Joint Position is meant to harmonise the application of the criteria for determining refugee status in the asylum procedures of the EU Member States. Given that one of the key elements of the EU asylum approximation process is the Dublin mechanism to allocate responsibility for processing an asylum application to one Member State only, the harmonised application of the criteria for determining refugee status in all Member States is essential for an equal treatment of asylum seekers in EU States and, hence, a fair and effective operation of the Dublin mechanism.

Yearly review of application guidelines

The Council has stated in the preamble of the Joint Position its intention to 'review the application of these guidelines once a year and, if appropriate, adapt them to developments in asylum applications'. This has yet to be done.

III. CONTENT

Structure

The Joint Position contains a preamble and 13 Chapters, which reflect on legal and technical concepts and aspects relevant in the context of applying the 1951 Refugee Convention's refugee definition. The Chapters are titled as the following:
– Recognition as a refugee
– Individual or collective determination of refugee status
– Establishment of the evidence required for granting refugee status
– 'Persecution' within the meaning of Article 1A of the Geneva Convention
– Origins of Persecution
– Civil war and other internal or generalised armed conflicts
– Grounds of persecution
– Relocation within the country of origin
– Refugee 'sur place'
– Conscientious objection, absence without leave and desertion
– Cessation of refugee status (Article 1C)
– Article 1D of the Geneva Convention
– Article 1F of the Geneva Convention

IV. ANALYSIS OF TEXT

Chapter 1: Recognition as refugee

This Chapter clarifies that the Joint Position is applicable only in the Refugee Status Determination (RSD) procedure. According to national or international law there might be another status, which could be invoked to permit a person to remain in the country for a reason not covered under the 1951 Refugee Convention.

Complementary forms of protection
It is important to highlight that even if a person for one or other reason does not qualify for the protection granted under the 1951 Refugee Convention, he/she might still be in need of international protection. Such subsidiary forms of protection have been covered in the legislation of most EU Member States.

Chapter 2: Individual or collective determination of refugee status

Individual assessment
In principle all 'applications will be examined individually', based on the facts put forward and taking into consideration the objective situation prevailing in the country of origin.

The requirement for an individual examination constitutes an important safeguard against the exclusion of whole groups of people from the protection of the 1951 Refugee Convention simply based on the general assessment of the situation in their country of origin. Even where a so-called safe country of origin list exists, cases have to be examined individually as to whether the claim should be distinguished from that of the rest of the group.

Group determination
In addition, it underlines the possibility of group determination and recognition, an element which could help to make procedure faster and more efficient, without hampering the interest of person in need of international protection.[3]

Chapter 3: Establishment of the evidence required for granting refugee status

The following important phrases of Chapter 3 should be highlighted:
1) 'It should be understood that once the credibility of the asylum seeker's statements has been sufficiently established, it will not be necessary to seek detailed

---

[3] In such cases the individual examination may be limited to determining whether the individual belongs to the group in question.

confirmation of the facts put forward and the asylum seeker should, unless there are good reasons to the contrary, be given the benefit of the doubt.'

2) 'The fact that an individual, prior to his departure from his country of origin, was not subject to persecution or directly threatened with persecution does not per se mean that he cannot in asylum proceedings claim a well-founded fear of persecution'.

Chapter 4: 'Persecution' within the meaning of Article 1A of the Geneva Convention

Given that the term 'persecution' is neither defined in the 1951 Refugee Convention, nor in the UNHCR Executive Committee's conclusion, Chapter 4 provides some guidelines, *but not a definition*, as to what could be understood by this term.

In order to constitute 'persecution' within the meaning of Article 1A, acts suffered or feared must be sufficiently serious by their nature or their repetition, inter alia human rights violations, and be based on one of the grounds mentioned in the refugee definition.

The guidelines given in this Chapter generally reflect current practice. An important element of the text in particular is the statement that 'the fact that these grounds (the grounds of persecution) are genuine or simply attributed to the person concerned by the persecutor is immaterial'. The guidelines also recognise the possible cumulative effect of types of persecution.

Chapter 5: Origins of persecution

In Chapter 5, the Joint Position distinguishes between two main roots of origin of persecution: a State, authority, party or organisation controlling the State on the one hand whatever status of that State or entity under international law[4], and so-called 'third parties'[5] on the other.

Criteria regarding 'legal' State action as persecution
By qualifying State persecution, the Joint Position provides guidelines as to when legal, administrative and police measures or prosecution might amount to persecution. The following main criteria are provided with regard to when in general 'legal' State actions amount to persecution:
– general measures to maintain public order, safeguard, State security, preserve public health, etc., do not themselves constitute sufficient grounds for granting refugee status, even if they include restriction or the use of force. Such measures

---

[4] De facto authorities and self proclaimed States are deemed in this context to have the same obligations of protecting persons and human rights as internationally recognized States.

[5] Third parties are often referred to as non-State agents.

only amount to persecution if they are implemented in a discriminatory manner and have sufficiently serious consequences that may give rise to well-founded fear in the sense of the 1951 Refugee Convention[6];
– measures concerning certain categories of the population are not necessarily illegitimate but may be considered as justifying fears of persecution – in particular if their aim has been condemned by the international community, where they are manifestly disproportionate, or their implementation leads to serious abuses aimed at treating a certain group differently and less favorably than the population as a whole[7];
– any administrative measures taken against an individual, leaving aside any consideration of general interest, which are sufficiently severe may be regarded as persecution, in particular if they are intentional, systematic and lasting[8];
– *prosecution* amounts to *persecution* where it includes a discriminatory element and where the consequences are sufficiently severe. This is particularly true in cases of discriminatory prosecution, discriminatory punishment or a breach of a criminal law provision on account of the grounds of persecution.[9]

Regarding the four points mentioned above, it must be considered whether an effective remedy exists which would put an end to the situation of abuse, and whether the applicant has guaranteed access to that effective remedy.[10]

Persecution by non-State agents

According to the Joint Position, persecution by non-State agents is considered to fall within the scope of the 1951 Refugee Convention in all cases where it is based on one of the grounds in Article 1A, is individual in nature, and 'encouraged or permitted' by the authorities.[11] If the State fails to act it has to be determined whether or not the failure to act was deliberate.[12]

In situations where a State is unable to or where no effective Government exists in the State, exists in the state, the Joint position refers MS to their national caselaw and points out the need to grant some form of protection, i.e. refugee status or an appropriate alternative protection according to national law.

---

[6] Chapter 5.1.1 a.
[7] Chapter 5.1.1 b.
[8] Chapter 5.1.1 c.
[9] Chapter 5.1.2.
[10] Chapter 5.1.1 c.
[11] Chapter 5.2.
[12] In essence, the text provides that where Governments have not acted to protect from persecution by third parties, each case is to be examined in light of national jurisprudence whether or not Government in-action was deliberate.

Future revision
The TEC (amended TEU) offers the legal basis for replacing the Joint Position by a Community instrument. The Council and Commission have indicated that modifications of the Joint Position may be necessary.

Chapter 6: Civil war and other internal or generalized armed conflicts

In Chapter 6, the Joint Position recognises in principle that persecution within the meaning of Article 1A of the 1951 Refugee Convention may occur in situations of civil war and other internal generalised armed conflicts under the following criteria:

– 'In such situations, persecution may stem either from the **legal** authority or third parties encouraged or tolerated by them, or from *de facto* authorities in control of part of the territory within which the state cannot afford its nationals protection';

– 'In principle, use of the armed forces does not constitute persecution where it is in accordance with international rules of war and internationally recognised practice (*inter alia the four 1949 Geneva Conventions*); however, it becomes persecution where, for instance, authority is established over a particular area and its attacks ... fulfill the criteria ... (*of persecution within the meaning of the 1951 Refugee Convention*)'.

Concerns relating to agents of persecution
Protection according to the 1951 Refugee Convention is not *per se* excluded in civil wars and other internal or generalised armed conflicts. However, the above-mentioned incomplete agreement between Member States relating to agents of persecution is recognisable here as well.

Chapter 7: Grounds of persecution

Chapter 7 of the Joint Position provides a comprehensive set of guidelines in respect of the grounds of persecution.

Gender as a social group
The Joint Position does not explicitly mention the concept of gender based persecution or women as a social group.[13]

Chapter 8: Relocation within the country of origin

The Joint Position expressly acknowledges that, in relation to the concept of the internal flight alternative, the protection offered in another part of the country

---

[13] Chapter 7.5 defines social groups as a group which 'normally comprises persons from the same background, with the same customs or the same social status, etc.'

must be effective and it must be reasonable for the individual to be expected to move there.

Applying the internal relocation alternative
In applying the internal flight alternative, it should be established first whether the fear of persecution that an individual experiences in one part of the country can be avoided by moving to another part, and second, whether it is possible and reasonable to expect the person to seek and obtain safety elsewhere in the country.

Chapter 9: Refugee 'sur place'

The Joint Position recognises in principle that a person need not necessarily have left his/her country on account of a well-founded fear of persecution. The Chapter outlines two main reasons for becoming a refugee after having left the country of origin:
– fear arising from a new situation in the country of origin after departure;[14]
– fear on account of activities outside the country of origin.[15]

The latter concept is the more problematic one as it entails the potential for abuse. Therefore, the Joint Position recognises the fear as relevant under the 1951 Refugee Convention if the post flight activities 'constitute the expression and continuation of convictions which s/he had held in his/her country of origin – unless the person was not yet able to establish convictions because of age – or can objectively be regarded as the consequences of asylum-related characteristics of the individual.'[16]

Cases of clear abuse
In cases of clear abuse, if it is clear that he/she expresses his/her convictions mainly for the purpose of creating the necessary conditions for being admitted as a refugee, the activities 'can not in principle furnish grounds for admission as refugee.'[17] However, he/she might still enjoy 'the right not to be returned to a country where his/her life, physical integrity or freedom would be in danger.'[18]

Chapter 10: Conscientious objections, absence without leave and desertion

The Joint Position in principal recognises that fear of punishment in these situations may furnish a refugee claim. Therefore, in addition to the criteria laid down

---

[14] Chapter 9.1.
[15] Chapter 9.2.
[16] Ibid.
[17] Ibid.
[18] Ibid.

in section 5.1 of the Joint position, Chapter 10 defines two main categories in which punishment for conscientious objection, absence without leave or desertion can amount to persecution:
- the conditions under which military duties are performed themselves constitute persecution;
- the performance of military duties were to have the effect of leading the persons concerned to participate in acts falling under the exclusion clauses in Article 1 of the 1951 Refugee Convention.

Chapters 11-13: Articles 1 C, 1D and 1 F of the 1951 Refugee Convention

Cessation of refugee status
In applying the cessation of refugee status clause in Article 1C of the 1951 Refugee Convention, Member States must take account of the individual nature of cessation decisions, and such decisions should be determined in an objective and verifiable manner.[19]

The Joint Position specifically mentions the considerable relevance of using CIREA[20] and UNHCR for the purposes of information related to the use of the cessation clause.

Application of the cessation clauses
The cessation clauses can be divided in to two broad sets. The first set comprises the clauses which relate to a change in personal circumstances of the refugee, brought about by the refugee's own act, and which results in the acquisition of national protection so that international protection is no longer necessary. The second set comprises the clauses, which relate to a change in the objective circumstances in connection with which the refugee has been recognised, so that international protection is no longer justified.

The cessation clauses are exhaustive. This means that the refugee's status is maintained until one of the cessation clauses can be invoked; in any case refugees should not be subjected to constant or regular reviews of their refugee status. In principle, the application of the cessation clauses is declaratory in nature, acknowledging that international refugee protection is no longer required.

Removal from international protection
Chapter 12 of the Joint Position interprets art 1D of the Geneva Convention as meaning that, if a person deliberately removes his/herself from the protection and

---

[19] Chapter 11.
[20] Center for Information, Reflection and Exchange on Asylum or 'clearing house' (also referred to as the Center for Information, Discussion/Research and Exchange on Asylum) established by a Decision by the Ministers Responsible for Immigration in light of the obligations stemming from the Dublin Convention.

assistance provided by organs or agencies of the UN other than UNHCR although such protection and assistance remain available, s/he shall not automatically be covered by the 51 Convention

Exclusion from international protection
The Joint position includes a Chapter, which illustrates the justifications for excluding certain people from international protection because of the seriousness of the crimes, which they have committed. The Joint Position explains the three categories of crimes set out in Article 1F of the 1951 Refugee Convention in further detail:
– crimes committed under Article 1F(a) are those defined in international instruments as they have been acceded to by the Member States, as well as those instruments from the United Nations or other international/regional organisations which the Member States have accepted;
– in relation to serious non-political crimes, the severity of the expected persecution must be weighed against the nature of the criminal offence, particularly cruel actions, even if committed with an allegedly political objective, may be classified as serious non political crimes. This applies both to the participants in the crime and to its instigators;
– acts contrary to the purposes and principles of the United Nations are explained as, in the first instance, those laid down by the Charter of the United Nations, particularly the maintenance of the peace, and regard for human rights and fundamental freedoms.

It is recalled that, due to the serious consequences of the decision for the asylum seeker or refugee, the Joint Position stresses that the exclusion clauses are to be applied only with care and after thorough consideration, and in accordance with the procedures laid down in national law.

4.3

RESOLUTION ON MINIMUM GUARANTEES FOR ASYLUM PROCEDURES[1]
(*Brussels, 21 June 1995*)

I. BACKGROUND

Introduction
On 20 June 1995 the EU Justice and Home Affairs Council agreed on the Resolution on Minimum Guarantees for Asylum Procedures.[2] Although not an EC law instrument[3], in Chapter VIII of the Resolution, Member States agree to 'take account of these principles in the case of all proposals for changes to their national legislation. In addition, Member States will strive to bring their national legislation into line with these principles by 1 January 1996'.

Common standards and exceptions
The Resolution can be considered as containing common guidelines for minimum standards in this area. They include some exceptions and derogation reflecting some of the particularities of current national practices.

In Chapter IX the Member States retain 'the right to enact national provisions on guarantees provided by procedures applicable to asylum seekers, which are more favorable than those contained in the common minimum guarantees'.

The Resolution and Amsterdam
This Resolution will be replaced by a binding EC law instrument on minimum standards for asylum procedures based on Article 63 TEC (European Council Vienna, Action Plan).

1. Asylum Procedures and the 1951 Refugee Convention

Asylum procedures and the 1951 Refugee Convention
Refugee Status Determination Procedures (RSD) commonly know as *asylum pro-*

---

[1] OJ No. C 274, 19.09.1996, p. 13.
[2] The Resolution must be read in conjunction with the London Resolutions on the 'Third Host Country' notion and on 'Manifestly Unfounded Claims' to which it refers several times.
[3] It is, however, politically binding on any State, which wishes to accede to the Union.

cedures are established to confirm formally whether a person meets the criteria provided for in Article 1A 2 of the 1951 Refugee Convention and is thus entitled to enjoy international protection. As long as it has not been decided that a person is not a refugee he/she is entitled to basic protection, in respect of the principle of non-refoulement (Article 33(1) of the 1951 Refugee Convention). This fundamental principle is in fact the *raison d'être* and rationale for establishing a national asylum procedure.

The 1951 Refugee Convention does not provide any specific guidance on asylum procedures; it is left to each contracting State to establish the procedure that it considers most appropriate, having due regard to its particular constitutional and administrative structure. The EU Resolution on Minimum Guarantees for Asylum Procedures is aimed at providing Member States with common guidelines and criteria with a view to harmonizing and strengthening the existing procedures.

2. Minimum Guarantees and 1951 Refugee Convention

Guiding international standards
As mentioned in Chapter II (paragraph 1) of the Resolution, asylum procedures will (have to) be applied in full compliance with the 1951 Refugee Convention and the 1967 New York Protocol relating to the Status of Refugees, and other obligations under international law in respect of refugees and human rights.[4]

Non-refoulement
In order to ensure effectively the principle of non-refoulement, no expulsion measure should be carried out as long as no decision has been taken on the asylum application.

II. PURPOSE

Introduction
With the Resolution on Minimum Guarantees for Asylum Procedures, the EU Member States have aimed at adopting common procedural guarantees regulating their asylum procedures with a view to arriving at equivalent and fair decisions on asylum applications.

---

[4] In particular, the procedures must comply fully with Article 1 of the 1951 Refugee Convention concerning the definition of a refugee, Article 33 relating to the principle of non-refoulement and Article 35 concerning co-operation with the Office of the United Nations High Commissioner for Refugees, including the facilitation of its duty of supervising the application of the Convention.

Relationship with the Dublin Convention
Harmonized standards in the asylum procedures are a way to ensure smooth implementation of the Dublin Convention of 15 June 1990, which pre-supposes that decisions on asylum applications are taken on the basis of equivalent procedures in all Member States.

II. CONTENT

Introduction
The Resolution consists of a preamble (I) and the following main Chapters:
- Universal principles concerning fair and effective asylum procedures
- Guarantees concerning the examination of asylum applications
- Rights of asylum seekers during examination, appeal and review procedures
- Additional safeguards for unaccompanied minors and women
- Residence where the criteria for classification as a refugee are met
- Other cases
- Further action
- More favourable provisions

Interpreting statements
Belgium, Ireland, Austria, Sweden and the United Kingdom clarified their interpretation of selected parts of questions of the Resolution through statements in the Council Minutes[5]. Please see the Annex for further details.

IV. ANALYSIS OF THE TEXT

1951 Refugee Convention and recognition of UNHCR's role
The 15 EU Member States – all signatories to the 1951 Refugee Convention – recognize the precedence of this international treaty as the main reference document for the setting up of RSD procedures. The supervisory role of UNHCR is also explicitly confirmed by the EU text.

1. Minimum guarantees for asylum procedures

1.1 *General standards*

National asylum legislation
The Resolution states that: 'The regulations on access to the asylum procedure, the basic features of the asylum procedure itself and the designation of the au-

---
[5] As such, the Minutes of Council meetings have no legal force.

thorities responsible for examination of asylum applications are to be laid down in the individual Member State's legislation'.[6] This is to promote transparency and the Rule of law in this sensitive area.

Instructions for authorities
The Resolution states that: 'The authorities responsible for border controls and the local authorities with which asylum applications are lodged must receive clear and detailed instructions so that the applications, together with all other information available, can be forwarded without delay to the competent authority for examination'.[7] In addition, border/local authorities and the asylum office should agree on clear provisions governing the stay, the physical care and transfer of the asylum seekers themselves. This can help to avoid refoulement and unnecessary detention of asylum seekers.

Lodging of asylum application
The Resolution states further that: 'An asylum seeker must have an effective opportunity to lodge his asylum application as early as possible'.[8]

Practice
The fair and effective implementation of these guarantees is crucial. It should be noted that, notwithstanding these procedural guarantees, asylum seekers may fail to communicate their request for asylum to the border/local authorities and/or may be ignored due to practical hindrances and in some cases returned to their country of origin.

Non-refoulement
The Resolution reaffirms the primacy of the principle of non-refoulement, as set out in Article 33 of the 1951 Refugee Convention, and therefore proscribes that no expulsion measure is carried out until a decision has been taken on the asylum application. It is worthwhile recalling that even if a person is excluded from lodging an asylum application, the binding non-refoulement principle is to be observed by the acting authorities.

Time limits
No formal deadlines, which may prevent an asylum seeker from applying for refugee status, are foreseen in the Resolution. The fact that the applicant must have an effective opportunity to apply 'as early as possible' illustrates that the prevailing circumstances, rather than formal deadlines, are seen as the decisive factor in this regard. Hence it could be concluded that they are not permitted.

---

[6] Paragraph 3.
[7] Ibid.
[8] Paragraph 10.

1.2. Competent Authorities

Qualified authorities

'The authorities responsible for the examination of the asylum application must be fully qualified in the field of asylum and refugee matters. To this effect, they must:
– have at their disposal specialized personnel with the necessary knowledge and experience in the field of asylum and refugee matters, who have an understanding of an applicant's particular situation;
– have access to precise and up-to-date information from various sources, including information from the UNHCR, concerning the situation prevailing in the countries of origin of asylum seekers and in transit countries;
– have the right to ask advice, whenever necessary, from experts on particular issues, e.g. a medical issue or an issue of a cultural nature'.[9]

Availability of staff

Furthermore, 'Member States must ensure that the competent authorities are adequately provided with staff and equipment so that they can discharge their duties promptly and under the best possible conditions'.[10]

Country of origin information

The reference to the qualification of the decision-taking body, the importance of up-to-date country of origin information, including information from UNHCR, and the right to ask advice from experts on particular issues are of special relevance as in terms of substance they go beyond of what is mentioned in other international instruments.

2. General rights of asylum seekers

Data protection

'Declarations made by the asylum seeker and other details of his application are very sensitive data, requiring protection. National law must therefore provide adequate data protection guarantees, particularly as against the authorities of the asylum seeker's country of origin'.[11]

Right to remain

'As long as the asylum application has not been decided on, the general principle applies that the applicant is allowed to remain in the territory of the State in which his application has been lodged or is being examined'.[12]

---

[9] Paragraph 6.
[10] Paragraph 9.
[11] Paragraph 11.
[12] Paragraph 12.

There are, however, exceptions to this general principle of the suspensive effect of the appeal particularly in accelerated procedures such as in cases considered to be manifestly unfounded, or in border procedures.

Where the national law of a Member State permits derogation from the principle of suspensive effect in certain cases, the asylum seeker should at least be able to apply to a court or independent review authority 'for leave to remain in the territory of the Member State temporarily during procedures before those bodies, on the grounds of the particular circumstances of his case; no expulsion may take place until a decision has been taken on this application'.[13]

Pre-procedural counseling
Asylum seekers must be informed of the procedure to be followed and of their rights and obligations during the procedure, in a language, which they can understand.[14] In particular:
– they must be given the services of an interpreter, whenever necessary, for submitting their case to the authorities concerned. These services must be paid for out of public funds, if the interpreter is appointed by the competent authorities;
– in accordance with the rules of the Member State concerned, they may call in a legal adviser or other counselor to assist them during the procedure;
– they must be given the opportunity at all stages of the procedure, to communicate with the Office of the United Nations High Commissioner for Refugees (UNHCR) or with other refuges organisations which may be working on behalf of the UNHCR in the Member State concerned, and vice versa.

NGOs
It is further mentioned that 'asylum seekers may enter into contact with other refugee organisations under procedures laid down by the Member States'.[15]

UNHCR
The position of UNHCR is explicitly spelled out: 'The representative of the Office of the UNHCR must be given the opportunity to be informed of the course of the procedure, to learn about the decisions of the competent authorities and to submit his observations'.[16]

Interview
Before a final decision is taken on the asylum application, the asylum seeker must be given the opportunity of a personal interview with an official qualified under national law.[17]

---

[13] Paragraph 17.
[14] Paragraph 13.
[15] Ibid.
[16] Ibid.
[17] Paragraph 14.

Rights of asylum seekers
The right to a personal interview, the right to remain in the country pending the final decision on the application, the guaranteed access to information and counseling by NGOs and/or UNHCR, and the right to data protection are necessary to provide a fair and efficient asylum determination procedure.[18]

Basic treatment
The MS shall adopt minimal standards concerning the reception conditions of asylum seekers within five years of the entry into force of the Amsterdam treaty.

3. Procedural guarantees

Independent decision taking
'Decisions will be taken independently in the sense that all asylum applications will be examined and decided upon individually, objectively and impartially'.[19]

Determination of refugee status
The Resolution highlights the need for national asylum legislation, regulating access to the procedure, the procedure itself and the competent authorities.[20] The Resolution also includes provisions on the actual decision-taking body and the applicant. The competent authority must 'of its own initiative, take into consideration and seek to establish all the relevant facts and give the applicant the opportunity to present a substantial description of the circumstances of the case and to prove them. For her/his part the applicant must present all the facts and circumstances known to him and give access to all the available evidence. Recognition of refugee status is not dependent on the production of any particular formal evidence'.[21]

Legal counseling during the procedure
As well as ensuring that asylum seekers have access to legal advise and the services of an interpreter[22], the Resolution states that: 'The decision on the asylum application must be communicated to the asylum seeker in writing. If the application is rejected, the asylum seeker must be informed of the reasons and of any possibility of having the decision reviewed. The asylum seeker must have the opportunity, inasmuch as national law so provides, to acquaint himself with or be informed of the main purport of the decision and any possibility of appeal, in a language which he understands'.[23]

---

[18] This reflects UNHCR ExCom Resolutions Nos. 8 & 30, as well as the Council of Europe Recommendation. No. R (81) 16.
[19] Paragraph 4.
[20] Paragraph 3.
[21] Paragraph 5.
[22] Paragraph 13.
[23] Paragraph 15.

Independent appeal authority

'In the case of a negative decision, provision must be made for an appeal to a court or a review authority which gives an independent ruling on individual cases under the conditions laid down in paragraph 4'.[24] It is to be understood that the review body is normally independent, and therefore different, from the first instance decision-taking body. The exercise of the right to an independent review procedure with suspensive effect is crucial to the quality and thoroughness of the decision-taking in the asylum procedure.

Adequate time for appeal

'The asylum seeker must be given an adequate period of time within which to appeal and to prepare his case when requesting review of the decision. These time limits must be communicated to the asylum seeker in good time'.[25]

Benefit of the doubt

Although not mentioned in the Resolution, the notion of the benefit of the doubt, which is an essential safeguard recognized in the asylum procedure in many countries, is expressly highlighted in par 3 of the Joint position on the harmonized implementation of the definition of the term 'refugee' etc.[26]

4. Additional safeguards for unaccompanied minors and women

Unaccompanied minors

'Provisions must be made for unaccompanied minors seeking asylum to be represented by a specifically appointed adult or institution if they do not have capacity under national law. During the interview, unaccompanied minors may be accompanied by that adult or representatives of that institution. Those persons are to protect the child's interests'.[27]

Maturity

'When examining an application for asylum from an unaccompanied minor, his mental development and maturity will be taken into account'.[28]

Women

'Member States must endeavor to involve skilled female employees and female interpreters in the asylum procedure where necessary, particularly where female

---

[24] Paragraph 8.

[25] Paragraph 16.

[26] This deficiency is corrected by the EU Joint Position on the Harmonised Application of the Definition of the Term 'Refugee', which in paragraph 3 highlights the standards of the evidence required and that the asylum seeker should be given the benefit of the doubt.

[27] Paragraph 26.

[28] Paragraph 27.

asylum seekers find it difficult to present the grounds for their application in a comprehensive manner owing to the experiences they have undergone or to their cultural origin'.[29]

International standards
Further important details with regard to the treatment of the unaccompanied minor asylum seekers can be found in the Council Resolution on Unaccompanied Third-Country Minors of 27 May 1997.

5. Special procedures

5.1. *Accelerated procedure for manifestly unfounded applications*

Manifestly unfounded asylum applications
'Manifestly unfounded asylum applications within the meaning of the Resolution adopted by the Immigration Ministers at their meeting on 30 November and 1 December 1992 will be dealt with in accordance with that Resolution. Subject to the principles laid down therein, the guarantees laid down in the present Resolution will apply'.[30] It should be recalled that manifestly unfounded claims are those where it is clear that none of the substantive criteria laid down in the 1951 Refugee Convention are met, either because there is clearly no substance to the applicant's claim to fear persecution in his/her own country, or because the claim is based on deliberate deception or is an abuse of asylum procedures.

Asylum applicants from EU Member States
'The Member States observe that, with due regard for the 1951 Geneva Refugee Convention, there should be no *de facto* or *de jure* grounds for granting refugee status to an asylum applicant who is a national of another Member State. On this basis a particularly rapid or simplified procedure will be applied to the application for asylum lodged by a national of another Member State, in accordance with each Member State's rules and practice, it being specified that the Member States continue to be obliged to examine individually every application for asylum, as provided by the Geneva Convention to which the Treaty on European Union refers'.[31]

Exclusion of appeal
By way of derogation from the right to appeal/review, 'Member States may exclude the possibility of lodging an appeal against a decision to reject an applica-

---

[29] Paragraph 28.
[30] Paragraph 18.
[31] Paragraph 20.

tion if, instead, an independent body which is distinct from the examining authority has already confirmed the decision'.[32]

Derogation from suspensive effect
Member States may provide for exceptions to the principle of the suspensive effect of the appeal in limited cases, under national law, when in consideration of objective criteria extraneous to the application itself the application is considered as manifestly unfounded in accordance with the relevant provisions of the Resolution adopted by the Immigration Ministers on 30 November and 1 December 1992. 'However, in such cases it should at least be guaranteed that the decision on the application is taken at a high level and that additional sufficient safeguards (e.g. the same assessment, before the execution of the decision, by another authority which must be of a central nature and have the necessary knowledge and experience in the field of asylum and refugee law) ensure the correctness of the decision'.[33]

In summary, important exceptions to the right of appeal and suspensive effect are allowed, namely when:
– in cases of rejection on manifestly unfounded grounds, the formal appeal to a court or review authority can be replaced by an independent administrative body, as long as this is distinct from the examining authority. No clear description of the role and qualification of this body is given;[34]
– the applicant is not granted the right to stay during the appeals/review procedure in manifestly unfounded cases, and where the safe third country notion is applied.

5.2. *Safe Third Country Notion*

Exceptions from standard procedure
Member States may provide for exceptions to the principle of suspensive effect of the review/appeal where, under national law, the host third country concept is applicable in accordance with the Resolution adopted by the Immigration Ministers at their meeting on 30 November and 1 December 1992. 'In such cases Member States may also provide (...) that the decision rejecting the application, its underlying reasons and the asylum seeker's rights may be communicated to him orally instead of in writing. Upon request, the decision will be confirmed in writing. The third country authorities must, where necessary, be informed that the asylum application was not examined as to substance'.[35]

---

[32] Paragraph 19.
[33] Paragraph 21.
[34] The reasons for allowing for such an exception are linked to current practices in Denmark where the competent independent body is an NGO.
[35] Paragraph 22.

Further exceptions

The exception to the right to an independent appeal, in cases of rejection based on the application of the safe third country notion, goes further than in cases where the application is rejected as manifestly unfounded applications, in so far as a confirmation of the negative decision by another central and qualified authority is not required in such cases. Furthermore, it is allowed that the written decision be communicated to the applicant only upon request.

Informing the receiving State

The third country authorities are to be informed about the fact that the application was not examined in substance, although it is not specified how, nor in which cases this is considered necessary.

5.3. Asylum applications at the border

Opportunity to lodge an asylum application

'Member States will adopt administrative measures ensuring that any asylum seeker arriving at the frontiers is afforded an opportunity to lodge an asylum application'.[36]

Manifestly unfounded applications

'Member States may, in as much a national law so provides, apply special procedures to establish, prior to the decision on admission, whether or not the application for asylum is manifestly unfounded. No expulsion measure will be carried out during this procedure'.[37]

Border procedures for manifestly unfounded applications

Where an application for asylum is manifestly unfounded, the asylum seeker may be refused admission. In such cases, the national law of a Member State may permit an exception to the general principle of the suspensive effect of the appeal (see above).

As in the case of rejection based on manifestly unfounded grounds, it must at least be ensured that the decision on the refusal of admission is taken by a ministry or comparable central authority and that additional sufficient safeguards (for example, prior examination by another central authority) ensure the correctness of the decision. Such authorities must be fully qualified in asylum and refugee matters.[38]

---

[36] Paragraph 23.
[37] Paragraph 24.
[38] Paragraphs 8 & 17. This exception reflects and confirms the current French practice. In airport and border cases the Ministry of Foreign Affairs, the French Central Refugee Office, is being consulted on return decisions prior to their execution. However, the Ministry's opinion is not seen as binding. To that end, the Ministry employs qualified agents from (OFPRA) the French Office for the

Border procedures for safe third country cases
Article 25 permits in safe third country cases for the border authority to reject an asylum application and return the applicant to the assumed safe country without safeguards as foreseen in the normal procedure.[39] In these cases neither the competent asylum authority nor any other central authority needs to be involved. The decision on the application taken by the border authority is only confirmed in writing upon request.

Guarantees in border procedures
However, the procedures, which are foreseen in Articles 24 and 25, are to be viewed without reference to the specific national context under which they were developed.

V. CONCLUSION

More protective standards
The Resolution provides – apart from the above-mentioned exceptions for special procedures – an elaborate set of comprehensive and detailed guidelines for asylum procedures, and marks an important step forward towards the standardisation of European asylum procedures.

Some EU Member States, which have recently brought in line their asylum legislation with EU standards, have established more protective standards and chosen not to implement the non-compulsory exceptional procedural elements.

Protection of Refugees and Stateless persons who conduct interviews with asylum seekers and draft the opinion of the Ministry.

[39] The rationale behind this exception is the German 'safe third country' clause, which allows for formal rejections of asylum application by border guards based on a so-called safe third country list which is drawn up and regularly up-dated by the competent authorities after a general assessment of the situation in the respective 'safe third country'.

4.4

RESOLUTION ON A HARMONISED APPROACH TO QUESTIONS CONCERNING HOST THIRD COUNTRIES
(30 November and 1 December 1992)

I. BACKGROUND

Introduction
The Ministers of the Member States of the European Communities responsible for Immigration, meeting in London on 30 November and 1 December 1992 adopted, together with the Resolution on Manifestly Unfounded Applications for Asylum and the Conclusions on Countries in which there is Generally No Serious Risk of Persecution, this Resolution dealing with the 'Host Third Country' notion.[1]

Harmonisation theme
Adopted after the signing, but before the entry into force, of the TEU I (Maastricht) in November 1993 the Resolution is the result of the then existing intergovernmental decision-making process. This process was guided by the objective to harmonise asylum policies, as defined by the Luxembourg Council in June 1991 and cleared by the Maastricht Council in December 1991.

Legal status
Similar to other instruments adopted in the pre-Maastricht phase, the Resolution is binding for any MS, which chooses to make use of the concept defined in it.[2]

The Resolution and Amsterdam
Though not explicitly mentioned in the new Article 63 TEU II (Amsterdam), this theme will most probably be part of the asylum related issues to be communitarised in the course of the five years transition period after the entering into force of the TEU II, particularly the instrument relating to procedural asylum law.

---

[1] The Host Third Country notion is commonly known as the 'Safe Third Country' notion.
[2] Although they are binding on any State which wishes to accede to the Union.

P.J. van Krieken (Ed.), The Asylum Acquis Handbook
© 2000, T.M.C.Asser Press, The Hague, the Röling Foundation and the authors

II. PURPOSE

Countering the increasing number of asylum seekers
Like all of the London Resolutions, the document reflects the priorities of the times which were very much focused on countering the increasing number of asylum seekers and sharing the burden for processing asylum applications with other signatories of the 1951 Refugee Convention.[3]

Concerns regarding refugees
With this Resolution the then EC Members wanted to address in particular their concerns with regard to 'the problem of refugees and asylum seekers unlawfully leaving countries where they have already been granted protection or have had a genuine opportunity to seek such protection'.[4]

Definition and harmonisation of national legislation
They therefore agreed on a definition and the basic principles on how to jointly apply the 'Host Third Country' notion. In addition, the Ministers wanted to bring in line their national legislation with the principles of the Resolution, at least by the time of the entry into force of the Dublin Convention.[5] Furthermore, they committed themselves to reviewing and – if necessary – amending the respective procedure in co-operation with the EU Commission and UNHCR.

III. CONTENT

Structure
The Resolution contains a preamble and the following four chapters:
– Procedure for application of the concept of host third country
– Substantive application: requirements and criteria for establishing whether a country is a host third country
– Dublin Convention
– Future action

Relevant criteria
The EU criteria relevant to the application of the 'safe third country' notion were complemented with procedural elements in the London Resolution on Manifestly Unfounded Applications[6] and the June 1995 Resolution on Minimum Guarantees

---

[3] Some 700.000 in 1992 (meanwhile the number was down to some 350,000 in 1998).
[4] As stated in the preamble to the Resolution.
[5] Which was foreseen at the time for 1 January 1995 (the Dublin Convention in fact entered into force in September/October 1997 for most of the EU Member States and January 1998 for Finland).
[6] Part 1(b).

for Asylum Procedures.⁷ Where appropriate reference is made in the following text to the relevant paragraph of these instruments.

IV. ANALYSIS OF THE TEXT

1. Procedure for application of the concept of host third country

Safe/host third country notion
As mentioned above, the same Council meeting in London in November/December 1992 which adopted the 'Host Third Country' Resolution also passed the Resolution on Manifestly Unfounded Applications for Asylum. This Resolution refers in paragraph 1(b) to the concept of host third country and allows for considering cases falling within this concept under the accelerated procedures.⁸

Principles for the procedural basis of application
The following principles should govern the procedural basis for applying the concept of host third country:
– the formal identification of a host third country in principle precedes the substantive examination of the application for asylum and its justification;
– the principle of the host third country is to be applied to all applicants for asylum, irrespective of whether or not they may be regarded as refugees;
– if a host third country is identified, the application for refugee status may not be examined and the asylum applicant may be sent to that country;
– if the asylum applicant cannot in practice be sent to a host third country, the provisions of the Dublin Convention will apply;
– any Member State retains the right, for humanitarian reasons, not to remove the asylum applicant to a host third country;
– third country authorities must, where necessary, be informed that the asylum application was not examined as to the substance.⁹

Need for procedural safeguards
The Resolution does not include all the relevant procedural elements, as essential provisions for exceptional procedures were only included in later instruments of the EU acquis on asylum. Hence, this Resolution needs to be read in conjunction with other EU texts, in particular with the Resolution on Minimum Guarantees for Asylum Procedures.

---

⁷ Articles 22 and 25 of the Resolution on Minimum Guarantees for Asylum Procedures.
⁸ Most of the countries applying the safe third country notion have established such procedures.
⁹ Article 25 of the Resolution on Minimum Guarantees for Asylum Procedures.

Need for safeguards
While international standards accept, in principle, that States can agree on parameters for the purpose of identifying the country responsible to examine the claim of an asylum seeker, the procedures applied in this regard should be surrounded by safeguards, which ensure that there will be no breach of the principle of non-refoulement

Member State exceptions
The Resolution on Minimum Guarantees for Asylum Procedures, in articles 22 to 25, allows for exceptions to these safeguards in accelerated procedures and border procedures in certain cases, including cases where the safe third country notion is applied.[10] Caution must be taken in such cases though, as the aim and purpose of the various safeguards is to ensure that no chain deportations, forcible returns to situations of persecution or 'refugee in orbit' situations occur.

State obligations
The responsibility of a State under the 1951 Refugee Convention is engaged whenever that State is presented with a request for asylum. The fact that a refugee has found, or could have found, protection elsewhere does not remove the obligation of a State to respect the principle of non-refoulement, even though it might be agreed that the primary responsibility for providing protection lies with another State.

2. **Requirements and criteria for establishing whether a country is a host third country**

Criteria
The Resolution provides a set of 'fundamental requirements'[11] to determine a safe third country, which should be assessed by the Member States in *each individual case:*
– life or freedom of the applicant must not be threatened in the safe third country within the meaning of Article 33 of the 1951 Refugee Convention;
– the applicant must not be exposed to torture or inhuman or degrading treatment;
– either protection was already granted, or there was the opportunity to seek protection, or clear evidence of admissibility to the safe third country;
– effective protection against refoulement (Article 33.1 of the 1951 Refugee Convention);

---

[10] Please see for further details under the respective parts of the Resolution on Minimum Guarantees for Asylum Procedures.
[11] Chapter 2.

In addition,
− Known practices in the third country, especially with regard to non-refoulement, and UNHCR information are taken into account.

Dublin Convention
The Resolution also determines the relations of the safe third country notion with the provisions of the Dublin Convention. The later provides a complex system of criteria to determine the responsibility for the examination of an asylum application among EU Member States which replaces the application of the safe third country notion between EU Member States. The safe third country notion remains applicable between EU Member States and non-EU Member States.

The safe third country notion and the Dublin Convention
According to the Resolution, the safe third country notion:
− precedes the Dublin mechanism, if the Member States decide to invoke the notion with regard to a non-Member State;
− cannot be used by a Member States to decline responsibilities pursuant to the Dublin mechanism;
can be applied also after having accepted the responsibility according to the Dublin Convention;
− does not hinder a Member State to voluntarily accept responsibility to examine an asylum application.[12]

V. CONCLUSIONS

Additional requirements
The individual assessment in each individual case is one of the essential safeguards enumerated in the Resolution.

---

[12] Chapter 3.

CONCLUSIONS ON COUNTRIES IN WHICH THERE IS GENERALLY NO SERIOUS RISK OF PERSECUTION
(*30 November and 1 December 1992*)

I. BACKGROUND

General
These Conclusions were adopted by the twelve Ministers responsible for Immigration of the (then) twelve Member States of the European Communities at their meeting in London on 30 November and 1 December 1992. The Conclusions relate to the Council Resolution on Manifestly Unfounded Applications for Asylum[1] which was adopted at the same meeting.

The Conclusion and Amsterdam
According to the Action Plan of the European Council Vienna the Conclusions might be reviewed and adopted by the JHA Council as a First Pillar instrument based on art. 63 TEC.[2]

II. PURPOSE

General
The purpose of the Conclusions is to develop a *concept*, usually referred to as the concept of 'safe' countries of origin[3], to assist in the establishing of a harmonised approach to asylum applications from countries which can be shown, in an objective and verifiable way, not to normally generate refugees.

Lack of procedures
The Conclusions list factors that a Member State can take into account when determining whether a country is one in which there is generally no serious risk of persecution. Once a Member State considers a country fits this criteria, the Mem-

---

[1] This Resolution is reviewed as a part of this Series.
[2] According to the Austrian Presidency's 'Action plan on establishing an area of freedom, security and justice' of 28 November 1998, the time frame for this adoption is within two years after the entry into force of TEU II.
[3] This concept or notion has also been referred to as the Safe Country of Origin Concept/Notion.

P.J. van Krieken (Ed.), The Asylum Acquis Handbook
© 2000, T.M.C.Asser Press, The Hague, the Röling Foundation and the authors

ber State may choose to apply the accelerated procedure of Article Two of the Resolution on Manifestly Unfounded Applications for Asylum to asylum applicants from that State.

III. CONTENT

Structure
The Conclusions is divided into six parts:
Part One: Definition
Part Two: Establishing a harmonised approach
Part Three: Assessments by a Member State
Part Four: Elements in the assessment
Part Five: Information based on wide range of sources
Part Six: Allowance for other elements of assessment

Definition of 'Safe country of origin' notion
Part One presents the definition of the 'safe country of origin'. It reads: *'This concept means that it is a country which can be clearly shown, in an objective and verifiable way, normally not to generate refugees or where it can be clearly shown, in an objective and verifiable way, that circumstances which might in the past have justified recourse to the 1951 Geneva Convention have ceased to exist'.*

Elements of assessment
Part Four of the Conclusions sets out the minimum elements in the assessment of 'safe' countries of origin. These elements are:
– Previous number of refugees and recognition rates
– Observance of human rights
– Existence of democratic institutions
– Stability

Sources of information
Part Five indicates that the assessment of the elements stated above should be based upon as wide a range of sources of information as possible, namely:
– Reports from diplomatic missions
– International organisations
– Non-governmental organisations
– Press
– UNHCR

IV. ANALYSIS OF TEXT

General
In principle, the notion of 'safe country of origin' is generally accepted and used:
– As a procedural tool to assign applications to accelerated procedures;
– In an evidentiary function (as a rebuttable presumption).

Application of the concept
As outlined in the Resolution on Manifestly Unfounded Applications for Asylum, the application of the accelerated procedures includes certain procedural safeguards such as an appeal or review possibility, and applicants are able to present specific indications which could outweigh any general presumption.

As foreseen under the abovementioned Resolution and the Resolution on Minimum Guarantees for Asylum Procedures[4], Member States must nevertheless consider the individual claims of all applicants from such countries, as it is impossible to exclude, as a matter of law, the possibility that an individual could have a well-founded fear of persecution in any particular country, however great its attachment to human rights and the rule of law.

Therefore, an assessment by an individual Member State of a country as one in which there is generally no serious risk of persecution should not automatically result in the refusal of all asylum applications from its nationals or their exclusion from individualised determination procedures, due to the importance of the possibility of an asylum seeker having a well-founded individual fear in their country of origin.

Evaluation of situation in country of origin
The text of the Conclusion suggests the following elements in determining whether a country of origin is 'safe':
1. Its record for not producing refugees – although low recognition rates can change suddenly, for example after a violent coup, but logic suggests that such a State immediately ceases to be safe as it does not any more fulfill the criteria;
2. Its observance of human rights – both through formal obligations and how in practice it meets those obligations, of which the latter aspect is clearly of more importance;
3. Its democratic institutions – which similarly in practice must offer effective protection and redress;
4. Stability – due to changing conditions in countries of origin, decisions on the 'safety' of a particular country must be reviewed over time.

Use of a wide range of resources
With regard to the information used for the assessment, the Conclusion stresses the need for a wide range of sources, including advice and reports from diplomatic missions, international and non-governmental organisations and press reports.

---

[4] OJ No. C 274, 19.09.1996, p. 13.

4.6

RESOLUTION ON MANIFESTLY UNFOUNDED APPLICATIONS FOR ASYLUM
(*30 November and 1 December 1992*)

The London Resolutions comprise of three instruments:
– *Resolution on Manifestly Unfounded Applications for Asylum*
– *Conclusions on Countries in which there is Generally No Serious Risk of Persecution*
– *Resolution on a Harmonised Approach to Questions concerning Host Third Countries*

These three instruments aimed to increase confidence between Member States and to standardise their approach in asylum policy, so as to close the loopholes for fraudulent asylum seekers and to make the process for genuine asylum seekers more efficient.

I BACKGROUND

General
The Resolution was adopted by the Ministers of the Member States of the European Communities responsible for Immigration prior to the entry into force of TEU I (Maastricht Treaty) in the context of the (then) existing inter-governmental cooperation. It is not an EC law instrument[1], but its elements are expected to be implemented in law and practice by the EU Member States.

Although no MS is under any obligation to introduce the concepts of 'Manifestly Unfounded', 'Host Third Country', 'Safe Country of Origin', 'Accelerated procedure' defined in these instruments into its national law or practice, any MS which chooses to do so has to do it in conformity with them and to implement fully the procedural guarantees laid down in the resolutions.

The Resolution and Amsterdam
A binding EC law instrument on minimal standards for asylum procedures based on art. 63 TEC (EC Vienna, Action Plan) shall regulate the questions covered by this Resolution.

---

[1] Although the Resolution is politically binding on any State which wishes to accede to the Union.

II. PURPOSE

General
The Resolution should be seen against the backdrop of a considerable increase in the number of asylum applications considered to be unfounded or abusive or otherwise not deserving of in-depth examination, and the resulting pressure on the asylum systems of the Member States.

The Resolution is therefore an attempt to standardise Member States' applications of the definition of 'manifestly unfounded' applications and the use of accelerated or simplified procedures to deal with such cases.

Apart from the 'manifestly unfounded' applications, the Resolution suggests further cases, which could give, rise to the application of accelerated procedures, which are not necessarily considered as 'manifestly unfounded'.

In adopting the Resolution, Member States expressed the aim of adapting their national laws to incorporate the principles of it as soon as possible (at the latest 1 January 1995).[2]

III. CONTENT

Structure
The Resolution contains a preamble and is structured into five main paragraphs which are further is divided into twelve Parts:

Preamble: Refers to guarantee of protection in the terms of the 1951 Refugee Convention and 1967 Protocol.

Paragraph One: Manifestly Unfounded Applications
– Definition and 'Safe third country' cases
– Accelerated procedure
– Elements of an accelerated procedures
– Minimum Standards for an accelerated procedure
– Applicant leaving Community territory

Paragraph Two: No Substance to Claim to Fear of Persecution
– Definition and procedure
– Internal flight alternative cases
– Safe country of origin cases

---

[2] They furthermore commit themselves to reviewing the operation of accelerated procedures from time to time, and examining whether any additional measures are necessary.

Paragraph Three: Deliberate Deception or Abuse of Asylum Procedures
- Definition
- Indicators for bad faith and well-founded fear of persecution
- Other cases for accelerated Procedures
- Further Action

Categories of manifestly unfounded applications
In Paragraph One two categories of manifestly unfounded applications are presented and the procedural elements for manifestly unfounded claims are outlined. The two categories are:
- No substance to claim fear of persecution;
- Deliberate deception or abuse of asylum procedures.

No substance
The first category of manifestly unfounded claims is further defined in Part Two and consists of those with 'no substance to claim fear of persecution' because:
- The grounds are outside the scope of the 1951 Refugee Convention but are related to the search for better living conditions;
- The application is totally lacking in substance, not containing circumstantial or personal details;
- The application is lacking any credibility by being inconsistent, contradictory or fundamentally improbable.[3]

Clear deceit or abuse
The second category of claims is further defined in Part Three and may be considered as manifestly unfounded since they constitute a deliberate deception or abuse of asylum procedures.

However, the Resolution clearly indicates that the elements outlined in this category constitute indications and shall only lead to the consideration of a claim in an accelerated procedure 'in the absence of satisfactory explanation for the applicant's behavior'.[4]

These factors cannot in themselves outweigh a well-founded fear of persecution according to Article 1A 2 of the 1951 Refugee Convention.

The indications for a clear deceit or abuse are outlined under Part 9 and can be seen in the following cases:
- Application based on false identity, forged or counterfeit document (maintaining their authenticity);
- Deliberate false representations about the claim;
- Destruction, damage or disposal in bad faith of passport, other documents or tickets relevant to the claim;

---

[3] Parts 6-8.
[4] Part 10.

– Deliberate failure to reveal previously lodged applications in one or more than one countries;
– Application to forestall impending expulsion despite earlier ample opportunity of applying;
– Flagrant failure to comply with substantive obligations imposed by rules of asylum procedure;
– Where an asylum application has previously been rejected in another Member State of the European Union[5].

Accelerated procedures
The Resolution leaves it open to the Member States to include manifestly unfounded asylum applications within an accelerated procedure. Such procedures need not include full examination at each level, and Member States can expedite the appeal stage provided they comply with the procedural guarantees laid down in the resolution.

Acceleration elements
Three specific elements are suggested to accelerated the procedure:
– Providing the initial decision as soon as possible;
– Completion of any appeal or review procedure as soon as possible;
– More simplified appeal and review procedures than those generally available.

Procedural safeguards
The Resolution contains the following procedural safeguards:
– Decision taken by the competent authority at the appropriate level fully qualified in asylum and refugee matters[6];
– Opportunity for a personal interview with qualified officials before any final decision is taken.[7]
   This would assume a full review of the claim at first instance, whereas the elements of accelerated procedure come in with regard to the appeal stage.

Other cases for accelerated procedures
Furthermore, the Member States may operate accelerated procedures for various other cases, without considering those 'manifestly unfounded'. This might be the situation if an applicant has transited a so-called 'host third country'[8] or without prejudice to the substance of the claim, where a case falls manifestly within the situation mentioned in Article 1F 1951 Refugee Convention, or the applicant constitutes a threat to national security.[9]

---
[5] Part 9(a-g).
[6] Part 4.
[7] Ibid.
[8] Part 1(b).
[9] Part 11.

Internal flight alternative
In addition, the Resolution suggests that Member States consider applying an accelerated procedure if the fear of persecution is 'clearly limited to a specific geographical area where effective protection is readily available for the individual in another part of his own country' (internal flight alternative).[10]

As an additional measure, the Resolution refers to consultations among Member States on this aspect as well as to consultations with UNHCR.[11]

'Safe' country of origin concept
The Resolution further leaves it open to Member States to include under the scope of an accelerated procedure applications of persons originating from countries in which there is generally no serious risk of persecution (safe country of origin).[12]

IV. ANALYSIS OF TEXT

1951 Refugee Convention and ExCom Conclusion No. 30
While interpreting the Resolution it is important to note that the preamble refers to the determination of Member States to guarantee protection in accordance with the terms of the 1951 Refugee Convention and 1967 Protocol, and refers to Conclusion No. 30 of the Executive Committee of UNHCR on 'The Problem of manifestly unfounded or abusive applications for refugee status or asylum'.

Furthermore the final paragraph refers to the need for consultations with UNHCR in the review of the implementation of the Resolution.[13]

Definition of clear abuse or deceit
Part 9 sets out the circumstances, which may constitute a manifestly unfounded application for the purposes of the Resolution. These include:
– where an application is based on a false identity or on forged or counterfeit documents, and the applicant has maintained that they are genuine when questioned, or has destroyed documents in bad faith;
– when an applicant has deliberately made false representations about his/her claim;
– when the applicant has deliberately failed to reveal a previous application for asylum in another Member State or a 'safe' third country;
– when an application is submitted in order to forestall an impending expulsion measure, provided that the applicant has had ample opportunity earlier to submit a claim;

---
[10] Part 7.
[11] Ibid.
[12] Part 8.
[13] Part 12.

— where an applicant has flagrantly failed to comply with substantive obligations imposed by national rules relating to asylum procedures.

The categories outlined under Part 9 in the Resolution reflect the notion of clearly fraudulent or abusive asylum applications, whereby there is a deliberate attempt, in bad faith, on the part of the individual to deceive the relevant authorities.

Indicators of bad faith
With regard to the indicators of 'bad faith' listed in Chapter 9 of the Resolution the following elements could be taken into thorough consideration:
— With regard to the use of forged or counterfeit documents it should be borne in mind that asylum seekers are often compelled to use forged documents, and will often insist on their genuineness until admitted into the country and the asylum procedure. Therefore an asylum seeker's lack of documentation or use of forged documentation should not by itself render his/her claim manifestly unfounded[14];
— The mere fact of having made false representations does not necessarily exclude a well-founded fear of persecution, and only if the representations appear to be false allegations of a material or substantive nature relevant for the status determination could the claim be considered fraudulent[15];
— Applications filed to forestall an expulsion order should only be considered as manifestly unfounded if the applicant is not in a position to give valid explanations for the delay[16];
— An application after the rejection of an asylum claim in another country should only be considered as manifestly unfounded if the previous examination of the merits of the claim was in conformity with agreed eligibility standards and the procedure comprised adequate procedural safeguards.[17]

Safe country of origin
In principle, there are no objections to process the concept of 'safe' country of origin under accelerated procedures as it is foreseen in Part 8 of the Resolution, if it is used:
— As a procedural tool to assign applications to accelerated procedures;
— In an evidentiary function (as a rebuttable presumption) provided that the accelerated procedures foresee sufficient procedural safeguards (including an ap-

---

[14] Part 9(a). It should be recalled that Article 31 of the 1951 Refugee Convention ensures that penalties are not imposed on individuals who enter or are present on the territory illegally without good reason. Caution should be taken so that applications are not automatically classified as manifestly unfounded purely on the basis of false, forged or counterfeit documents or identities.
[15] Part 9(b).
[16] Part 9(e).
[17] Part 9(g).

peal or review possibility) and an effective possibility to rebut the presumption of the existence of safety in the country of origin.[18]

Procedural safeguards according to the Resolution on Minimum Guarantees
The Resolution should be read in conjunction with the resolution on minimal guarantees in asylum procedures, where the nature and scope of the possible exceptions to normal procedure and of the compensatory safeguards are described more in full.

V. CONCLUSIONS

Accelerated procedures for claims considered as manifestly unfounded, i.e. which are obviously without foundation, have generally proven useful in reducing the waiting period for the applicant and in helping discourage abusing claims in the Member States.

The purpose of an accelerated procedure is not only to reject very fast manifestly unfounded and clearly abusive applications but also to be a tool to quickly detect cases which have been erroneously channelled into that procedure.

---

[18] For further details concerning the 'safe country of origin' notion, please see the Chapter on the respective conclusion adopted in the London 1992.

4.7

COUNCIL RESOLUTION ON UNACCOMPANIED MINORS WHO ARE NATIONALS OF THIRD COUNTRIES
(*Brussels, 26 June 1997*)[1]

I. BACKGROUND

General
On 26 June 1997, the European Ministers responsible for Justice and Home Affairs adopted the Council Resolution on Unaccompanied Minors who are Nationals of Third Countries, in recognition of the vulnerable situation of all unaccompanied minors, both asylum seekers and migrants. A child's requirement for special safeguards and care justifies the laying down of common guidelines for dealing with such situations.

UN Convention on the Rights of the Child
The Council Resolution states in the preamble that it is without prejudice to the international commitments entered into by the Member States pursuant to the UN Convention on the Rights of the Child.[2] The UN Convention is the most widely ratified international instrument, with only two countries in the world[3] not being signatories to its provisions.

Therefore, in reflection of Article 3 of the UN Convention, the Council Resolution ensures that 'the best interests of the child shall be a primary consideration'.

Definition of unaccompanied minor
The Resolution defines an 'unaccompanied minor' as a third country national below the age of eighteen, who arrives on the territory of the Member States unaccompanied or not awaited at arrival by an adult responsible for it whether by law or custom. The Resolution can also be applied to minors of third countries who are left unaccompanied after they have entered the territory of the Member States

---

[1] OJ No. C 221, 19.07.1997, p. 23.
[2] Adopted and opened to signature, ratification and accession by UN General Assembly Resolution 44/25 of 20 November 1989.
[3] The United States of America and Somalia.

P.J. van Krieken (Ed.), *The Asylum Acquis Handbook*
© 2000, T.M.C.Asser Press, The Hague, the Röling Foundation and the authors

II. PURPOSE

Guidelines on treatment
The Resolution establishes guidelines for the treatment of unaccompanied minors (UAM) with regard to reception, stay and return conditions, and the handling of their applications for asylum, taking into consideration their particular needs and their vulnerable situation. The Resolution recognises especially the need to provide, as soon as possible, the assistance of a legal guardian, either a specifically appointed adult representative or an institution.

The Resolution also recognises the need to quickly establish the unaccompanied minor's identity and then to trace their parents or relations, and to reunite them if this is feasible or possible. However, irrespective of their legal status, unaccompanied minors should be entitled to the necessary protection and care in accordance with the national law.

Although the Resolution only sets out guidelines, the competent authorities in each Member State must be notified of the contents of the Resolution[4], and the guidelines must be taken into account in all proposals for changes to national legislation.[5] The Resolution must also be read in light of the Council Resolution on Minimum Guarantees for Asylum Procedures[6] which requires Member States to make provisions for the representation and protection of unaccompanied minor asylum seekers.

More favourable provisions
The intention of the Resolution was to set out guidelines for national authorities to follow in dealings with unaccompanied minors from third countries. However, the text stresses in two separate articles[7] that Member States are free to allow more favourable conditions under their national laws, thereby ensuring that unaccompanied minors can receive the greatest level of protection possible.

Yearly review of application guidelines
The application of the guidelines is to be reviewed once a year by the Council, in conjunction with the Commission and in consultation with UNHCR, and if appropriate the guidelines will be adapted to meet the developments in asylum and immigration policy. This review procedure has not been implemented since the Resolution was adopted.

---

[4] Article 1(5).
[5] Article 6(1).
[6] OJ No. C 274, 19.09.1996, p. 3.
[7] Article 1(4) and Article 6(2).

III. CONTENT

Structure
The Resolution contains a preamble, six articles and an Annex, setting out the rights of unaccompanied minors and of the Member States. These provisions relate to both unaccompanied minor asylum seekers and other migrants. The articles are titled as the following:
– Scope and purpose
– Admission
– Minimum guarantees for all unaccompanied minors
– Asylum procedure
– Return of unaccompanied minors
– Final provisions
– Annex. Measures to combat trafficking in minors, and measures to prevent illegal entry.

IV. ANALYSIS OF TEXT

The Resolution was intended to deal with all unaccompanied minors who are nationals of third countries; be they migrants or asylum seekers. The original draft Resolution was only intended to cover migrants, and not asylum seekers, but the Member States decided that it was necessary to include specific provisions and safeguards for unaccompanied minor asylum seekers. It is important to remember that the text covers two specific groups of minors – and some of the provisions apply solely to one group; while others, such as the minimum guarantees, apply to both.

Article 2: Admission of unaccompanied minors

In Article 2, Member States retain the right to refuse entry to their territory for unaccompanied minors. This provision does not apply to unaccompanied minors who apply for asylum, as in this case the Resolution on Minimum Guarantees for Asylum Procedures applies. Member States should co-operate in preventing the unauthorised entry or illegal residence of unaccompanied minors on their territory.

When unaccompanied minors remain at the border pending a decision, they must receive all necessary material support, such as food, accommodation, sanitary facilities and medical care.[8]

---

[8] Article 2(3).

Article 3: Minimum guarantees for all unaccompanied minors

All unaccompanied minors, whether they are asylum seekers or not, require a basic standard of treatment, and Article 3 sets out the minimum guarantees for such treatment.

The first task for the competent authorities is to establish the individual's identification. This must be done with sensitivity to the child's age and maturity, and any information that is obtained must be treated with confidentiality, particularly in the case of asylum seekers. The importance of such information is that it may enhance the prospects of family reunion for the minor;

It is generally in the minor's best interest to facilitate family reunification, therefore the competent authorities should endeavour to trace any family members, regardless of their legal status and without prejudice to any application for residence. Unaccompanied minors are also encouraged to contact organisations, and the International Committee of the Red Cross in particular, to help in tracing family members. Once again, confidentiality of any information, especially for asylum seekers, is essential;

The Resolution guarantees that all unaccompanied minors are provided the necessary representation, either through a legal guardian, representation by a (national) organisation, or by other appropriate representation. Such representation must ensure, in accordance with national law, that the minor's needs (for example legal, social, medical and psychological) are duly met;

When it is assumed that an unaccompanied minor will remain on the territory of the Member State for a prolonged period, they must be granted the same right to general education that nationals receive, or special provisions must be made for them;

Unaccompanied minors must receive appropriate medical treatment for their immediate needs. Special treatment must also be available for those who have suffered any form of neglect, exploitation, or abuse, torture or any other form of cruel, inhuman or degrading treatment or punishment, or armed conflict. Due to the traumatic situations which an unaccompanied minor might have fled from, and finding themselves alone in an alien environment, the availability of appropriate psychological treatment is essential.

Article 4: Asylum procedure

Right to asylum
Every unaccompanied minor should have the right to apply for asylum.[9] However, Member States may reserve the right to require minors under a certain age

---

[9] Article 4(1).

to apply for asylum only if they have the assistance of a legal guardian, or a specifically appointed adult representative or institution.

Asylum claims from minors should be treated as a matter of absolute priority[10], and during all interviews unaccompanied minors should be represented by their legal guardian or other responsible person. The importance of specific training for officers conducting interviews is expressly recognised. Furthermore, as well as objective facts and circumstances, the minor's stage of development, psychological maturity and his/her possibly limited knowledge of conditions in the country of origin should always be taken into account.[11]

Appropriate reception facilities
Member States have an obligation to provide appropriate reception facilities such as with adult relatives, foster families, specialised reception centres or other suitable accommodation. Minors over the age of 16 may be placed in reception centres for adult asylum seekers.[12]

The Resolution does not exclude the possibility of unaccompanied minors being held in detention or 'closed centres'. However, as a minimum, Article 37 of the Convention on the Rights of the Child states that detention of minors must be used 'only as a measure of last resort and for the shortest appropriate period of time'.

Burden of proof and age assessment
In principle, the burden of proof regarding the minor's age rests on the minor himself or herself[13], although it may be necessary to carry out an objective age assessment. If so, this must be carried out by qualified medical personnel and with the consent of the minor or their representative.

Long-term arrangements
Once an unaccompanied minor has been granted refugee status or any other permanent right of residence they should be provided with long-term arrangements for accommodation.[14] However, if it is in the best interests of the child, the priority should be family reunification and possible voluntary repatriation. Otherwise, the integration of the child into the host country should be facilitated, for example though a structured orientation programmes.

---

[10] However, certain Member States do not process such asylum claims as a matter of urgency due to the need to obtain all of the facts relating to the minor's asylum application beforehand.
[11] Article 4(6).
[12] Article 4(4).
[13] Article 4(3).
[14] Article 4(7).

Article 5: Return of unaccompanied minors

Adequate reception and care
An unaccompanied minor can only be returned to his/her country of origin, or to a third country that is prepared to accept him/her, if adequate reception and care is available, and in line with Article 3 of the Convention of the Rights of the Child.[15] Care can be provided by parents or other adults who can take care of the child, or by governmental or non-governmental bodies. If these conditions are not present, the minor must remain on the territory of the Member States.[16]

If return is being considered, the competent authorities in the Member States must co-operate with the authorities of the country of origin or with the authorities of a third country, with international organisations such as UNHCR or UNICEF, or with NGO's, prior to departure to determine the availability of reception and care facilities in the country to where the minor might be returned to.

Any procedures with a view to the removal of a minor from the territory must comply with the Member States' obligations under international instruments such as the 1951 Refugee Convention or the ECHR.[17]

Annex: Trafficking and illegal entry

Measures to combat trafficking in minors
As unaccompanied minors are particularly vulnerable to exploitation, the Member States agreed to take all measures to prevent the trafficking and exploitation of minors, and to co-operate in this regard.

Measures to prevent illegal entry
Member States are allowed to take certain measures to prevent the unauthorised arrival of unaccompanied minors on their territory. These measures may include: collaboration with competent authorities or bodies such as airline companies, observation at airports of flights coming from sensitive countries, and application of carriers' liability legislation.

Status of the Annex
These measures are in an Annex to the Resolution, rather than in the body of the text, because they do not constitute part of the structure to protect unaccompanied minors.

However, any such measures must not reduce the right of unaccompanied minors to arrive on the territory of the EU if they wish to exercise their right to

---

[15] Article 5(1).
[16] Article 5(2).
[17] Article 5(4).

claim asylum.[18] This is emphasised in the preamble of the Resolution which expressly refers to Article 22 of the Convention on the Rights of the Child regarding the protection of child asylum seekers or refugees; as well as the great importance which Member States, as a result of their common humanitarian tradition, place on the protection of refugees.

V. CONCLUSIONS

In general, the text of the Resolution represents an opportunity for substantial protection for unaccompanied minors, including comprehensive guarantees for family tracing and family reunification, basic care and reception, legal representation or guardianship, educational and medical treatment.

In ensuring that the guarantees are implemented, the involvement of a central, competent body including child welfare personnel in integration or in aiding voluntary repatriation has been shown to be of benefit.[19]

---

[18] As set out in Article 4(1) of the Resolution.
[19] An example of good practice in this regard is the Children's Panel of the Refugee Council in the UK. The Government refers all unaccompanied minor asylum seekers to the Children's Panel, which is then responsible for organising the welfare of the child during the asylum procedure.

4.8

COUNCIL RECOMMENDATIONS CONCERNING READMISSION AGREEMENTS
(*Brussels, 30 November 1994 and 24 July 1995*)

I. BACKGROUND

General

Readmission agreements are bilateral contracts normally signed between an EU Member State and a non-EU Member State which are designed to facilitate the return, between the signatory States to the agreement, of nationals who have entered in an irregular manner, as well as asylum seekers from third countries who have been rejected and/or determined as manifestly unfounded cases.

The Council of Ministers for Justice and Home Affairs of the European Union have adopted two recommendations in this field:
1) Council Recommendation of 30 November 1994 concerning a Specimen Bilateral Readmission Agreement between a Member State of the European Union and a Third Country[1];
2) Council Recommendation of 24 July 1995 on the Guiding Principles to be followed in Drawing up Protocols on the Implementation of Readmission Agreements[2].

Although the Council Recommendations concerning readmission agreements are part of the EU acquis on migration rather than asylum, they are included here as readmission agreements are used, *inter alia*, as a legal basis for the return of asylum seekers to third countries.

Readmission agreements and Amsterdam

The entry into force of TEU II (Amsterdam) on 1 May 1999, conferred new powers on the EC in the field of immigration and asylum.

---

[1] OJ No. C 274, 19.09.1996, p. 20.
[2] OJ No. C 274, 19.09.1996, p. 25.

II. PURPOSE

Standardisation of related practices
By suggesting a model agreement and providing guidelines regarding the facilitation of returns under these agreements the EU intends to standardise the related practice of its Member States. The latter is an indispensable precondition to establishing a joint external border and to creating a common area of freedom, security and justice.

Increase in readmission agreements
The ever increasing number of cross-border movements and, as a side effect, the phenomena of unauthorized immigration has in the past few years triggered a 'boom' of so-called readmission agreements among almost all European States.

The benefit of such, normally bilateral, agreements can be seen in the explicit commitment of the contracting States to readmit not only their own nationals, but also third-country nationals who either entered the other contracting State via the external frontier[3], or for whose entry the contracting State can be held responsible.[4]

III. CONTENT

Structure of 30 November 1994 Recommendation
The Council Recommendation concerning a Specimen Bilateral Readmission Agreement, of 30 November 1994, is divided into the following 13 articles:
1. Readmission of own nationals
2. Readmission in the case of third-country nationals who entered via the external frontier
3. Readmission of nationals of third countries by the Contracting Party responsible for the entry
4. Residence permits
5. Time limits
6. Time limit after which the readmission obligation will lapse
7. Transit
8. Data protection
9. Costs

---

[3] An external frontier is defined as 'the first frontier to have been crossed which is not a frontier common to the Contracting Parties', Council Recommendation concerning a Specimen Bilateral Readmission Agreement, Article 2(2).

[4] For example, if a Contracting Party has issued a valid visa or valid residence permit to the individual, Council Recommendation concerning a Specimen Bilateral Readmission Agreement, Article 3(1).

10. Committee of Experts
11. Clause stipulating that international agreements/conventions shall not be affected
12. Entry into force
13. Suspension, termination

Council Recommendation of 30 November 1994
The specimen readmission agreement provides the main provisions necessary to govern the relations between two or more States on the readmission of persons residing without authorization in the respective countries. The following listed groups are covered under the agreement:
– nationals, or persons who have been deprived of their nationality in one contracting State while there were staying in the other contracting State;[5]
– third-country nationals who entered via the external border, unless they have been in possession of a valid residence permit issued by the requesting contracting State. The Contracting Parties will give priority to deporting nationals from an adjacent State to their country of origin;[6]
– third-country nationals for whose entry the requested contracting State is responsible.[7]

Permission of residence
For readmission agreements, temporary permission to reside on the territory of one contracting State in connection with the processing of an asylum application is not recognised as a residence permit.[8] Subsequently, asylum seekers, even those provided with a temporary residence permit, are subject to readmission agreements.[9] However, to avoid 'refugee in orbit' situations[10], it is necessary to ensure that the effect of readmission agreements is suspended for asylum seekers once the material asylum procedure has commenced in a Member State.

Readmission requests
Within a maximum of 15 days the requested contracting State is expected to reply to a request for the readmission of an individual. If the readmission is approved, in principle the requested contracting State is supposed to facilitate the

---

[5] Article 1.
[6] Article 2.
[7] Article 3.
[8] Article 4.
[9] The rationale behind this provision can be seen in the possibility to use readmission agreements to facilitate returns of asylum seekers to another State identified as responsible for the examination of an asylum claim.
[10] The disadvantages of which the Member States explicitly recognised in the preamble to the Dublin Convention.

return within a maximum of one month. The time limit may be extended upon application by the requesting State.[11]

Transit of third-country nationals
Contracting States shall allow for transit of third-country nationals through their State upon request if the admission to third States of transit or destination (country of origin preferred) is assured.[12]

Transport costs
Transports cost shall in general be borne by the requesting contracting State.[13]

Monitoring
Further provisions are made for data protection (Article 8), and the interpretation and monitoring of the application of the readmission agreement by a Committee of Experts (Article 10).

Precedence of international standards
The Council Recommendation expressly states in Article 11 that international agreements and conventions will not be affected by the provisions of such readmission agreements. This applies in particular to the 1951 Refugee Convention, the ECHR, the Dublin Convention (and other international conventions on asylum), international conventions on extradition and transit, and international conventions and agreements on the readmission of foreign nationals.

Structure of 24 July 1995 Recommendation
The Council Recommendation on the Guiding Principles to be followed in Drawing up Protocols on the Implementation of Readmission Agreements consists of a preamble and the following six main points:
– Readmission procedures
– Means of identifying persons to be readmitted
– Designation of the competent authorities
– Conditions for transit of third-country nationals under escort
– Data Protection
– Conditions of applicability of the protocol

IV. ANALYSIS OF THE TEXT

Special obligations
Though the specimen for bilateral readmission agreements does not provide special provisions for asylum seekers and refugees, Article 11 of the specimen ac-

---

[11] Article 5.
[12] Article 7.
[13] Article 9.

knowledges that States have a duty to comply with certain obligations, such as those outlined in the 1951 Refugee Convention, the 1967 Protocol, the ECHR and other international agreements/conventions.[14] Subsequently, in principle the returnee might invoke the international protection standards against the return decision taken under the readmission agreement.

Return procedures and related standards of proof
There is an obligation to inform a safe third country that a claim has not been examined in substance, if this deems necessary (n.22 of the minimum guarantees). In general, if a person is returned to some other country, his claim must have been rejected in substance, otherwise this would be a violation of the principle of non-refoulement.

The Council Recommendation on Guiding Principles to be followed in Drawing up Protocols on the Implementation of Readmission Agreements (24 July 1995) provides a detailed and structured description of the return procedures and the related standards of proof. These include: the record of the return/readmission of a person under a simplified procedure (48 hours/persons apprehended in border areas), the request for readmission/transit under the normal procedure, and the record of the return/readmission in the normal procedure.

These help to avoid misunderstandings and confusion in the course of the proceedings, the disadvantages of which are often placed on the returnees.

There is no obligation on the part of the sending State to inform the receiving State of the fact that the asylum application has not been examined in substance.[15]

However, the Council Recommendation concerning a Specimen Bilateral Readmission Agreement of 30 November 1994 stipulates that in cases of transit the date of the asylum application, the present stage of the procedure and the content of any decision may be transmitted to the competent authorities.[16]

Identified concerns
In order to safeguard the not specifically mentioned rights of asylum seekers, readmission procedures must be applied in accordance with the minimum guarantees in order to avoid cases in which asylum seekers can not benefit from the asylum procedures in the receiving State, because the authorities of the receiving State were not aware that the person concerned had asked for asylum or had assumed that his claim had been reviewed in substance and the status was refused.

---

[14] For example, the Dublin Convention shall not be affected.

[15] Only the form for a request for readmission/transit of a person includes a paragraph (4.6) on applications for asylum.

[16] The issuing of such instruction is not only relevant in the context of the conclusion of readmission agreements, but also when implementing the Resolution on Minimum Guarantees for Asylum Procedures.

4.9

THE CONVENTION DETERMINING THE STATE RESPONSIBLE FOR EXAMINING APPLICATION FOR ASYLUM LODGED IN ONE OF THE MEMBER STATES OF THE EUROPEAN COMMUNITIES
(Dublin, 15 June 1990)[1]

I. BACKGROUND

General
On 1 September 1997, the Convention Determining the State Responsible for Examining Applications for Asylum Lodged in one of the Member States of the European Communities (known as the 'Dublin Convention') entered into force in the eleven European Union (EU) Member States which had signed the instrument in June 1990 and in Denmark which had signed and ratified the Convention in June 1991. In Austria and Sweden, the Convention entered into force on 1 October 1997, and in Finland on 1 January 1998.

Comparison of the Dublin Convention and Schengen Implementation Agreement
The Dublin Convention has replaced the essentially similar provisions on asylum law in Articles 28-38 of the Convention implementing the Schengen Agreement[2], applied by the Schengen States since March 1995. Like those provisions, the Dublin Convention establishes uniform criteria for determining the State responsible for examining applications for asylum. The possibility that no contracting State might consider itself responsible for examining an application for asylum is eliminated through the application of objective responsibility criteria, which at the same time aim to prevent asylum seekers submitting applications for asylum in several Member States simultaneously or in succession.[3]

Dublin Convention and the Treaty on European Union having incorporated the Schengen Agreements, both the Dublin Convention and the Schengen Agreement

---

[1] OJ No. C 254, 19.08.1997, p. 1.
[2] The Schengen Agreement has been signed fully by 13 of the 15 Members of the EU. At present, Ireland, and the United Kingdom are not Contracting Parties to the Schengen Agreement.
[3] For more information regarding the Schengen Convention see the Annex.

P.J. van Krieken (Ed.), The Asylum Acquis Handbook
© 2000, T.M.C.Asser Press, The Hague, the Röling Foundation and the authors

share the common objective of contributing to the establishment of an area without internal frontiers. The Dublin Convention lists as an additional, important, objective the harmonisation of asylum policies in the European Union.

II. PURPOSE

Establishment of a common European asylum system
The Dublin Convention provides for the establishment of a mechanism to determine responsibilities for examining an asylum claim in one of the contracting States. This principle is meant to avoid 'forum shopping', whereby an asylum seeker claims asylum in a number of Member States, as well as 'asylum seeker in orbit' situations, whereby an asylum seeker is transferred between States with no State willing to take responsibility for examining in substance their claim to asylum. Therefore, the Dublin Convention can be considered as a first and important step in the establishment of a common European asylum system. The TEU II (Amsterdam) lists the mechanism and criteria for the determination of the State responsible for examining an asylum application as a key element of a future asylum policy (Article 63).

According to the Action Plan of the European Council Vienna the Convention – which was the product of intergovernmental co-operation in the Council – will have to be replaced by a Community ('First Pillar') instrument based on Article 63 1) a TEC within a period of five years after the entry into force of TEU II. In accordance with the new Article 249(1)&(2) of the EC Treaty, the legal instrument should take the form of a Regulation.

III. CONTENT

Structure
The Dublin Convention[4] contains a preamble and 22 articles, which include:
– Article 1 provides a list of definitions for the purposes of the Convention;
– Article 2 reaffirms the commitment of the signatories to the 1951 Refugee Convention and 1967 Protocol;
– Article 3 sets out the basic principle that only one Member State should examine a request for asylum;

---

[4] As well as the Convention itself, regard must also be given to the Council Conclusions of 27 May 1997 concerning the Practical Implementation of the Dublin Convention (OJ No. C 191, 23.06.1997, p. 27), and the Implementing Guidelines adopted by the Council regarding the Application of the Dublin Convention of 9 September 1997 (OJ No. L 281, 14.10.1997, p. 1).

– Articles 4-8 can be considered the key articles as they constitute the mechanism to assign responsibility and deal with the various situations where it has to be decided which Member State has to assume responsibility for examining an application;
– Article 9 allows a Member State to decide for humanitarian reasons to examine a claim for asylum at the request of another Member State;
– Articles 10-13 deal with the practical implementation of the Convention;
– Articles 14 and 15 deal with information exchange and communications between the Member States;
– Articles 16 and 17 deal with difficulties which may arise from the implementation of Dublin;
– Article 18 refers to the Committee, which is to be set up as the governing structure of the Dublin Convention.

IV. ANALYSIS OF TEXT

A. General framework

Avoiding 'orbit' situations
The preamble of the Dublin Convention states explicitly that, in applying the Convention, Member States need to avoid so-called 'applicants in orbit' situations, in which asylum seekers are referred successively from one Member State to another without any of these States taking responsibility for examining the application.

Avoiding 'forum shopping'
Article 3(2) of the Convention stipulates that an asylum application should be processed by a single Member State. In theory, once a decision on an asylum application has been taken, there is no possibility for a repeat application in another Member State. The Dublin mechanism, therefore, is aimed at discouraging asylum seekers from applying for asylum in several Member States simultaneously or in succession.

Precedence of national law
Once the responsible Member State has accepted the application, it will process the claim according to its national law and procedure (Article 3(3)). This may include the use of the 'safe third country' notion (Article 3(5)) as laid down in national law or applied in national practice. This means that, in practice, application of the Dublin provisions does not always guarantee a material examination of the application.

Time limits and appeals

In practical terms, the Dublin Convention sets out a complex system for determining responsibility. If a Member State wishes to request another Member State to accept responsibility for an asylum seeker, it must do so as quickly as possible, and at the latest within six months. If the request is not made within the six-month time period, the responsibility for examining the asylum application will rest with the State in which the application was lodged.[5]

If an asylum seeker lodges an asylum application in one Member State, after withdrawing his/her application in another Member State, they shall be sent back to the original Member State. However, if he/she left the territory of the Member States at least three months previously, or has been granted a residence permit for three months or longer by the second Member State, that Member State shall examine the request for asylum.[6]

It should be noted that Article 11(5) of the Convention implies that an asylum seeker can lodge an appeal against a transfer to another Member State considered to be responsible for processing his/her claim if the national law of the Member State so provides, although this is not otherwise expressly mentioned in the text of the Convention.

B. Fair and transparent procedures

Hierarchy in applying criteria for determining responsibility

Article 3(2) of the Convention stipulates that the criteria for the determination of responsibility should be applied in the order in which they appear in the text; i.e. first the family reunion criterion (Article 4), followed by criteria related to the Member State having issued a residence permit or (transit) visa (Article 5), the Member State to which the asylum seeker irregularly entered into the common territory (Article 6), the Member State being responsible for controlling the asylum seeker's entry into the common territory (Article 7), or, in case no other criteria can be applied, the Member State where the application is lodged (Article 8).

Recent experiences with the implementation of the Convention provisions in border procedures show that the establishment of a clear order of priority in applying them is essential. For instance, the family reunion criteria prevail over the other criteria, such as those linked to the fact that the asylum application was made in transit or at the border.

---

[5] Article 11(1).
[6] Article 3(7).

Notification of asylum applicant
It is important to provide the asylum seeker and his/her legal counsel with timely and sufficiently detailed information as regards the application of the Dublin provisions in his/her particular case, including information on transfer. Article 19 of the Implementing Guidelines[7] state that the applicant shall be informed as soon as possible once a request for a transfer of responsibility has been made, including information as to the time and place to which the applicant should report on arrival in the second Member State.

Decision in writing and review
For the sake of clarity and so that asylum applicants are not left in doubt as regards the likely outcome of their applications, the decision concerning allocation of responsibility, including possible transfer, should be issued in writing.[8]

C. The 'safe third country' notion

Removals to third countries
Article 3(5) allows for the removal of the asylum seeker by the responsible State to a 'safe third country' outside the Dublin space. However, in order to ensure that the application of the Dublin provisions does not result in chain deportation and, ultimately, cases of refoulement, such removals must be in compliance with the 1951 Refugee Convention.

Need for additional safeguards
It has been recognised therefore, that additional implementing guidelines regarding the application of Article 3(5), in accordance with a proper application of the safe third country notion[9], might be necessary. This has been made trough the resolution on a 'Harmonized Approach to Questions concerning Host Third Countries'.

Precedence of Dublin over the safe third country notion
With the entry into force of the Dublin Convention, the 'safe third country' notion is no longer applicable by the Contracting Parties. The legally binding Dublin provisions have precedence over the concept the 'safe third country'. This concept continues to be applicable to non-EU countries only.

---

[7] Decision No. 1/97 of the Committee set up by Article 18 of the Dublin Convention, concerning provisions for the implementation of the Convention.

[8] This would also reflect Article 15 of the Council Resolution on Minimum Guarantees for Asylum Procedures.

[9] See the Chapter on the Resolution on a Harmonised Approach to Questions concerning Host Third Countries.

D. Humanitarian clause and family unity

Members of the same family risk having their applications processed in different Member States following a strict application of the Dublin criteria. This can be the case, for instance, when members of the same family are in possession of visa issued by embassies of different Member States, or where they have crossed different external borders when entering the common territory in an irregular manner.

Decisions taken for humanitarian reasons
In such situations, Member States may agree that the applications are processed by one and the same State, with reference to Article 9 of the Dublin Convention which allows for such a decision to be taken for humanitarian reasons, based in particular on family or cultural grounds.

E. The sovereignty clause

Article 3(4) of the Convention stipulates that each Member State shall retain the right to examine an asylum application, even if such examination is not its responsibility under the Dublin criteria – provided that the asylum seeker agrees thereto.

This sovereignty or clause was included in order to respect some Member States' constitutional obligations related to the right to asylum and maintain their sovereignty in dealing with asylum procedures.

Applicant's interest
Care must be taken if this clause is invoked on the presumption that the application is manifestly unfounded, and dealt with in an accelerated procedure, so as not to result in the expeditious return of the asylum seeker to his home country or a third country.

F. Difficulties to applying the Dublin Convention

In search of less strict means of proof
Member States have adopted measures allowing for applying criteria for the use of means of proof in a more flexible and less restrictive manner[10], assuming responsibility for the examination of an asylum claim on the basis of indicative evidence alone, taking into account general evidence relating to asylum applicants of

---

[10] Implementing Guidelines adopted by the Council regarding the Application of the Dublin Convention of 9 September 1997, OJ No. L 281, 14.10.1997, p. 1.

the same nationality or social group (such as travel routes, or ways and means of presentation of asylum applications).

Extension of the EURODAC Convention
The system is to be complemented by EURODAC, an Automated fingerprint identification system (AFIS) which provides for the fingerprinting of all asylum seekers within the EU, so that these fingerprints can be sent to a Central Unit where it will be determined whether the individual has previously claimed asylum in another Member State. Therefore, another proposed solution to the improved operation of the Dublin provisions is to extend the scope of the EURODAC Convention to the collection, storage, exchange and comparison of fingerprints of all illegally entering migrants controlled at the border who cannot be immediately refused entry, rather than solely processing the fingerprints of asylum seekers.

Issuing visas
Furthermore, the procedures for issuing visas to allow for entry into the common territory differ from one Member State to the other. In order to ensure a fair application of Article 5, Member States are currently reviewing the criteria, which govern the issuing of visas by their diplomatic missions in countries of origin

Towards durable solutions Member States still have some way to go before the Dublin mechanism can function to full satisfaction. Solutions to the various obstacles can be found partially in adopting further implementing guidelines, which should address the problems, listed above.

Now that the Dublin mechanism needs to be replaced with a community law instrument pursuant to Article 63 of the treaty establishing the EC, the question arises wether the system should be substantially amended.

V. CONCLUSIONS

Approximation of asylum laws
The fair and effective functioning of the Dublin system is not only dependent on the co-operation of the asylum seeker and the streamlining of procedures. A decisive impetus to the improvement of the system can be expected if national asylum procedures and elements of material asylum law are approximated on the basis of minimum guarantees decided by the Council in accordance to Article 63 TEC.

Fair and equitable application of Dublin
Such a harmonisation of procedures and criteria for refugee status determination can have a positive impact on the fair and equitable application of the Dublin mechanism. Practical co-operation has certainly contributed to a climate, which is conducive to further harmonisation of procedural and material asylum law.

5. ADDITIONAL TEXTS

Apart from the texts which have been included in the Acquis list, reference should be had to some of the underlying and related texts as well. Of relevance in this context are first of all the 'Treaty of Amsterdam', Art. 63 in particular, the Vienna Action Plan and the Tampere Milestones. But regard should also be had to Schengen, Eurodac and related UNHCR material.

In this Chapter references to all these texts will be made. Of particular importance is 'Schengen', although it is, as such, not part of the asylum acquis. It should be duly noted that 'Schengen' is part of the acquis communautaire since 1 May 1999, the date on which the Treaty of Amsterdam entered into force. It is recalled that one of the Protocols annexed to the Treaty of Amsterdam (in fact: annexed to the Treaty on European Union and to the Treaty establishing the European Community, as the Treaty of Amsterdam indicated how the latter Treaties had to be amended) covers this 'merger' : the Protocol Integrating the Schengen Acquis into the Framework of the European Union. 'Schengen', however has not been included in this Handbook.

Other material of use and relevance are instruments relating to intra-Union extradition as well as the issue of asylum applications submitted by nationals of fellow Member States. The Protocol on this subject has been duly included, also because it will have an impact on the asylum applications submitted by new Members of the Union.

Of the utmost importance, in due time, will be the Eurodac instrument. It goes without saying that the concept and details of Eurodac are not without discussion, in particular concerning the issue illegal migrant vs asylum seeker. Under the heading of this Chapter the draft Eurodac Convention, the draft Eurodac Protocol as well as the draft Commission's Regulations have been included. For the relevance of Eurodac for e.g. the implementation of the Dublin Convention reference should also be made to the Commission's (inofficial) Commentary on Dublin, in which indeed attention has been paid to Eurodac.

Finally, in this Chapter a list has been included of the Conclusions adopted by UNHCR's Executive Committee, as well as the Introduction to and the Conclusion of UNHCR's Handbook. Hence:

5.1	Title IV of the Consolidated Version of the Treaty Establishing the European Community	283
5.2	Protocol on Asylum for National of Member States of the European Union	287
5.3	Convention relating to Extradition between the Member States of the European Union	288
5.4	Vienna Action Plan	293
5.5	Tampere Milestones	304
5.6.a	Draft Eurodac Convention	310
5.6.b	Draft Eurodac Protocol	320
5.6.c	Draft Eurodac Regulation	324
5.7	List ExCom Conclusions	344
5.8	UNHCR Handbook, Introduction and Conclusion	347

CONSOLIDATED VERSION OF THE TREATY ESTABLISHING THE EUROPEAN COMMUNITY[1]

TITLE IV: VISAS, ASYLUM, IMMIGRATION AND OTHER POLICIES RELATED TO FREE MOVEMENT OF PERSONS

ARTICLE 61

In order to establish progressively an area of freedom, security and justice, the Council shall adopt:
(a) within a period of five years after the entry into force of the Treaty of Amsterdam[2], measures aimed at ensuring the free movement of persons in accordance with Article 14, in conjunction with directly related flanking measures with respect to external border controls, asylum and immigration in accordance with the provisions of Articles 62(2), 62(3), 63(1)(a) and 63(2)(a) and measures to prevent and combat crime in accordance with the provisions of Article 31(e) of the Treaty on European Union;
(b) other measures in the fields of asylum, immigration and safeguarding the rights of nationals of third countries, in accordance with the provisions of Article 63;
(c) measures in the field of judicial cooperation in civil matters as provided for in Article 65;
(d) appropriate measures to encourage and strengthen administrative cooperation, as provided for in Article 66;
(e) measures in the field of police and judicial cooperation in criminal matters aimed at a high level of security by preventing and combating crime within the Union in accordance with the provisions of the Treaty on European Union.

---

[1] The so-called 1997 Treaty of Amsterdam resulted in two major documents:
1) The Consolidated Version of the Treaty on European Union, which is, in fact, an amendment of the 1991 Maastricht Treaty, and
2) Consolidated Version of the Treaty Establishing the European Community, which, in fact, is an amended version of the, already quite often amended 1957 Rome Treaty,
The 'Treaty of Amsterdam' basically indicates how the Treaties on Union and Community should be amended, hence the 'consolidated texts.'
Both Treaties carry a number of Protocols, one of which on the inclusion of the Schengen Acquis into the Union Acquis (not reproduced in this Handbook), another one on the issue of the granting of asylum to nationals of EU Member States (hereinbelow).
The Articles 61-68 as – partly – reproduced herein are part of Title IV (ex Title IIIa) on Visas, Asylum, Immigration and Other Policies Related to Free Movement of Persons. Originally these articles fell under Article 73 (i thru q).

[2] Ed.: The Treaty of Amsterdam entered into force on 1 May 1999. The period referred to runs, therefore thru 30 April 2004. But note the last sentence of this Article, referring to 2(b), 3(a) and 4.

P.J. van Krieken (Ed.), The Asylum Acquis Handbook
© 2000, T.M.C.Asser Press, The Hague, the Röling Foundation and the authors

ARTICLE 62

The Council, acting in accordance with the procedure referred to in Article 67, shall, within a period of five years after the entry into force of the Treaty of Amsterdam, adopt

(1) measures with a view to ensuring, in compliance with Article 14, the absence of any controls on persons, be they citizens of the Union or nationals of third countries when crossing border;

(2) measures on the crossing of the external borders of the Member States which shall establish:
(a) standards and procedures to be followed by Member States in carrying out checks on persons at such borders;
(b) rules on visas for intended stays of no more than three months, including:
(i) the list of third countries whose nationals must be in possession of visas when crossing the external borders and those whose nationals are exempt from that requirement;
(ii) the procedures and conditions for issuing visas by Member States;
(iii) a uniform format for visas;
(iv) rules on a uniform visa;

(3) measures setting out the conditions under which nationals of third countries shall have the freedom to travel within the territory of the Member States during a period of no more than three months.

ARTICLE 63

The Council, acting in accordance with the procedure referred to in Article 67, shall, within a period of five years after the entry into force of the Treaty of Amsterdam, adopt:

(1) measures on asylum, in accordance with the Geneva Convention of 28 july 1951 and the Protocol of 31 January 1967 relating to the status of refugees and other relevant treaties, within the following areas:
(a) criteria and mechanisms for determining which Member State is responsible for considering an application for asylum submitted by a national of a third country in one of the Member States,
(b) minimum standards on the reception of asylum seekers in Member States,
(c) minimum standards with respect to the qualification of nationals of third countries as refugees,
(d) minimum standards on procedures in Member States for granting or withdrawing refugee status;

(2) measured on refugees and displaced persons within the following areas:
(a) minimum standards for giving temporary protection to displaced persons from third countries who cannot return to their country of origin and for persons who otherwise need international protection,
(b) promoting a balance of effort between Member States in receiving and bearing the consequences of receiving refugees and displaced persons;

(3) measures on immigration policy within the following areas:
(a) conditions of entry and residence, and standards on procedures for the issue by Member States of long term visas and residence permits, including those of family reunion,
(b) illegal immigration and illegal residence, including repatriation of illegal residents;

(4) measures defining the rights and conditions under which nationals of third countries who are legally resident in a Member State may reside in other Member States.

Measures adopted by the Council pursuant to points 3 and 4 shall not prevent any Member State from maintaining or introducing in the areas concerned national provisions which are compatible with this Treaty and with international agreements

Measures to be adopted pursuant to points 2(b), 3(a) and 4 shall not be subject to the five year period referred to above.

ARTICLE 64

1. This Title shall not affect the exercise of the responsibilities incumbent upon Member States, with regard to the maintenance of law and order and the safeguarding of internal security.

2. In the event of one or more Member States being confronted with an emergency situation characterised by a sudden inflow of nationals of third countries and without prejudice to paragraph 1, the Council may, acting by qualified majority on a proposal from the Commission, adopt provisional measures of a duration not exceeding six months for the benefit of the Member States concerned.

(Art. 65, on judicial cooperation in civil matters having cross-border implications: not reproduced)

ARTICLE 66

The Council, acting in accordance with the procedure referred to in Article 67, shall take measures to ensure cooperation between the relevant departments of the administrations of the Member States in the areas covered by this Title, as well as between those departments and the Commission.

ARTICLE 67

1. During a transitional period of five years following the entry into force of the Treaty of Amsterdam, the Council shall act unanimously on a proposal from the Commission or on the initiative of a Member State and after consulting the European Parliament.

2. After this period of five years:
– the Council shall act on proposals from the Commission; the Commission shall examine any request made by a Member State that it submit a proposal to the Council;

— the Council, acting unanimously after consulting the European Parliament, shall take a decision with a view to providing for all or for parts of the areas covered by this Title to be governed by the procedure referred to in Article 251[3] and adapting the provisions relating to the powers of the Court of Justice.

3. By derogation from paragraphs 1 and 2, measures referred to in Article 62(2)(b)(i) and (iii) shall, from the entry into force of the Treaty of Amsterdam, be adopted by the Council acting by a qualified majority on a proposal by the Commission and after consulting the European Parliament.

4. By derogation from paragraph 2, measures referred to in Article 62(2)(b)(ii) and (iv) shall, after a period of five years following the entry into force of the Treaty of Amsterdam, be adopted by the Council in accordance with the procedure referred to in Article 251.

ARTICLE 68

1. Article 234[4] shall apply to this Title under the following circumstances and conditions: where a question on the interpretation of this Title or on the validity or interpretation of acts of the institutions of the Community based on this Title is raised in a case pending before a court or tribunal of a Member State against whose decisions there is no judicial remedy under national law, that court or tribunal shall, if it considers that a decision on the question is necessary to enable it to give judgment, request the Court of Justice to give a ruling thereon.

2. In any event, the Court of Justice shall not have jurisdiction to rule on any measure or decision taken pursuant to Article 62(1) relating to the maintenance of law and order and the safeguarding of internal security.

3. The Council, the Commission, or a Member State may request the Court of Justice to give a ruling on a question of interpretation of this Title or of acts of the institutions of the Community based on this Title. The ruling given by the Court of Justice in response to such a request shall not apply to judgments of courts or tribunals of the Member States which have become res judicata.

ARTICLE 69

The application of this Title shall be subject to the provisions of the Protocol on the position of the United Kingdom and Ireland and to the Protocol on the position of Denmark and without prejudice to the Protocol on the application of certain aspects of Article 14 of the Treaty establishing the European Community to the United Kingdom and Ireland.

---

[3] Ed.: Art. 251 lays down procedures for adoption of an act (Council, qualified majority; Parliament rejection by an absolute majority; Conciliation Committee, etc).
[4] Ed.: Art. 234 indicates on which issues the Court of Justice shall have jurisdiction to give preliminary rulings.

5.2

PROTOCOL ON ASYLUM FOR NATIONALS OF MEMBER STATES OF THE EUROPEAN UNION

THE HIGH CONTRACTING PARTIES;

WHEREAS pursuant to the provisions of Article F(2) of the Treaty on European Union the Union shall respect fundamental rights as guaranteed by the European Convention for the Protection of Human Rights and Fundamental Freedoms signed in Rome on 4 November 1950;

WHEREAS the Court of Justice of the European Communities has jurisdiction to ensure that in the interpretation and application of Article F(2) of the Treaty on European Union the law is observed by the European Community;

WHEREAS pursuant to Article O of the Treaty on European Union any European State, when applying to become a Member of the Union, must respect the principles set out in Article F(1) of the Treaty on European Union;

BEARING IN MIND that Article 236 of the Treaty establishing the European Community establishes a mechanism for the suspension of certain rights in the event of a serious and persistent breach by a Member State of those principles;

RECALLING that each national of a Member State, as a citizen of the Union, enjoys a special status and protection which shall be guaranteed by the Member States in accordance with the provisions of Part Two of the Treaty establishing the European Community;

BEARING IN MIND that the Treaty establishing the European Community establishes an area without internal frontiers and grants every citizen of the Union the right to move and reside freely within the territory of the Member States;

RECALLING that the question of extradition of nationals of Member States of the Union is addressed in the European Convention on Extradition of 13 December 1957 and the Convention of 27 September 1996 drawn up on the basis of Article K.3 of the Treaty on European Union relating to extradition between the Member States of the European Union;

WISHING to prevent the institution of asylum being resorted to for purposes alien to those for which it is intended;

WHEREAS this Protocol respects the finality and the objectives of the Geneva Convention of 28 July 1951 relating to the status of refugees;

HAVE AGREED UPON the following provisions which shall be annexed to the Treaty establishing the European Community,

(SOLE ARTICLE)

Given the level of protection of fundamental rights and freedoms by the Member States of the European Union, Member States shall be regarded as constituting safe countries of origin in respect of each other for all legal and practical purposes in relation to asylum matters. Accordingly, any application for asylum made by a national of a Member State may be taken into consideration or declared admissible for processing by another Member State only in the following cases:

(a) if the Member State of which the applicant is a national proceeds after the entry into force of the Treaty of Amsterdam, availing itself of the provisions of Article 15 of the Convention for the Protection of Human Rights and Fundamental Freedoms, to take measures derogating in its territory from its obligations under that Convention;

(b) if the procedure referred to in Article F.1(1) of the Treaty on European Union has been initiated and until the Council takes a decision in respect thereof;

(c) if the Council, acting on the basis of Article F.1(1) of the Treaty on European Union has determined, in respect of the Member State which the applicant is a national, the existence of a serious and persistent breach by that Member State of principles mentioned in Article F(1);

(d) if a Member State should so decide unilaterally in respect of the application of a national of another Member State; in that case the Council shall be immediately informed the application shall be dealt with on the basis of the presumption that it is manifestly unfounded without affecting in any way, whatever the cases may be, the decision-making power of the Member State.

5.3

CONVENTION DRAWN UP ON THE BASIS OF ARTICLE K.3 OF THE TREATY ON EUROPEAN UNION, RELATING TO EXTRADITION BETWEEN THE MEMBER STATES OF THE EUROPEAN UNION[5]

THE HIGH CONTRACTING PARTIES to this Convention, Member States of the European Union,

REFERRING to the Act of the Council of the European Union of 27 September 1996,
DESIRING to improve judicial cooperation between the Member States in criminal matters, with regard both to prosecution and to the execution of sentences,
RECOGNIZING the importance of extradition in judicial cooperation for the achievement of these objectives,
STRESSING that Member States have an interest in ensuring that extradition procedures operate efficiently and rapidly in so far as their systems of government are based on democratic principles and they comply with the obligations laid down by the Convention for the Protection of Human Rights and Fundamental Freedoms signed in Rome on 4 November 1950,
EXPRESSING their confidence in the structure and operation of their judicial systems and in the ability of all Member States to ensure a fair trial,
BEARING IN MIND that by Act of 10 March 1995 the Council drew up the Convention on simplified extradition procedure between the Member States of the European Union,
TAKING ACCOUNT of the interest in concluding a Convention between the Member

---

[5] Official Journal C 313, 23/10/1996 p. 0012 – 0023 496A1023(02).

States of the European Union supplementing the European Convention on Extradition of 13 December 1957 and the other Conventions in force on the matter,

CONSIDERING that the provisions of those Conventions remain applicable for all matters not covered by this Convention,

HAVE AGREED AS FOLLOWS:

Article 1
General provisions
1. The purpose of this Convention is to supplement the provisions and facilitate the application between the Member States of the European Union:
– of the European Convention on Extradition of 13 December 1957 (hereinafter referred to as the 'European Convention on Extradition`);
– the European Convention on the Suppression of Terrorism of 27 January 1977 (hereinafter referred to as the 'European Convention on the Suppression of Terrorism`);
– the Convention of 19 June 1990 applying the Schengen Agreement of 14 June 1985 on the gradual abolition of checks at their common borders in relations between the Member States which are party to that Convention, and
– the first chapter of the Treaty on Extradition and Mutual Assistance in Criminal Matters between the Kingdom of Belgium, the Grand-Duchy of Luxembourg and the Kingdom of the Netherlands of 27 June 1962, as amended by the Protocol of 11 May 1974 (hereinafter referred to as the 'Benelux Treaty`) in relations between the Member States of the Benelux Economic Union.
2. Paragraph 1 shall not affect the application of more favourable provisions in bilateral or multilateral agreements between Member States, nor, as provided for in Article 28(3) of the European Convention on Extradition, shall it affect extradition arrangements agreed on the basis of uniform or reciprocal laws providing for the execution in the territory of a Member State of warrants of arrest issued in the territory of another Member State.

Article 2
Extraditable offences
1. Extradition shall be granted in respect of offences which are punishable under the law of the requesting Member State by deprivation of liberty or a detention order for a maximum period of at least 12 months and under the law of the requested Member State by deprivation of liberty or a detention order for a maximum period of at least six months.
2. Extradition may not be refused on the grounds that the law of the requested Member State does not provide for the same type of detention order as the law of the requesting Member State.
3. Article 2(2) of the European Convention on Extradition and Article 2(2) of the Benelux Treaty shall also apply where certain offences are punishable by pecuniary penalties.

Article 3
Conspiracy and association to commit offences
1. Where the offence for which extradition is requested is classified by the law of the requesting Member State as a conspiracy or an association to commit offences and is punishable by a maximum term of deprivation of liberty or a detention order of at least 12 months, extradition shall not be refused on the ground that the law of the requested Member State does not provide for the same facts to be an offence, provided the conspiracy or the association is to commit:

(a) one or more of the offences referred to in Articles 1 and 2 of the European Convention on the Suppression of Terrorism; or
(b) any other offence punishable by deprivation of liberty or a detention order of a maximum of at least 12 months in the field of drug trafficking and other forms of organized crime or other acts of violence against the life, physical integrity or liberty of a person, or creating a collective danger for persons.
2. For the purpose of determining whether the conspiracy or the association is to commit one of the offences indicated under paragraph 1(a) or (b) of this Article, the requested Member State shall take into consideration the information contained in the warrant of arrest or order having the same legal effect or in the conviction of the person whose extradition is requested as well as in the statement of the offences envisaged in Article 12(2)(b) of the European Convention on Extradition or in Article 11(2)(b) of the Benelux Treaty.
3. When giving the notification referred to in Article 18(2), any Member State may declare that it reserves the right not to apply paragraph 1 or to apply it under certain specified conditions.
4. Any Member State which has entered a reservation under paragraph 3 shall make extraditable under the terms of Article 2(1) the behaviour of any person which contributes to the commission by a group of persons acting with a common purpose of one or more offences in the field of terrorism as in Articles 1 and 2 of the European Convention on the Suppression of Terrorism, drug trafficking and other forms of organized crime or other acts of violence against the life, physical integrity or liberty of a person, or creating a collective danger for persons, punishable by deprivation of liberty or a detention order of a maximum of at least 12 months, even where that person does not take part in the actual execution of the offence or offences concerned; such contribution shall be intentional and made having knowledge either of the purpose and the general criminal activity of the group or of the intention of the group to commit the offence or offences concerned.

Article 4
Order for deprivation of liberty in a place other than a penitentiary institution
Extradition for the purpose of prosecution shall not be refused on the ground that the request is supported, pursuant to Article 12(2)(a) of the European Convention on Extradition or Article 11(2)(a) of the Benelux Treaty, by an order of the judicial authorities of the requesting Member State to deprive the person of his liberty in a place other than a penitentiary institution.

Article 5
Political offences
1. For the purposes of applying this Convention, no offence may be regarded by the requested Member State as a political offence, as an offence connected with a political offence or an offence inspired by political motives.
2. Each Member State may, when giving the notification referred to in Article 18 (2), declare that it will apply paragraph 1 only in relation to:
(a) the offences referred to in Articles 1 and 2 of the European Convention on the Suppression of Terrorism; and
(b) offences of conspiracy or association – which correspond to the description of behaviour referred to in Article 3(4) – to commit one or more of the offences referred to in Articles 1 and 2 of the European Convention on the Suppression of Terrorism.

3. The provisions of Article 3(2) of the European Convention on Extradition and of Article 5 of the European Convention on the Suppression of Terrorism remain unaffected.
4. Reservations made pursuant to Article 13 of the European Convention on the Suppression of Terrorism shall not apply to extradition between Member States.

Article 6
Fiscal offences (...)

Article 7
Extradition of nationals
1. Extradition may not be refused on the ground that the person claimed is a national of the requested Member State within the meaning of Article 6 of the European Convention on Extradition.
2. When giving the notification referred to in Article 18(2), any Member State may declare that it will not grant extradition of its nationals or will authorize it only under certain specified conditions.
3. Reservations referred to in paragraph 2 shall be valid for five years from the first day of application of this Convention by the Member State concerned. However, such reservations may be renewed for successive periods of the same duration.
Twelve months before the date of expiry of the reservation, the depositary shall give notice of that expiry to the Member State concerned.
No later than three months before the expiry of each five-year period, the Member State shall notify the depositary either that it is upholding its reservation, that it is amending it to ease the conditions for extradition or that it is withdrawing it.
In the absence of the notification referred to in the preceding subparagraph, the depositary shall inform the Member State concerned that its reservation is considered to have been extended automatically for a period of six months, before the expiry of which the Member State must give notification. On expiry of that period, failure to notify shall cause the reservation to lapse.

Article 8
Lapse of time
1. Extradition may not be refused on the ground that the prosecution or punishment of the person would be statute-barred according to the law of the requested Member State.
2. The requested Member State shall have the option of not applying paragraph 1 where the request for extradition is based on offences for which that Member State has jurisdiction under its own criminal law.

Article 9
Amnesty
Extradition shall not be granted in respect of an offence covered by amnesty in the requested Member State where that State was competent to prosecute the offence under its own criminal law.

Article 10
Offences other than those upon which the request for extradition is based (...)

Article 11
Presumption of consent of the requested Member State (...)

Article 12
Re-extradition to another Member State (...)

Article 13
Central authority and transmission of documents by facsimile (...)

Article 14
Supplementary information (...)

Article 15
Authentication (...)

Article 16
Transit (...)

Article 17
Reservations
No reservations may be entered in respect of this Convention other than those for which it makes express provision.

Article 18
Entry into force (...)

Article 19
Accession of new Member States
1. This Convention shall be open to accession by any State that becomes a member of the European Union.
2. The text of this Convention in the language of the acceding State, drawn up by the Council of the European Union, shall be authentic.
3. The instruments of accession shall be deposited with the depositary.
4. This Convention shall enter into force with respect to any State that accedes to it 90 days after the deposit of its instrument of accession or on the date of entry into force of this Convention if it has not already entered into force at the time of expiry of the said period 90 days.
5. Where this Convention is not yet in force at the time of the deposit of their instrument of accession, Article 18(4) shall apply to acceding Member States.

Article 20
Depositary (...)

ANNEX

Joint Declaration on the right of asylum
The Member States declare that this Convention is without prejudice either to the right of

asylum to the extent to which it is recognized by their respective constitutions or to the application by the Member States of the provisions of the Convention relating to the Status of Refugees of 28 July 1951, as supplemented by the Convention relating to the Status of Stateless Persons of 28 September 1954 and by the Protocol relating to the Status of Refugees of 31 January 1967.

(...)

Declaration on the concept of 'nationals'
The Council takes note of the Member States' undertaking to apply the Council of Europe Convention of 21 March 1983 on the Transfer of Sentenced Persons in respect of the nationals of each Member State within the meaning of Article 3(4) of the said Convention. The Member States' undertaking mentioned in the first paragraph is without prejudice to the application of Article 7(2) of this Convention.

(...)

Council declaration on the follow up to the Convention
The Council declares:
(a) that it considers that there should be a periodic review, on the basis of information supplied by the Member States, of:
– the implementation of this Convention;
– the functioning of this Convention after its entry into force;
– the possibility for Member States to amend the reservations entered in the framework of this Convention with a view to easing the conditions for extradition or withdrawing its reservations;
– the general functioning of extradition procedures between the Member States;
(b) that it will consider, one year after entry into force of this Convention, whether jurisdiction should be given to the Court of Justice of the European Communities.

5.4

VIENNA ACTION PLAN

Document submitted to the Vienna European Council: 13844/98
Brussels, 11 December 1998, Nr. 13844/98

Action Plan of the Council and the Commission
on how best to implement the provisions of the Treaty of Amsterdam
on an area of freedom, security and justice.

TABLE OF CONTENTS

PART I: INTRODUCTION
A. An Area of Freedom
B. An Area of Security

C. An Area of Justice
D. Enlargement
E. Relations with Third Countries and International Organizations
F. Structure of Work in the Field of Justice and Home Affairs

PART II: PRIORITIES AND MEASURES
A. Selection criteria for priorities
B. Policies related to free movement of persons
   I. Measures in the field of asylum, external borders and immigration
   II. Judicial cooperation in civil matters
C. Provisions on police and judicial cooperation in criminal matters
   I. Police cooperation
   II. Judicial cooperation in criminal matters
   III. Approximation of rules on criminal matters
   IV. Horizontal issues

PART I – INTRODUCTION

1. The European Council, meeting at Cardiff called on the Council and the Commission to submit at its meeting in Vienna an action plan on 'how best to implement the provisions of the Treaty of Amsterdam on an area of freedom, security and justice'.

Heads of State and Government at Pörtschach further confirmed the importance they attach to this subject by agreeing to hold a special European Council in Tampere in October 1999.

Under the Amsterdam Treaty, the areas of visa, asylum, immigration and other policies related to free movement of persons, like judicial cooperation in civil matters, are transferred from the EU's third pillar to its first pillar (albeit not all of the first pillar procedures will be applicable), whereas provisions on police and judicial cooperation in criminal matters contained in the new Title VI of the TEU remain within the EU's third pillar. In addition to these changes in responsibilities, the Amsterdam Treaty also lays down the broad lines of action in the areas currently assigned to the third pillar.

2. When the Cardiff European Council called on the Council and the Commission to present the Action Plan, it clearly indicated its view that those provisions offer new opportunities to tackle an area of major public concern and thus to bring the European Union closer to the people.

3. Without underestimating what has already been achieved in this area under the EC Treaty, under the Title VI provisions of the Maastricht Treaty and within Schengen, it is worth recalling the reasons why the new provisions adopted in Amsterdam open up improved possibilities. First, the objective of maintaining and developing the Union as an area of freedom, security and justice is asserted and the various aspects involved are reviewed. Secondly, the Union has been given the necessary framework in which to accommodate it and the instruments required have been strengthened and at the same time, thanks to the enhanced role foreseen for the European Court of Justice and the European Parliament, made subject to tighter judicial and democratic review. The Community method is extended: several of the areas of the current 'third pillar' are brought under Community arrangements and restrictions which used to apply to the Community institu-

ions in the areas of police and criminal justice cooperation have been lifted. Access to the Community budget has been made less cumbersome. Finally, the integration of Schengen recognizes the efforts of the Member States which embarked on this cooperation and gives the Union a base on which to build further.

4. In drawing up this action plan, the Council and the Commission take as their starting point that one of the keys to its success lies in ensuring that the spirit of interinstitutional cooperation inherent in the Amsterdam Treaty is translated into reality. This applies in particular to the new responsibilities, including an extended right of initiative, which Amsterdam bestows on the Commission. What is important is not so much where the right of initiative lies, be it shared or exclusive, as the way in which this right is exercised. In any case the Treaty provides that for the five years earmarked for the full attainment of the free movement of persons, the right of initiative will be shared between the Commission and the Member States for matters transferred to the Community framework.

5. Although any action plan drawn up must, in concrete terms, necessarily reflect the priorities and timetable set out in the Amsterdam Treaty itself, it needs to reflect also the general approach and philosophy inherent in the concept of an 'area of freedom, security and justice'. These three notions are closely interlinked. Freedom loses much of its meaning if it cannot be enjoyed in a secure environment and with the full backing of a system of justice in which all Union citizens and residents can have confidence. These three inseparable concepts have one common denominator – people – and one cannot be achieved in full without the other two. Maintaining the right balance between them must be the guiding thread for Union action. It should be noted in this context that the Treaty instituting the European Communities (article 61 ex article 73 I a), makes a direct link between the measures establishing freedom of movement of persons and the specific measures seeking to combat and prevent crime (article 31 e TEU), thus creating a conditional link between the two areas.

A. **An area of freedom**

a) *A wider concept of freedom*

6. Freedom in the sense of free movement of people within the European Union remains a fundamental objective of the Treaty, and one to which the flanking measures associated with the concepts of security and justice must make their essential contribution. The Schengen achievement has shown the way and provides the foundation on which to build. However, the Treaty of Amsterdam also opens the way to giving 'freedom' a meaning beyond free movement of people across internal borders. It is also freedom to live in a law-abiding environment in the knowledge that public authorities are using everything in their individual and collective power (nationally, at the level of the Union and beyond) to combat and contain those who seek to deny or abuse that freedom. Freedom must also be complemented by the full range of fundamental human rights, including protection from any form of discrimination as foreseen by Articles 12 and 13 of TEC and 6 of the TEU.

7. Another fundamental freedom deserving special attention in today's fast-developing information society is that of respect for privacy and in particular the protection of per-

sonal data. When, in support of the development of police and judicial cooperation in criminal matters, personal data files are set up and information exchanged, it is indeed essential to strike the right balance between public security and the protection of individuals' privacy.

b) *Immigration and asylum policies*

8. When looking at the priorities ahead, different considerations must apply to immigration policy on the one hand and asylum policy on the other. Future work in these areas will essentially be determined by the fact that the new Treaty itself contains an obligation to take action within 5 years in a wide range of immigration and asylum-related areas involving both substance and procedure. An impressive amount of work has already been carried out. However, the instruments adopted so far often suffer from two weaknesses: they are frequently based on 'soft law', such as resolutions or recommendations that have no legally binding effect. And they do not have adequate monitoring arrangements. The commitment in the Amsterdam Treaty to use European Community instruments in the future provides the opportunity to correct where necessary these weaknesses. Particular priority needs to be attached to combating illegal immigration on the one hand, while on the other hand ensuring the integration and rights of those third country nationals legally present in the Union as well as the necessary protection for those in need of it even if they do not meet fully the criteria of the Geneva Convention.

B. **An area of security**

9. The full benefits of any area of freedom will never be enjoyed unless they are exercised in an area where people can feel safe and secure.

10. The agreed aim of the Treaty is not to create a European Security area in the sense of a common territory where uniform detection and investigation procedures would be applicable to all law enforcement agencies in Europe in the handling of security matters. Nor do the new provisions affect the exercise of the responsibilities incumbent upon Member States to maintain law and order and safeguard internal security.

11. Amsterdam rather provides an institutional framework to develop common action among the Member States in the indissociable fields of police cooperation and judicial cooperation in criminal matters and thus not only to offer enhanced security to their citizens but also to defend the Union's interests, including its financial interests. The declared objective is to prevent and combat crime at the appropriate level, 'organised or otherwise, in particular terrorism, trafficking in persons and offenses against children, illicit drug trafficking and illicit arms trafficking, corruption and fraud'.

a) Organised crime
(...)
b) Drugs
(...)
c) Europol
(...)

C. An area of justice

15. The new impetus and instruments introduced by Amsterdam provide the opportunity to examine what the area of 'justice' should seek to achieve, while respecting the reality that, for reasons deeply imbedded in history and tradition, judicial systems differ substantially between Member States. The ambition is to give citizens a common sense of justice throughout the Union. Justice must be seen as facilitating the day-to-day life of people and bringing to justice those who threaten the freedom and security of individuals and society. This includes both access to justice and full judicial cooperation among Member States. What Amsterdam provides is a conceptual and institutional framework to make sure that those values are defended throughout the Union.

Both in civil and criminal matters speedy ratification and effective implementation of adopted conventions are crucial for achieving an area of Justice.

a) Judicial cooperation in civil matters
(...)
b) Judicial cooperation in criminal matters
(...)
c) Procedures
(...)
d) Cross-border litigation
(...)

D. Enlargement

21. There is an important link with the enlargement process, in particular with the pre-accession strategy.

The countries applying for membership of the European Union are well aware that Justice and Home Affairs will have a special significance for their applications. However, the JHA *acquis* is different in nature from other parts of the Union's *acquis*. Much still needs to be done and the *acquis* will therefore be developing constantly over the pre-accession years. The adoption of the Action Plan will have the additional advantage of setting out for the benefit of the applicant countries a clear and comprehensive statement of the Union's priorities in this area.

E. Relations with third countries and international organisations

22. The advances introduced by the Amsterdam Treaty will also enhance the Union's role as a player and partner on the international stage, both bilaterally and in multilateral fora. As a result, and building on the dialogue that it has already started in Justice and Home Affairs cooperation with an increasing number of third countries and international organisations and bodies (e.g. Interpol, UNHCR, Council of Europe, G8 and the OECD), this external aspect of the Union's action can be expected to take on a new and more demanding dimension. Full use will need to be made of the new instruments available under the Treaty. In particular, the communautarisation of the matters relating to asylum, immigration and judicial cooperation in civil matters permit the Community – to the extent permit-

ted by the established case law of the European Court of Justice related to the external competence of the Community – to exercise its influence internationally in these matters. In those subjects which remain in Title VI of TEU, the Union can also make use of the possibility for the Council to conclude international agreements in matters relating to Title VI of the Treaty, as well as for the Presidency, assisted by the Secretary General of the Council and in full association with the Commission, to represent the Union in these areas.

F. Structure of work in the field of justice and home affairs

23. The new provisions of the Amsterdam Treaty as well as its Protocol integrating the Schengen acquis into the framework of the European Union, with their emphatically cross-pillar characteristic, will need to be reflected also in the working structures of the Council. It was clearly not the intention of the Treaty to compartmentalise the way in which the different components of this area of freedom, security and justice are handled as between the structures of the European Community on the one hand and the European Union on the other, particularly since in both cases the responsibility for taking the objective forward will fall irrespective whether they are 1st or 3rd pillar competence, to the Council in its composition of Ministers of Justice and Home Affairs. It will therefore be essential to establish before the entry into force of the treaty of Amsterdam for this purpose appropriate arrangements which both respect the provisions of the Treaty and facilitate the coordinating role of the Committee of Permanent Representatives.

It will also be important to establish the appropriate arrangement to cover the particular case of the Schengen Information System in order to ensure smooth transition, with no reduction in the system's efficiency. A discussion could, also, be started in the medium term on the prospects for developing SIS II after it has been expanded.

Work on the necessary structural arrangements, including reflexions on the need for further coordination in the fields of migration and asylum as well as in the area of civil law by Committees composed of high officials is already under way within the K4 Committee acting on the basis of art. K4 par.1. of the TEU.

This reform of the working structures should be based on the following principles: rationalisation and simplification (an appropriate number of working Parties to meet the objectives laid down in the Treaty, no duplication), specialisation and responsibility (Working Parties to consist of experts having an adequate degree of responsibility in their Member States, appropriate allowance for operational structures – Europol, European judicial network), continuity (permanence of Working Parties to reflect the permanent objectives of the Treaty, mechanism for following-up all the instruments adopted), transparency (clarity of terms of reference and of relations between Working Parties) and flexibility (possibility of extremely short-term adjustment of structures to deal with new problems requiring urgent specific handling).

The entry into force of the Treaty of Amsterdam also raises a number of legal questions resulting from the transition of certain policies from the third pillar to the first pillar as well as from the transition to new forms of acts and procedures in the third pillar. This concerns, for example, the question of how to handle conventions in the field to be transferred to Community competence which will be signed but not yet ratified at the time of entry into force of the Treaty of Amsterdam.

PART II – PRIORITIES AND MEASURES

II.A. Selection criteria for priorities

24. A number of principles have determined the way in which the Council and the Commission have identified – and intend to implement – the measures listed in this Part:
i) The *Amsterdam Treaty* itself has set out some clear guidance on the measures to which priority importance must be attached, particularly during the first five years after its entry into force. The Action Plan must respect this guidance;
ii) The principle of *subsidiarity*, which applies to all aspects of the Union's action, is of particular relevance to the creation of an area of freedom, security and justice;
iii) The principle of *solidarity* among Member States and between them and the European institutions, should apply in facing the transnational challenges presented by organised crime and migration movements;
iv) *Operational efficiency* in implementing the legal framework established by the Treaty is no less important than the legislative framework itself. Measures taken shall meet factual needs and add value In this context, working methods which have proved already their worth, for example in the Schengen context, should find their place in the Union's Action Plan;
v) *Responsibility for safeguarding of internal security rests with Member States*. It is therefore important, when developing European cooperation, to take into account national interests and common approaches as well as differences;
vi) A *realistic approach* requires, when selecting priorities, the resources and time available to be taken into account.

25. According to art. 2 of the TEU, the Union shall set itself the objective to maintain and develop an area of freedom, security and justice in which the free movement of persons is assured in conjunction with appropriate measures with respect to external borders, asylum, immigration and the prevention and combatting of crime. The mutual interdependence between the different aspects of this overall objective is confirmed by art. 61, a) which mentions art. 31 (e) of the TEU. It is therefore in the interest of as high level as possible of security for the public that some activities in one area be meshed in timing and substance with those in the other.

26. Integration of the Schengen acquis into the framework of the European Union will have as a consequence that as from the date of entry into force of the Treaty of Amsterdam the objectives of the Community as set out in the entire Article 62 TEC and to a large extent in Article 63(3)(b) of the TEC in their versions of the Treaty of Amsterdam will largely have been realized in respect of 10 Member States, and in respect of 13 Member States as from the date of the decision of the Council referred to in Article 2(2) of the Schengen Protocol. This is to say that much of the substantive work will have been done far in advance of the 5 years time limit set by the Articles concerned. It would permit the Council to concentrate initially particularly on other objectives of the Community and the Union in the field of Justice and Home Affairs for the realization of which a maximum time limit of 5 years has been determined (Article 63(1)) and (2)(a) TEC and Article 30(2) TEU, for example and to deal with matters which would require urgent handling or which become politically important.

In order to put the priorities listed in those Articles into practice, efforts will have to be made to adopt measures detailed in the following sections.

27. In the context of the Treaty requirements, account should also be taken of the position of the United Kingdom and Ireland under the Protocols to the Amsterdam Treaty and, in setting priorities, of existing plans and the need to continue taking forward present medium-term work programmes.

28. In establishing substantive and political priorities, first consideration has had to be given in particular to those projects on which work is already in hand at present or for which work is likely still to be in progress at the time of entry into force of the Amsterdam Treaty. It has basically been attempted here, in fully adjusting to the new environment, to ensure maximum continuity.

29. In legislative work, account has also had to be taken of the existing third-pillar 'acquis'; making it necessary to decide which, if any, of the present provisions should be replaced by more effective ones. Those classifiable as 'soft law' formed the prime candidates for this purpose.

30. The entry into force of the Treaty of Amsterdam is likely to have the effect of increasing the case-load of the European Court of Justice, whereas an Area of freedom, security and justice precisely requires judicial proceedings to be as expedient as possible. It is therefore in the interest of both the Member States and the individuals concerned that priority be given to examining jointly with the Court all possible means to shorten the average length of procedures before the Court, in particular of requests for preliminary rulings under Title VI TEU and Title IV TEC.

31. The levels of priority set out below become effective, logically, upon entry into force of the Amsterdam Treaty. The priority measures are to be found in two categories. On the one hand, the actions and measures for which it is important that they are implemented or adopted within two years from the entry into force of the Treaty of Amsterdam (hereinafter referred to as *'measures to be taken within 2 years'*), and on the other hand the actions and measures which must be adopted or implemented within 5 years following the entry into force of the Treaty or, at least, to commence elaboration of the actions and measures in the area (hereinafter referred to as *'measures to be taken within 5 years'*). However, a start may have to be made on many activities in the first level of priority without delay upon adoption of this action plan as they require preparatory work, e.g. in technical working parties, which should if possible have been completed by the date of the entry into force. Such particularly urgent measures are specifically indicated below.

II.B. Policies related to free movement of persons

II.B.I. *Measures in the field of asylum, external borders and immigration*

32. The objective is to introduce the area of freedom within the next five years. As a result, to ensure increased security for all European citizens, achieving this objective requires accompanying measures to be drawn up, particularly in the areas of external border

VIENNA ACTION PLAN 301

controls and the combating of illegal immigration while full account is taken of the principles set out in Article 6 of the TEU and Articles 12 and 13 of the TEC. The HCR will be consulted on asylum issues when necessary.

33. The measures to be drawn up must take due account of the fact that the areas of asylum and immigration are separate and require separate approaches and solutions.

34. An overall migration strategy should be established in which a system of European solidarity should figure prominently. The experiences gained and progress achieved through cooperation in the Schengen framework should prove particularly pertinent as regards short term residence (up to three months), the fight against illegal immigration as well as the controls at external borders.

An overall priority should be to improve the exchange of statistics and information on asylum and immigration. This exchange should include statistics on asylum and immigration, information on the status of third country nationals and national legislation and policy on the basis of the Commission's Action Plan.

35. In order to complete the area of free movement, it is crucial for there to be a swift and comprehensive extension of the principles of the free movement of persons in accordance with the Protocol integrating the Schengen acquis into the framework of the EU.

Measures to be taken within two years

36. The following measures should be taken within two years after the entry into force of the Treaty:

a) Measures in the fields of asylum and immigration
Assessment of countries of origin in order to formulate a country specific integrated approach.

b) Measures in the field of asylum
i) Effectiveness of the Dublin Convention: continued examination of the criteria and conditions for improving the implementation of the Convention and of the possible transformation of the legal basis to the system of Amsterdam (Article 63(1)(a) TEC).
A study should be undertaken to see to what extent the mechanism should be supplemented inter alia by provisions enabling the responsibility for dealing with the members of the same family to be conferred upon one Member State where the application of the responsibility criteria would involve a number of States and by provisions whereby the question of protection when a refugee changes his country of residence can be resolved satisfactorily.
ii) The implementation of Eurodac.
iii) Adoption of minimum standards on procedures in Member States for granting or withdrawing refugee status (Article 63(1) (d) TEC) with a view, inter alia, to reducing the duration of asylum procedures. In this context, a special attention shall be paid to the situation of children.
iv) Limit 'secondary movements' by asylum seekers between Member States.
v) Defining minimum standards on the reception of asylum seekers with a particular at-

tention to the situation of children (Article 63(1) (b) TEC).
vi) Undertake a study with a view to establishing the merits of a single European asylum procedure.

c) Measures in the field of immigration
i) Instrument on the lawful status of legal immigrants.
ii) Establish a coherent EU policy on readmission and return.
iii) Combat illegal immigration (Article 63(3)(b) TEC) through, inter alia, information campaigns in transit countries and in the countries of origin.
In line with the priority to be given to controlling migration flows, practical proposals for combating illegal immigration more effectively need to be brought forward swiftly.

d) Measures in the fields of external borders and free movement of persons:
i) Procedure and conditions for issuing visas by Member States (resources, guarantees of repatriation or accident and health cover) as well as the drawing up of a list of countries whose nationals are subject to an airport transit visa requirement (abolition of the current grey list).
ii) Define the rules on a uniform visa (Article 62(iv) TEC)
iii) Draw up a Regulation on countries:
– whose nationals are exempt from any visa requirement in the Member States of the European Union;
– whose nationals are subject to a visa requirement in the Member States of the European Union (Article 62(2)(b)(i) TEC).
iv) Further harmonising Member States' laws on carriers' liability.

Measures to be taken as quickly as possible in accordance with the provisions of the Treaty of Amsterdam:

37. a) Minimum standards for giving temporary protection to displaced persons from third countries who cannot return to their country of origin (Article 63(2)(a) TEC).
b) Promoting a balance of effort between Member States in receiving and bearing the consequences of receiving displaced persons (Article 63(2)(b) TEC).

Measures to be taken within five years

38. The following measures should be taken within five years after the entry into force of the Treaty:
a) Measures in the fields of asylum and immigration
Identification and implementation of the measures listed in the European migration strategy
b) Measures in the field of asylum
i) Adoption of minimum standards with respect to the qualification of nationals of third countries as refugees.
ii) Defining minimum standards for subsidiary protection to persons in need of international protection (Article 63(2) (a) second part).
c) Measures in the field of immigration
i) Improvement of the possibilities for the removal of persons who have been refused the

right to stay through improved EU co-ordination implementation of readmission clauses and development of European official (Embassy) reports on the situation in countries in origin.

i) Preparation of rules on the conditions of entry and residence, and standards on procedures for the issue by Member States of long-term visas and residence permits, including those for the purposes of family reunion (Article 63(3)(a) TEC).

The question of giving third-country nationals holding residence permits the freedom to settle in any Member State of the Union will shortly be discussed by the relevant working party.

ii) Determination of the rights and conditions under which nationals of third countries who are legally resident in a Member State may reside in other Member States (Article 3(4) TEC).

Within the competent Council bodies discussions could be held, taking account of the consequences for social equilibrium and the labour market, on the conditions under which, like Community nationals and their families, third country nationals could be allowed to settle and work in any Member State of the Union.

In these two last fields, although the Amsterdam Treaty does not request action to be accomplished in a five year period, efforts should be made towards an improvement of the situation in due time.

d) Measures in the fields of external borders and free movement of persons:

i) Extension of the Schengen representation mechanisms with regard to visas:

A discussion could be initiated on the possibility of establishing an arrangement between the Member States, which will improve the possibility of preventing visa applicants from abusing the foreign representations of one or more Member States in order to gain access to another Member State, which at the time of application was the actual intended country of destinations.

ii) Attention will be given to new technical developments in order to ensure – as appropriate – an even better security of the uniform format for visas (sticker).

II.B.II. Judicial cooperation in civil matters
(..)
II.C. Police and judicial cooperation in criminal matters
(..)
II.C.I. Police cooperation
(..)
II.C.II. Judicial cooperation in criminal matters
(..)
II.C.III. Approximation of the rules on criminal matters
(..)
II.C.IV. Horizontal [issues] problems
(..)

THE TAMPERE MILESTONES

PRESIDENCY CONCLUSIONS

TAMPERE EUROPEAN COUNCIL
15 AND 16 OCTOBER 1999

The European Council held a special meeting on 15 and 16 October 1999 in Tampere on the creation of an area of freedom, security and justice in the European Union. At the start of proceedings an exchange of views was conducted with the President of the European Parliament, Mrs Nicole Fontaine, on the main topics of discussion.

The European Council is determined to develop the Union as an area of freedom, security and justice by making full use of the possibilities offered by the Treaty of Amsterdam. The European Council sends a strong political message to reaffirm the importance of this objective and has agreed on a number of policy orientations and priorities which will speedily make this area a reality.

The European Council will place and maintain this objective at the very top of the political agenda. It will keep under constant review progress made towards implementing the necessary measures and meeting the deadlines set by the Treaty of Amsterdam, the Vienna Action Plan and the present conclusions. The Commission is invited to make a proposal for an appropriate scoreboard to that end. The European Council underlines the importance of ensuring the necessary transparency and of keeping the European Parliament regularly informed. It will hold a full debate assessing progress at its December meeting in 2001.

In close connection with the area of freedom, security and justice, the European Council has agreed on the composition, method of work and practical arrangements (attached in the annex) for the body entrusted with drawing up a draft Charter of fundamental rights of the European Union. It invites all parties involved to ensure that work on the Charter can begin rapidly.

(...)

TOWARDS A UNION OF FREEDOM, SECURITY AND JUSTICE:
THE TAMPERE MILESTONES

From its very beginning European integration has been firmly rooted in a shared commitment to freedom based on human rights, democratic institutions and the rule of law. These common values have proved necessary for securing peace and developing prosperity in the European Union. They will also serve as a cornerstone for the enlarging Union.

The European Union has already put in place for its citizens the major ingredients of a shared area of prosperity and peace: a single market, economic and monetary union, and the capacity to take on global political and economic challenges. The challenge of the Amsterdam Treaty is now to ensure that freedom, which includes the right to move freely throughout the Union, can be enjoyed in conditions of security and justice accessible to all. It is a project which responds to the frequently expressed concerns of citizens and has a direct bearing on their daily lives.

This freedom should not, however, be regarded as the exclusive preserve of the Union's own citizens. Its very existence acts as a draw to many others world-wide who cannot enjoy the freedom Union citizens take for granted. It would be in contradiction with Europe's traditions to deny such freedom to those whose circumstances lead them justifiably to seek access to our territory. This in turn requires the Union to develop common policies on asylum and immigration, while taking into account the need for a consistent control of external borders to stop illegal immigration and to combat those who organise it and commit related international crimes. These common policies must be based on principles which are both clear to our own citizens and also offer guarantees to those who seek protection in or access to the European Union.

The aim is an open and secure European Union, fully committed to the obligations of the Geneva Refugee Convention and other relevant human rights instruments, and able to respond to humanitarian needs on the basis of solidarity. A common approach must also be developed to ensure the integration into our societies of those third country nationals who are lawfully resident in the Union.

The enjoyment of freedom requires a genuine area of justice, where people can approach courts and authorities in any Member State as easily as in their own. Criminals must find no ways of exploiting differences in the judicial systems of Member States. Judgements and decisions should be respected and enforced throughout the Union, while safeguarding the basic legal certainty of people and economic operators. Better compatibility and more convergence between the legal systems of Member States must be achieved.

People have the right to expect the Union to address the threat to their freedom and legal rights posed by serious crime. To counter these threats a common effort is needed to prevent and fight crime and criminal organisations throughout the Union. The joint mobilisation of police and judicial resources is needed to guarantee that there is no hiding place for criminals or the proceeds of crime within the Union.

The area of freedom, security and justice should be based on the principles of transparency and democratic control. We must develop an open dialogue with civil society on the aims and principles of this area in order to strengthen citizens' acceptance and support. In order to maintain confidence in authorities, common standards on the integrity of authorities should be developed.

The European Council considers it essential that in these areas the Union should also develop a capacity to act and be regarded as a significant partner on the international scene. This requires close co-operation with partner countries and international organisations, in particular the Council of Europe, OSCE, OECD and the United Nations.

The European Council invites the Council and the Commission, in close co-operation with the European Parliament, to promote the full and immediate implementation of the Treaty of Amsterdam on the basis of the Vienna Action Plan and of the following political guidelines and concrete objectives agreed here in Tampere.

A. A Common EU Asylum and Migration Policy

The separate but closely related issues of asylum and migration call for the development of a common EU policy to include the following elements.

I. *Partnership with countries of origin*

The European Union needs a comprehensive approach to migration addressing political, human rights and development issues in countries and regions of origin and transit. This requires combating poverty, improving living conditions and job opportunities, preventing conflicts and consolidating democratic states and ensuring respect for human rights, in particular rights of minorities, women and children. To that end, the Union as well as Member States are invited to contribute, within their respective competence under the Treaties, to a greater coherence of internal and external policies of the Union. Partnership with third countries concerned will also be a key element for the success of such a policy, with a view to promoting co-development.

In this context, the European Council welcomes the report of the High Level Working Group on Asylum and Migration set up by the Council, and agrees on the continuation of its mandate and on the drawing up of further Action Plans. It considers as a useful contribution the first action plans drawn up by that Working Group, and approved by the Council, and invites the Council and the Commission to report back on their implementation to the European Council in December 2000.

II. *A Common European Asylum System*

The European Council reaffirms the importance the Union and Member States attach to absolute respect of the right to seek asylum. It has agreed to work towards establishing a Common European Asylum System, based on the full and inclusive application of the Geneva Convention, thus ensuring that nobody is sent back to persecution, i.e. maintaining the principle of non-refoulement.

This System should include, in the short term, a clear and workable determination of the State responsible for the examination of an asylum application, common standards for a fair and efficient asylum procedure, common minimum conditions of reception of asylum seekers, and the approximation of rules on the recognition and content of the refugee status. It should also be completed with measures on subsidiary forms of protection offering an appropriate status to any person in need of such protection. To that end, the Council is urged to adopt, on the basis of Commission proposals, the necessary decisions according to the timetable set in the Treaty of Amsterdam and the Vienna Action Plan. The European Council stresses the importance of consulting UNHCR and other international organisations.

In the longer term, Community rules should lead to a common asylum procedure and a uniform status for those who are granted asylum valid throughout the Union. The Commission is asked to prepare within one year a communication on this matter.

The European Council urges the Council to step up its efforts to reach agreement on the issue of temporary protection for displaced persons on the basis of solidarity between Member States. The European Council believes that consideration should be given to making some form of financial reserve available in situations of mass influx of refugees for temporary protection. The Commission is invited to explore the possibilities for this.

The European Council urges the Council to finalise promptly its work on the system for the identification of asylum seekers (Eurodac).

III. *Fair treatment of third country nationals*

The European Union must ensure fair treatment of third country nationals who reside legally on the territory of its Member States. A more vigorous integration policy should aim at granting them rights and obligations comparable to those of EU citizens. It should also enhance non-discrimination in economic, social and cultural life and develop measures against racism and xenophobia.

Building on the Commission Communication on an Action Plan against Racism, the European Council calls for the fight against racism and xenophobia to be stepped up. The Member States will draw on best practices and experiences. Co-operation with the European Monitoring Centre on Racism and Xenophobia and the Council of Europe will be further strengthened. Moreover, the Commission is invited to come forward as soon as possible with proposals implementing Article 13 of the EC Treaty on the fight against racism and xenophobia. To fight against discrimination more generally the Member States are encouraged to draw up national programmes.

The European Council acknowledges the need for approximation of national legislations on the conditions for admission and residence of third country nationals, based on a shared assessment of the economic and demographic developments within the Union, as well as the situation in the countries of origin. It requests to this end rapid decisions by the Council, on the basis of proposals by the Commission. These decisions should take into account not only the reception capacity of each Member State, but also their historical and cultural links with the countries of origin.

The legal status of third country nationals should be approximated to that of Member States' nationals. A person, who has resided legally in a Member State for a period of time to be determined and who holds a long-term residence permit, should be granted in that Member State a set of uniform rights which are as near as possible to those enjoyed by EU citizens; e.g. the right to reside, receive education, and work as an employee or self-employed person, as well as the principle of non-discrimination vis-à-vis the citizens of the State of residence. The European Council endorses the objective that long-term legally resident third country nationals be offered the opportunity to obtain the nationality of the Member State in which they are resident.

IV. *Management of migration flows*

The European Council stresses the need for more efficient management of migration flows at all their stages. It calls for the development, in close co-operation with countries of origin and transit, of information campaigns on the actual possibilities for legal immigration, and for the prevention of all forms of trafficking in human beings. A common active policy on visas and false documents should be further developed, including closer co-operation between EU consulates in third countries and, where necessary, the establishment of common EU visa issuing offices.

The European Council is determined to tackle at its source illegal immigration, especially by combating those who are engaged in trafficking in human beings and economic exploitation of migrants. It urges the adoption of legislation foreseeing severe sanctions against this serious crime. The Council is invited to adopt by the end of 2000, on the basis of a proposal by the Commission, legislation to this end. Member States, together with Europol, should direct their efforts to detecting and dismantling the criminal networks involved. The rights of the victims of such activities shall be secured with special emphasis on the problems of women and children.

The European Council calls for closer co-operation and mutual technical assistance between the Member States' border control services, such as exchange programmes and technology transfer, especially on maritime borders, and for the rapid inclusion of the applicant States in this co-operation. In this context, the Council welcomes the memorandum of understanding between Italy and Greece to enhance co-operation between the two countries in the Adriatic and Ionian seas in combating organised crime, smuggling and trafficking of persons.

As a consequence of the integration of the Schengen acquis into the Union, the candidate countries must accept in full that acquis and further measures building upon it. The European Council stresses the importance of the effective control of the Union's future external borders by specialised trained professionals.

The European Council calls for assistance to countries of origin and transit to be developed in order to promote voluntary return as well as to help the authorities of those countries to strengthen their ability to combat effectively trafficking in human beings and to cope with their readmission obligations towards the Union and the Member States.

The Amsterdam Treaty conferred powers on the Community in the field of readmission. The European Council invites the Council to conclude readmission agreements or to include standard clauses in other agreements between the European Community and relevant third countries or groups of countries. Consideration should also be given to rules on internal readmission.

B. A Genuine European Area of Justice

In a genuine European Area of Justice individuals and businesses should not be prevented or discouraged from exercising their rights by the incompatibility or complexity of legal and administrative systems in the Member States.

V. *Better access to justice in Europe*
(...)

VI. *Mutual recognition of judicial decisions*

Enhanced mutual recognition of judicial decisions and judgements and the necessary approximation of legislation would facilitate co-operation between authorities and the judicial protection of individual rights. The European Council therefore endorses the principle of mutual recognition which, in its view, should become the cornerstone of judicial co-operation in both civil and criminal matters within the Union. The principle should apply both to judgements and to other decisions of judicial authorities.

In civil matters the European Council calls upon the Commission to make a proposal for further reduction of the intermediate measures which are still required to enable the recognition and enforcement of a decision or judgement in the requested State. As a first step these intermediate procedures should be abolished for titles in respect of small consumer or commercial claims and for certain judgements in the field of family litigation (e.g. on maintenance claims and visiting rights). Such decisions would be automatically recognised throughout the Union without any intermediate proceedings or grounds for reusal of enforcement. This could be accompanied by the setting of minimum standards on specific aspects of civil procedural law.

With respect to criminal matters, the European Council urges Member States to speedily ratify the 1995 and 1996 EU Conventions on extradition. It considers that the formal extradition procedure should be abolished among the Member States as far as persons are concerned who are fleeing from justice after having been finally sentenced, and replaced by a simple transfer of such persons, in compliance with Article 6 TEU. Consideration should also be given to fast track extradition procedures, without prejudice to the principle of fair trial. The European Council invites the Commission to make proposals on this matter in the light of the Schengen Implementing Agreement.

The principle of mutual recognition should also apply to pre-trial orders, in particular to those which would enable competent authorities quickly to secure evidence and to seize assets which are easily movable; evidence lawfully gathered by one Member State's authorities should be admissible before the courts of other Member States, taking into account the standards that apply there.

The European Council asks the Council and the Commission to adopt, by December 2000, a programme of measures to implement the principle of mutual recognition. In this programme, work should also be launched on a European Enforcement Order and on those aspects of procedural law on which common minimum standards are considered necessary in order to facilitate the application of the principle of mutual recognition, respecting the fundamental legal principles of Member States.

VII. *Greater convergence in civil law*
(...)

C. A Unionwide Fight Against Crime

The European Council is deeply committed to reinforcing the fight against serious organised and transnational crime. The high level of safety in the area of freedom, security and justice presupposes an efficient and comprehensive approach in the fight against all forms of crime. A balanced development of unionwide measures against crime should be achieved while protecting the freedom and legal rights of individuals and economic operators.

VIII. *Preventing crime at the level of the Union*
(...)

IX. *Stepping up co-operation against crime*
(...)

X. *Special action against money laundering*
(...)

D. Stronger External Action

The European Council underlines that all competences and instruments at the disposal of the Union, and in particular, in external relations must be used in an integrated and consistent way to build the area of freedom, security and justice. Justice and Home Affairs concerns must be integrated in the definition and implementation of other Union policies and activities.

Full use must be made of the new possibilities offered by the Treaty of Amsterdam for external action and in particular of Common Strategies as well as Community agreements and agreements based on Article 38 TEU.

Clear priorities, policy objectives and measures for the Union's external action in Justice and Home Affairs should be defined. Specific recommendations should be drawn up by the Council in close co-operation with the Commission on policy objectives and measures for the Union's external action in Justice and Home Affairs, including questions of working structure, prior to the European Council in June 2000.

The European Council expresses its support for regional co-operation against organised crime involving the Member States and third countries bordering on the Union. In this context it notes with satisfaction the concrete and practical results obtained by the surrounding countries in the Baltic Sea region. The European Council attaches particular importance to regional co-operation and development in the Balkan region. The European Union welcomes and intends to participate in a European Conference on Development and Security in the Adriatic and Ionian area, to be organised by the Italian Government in Italy in the first half of the year 2000. This initiative will provide valuable support in the context of the South Eastern Europe Stability Pact.

(...)

5.6.a

EUROPEAN UNION Brussels, 17 November 1998
THE COUNCIL 12942/98

DRAFT COUNCIL ACT of drawing up the Convention concerning the establishment of 'Eurodac' for the comparison of fingerprints of applicants for asylum

THE COUNCIL OF THE EUROPEAN UNION,
Having regard to the Treaty on European Union, and in particular Article K.3(2)(c) thereof,
whereas asylum policy is regarded as a matter of common interest for the Member States under Article K.1(1) of the Treaty; whereas it is necessary to set up a computerized system for comparison of fingerprints of persons seeking asylum in a Member State in order effectively to apply the Convention determining the State responsible for examining applications for asylum lodged in one of the Member States of the European Communities (signed at Dublin on 15 June 1990), and in particular Article 15 thereof;
having decided that the Convention, the text of which is given in the Annex and which has been signed today by the Representatives of the Governments of the Member States, is hereby drawn up;
having examined the views of the European Parliament, following the consultation conducted by the Presidency in accordance with Article K.6 of the Treaty on European Union;

RECOMMENDS that it be adopted by the Member States in accordance with their respective constitutional requirements and in such manner that it will enter into force at the same time as a Protocol extending the scope ratione personae of this Convention for the purpose of further facilitating the application of the Dublin Convention. (...)

ANNEX: CONVENTION

drawn up on the basis of Article K.3 of the Treaty on European Union concerning the establishment of 'Eurodac' for the comparison of fingerprints of applicants for asylum;

THE HIGH CONTRACTING PARTIES to this Convention, Member States of the European Union;

REFERRING to the Act of the Council of the European Union of (...),

RECALLING the objective of harmonization of the Member States' asylum policies, set by the Strasbourg European Council on 8 and 9 December 1989 and further developed by the Maastricht European Council on 9 and 10 December 1991 and the Brussels European Council on 10 and 11 December 1993 as well as in the Commission communication on 23 February 1994 on immigration and asylum policies;

DETERMINED, in keeping with their common humanitarian tradition, to guarantee adequate protection to refugees in accordance with the terms of the Geneva Convention of 28 July 1951, as amended by the New York Protocol of 31 January 1967, relating to the Status of Refugees, and to continue the dialogue begun with the United Nations High Commissioner for Refugees on any issues relating to application of this Convention;

CONSIDERING the joint objective of an area without internal frontiers in which the free movement of persons is ensured, in accordance with Article 7a of the Treaty establishing the European Community;

AWARE of the need, in pursuit of this objective, to take measures to avoid any situations arising which would result in applicants for asylum being left in doubt for too long as to the likely outcome of their applications and concerned to provide all applicants for asylum with a guarantee that their applications will be examined by one of the Member States and to ensure that applicants for asylum are not referred successively from one Member State to another without any of these States acknowledging itself to be competent to examine the application for asylum;

CONSIDERING that the specific aim of the Dublin Convention of 15 June 1990 determining the State responsible for examining applications for asylum lodged in one of the Member States of the European Communities is to meet that concern;

CONSIDERING that for the purposes of applying the Dublin Convention it is necessary to establish the identity of applicants for asylum;

CONSIDERING that fingerprints constitute an important element in establishing the exact identity of such persons and considering that it is necessary to set up a system for the comparison of their fingerprints;

WHEREAS the provisions of this Convention may only be applied in compliance with the European Convention for the Protection of Human Rights and Fundamental Freedoms, signed in Rome on 4 November 1950;

CONSIDERING that the processing of such data must observe the strictest standards of confidentiality and is only possible with due regard for the Council of Europe Convention for the Protection of Individuals with regard to Automatic Processing of Personal Data, signed at Strasbourg on 28 January 1981;

HAVE AGREED ON THE FOLLOWING PROVISIONS:

Article 1
Purpose of 'Eurodac'
1. A system known as 'Eurodac' is hereby established, the sole purpose of which shall be to assist in determining the Member State which is responsible pursuant to the Dublin Convention for examining an application for asylum lodged in a Member State.
2. To that end, Eurodac shall consist of:
– the Central Unit referred to in Article 3,
– a computerized central database in which the data referred to in Article 5(1) are recorded and stored for the purpose of comparing the fingerprints of applicants for asylum,
– means of transmission between the Member States and the central database.

The rules governing Eurodac shall also apply to operations effected by the Member States as from the transmission of data to the Central Unit until use is made of the results of the comparison.
3. Without prejudice to the use of data intended for Eurodac by the Member State of origin in databases set up under the latter's national law, fingerprints and other personal data may be processed in Eurodac only for the purposes set out in Article 15(1) of the Dublin Convention.

Article 2
Definitions
For the purposes of this Convention:
1. 'The Dublin Convention' shall mean the Convention determining the State responsible for examining applications for asylum lodged in one of the Member States of the European Communities, signed at Dublin on 15 June 1990.
2. Unless stated otherwise, the terms defined in Article 1 of the Dublin Convention shall have the same meaning in this Convention.
3. An 'applicant for asylum' shall mean an alien who has made an application for asylum or on whose behalf such an application has been made.
4. 'Transmission of data' shall mean:
– communication of personal data from Member States to the Central Unit for recording in the central database and communication to Member States of the results of the comparison made by the Central Unit, and
– recording of personal data directly by Member States in the central database and direct communication of the results of the comparison to such Member States.
5. 'Personal data' shall mean any information relating to an identified or identifiable natural person; an identifiable person is one who can be identified, directly or indirectly, in particular by reference to an identification number or to one or more factors specific to his physical identity.
6. 'Member State of origin' shall mean the Member State which transmits the personal data to the Central Unit and receives the results of the comparison.

Article 3
Central Unit
1. A Central Unit shall be established within the Commission which shall be responsible for operating the central database of fingerprints of applicants for asylum on behalf of the Member States. The Central Unit shall be equipped with a computerized fingerprint recognition system.

2. Data on applicants for asylum which are processed at the Central Unit shall be processed on behalf of the Member State of origin.
3. The Commission shall submit to the Council and the European Parliament an annual report on the activities of the Central Unit.

Article 4
Procedure
1. Each Member State shall promptly take the fingerprints of every applicant for asylum of at least 14 years of age and shall promptly transmit the data referred to in Article 5(1), points 1 to 6, to the Central Unit. The procedure for taking fingerprints shall be determined in accordance with the national practice of the Member State concerned. The applicant for asylum shall be informed of the purpose of taking his/her fingerprints as provided for in Article 13(1).
2. The data referred to in Article 5(1) shall be immediately recorded in the central database:
(i) by the Central Unit or,
(ii) insofar as the technical conditions for such purposes are met, directly by the Member State of origin.
3. Fingerprint data within the meaning of point 2 of Article 5(1) transmitted by any Member State shall be compared by the Central Unit with the fingerprint data transmitted by other Member States and already recorded in the central database.
4. Any Member State may request that the comparison referred to in paragraph 3 should cover the fingerprint data previously transmitted by it, in addition to the data from other Member States.
5. The Central Unit shall forthwith communicate the results of the comparison to the Member State of origin, together with the data referred to in Article 5(1), relating to those fingerprints which, in the opinion of the Central Unit, are so similar as to be considered as matching with the fingerprints which were transmitted by that Member State. Direct transmission to the Member State of origin of the results of the comparison shall be permissible where the technical conditions for such purpose are met.
6. The results of the comparison shall be immediately checked in the Member State of origin. Final identification shall be made by the Member State of origin in cooperation with the Member States concerned, pursuant to Article 15 of the Dublin Convention. Information received from the Central Unit relating to any data mismatch or other data found to be unreliable shall be erased by the Member State of origin as soon as the mismatch or unreliability of the data is established.
7. The Council shall adopt the implementing rules which are necessary to give effect to the procedures provided for in this Article.

Article 5
Recording of data
1. Only the following data shall be recorded in the central database:
1. Member State of origin, place and date of the application for asylum;
2. fingerprints pursuant to the rules for implementing this Convention adopted by he Council;
3. sex;

4. reference number used by the Member State of origin;
5. date on which the fingerprints were taken;
6. date on which the data were transmitted to the Central Unit;
7. date on which the data were entered in the central database;
8. details in respect of the recipient(s) of the data transmitted and the date(s) of transmission(s).
2. After recording the data in the central database, the Central Unit shall destroy the media used for transmitting the data, unless the Member State of origin has requested their return.

Article 6
Data storage
Each set of data, as referred to in Article 5 (1), shall be stored in the central database for ten years from the date on which the fingerprints were last taken. Upon expiry of this period, the Central Unit shall automatically erase the data from the central database.

Article 7
Advance data erasure
Notwithstanding the provisions of Article 6, data relating to a person who has acquired citizenship of a Member State shall be erased from the central database. In conformity with Article 11(3), such erasure shall be carried out by the Member State of origin either directly or, at the request of the latter, by the Central Unit, as soon as that Member State becomes aware that the person has acquired citizenship of a Member State.

Article 8
Blocking of data
1. Notwithstanding the provisions of Article 6, data relating to a person who in accordance with the Geneva Convention of 28 July 1951, as amended by the New York Protocol of 31 January 1967, has been recognised and admitted as a refugee in a Member State shall be blocked in the central database. Such blocking shall be carried out by the Central Unit on the instructions of the Member State of origin.
2. Five years after Eurodac begins its activities, the Council shall, on the basis of reliable statistics compiled by the Central Unit on persons who have lodged an application for asylum in a Member State after having been recognised and admitted as refugees as defined in paragraph 1 in another Member State, unanimously adopt a procedure enabling it to decide whether the data relating to persons who have been recognised and admitted as refugees in a Member State should either:
(a) be unblocked and be stored in accordance with Article 6 for the purpose of the comparison provided for in Article 4(3). In such case, the procedure mentioned in paragraph 1 shall no longer apply; or
(b) be erased in advance once a person has been recognised and admitted as a refugee. In such case:
– data which have been blocked in accordance with paragraph 1 shall be erased immediately by the Central Unit; and
– with regard to data relating to persons who are subsequently recognised and admitted as refugees, the last sentence of Article 7 shall apply mutatis mutandis.
3. The Council shall adopt implementing rules concerning compilation of the statistics referred to in paragraph 2.

Article 9

Responsibility for data use

1. The Member State of origin shall be responsible for ensuring that:

a) fingerprints are taken lawfully;

b) fingerprints and the other data referred to in Article 5(1) are lawfully transmitted to the Central Unit;

c) data are accurate and up-to-date when they are transmitted to the Central Unit;

d) without prejudice to the responsibilities of the Commission, data in the central database are lawfully recorded, stored, corrected and erased;

e) the results of fingerprint comparisons transmitted by the Central Unit are lawfully used.

2. In accordance with Article 10, the Member State of origin shall ensure the security of these data before and during transmission to the Central Unit as well as the security of the data it receives from the Central Unit.

3. The Member State of origin shall be responsible for the final identification of the data pursuant to Article 4(6).

4. The Commission shall ensure that the Central Unit is operated in accordance with the provisions of the Convention and with the implementing rules adopted by the Council. (...)

5. Member States shall ensure that use of data recorded in the central database contrary to the purpose of Eurodac as laid down in Article 1(1) shall be subject to appropriate penalties.

Article 10

Security

1. The Member State of origin shall take the necessary measures to:

(a) prevent any unauthorized person from having access to national installations in which the Member State carries out operations in accordance with the aim of Eurodac (checks at the entrance to the installation); [(b) control of data media; (c) control of data recording; (d) control of data entry; (e) control of access; (f) control of transmission; (g) control of transport.]

2. As regards the operation of the Central Unit, the Commission shall be responsible for applying the abovementioned measures.

Article 11

Access to and correction or erasure of data recorded in Eurodac

1. The Member State of origin shall have access to data which it has transmitted and which are recorded in the central database in accordance with the provisions of this Convention. No Member State may conduct searches in the data transmitted by another Member State, nor may it receive such data apart from data resulting from the comparison referred to in Article 4(5). (...)

2. If a Member State or the Central Unit has evidence to suggest that data recorded in the central database are factually inaccurate, it shall advise the Member State of origin as soon as possible. In addition, if a Member State has evidence to suggest that data were recorded in the central database contrary to this Convention, it shall similarly advise the Member State of origin as soon as possible. The latter shall check the data concerned and, if necessary, amend or erase without delay.

Article 12
Damages
1. The Member State of origin shall, in accordance with its national law, be liable for any damage caused to persons or other Member States resulting from the illegal use of the results of the fingerprint comparisons transmitted by the Central Unit.
2. The European Community shall be liable, in accordance with Article 215, second paragraph, of the Treaty establishing the European Community, for any damage caused to persons or Member States through the fault of persons working in the Central Unit in breach of their duties under this Convention. Article 178 of the Treaty establishing the European Community shall be applicable.
3. The European Community shall likewise be liable for damage to the central database. However, if the damage is due to the failure of a Member State to comply with its obligations under this Convention, that Member State shall be liable, unless the Commission failed to take reasonable steps to prevent the damage from happening or to minimise its impact.
4. Claims for compensation against a Member State for the damage referred to in paragraphs 1 and 3 shall be governed by the provisions of national law of the defendant Member State.

Article 13
Rights of the data subject
1. Member States shall inform the applicant for asylum, when taking his/her fingerprints, of the purpose, as defined in Article 1(1), of taking the prints and of his/her rights under this Article and their procedural practices.
2. In each Member State any person may, in accordance with the laws, regulations and procedures of the State, exercise a right of access to data concerning him/her recorded in the central database. Such access to data may be granted only by a Member State. The person will be informed of the data relating to him/her recorded in the central database and of the Member State which transmitted them to the Central Unit.
3. If the person contests the accuracy of the data or the lawfulness of recording them in the central database, he/she may ask for data which are factually inaccurate to be corrected or for data recorded unlawfully to be erased. The correction and erasure shall be carried out by the Member State which transmitted the data in accordance with its laws, regulations and procedures. (...)
10. The national supervisory authority of the Member State which transmitted the data shall assist any person resident in another Member State to exercise his/her right to correct or erase data. Such assistance shall be granted in accordance with its laws, regulations and procedures giving effect to the Council of Europe Convention for the Protection of Individuals with regard to Automatic Processing of Personal Data, signed at Strasbourg on 28 January 1981. Requests for such assistance may be made to the national supervisory authority of the Member State of residence, which shall transmit the requests to the authority of the Member State which transmitted the data. Alternatively, the data subject may apply for assistance directly to the joint supervisory authority set up in Article 15. (...)

Article 14
National supervisory authority
1. Each Member State shall designate a national supervisory authority or authorities responsible for personal data protection in that Member State. The task of the national su-

supervisory authority shall be to monitor independently, in accordance with its respective national law, the lawfulness of the processing, in accordance with the provisions of this Convention, of personal data by the Member State in question, as well as of their transmission to the Central Unit, and to examine whether this violates the rights of the data subject. For this purpose, the supervisory authority shall have access to the data processed by the Member State concerned. The Member State shall also make available to the national supervisory authority any information which it requests and allow it access to all documents and files, as well as all premises, at all times.

2. Each Member State shall ensure that its national supervisory authority has access to advice from persons with sufficient knowledge of fingerprint data.

3. Any person may ask the national supervisory authority to ensure that the recording and transmission of data concerning him/her to the Central Unit and the retrieval and use of such data by the Member State in question are lawful. This right shall be exercised in accordance with the national law applicable to the national supervisory body of which the request is made.

Article 15
Joint supervisory authority

1. An independent joint supervisory authority shall be set up, consisting of a maximum of two representatives from the supervisory authorities of each Member State. Each delegation shall have one vote.

2. The joint supervisory authority shall have the task of monitoring the activities of the Central Unit to ensure that the rights of data subjects are not violated by the processing or use of the data held by the Central Unit. In addition, it shall monitor the lawfulness of the transmission of personal data to the Member States by the Central Unit.

3. The joint supervisory authority shall also be competent for the examination of implementation or interpretation problems in connection with the operation of Eurodac, for the examination of possible difficulties during checks by the national supervisory authorities and for drawing up proposals for common solutions to existing problems.

4. In the performance of its duties, the joint supervisory authority shall, if necessary, be actively supported by the national supervisory authorities.

5. The joint supervisory authority shall have access to advice from persons with sufficient knowledge of fingerprint data.

6. The Commission shall assist the joint supervisory authority in the performance of its tasks. In particular, it shall supply information requested by the joint supervisory body, give it access to all documents and paper files as well as access to the data stored in the system and allow it access to all its premises, at all times.

7. The joint supervisory authority shall unanimously adopt its rules of procedure.

8. Reports drawn up by the joint supervisory authority shall be forwarded to the bodies to which the national supervisory authorities submit their reports, as well as to the Council for information. In addition, the joint supervisory authority may submit comments or proposals for improvement regarding its remit to the Council at any time.

9. In the performance of their duties, the members of the joint supervisory authority shall not receive instructions from any government or body.

10. The joint supervisory authority shall be consulted on that part of the draft operating budget of the Eurodac Central Unit which concerns it. Its opinion shall be annexed to the draft budget in question.

11. The joint supervisory authority shall be disbanded upon the establishment of the Cen-

tral Unit supervisory authority under Article 286(2) of the EC Treaty as inserted by the Treaty of Amsterdam. The independent supervisory authority shall take over the tasks of the joint supervisory authority and shall exercise for the purposes of the supervision of the Central Unit all the powers attributed to it by virtue of the act under which the independent supervisory authority is established. For the purpose of this Convention, the independent supervisory authority shall be referred to as the 'Central Unit supervisory authority'.
12. The Council may adopt such supplementary measures as it considers necessary to enable the Central Unit supervisory authority to perform its duties.

Article 16
Costs
1. The costs incurred in connection with the establishment and operation of the Central Unit shall be borne by the budget of the European Communities.
2. The costs incurred by national units and for their connection to the central database shall be borne by each Member State.
3. The costs of transmission of data from the Member State of origin and of the findings of the comparison to that State shall be borne by the State in question.

Article 17
Jurisdiction of the Court of Justice
1. The Court of Justice shall have jurisdiction to rule on any dispute between Member States regarding the interpretation or the application of this Convention whenever such dispute cannot be settled by the Council within six months of its being referred to the Council by one of its members.
2. The Court of Justice shall have jurisdiction to rule on any dispute between one or more Member States and the Commission of the European Communities regarding the interpretation or the application of this Convention whenever such dispute cannot be settled through negotiation.
3. Any court in a Member State may ask the Court of Justice to give a preliminary ruling on a matter concerning the interpretation of this Convention.
4. The competence of the Court of Justice provided for in paragraph 3 shall be subject to its acceptance by the Member State concerned in a declaration to that effect made at the time of the notification referred to in Article 20(2) or at any subsequent time.
5. A Member State making a declaration under paragraph 4 may restrict the possibility of asking the Court of Justice to give a preliminary ruling to those of its courts against the decisions of which there is no judicial remedy under national law.
6. (a) The Statute of the Court of Justice of the European Community and its Rules of Procedure shall apply; (b) In accordance with that Statute, any Member State, whether or not it has made a declaration under paragraph 4, shall be entitled to submit statements of case or written observations to the Court of Justice in cases which arise under paragraph 3.
7. After the entry into force of the Treaty of Amsterdam amending the Treaty on European Union, the Treaties establishing the European Communities and certain related acts:
– paragraphs 1 to 5 and paragraph 6(b) of this Article shall cease to apply; and
– all the relevant provisions of the Treaty establishing the European Community as amended by the Treaty of Amsterdam, concerning the powers of the Court of Justice, including Article 68, shall apply mutatis mutandis and for such purposes, references to 'this

Treaty' in the said provisions or in provisions to which they refer, and references to 'this Title' in the case of Article 68, shall be taken as meaning references to 'this Convention'.

Article 18
Supervision of implementation
The Council shall supervise the implementation and application of the provisions of this Convention to ensure that Eurodac operates effectively. (...)

Article 19
Reservations
This Convention shall not be subject to any reservations.

Article 20
Entry into force
1. This Convention shall be subject to adoption by the Member States in accordance with their respective constitutional requirements.
2. Member States shall notify the Secretary-General of the Council of the European Union of the completion of the procedures necessary under their constitutional requirements for adopting this Convention.
3. Article 4(7) and Article 8(3) of this Convention shall enter into force on the day following the notification referred to in paragraph 2 by the State which, being a member of the European Union on the date of adoption by the Council of the Act drawing up this Convention, is the last to complete that formality. The other provisions of this Convention shall enter into force on the first day of the third month after that notification, provided that a Protocol extending the scope ratione personae of this Convention for the purpose of further facilitating the application of the Dublin Convention, enters into force on the same date.
4. Without prejudice to paragraph 3, Eurodac shall not begin its activities pursuant to this Convention until the implementing rules referred to in Articles 4(7) and 8(3) have been adopted.

Article 21
Territorial scope
As regards the United Kingdom, the provisions of this Convention shall apply only to the United Kingdom of Great Britain and Northern Ireland.

Article 22
Accession
1. This Convention shall be open to accession by any State that becomes a member of the European Union. (...)

Article 23
Depositary (...)

5.6.b

EUROPEAN UNION Brussels, 26 February 1999
THE COUNCIL (6324/99)

DRAFT EURODAC PROTOCOL

Draft Council Act drawing up a Protocol extending the scope ratione personae of the Convention concerning the establishment of 'Eurodac' for the comparison of fingerprints of applicants for asylum
1. At its session on 3/4 December 1998, the (Justice and Home Affairs) Council recorded agreement, subject to parliamentary scrutiny reservations from the Danish, Italian and United Kingdom delegations, on the content of the draft Eurodac Convention which was to be 'frozen' pending the entry into force of the Treaty of Amsterdam. The Council noted that once that treaty entered into force, the Commission would put forward a proposal for a Community legal instrument incorporating the content of the draft convention.
2. With regard to the draft Protocol to the draft Eurodac Convention (extending the scope ratione personae of the draft Convention), the Council, on the one hand, agreed to forward the text as set out in 12298/98 to the European Parliament for opinion and, on the other hand, invited the Permanent Representatives Committee to continue examination of the outstanding questions on the text with a view to enabling the Council, in the light of the European Parliament's opinion, to reach agreement on the draft Protocol at its next session.
3. The Eurodac Working Party has devoted several meetings to the examination of the draft Protocol and, at its meeting on 16/17 February 1999 reached broad agreement on the text set out in the Annex hereto.
4. On 23 February 1999, the K4 Committee confirmed the agreement (7) in the Working Party.
(7) Italian and United Kingdom delegations maintained parliamentary scrutiny reservations. Several delegations maintained linguistic reservations.
5. The Permanent Representatives Committee is invited to suggest that the Council
– record agreement on the content of the draft Protocol to the draft Eurodac Convention as set out in the Annex;
– decide to 'freeze' the text of the draft Protocol pending the entry into force of the Treaty of Amsterdam;
– note that the Commission will, upon entry into force of that Treaty, put forward a proposal for a Community instrument incorporating the content of the draft Protocol taking account of the Opinion which the European Parliament is expected to deliver shortly.

ANNEX: DRAFT
COUNCIL ACT of drawing up a Protocol extending the scope ratione personae of the Convention concerning the establishment of 'Eurodac' for the comparison of fingerprints of applicants for asylum
THE COUNCIL OF THE EUROPEAN UNION,

Having regard to the Treaty on European Union, and in particular Article K.3(2)(c) thereof,

Whereas asylum policy is regarded as a matter of common interest for the Member States under Article K.1(1) of the Treaty;

Whereas the Council has drawn up a Convention concerning the establishment of 'Eurodac' for the comparison of fingerprints of applicants for asylum (the 'Eurodac Convention'), for the purposes of applying the Convention determining the State responsible for examining applications for asylum lodged in one of the Member States of the European Communities, signed at Dublin on 15 June 1990 particular Article 15 thereof;

Whereas it is also necessary, in order effectively to apply the Dublin Convention, and in particular Article 6 thereof, to make provision for communicating to 'Eurodac' the fingerprints of persons apprehended in connection with the irregular crossing of the external border of a Member State;

Whereas it is also desirable in order effectively to apply the Dublin Convention, and in particular Article 10, paragraph 1(c) and (e) thereof, to allow for each Member State to check whether an alien found illegally present on its territory has applied for asylum in another Member State.

Having decided that a Protocol supplementing the Eurodac Convention to that effect, the text of which is given in the Annex and which has been signed today by the Representatives of the Governments of the Member States, is hereby drawn up;

Having examined the views of the European Parliament, following the consultation conducted by the Presidency in accordance with Article K.6 of the Treaty on European Union;

RECOMMENDS that it be adopted by the Member States in accordance with their respective constitutional requirements and in such manner that it will enter into force at the same time as the Eurodac Convention.

Done at (...), For the Council, The President

Annex
PROTOCOL
drawn up on the basis of Article K.3 of the Treaty on European Union,
extending the scope ratione personae of the Convention concerning the establishment of 'Eurodac' for the comparison of fingerprints of applicants for asylum

THE HIGH CONTRACTING PARTIES to this Protocol, Member States of the European Union,

REFERRING to the Act of the Council of the European Union of (...),

RECOGNISING that the Convention signed at Dublin on 15 June 1990, determining the State responsible for examining applications for asylum lodged in one of the Member States of the European Communities, is a measure relating to the free movement of persons in accordance with the objective set out in Article 7a of the Treaty establishing the European Community;

RECALLING that for the purposes of applying the Dublin Convention, and in particular Article 15 thereof, the Council has drawn up a Convention concerning the establishment of 'Eurodac' for the comparison of fingerprints of applicants for asylum;

WHEREAS it is also necessary in order effectively to apply the Dublin Convention, and in particular Article 6 thereof, to make provision for communicating to 'Eurodac' the fingerprints of persons apprehended in connection with the irregular crossing of the external border of a Member State;

WHEREAS it is also desirable in order effectively to apply the Dublin Convention, and in particular Article 10, paragraph 1(c) and (e) thereof, to allow for each Member State to use 'Eurodac' for checking whether an alien found illegally present on its territory has applied for asylum in another Member State.

HAVE AGREED ON THE FOLLOWING PROVISIONS:

Article 1

Extension of 'Eurodac'

The provisions of the Convention concerning the establishment of 'Eurodac' for the comparison of fingerprints of applicants for asylum, hereinafter referred to as 'the Eurodac Convention', shall be extended, subject to the provisions of this Protocol, to fingerprint data on certain other aliens, for the purpose of assisting in determining the Member State which is responsible under the Dublin Convention of 15 June 1990 for examining an application for asylum lodged in a Member State, as well as for the purpose of otherwise facilitating the application of the latter Convention.

Article 2

Definitions

Unless otherwise stated, the terms defined in Article 2 of the Eurodac Convention and in Article 1 of the Dublin Convention of 15 June 1990 shall have the same meaning in this Protocol.

Article 3

Collection and communication of fingerprint data on aliens who irregularly cross an external border

1. Each Member State shall promptly take the fingerprints of every alien of at least fourteen years of age who is apprehended by the competent control authorities in connection with the irregular crossing by land, sea or air of the border of that Member State having come from a third country and who is not turned back.

2. The Member State concerned shall promptly communicate the fingerprints of any alien as referred to in paragraph 1 above to the Eurodac Central Unit, together with the other relevant data referred to in Article 5(1) of the Eurodac Convention.

Article 4

Recording of data on aliens who irregularly cross an external border

1. Data communicated to the Central Unit pursuant to Article 3 of this Protocol shall be recorded in the central database for the sole purpose of comparison with data on applicants for asylum transmitted subsequently to the Central Unit. The Central Unit shall therefore not compare data communicated to it pursuant to Article 3 with any data previously recorded in the central database, nor with data subsequently communicated to the Central Unit pursuant to Article 3.

2. In so far as the provisions of the Eurodac Convention apply to data on an alien as referred to in Article 3 of this Protocol, references to the 'Member State of origin' shall be taken as meaning the Member State which communicates such data to the Central Unit.

Article 5
Storage of data on aliens who irregularly cross an external border
1. Each set of data relating to an alien as referred to in Article 3 of this Protocol shall be stored in the Eurodac central database for two years from the date on which the fingerprints of the alien were taken. Upon expiry of this period, the Central Unit shall automatically erase the data from the central database.
2. Notwithstanding the provisions of paragraph 1 above, the data relating to an alien as referred to in Article 3 shall be erased from the central database immediately when the Member State of origin becomes aware of either of the following circumstances before the two-year period mentioned in paragraph 1 has expired:
(a) the alien has been issued with a residence permit; or
(b) the alien has left the territory of the Member States.

Article 6
Rights of the data subject
The right of any alien as referred to in Article 3 to have access to data concerning him/her in the central database shall be exercised in accordance with the law of the Member State before which he/she invokes that right. If the national law so provides, the national supervisory authority provided for in Article 14 of the Eurodac Convention shall decide whether information shall be communicated and by what procedures. In the case referred to in the previous sentence, a Member State which did not transmit the data may communicate information concerning such data only if it has previously given the Member State of origin an opportunity to state its position.

Article 7
Comparison of fingerprints of aliens found illegally present in a Member State
1. With a view to checking whether an alien found illegally present within its territory has previously lodged an application for asylum in another Member State, each Member State may communicate to the Central Unit fingerprints it may have taken of any such alien of at least fourteen years of age. As a general rule there are grounds for checking whether the alien has previously lodged an application for asylum in another Member State where:
– the alien declares that he/she has lodged an application for asylum but without indicating the Member State in which he/she made the application;
– the alien does not request asylum but objects to being returned to his/her country of origin by claiming that he/she would be in danger, or
– the alien otherwise seeks to prevent his/her removal by refusing to cooperate in order to establish his/her identity, in particular by showing no or false identity papers.
2. The fingerprints of an alien as referred to in paragraph 1 shall be communicated to the Central Unit solely for the purpose of comparison with the fingerprints of applicants for asylum transmitted by other Member States and already recorded in the central database. The fingerprints of such an alien shall not be stored in the central database, nor shall they be compared with the data communicated to the Central Unit pursuant to Article 3 of this Protocol.
3. The Central Unit shall destroy the fingerprints communicated to it under paragraph 1 above forthwith, once the results of the comparison have been communicated to the Member State of origin.

Article 8
Application of provisions of the Eurodac Convention
Unless otherwise stated in this Protocol or unless a different intention appears from the context, all the provisions of the Eurodac Convention shall apply mutatis mutandis to this Protocol.

Article 9
Reservations
This Protocol shall not be subject to any reservations.

Article 10
Entry into force (...)

Article 11
Accession
1. This Protocol shall be open to accession by any State that becomes a member of the European Union. (...)

Article 12
Depositary (...)

5.6.c

PROPOSAL FOR A COUNCIL REGULATION (EC) CONCERNING THE ESTABLISHMENT OF 'EURODAC' FOR THE COMPARISON OF THE FINGERPRINTS OF APPLICANTS FOR ASYLUM AND CERTAIN OTHER ALIENS

EXPLANATORY MEMORANDUM

CONTENTS

1. GENERAL
1.1 Context
1.2 Negotiations for a Convention and Protocol

2. PROPOSAL FOR COUNCIL REGULATION
2.1 Subject-matter
2.2 Legal basis

3. JUSTIFICATION FOR PROPOSAL IN TERMS OF PROPORTIONALITY AND SUBSIDIARITY PRINCIPLE

4. INDIVIDUAL PROVISIONS
4.1 General objective
4.2 Continuity
4.3 Adaptation

4.4 Concordance table
4.5 Individual Articles

1. GENERAL

1.1 Context

Under Article 2 of the Treaty on European Union, the Member States set themselves the objective of maintaining and developing the Union as an area of freedom, security and justice, in which the free movement of persons is assured in conjunction with appropriate measures with respect to external border controls, asylum, immigration and the prevention and combating of crime.

One way in which the Union is to achieve this aim is through the adoption, within five years after the entry into force of the Treaty of Amsterdam, of measures on asylum, in accordance with the Geneva Convention of 28 July 1951 and other relevant treaties (Article 63(1)). Under Article 61, the Council is also to adopt any necessary directly related flanking measures with respect to, inter alia, asylum. Article 61 refers explicitly to the adoption of flanking measures under Article 63(1)(a), which provides for the adoption of measures on criteria and mechanisms for determining which Member State is responsible for considering an application for asylum submitted by a national of a third country in one of the Member States.

The Dublin Convention of 15 June 1990, to which all Member States are party, provides a mechanism for determining the State responsible for examining applications for asylum lodged in one of the Member States of the European Communities. The Member States considered that it would, however, be problematic to implement the Convention solely on the basis of the evidence provided by identity cards and passports, since these can easily be disposed of or destroyed. In December 1991, Ministers responsible for immigration meeting in the Hague therefore agreed that a feasibility study for a Community wide fingerprint system for asylum applicants should be undertaken. Work has been ongoing since then to develop a system for the computerized comparison of fingerprints in order to facilitate the application of the relevant rules for determining which Member State is responsible for considering an application for asylum.

1.2 Negotiations for a Convention and Protocol

In March 1996, Member States began negotiations on a Convention to establish a definitive identification system based on the comparison of the fingerprints of asylum seekers. The Eurodac system would function through the collection of fingerprint data by Member States and its transmission to a Central Unit, which would compare individual sets of fingerprints against the data retained in the system at the request of a Member State. The text of a draft Convention under Title VI of the Treaty on European Union was prepared and consensus was reached within the Council (Justice and Home Affairs) in December 1998 to 'freeze' the text pending the entry into force of the Treaty of Amsterdam.

In addition, Member States also prepared a draft Protocol, which was intended to further facilitate the application of the Dublin Convention by providing for the collection of fingerprint data relating to persons apprehended in connection with the irregular crossing of an external border. This data would be available for the purposes of comparison with the fingerprints of people who subsequently claimed asylum in one of the Member States. In addition, the Protocol provided a facility to make checks with Eurodac in certain circumstances to determine whether a person found illegally present within a Member State had previously claimed asylum in another Member State. Again, the Council (Justice and Home Affairs) noted consensus on the draft Protocol and agreed, in March 1999, to 'freeze' this text also.

The subject matter covered by the frozen texts now falls within the scope of Article 63(1)(a) of the Treaty establishing the European Community. The present draft Eurodac Regulation fulfils the remit given to the Commission by the Council (Justice and Home Affairs) in December 1998 and March 1999 to bring forward after the entry into force of the Treaty of Amsterdam a proposal for a Community instrument incorporating the frozen texts.

2. PROPOSAL FOR COUNCIL REGULATION

Since the acts drawing up the draft Eurodac Convention and draft Eurodac Protocol were not formally adopted and the Convention and Protocol were not signed, their provisions are clearly not applicable. The Council (Justice and Home Affairs) decided at its meetings on 3-4 December 1998 and 12 March 1999 to 'freeze' the texts of the Convention and the Protocol, and invited the Commission to put forward a proposal for a Community legal instrument after the entry into force of the Treaty of Amsterdam.

2.1 Subject-matter

This proposal for a Regulation is the first proposal of the Commission in the field of asylum under Title IV of the Treaty establishing the European Community. Its purpose is to assist in determining the Member State which is responsible pursuant to the Dublin Convention for examining an application for asylum lodged in a Member State and otherwise to facilitate the application of the Dublin Convention under the conditions set out in the proposal. The Commission has incorporated the substance of the draft Convention and draft Protocol in its proposal for a Regulation, subject to the adaptation set out in section 4.3 of this explanatory memorandum.

The proposal has been made in order to facilitate the ongoing work of the institutions following the entry into force of the Treaty of Amsterdam. The subject matter should be viewed in the context of the broader work programme set out in new Title IV of the Treaty establishing the European Community, and in particular in Article 63 paragraphs (1) and (2).[6]

2.2 Legal basis

The subject matter covered by the frozen draft Convention and Protocol is now within the ambit of Article 63(1)(a) of the Treaty. Article 61(a) of the Treaty specifies the need for

---

[6] A full account of this work programme is contained in section B of the Commission Working Document 'Towards common standards on asylum procedures', Brussels, 3.3.1999, SEC(1999) 271 final.
(Ed.: see Ch. 4.1).

flanking measures inter alia on asylum in accordance with Article 63(1)(a).

The form chosen for the instrument – a Regulation – is warranted in view of the need to apply strictly defined and harmonised rules in relation to the storage, comparison and erasure of fingerprints, for otherwise the system would not work. These rules constitute a set of precise, unconditional provisions that are directly and uniformly applicable in a mandatory way and, by their very nature, require no action by the Member States to transpose them into national law.

The instrument falls to be adopted by the procedure of Article 67 of the Treaty, which provides that, during a transitional period of five years, the Council is to act unanimously on a proposal from the Commission or on the initiative of a Member State and after consulting the European Parliament.

The new Title IV of the EC Treaty, which applies to the matters covered by this proposal for a Regulation, is not applicable to the United Kingdom and Ireland, unless they 'opt in' in the manner provided by the Protocol on the position of the United Kingdom and Ireland which is annexed to the Treaties. At the Council meeting (Justice and Home Affairs) on 12 March 1999, these two Member States announced their intention of being fully associated with Community activities in the field of asylum. It will be for them to embark on the appropriate procedure under the Protocol in due course.

Title IV of the EC Treaty is likewise not applicable to Denmark, by virtue of the Protocol on the position of Denmark which is annexed to the Treaties. Denmark has so far given no notice of an intention to embark on a procedure to participate in the Eurodac system.

The current proposal for a Regulation has been drafted on the basis of the current situation. If the position were to change in relation to one or more of the Member States mentioned above, the requisite adjustments will have to be made.

The Commission is ready, if necessary, to come forward with additional recitals and operative provisions in order to motivate fully the territorial scope of the Regulation.

The Commission notes that according to the terms of Article 7 of the agreement concluded by the Council of the European Union and the Republic of Iceland and the Kingdom of Norway concerning the latters' association to the implementation, application and development of the Schengen acquis, it will be necessary to conclude an appropriate arrangement on criteria and mechanisms for establishing the State responsible for considering an application for asylum lodged in one of the Member States of the European Union or in Iceland or Norway, and such an agreement will entail an extension of the Eurodac system to these two States.

3. JUSTIFICATION FOR PROPOSAL IN TERMS OF PROPORTIONALITY AND SUBSIDIARITY PRINCIPLE

What are the objectives of the proposal in relation to the obligations imposed on the Community?

The objectives of the measure are to assist in determining the Member State which is responsible pursuant to the Dublin Convention for examining an application for asylum lodged in a Member State and otherwise to facilitate the application of the Dublin Convention under the conditions set out in the proposal. These objectives are consistent with the objective under Title IV of the Treaty establishing the European Community of establishing an area of freedom, security and justice. To establish such an area, the Community is to adopt measures aimed at ensuring the free movement of persons, in conjunction with directly related flanking measures inter alia on asylum under Article 63(1)(a) of the Treaty. Article 63(1)(a) of the Treaty requires the Community to adopt measures on criteria and mechanisms for determining which Member State is responsible for considering an application for asylum submitted by a national of a third country in one of the Member States.

Does the measure satisfy the criteria of subsidiarity?
Its objectives can not be attained by the Member States acting alone and must therefore, by reason of the cross-border impact, be obtained at Community level.

Does the measure satisfy the criteria of proportionality?
The proposed instrument is confined to the minimum needed for the attainment of these objectives and does not exceed what is necessary for that purpose.

The measures proposed in the Regulation are consistent with the aim of facilitating the application of the Dublin Convention in the light of the fact that many applicants for asylum in the European Union are not properly documented, and there is a lack of evidence about their identity, which makes it difficult to establish whether they have previously lodged an application for asylum or how they entered the Union.

Articles 8-10 of the Regulation provide for the comparison of fingerprint data of persons apprehended in connection with the irregular crossing of the external frontier with fingerprint data relating to persons subsequently claiming asylum in one of the Member States. The detection of a match, indicating that an asylum applicant has previously crossed the external border irregularly, facilitates the application of Article 6 of the Dublin Convention, which establishes broadly that the Member State which a person first entered irregularly from a third country is responsible for considering any subsequent application for asylum.

Article 11 allows a Member State to compare fingerprint data taken from a person found illegally present on its territory against data relating to asylum applicants in order to check whether the person concerned has previously claimed asylum in another Member State. The existence of a match allows the application of Articles 10(1)(c) and 10(1)(e) of the Dublin Convention, which provide for the return of such persons to the Member State in which the asylum claim is being or has been examined.

4. INDIVIDUAL PROVISIONS

4.1 General objective

The objective of Eurodac is to assist in determining the Member State which is responsible pursuant to the Dublin Convention for examining an application for asylum lodged in a Member State and otherwise to facilitate the application of the Dublin Convention under the conditions set out in the proposal. To this end, it provides for the establishment of a Central Unit within the Commission which will be equipped with a computerized central database for comparing the fingerprints of asylum applicants and certain other persons.

The draft regulation provides for the fingerprints of three different groups of people to be transmitted or communicated to the Central Unit and processed within the Central database:

(a) Applicants for asylum (Articles 4 – 7). The Regulation creates an obligation to take the fingerprints of applicants for asylum and transmit them to the Eurodac Central Unit. This data will immediately be compared with fingerprint data on asylum applicants and on people covered by paragraph (b) below which is already stored in the Central Unit. Matches will be transmitted to the Member State of origin for final verification, and the Member States concerned will then use the evidence provided to apply the procedures of the Dublin Convention. Data will normally be stored for ten years, but will be erased in advance if the applicant for asylum obtains citizenship of the Union. (In addition, Article 12 provides that if the person concerned obtains refugee status, their data will be blocked in the central database and statistics will be compiled.)

(b) Persons apprehended in connection with the irregular crossing of an external border (Articles 8 – 10). The Regulation creates an obligation to take the fingerprints of persons apprehended in connection with the irregular crossing of the external border of the European Union and transmit them to the Central Unit. This data is stored in the Central Unit for a maximum of two years. Fingerprint data on asylum applicants which is subsequently transmitted to the Central Unit under paragraph (a) above is also compared against this data. The detection of a match, indicating that an asylum applicant had previously crossed the external border of the Union irregularly and entered a specified Member State, facilitates the application of Article 6 of the Dublin Convention. The data is erased before the expiry of the two year period if the person in question is granted a residence permit, leaves the territory of the Union, or becomes a citizen of the Union.

(c) Persons found illegally present within the territory of a Member State (Article 11). The Regulation allows a Member State, if it has fingerprinted a person found illegally present on its territory, to transmit this data to Eurodac in certain circumstances in order to check whether the person concerned has previously claimed asylum in another Member State. In the event that Eurodac identifies a match, the data is transmitted back to the Member State of origin for final checking. The existence of a match can facilitate the application of Articles 10(1)(c) and 10(1)(e) of the Dublin Convention. Data relating to persons found illegally present in a Member State is destroyed as soon as the comparison within Eurodac has been carried out.

The Regulation contains detailed provisions (Articles 13 – 20) on data use, data protection, responsibility and security to ensure that stringent standards of protection in accordance inter alia with Directive 95/46/EC and Article 286 of the Treaty are applied.

4.2 Continuity

The Commission has incorporated the substance of the frozen draft Convention and draft Protocol to ensure continuity in the results of the negotiations, but has omitted such provisions as would be incompatible with the nature of the proposed legal instrument and the framework for cooperation in the field of asylum established by Title IV of the Treaty establishing the European Community as amended by the Treaty of Amsterdam.

4.3 Adaptation

The obvious differences between a Third Pillar Convention and Protocol on the one hand and a Community Regulation on the other warrants departures from the frozen draft Convention and Protocol texts in a number of respects:

– Jurisdiction of the Court of Justice: unlike Article 17 of the Convention, the Regulation does not need to confer jurisdiction on the Court of Justice, given the provisions of Article 68 and other normally applicable provisions of the Treaty;
– Implementing provisions: Article 18 of the draft Convention foresees supervision of implementation and application by the Council, and the adoption of implementing measures by the Council. The first aspect will automatically fall to the Commission under Articles 211 and 226 of the Treaty. As far as the second aspect is concerned, the Regulation confers on the Commission powers of implementation to adopt provisions to give effect to it, with the assistance of a regulatory committee (Procedure III(a) of the 'comitology' decision), in accordance with Articles 202 and 211 of the Treaty.
– Formal provisions: Articles 19 (reservations), 22 (accession) and 23 (depositary) of the frozen draft Convention, and the corresponding provisions in the frozen draft Protocol (Articles 9, 11 and 12) would be out of place in a Community instrument.
– Entry into force and applicability: in relation to entry into force (Article 20 of the frozen draft Convention and Article 10 of the frozen draft Protocol), Article 249 and 254 of the Treaty are applicable to the entry into force of the Regulation. In addition Article 26 of the Regulation contains a new provision, which takes account of the fact that there will no longer be a ratification period during which Member States and the Commission will be able to make the necessary technical arrangements by introducing a two stage approach to entry into force and applicability.
– Territorial scope: Article 21 of the frozen draft Convention makes provision in relation to the United Kingdom, but no corresponding provision appears in the Regulation. As explained in section 2.2 above, the proposal has been drafted on the basis of the current legal situation under new Title IV of the EC Treaty and the Protocol on the position of the United Kingdom and Ireland which is annexed to the Treaties. If the United Kingdom applies the procedure of Article 3 of the Protocol, appropriate adjustments will have to be made in the text of the Regulation. It is, however, necessary to make provision in the Regulation (see Article 25) to ensure that the territorial scope of the Eurodac Regulation is aligned with the territorial scope of the Dublin Convention which it is implementing. The normal scope of application in accordance with Article 299 of the Treaty has therefore been limited.
– Monitoring and evaluation: a new Article has been included in the Regulation (Article 23) on monitoring and evaluation in the context of Sound and Efficient Management 2000, underpinned by Article 2 of the Financial Regulation ((EEC) No 1231/77).
– Integration into a single legal instrument: the technique of negotiating a draft Convention and a draft Protocol in parallel was unorthodox, even under the previous Title VI of the Treaty on European Union. For reasons of legislative orthodoxy, the Commission has integrated the frozen draft Convention and Protocol texts into a single legal instrument. This entails the suppression of Articles 2 and 8 of the Protocol, and numerous consequential changes throughout the text of the Regulation.
– Alignment with the data protection regime established under the Treaty establishing the European Community: Directive 95/46/EC of the European Parliament and the Council of 24 October 1995 on the protection of individuals with regard to the processing of personal data and on the free movement of such data applies to the processing of personal data in the course of activities which fall within the scope of Community law. Since the Eurodac system is set up on the basis of Title IV of the Treaty (Visas, asylum, immigration and other policies related to free movement of persons), the processing of personal data car-

ried out by the Member States within the context of the Eurodac system is subject to the principles laid down by Directive 95/46/EC. In addition, the national data protection supervisory authorities established under the Directive are responsible for monitoring the processing of personal data by the Member States in the framework of Eurodac. By virtue of Article 286 of the Treaty, Directive 95/46/EC also applies to the processing of personal data by the Central Unit, since the Central Unit will be established within the Commission. The Central Unit will be subject to the Regulation which the Commission will propose under Article 286 of the Treaty, and to supervision by the independent supervisory body referred to in Article 286. Articles 13 to 20 of this Regulation clarify and specify some of the principles laid down in Directive 95/46/EC in relation to the specific situation of Eurodac. Amendments have been made to the frozen Convention text to ensure that the Regulation is consistent with the requirements laid down in Directive 95/46/EC. Article 6 of the frozen Protocol text, which restricted the right of access of persons apprehended in connection with the irregular crossing of an external border, has not been incorporated in the Regulation, since it is incompatible with Directive 95/46/EC.

4.4 (...)

4.5 Individual Articles

CHAPTER I – GENERAL PROVISIONS

Article 1 – Purpose of 'Eurodac'
This Article sets out the nature and purpose of the Eurodac system. Paragraph 1 establishes a direct and exclusive link with the Convention determining the State responsible for examining an application for asylum lodged in one of the Member States of the European Communities (the 'Dublin Convention').

Paragraph 2 provides that Eurodac consists of the Central Unit, a computerised central database for recording and storing fingerprints, and the means of transmission between the Member States and the central database. This paragraph also specifies that Eurodac's rules shall apply to operations carried out in the Member State from the point when data is transmitted to the Central Unit until the point where use is made of the results of the comparison.

Paragraph 3 provides that processing of fingerprints and other data in Eurodac may only be for the purposes set out in Article 15(1) of the Dublin Convention. These purposes are: determining the Member State which is responsible for examining the application for asylum; examining the application for asylum; and implementing any obligation arising under the Dublin Convention. Under paragraph 3, the fingerprints which a Member State takes and communicates to the Eurodac central unit may also be used in databases set up under that Member State's national law for another purpose.

Article 2 – Definitions
This Article defines terms used in the Regulation. In general, terms defined in Article 1 of the Dublin Convention have the same meaning in the Eurodac Regulation (paragraph 2). The definition of 'applicant for asylum' for the purpose of Eurodac does, however, specify that it covers persons on whose behalf an asylum application has been made. This

is designed in particular to cover minors aged between 14 and 18, on whose behalf an application may be lodged by a guardian or legal representative.

The definition of 'personal data' is slightly different from the one in the Convention text which was frozen by the Council. In addition, a definition of 'processing of personal data' has been added. These changes are designed to bring the text fully in line with Directive 95/46/EC of the European Parliament and of the Council of 24 October 1995 on the protection of individuals with regard to the processing of personal data and on the free movement of such data.

The definition of 'transmission of data' covers both the communication of data to the Central Unit for recording in the central database and the communication of the results of the comparison back to the relevant Member State. The second indent of the definition is designed to cover situations where the available technology permits a Member State to record data directly in the central database.

The definition of 'Member State of origin' is slightly different for asylum applicants and persons found illegally present within the territory of a Member State on the one hand and for persons apprehended in connection with the irregular crossing of an external border on the other hand. The difference simply reflects the fact that for the latter category there is no immediate comparison, so there are no results to communicate to the Member State in question. Point (f) effectively incorporates Article 4, paragraph 2, of the frozen Eurodac Protocol text.

Article 3 – Central Unit
Article 3 deals with arrangements for the Central Unit. It provides that this will be located within the Commission. The Article provides in effect that the Member States are controllers of the data which they communicate to the Central Unit, and the Commission is the processor. The computerised fingerprint recognition system which will compare the fingerprints will be located in the Central Unit.

Paragraph 3 provides for the adoption of implementing rules relating to the compilation of statistical data by the Central Unit. Such statistical data will clearly be valuable since it would otherwise be impossible to evaluate the effectiveness of the Eurodac system. There is no corresponding provision in the frozen Convention text, but it is essential that the performance and utility of Eurodac can be properly monitored. The Council has of its own initiative prepared draft implementing rules on this point.

CHAPTER II – APPLICANTS FOR ASYLUM

Article 4 – Collection, transmission and comparison of fingerprints
This Article deals with the procedure for taking, transmitting, storing and comparing the fingerprints of asylum applicants.

Paragraph 1 creates an obligation for each Member State to fingerprint every asylum applicant aged at least 14 years of age. The procedure for taking the fingerprints is, however, left to the national practice of the Member State concerned (although the Member States do of course have obligations under the European Convention for the Protection of Human Rights and Fundamental Freedoms, with which they will have to comply). The fingerprint data must be transmitted to the Central Unit together with other data specified in Article 5. A reference in the corresponding article of the frozen Convention text to informing the applicant of the reasons why his fingerprints have been taken has been removed. The issue of providing information to the applicant is dealt with fully in Article 18(1) of the Regulation, and in addition Article 10 of Directive 95/46/EC is applicable in the context of the Regulation.

Paragraph 2 provides for the immediate recording in the central database of the data transmitted to it under paragraph 1.

Paragraph 3 provides that each new set of fingerprints of an asylum applicant which is received by the Central Unit must be compared against the fingerprint data on asylum applicants which has been supplied by other Member States and already been stored in the central database. This procedure is designed to ensure that all multiple asylum applications within the territory of the Member States can be detected.

Paragraph 4 allows a Member State to request that the fingerprints of asylum applicants which it transmits to the Central Unit are also compared with the fingerprint data on asylum applicants which it has itself previously transmitted to the Central Unit. This facility means that a Member State would not necessarily need to have a separate system for comparing the fingerprints of asylum applicants at the national level.

Paragraphs 5 and 6 set out the procedure in relation to the results of the comparison. If the Central Unit does not detect a match, it simply communicates this result to the Member State of origin. If the Central Unit does detect an apparent match, it must communicate this fact together with the data listed in Article 5(1) relating to the matching fingerprints to the Member State of origin. The Member State of origin nevertheless remains responsible for checking the comparison. That Member State and the other Member States concerned must then apply the procedures set out in the Dublin Convention in order to determine which state is responsible for considering the asylum application and whether the asylum applicant can be transferred. Paragraph 6 also provides that if checking and verification at the national level shows that the apparent match detected by the Central Unit is not in fact a genuine match or that the data is otherwise unreliable, the Member State of origin shall erase the data as soon as this is established.

Paragraph 7 provides for the adoption of implementing rules setting out the detailed procedures necessary for the application of this Article. The frozen Convention text envisaged that the Council would adopt implementing measures, and that this would be done by two-thirds majority. This has been amended in the light of the communitarisation of asylum policy. The paragraph now envisages delegation of this implementing power to the Commission in accordance with Article 202 of the Treaty establishing the European Community. The comitology procedure selected and set out in Article 22 of this Regulation is Procedure III(a) in Council Decision 87/373/EEC of 13 July 1987 laying down the procedures for the exercise of implementing powers conferred on the Commission.

Article 5 – Recording of data
Article 5 relates to the recording of data. Paragraph 1 provides an exhaustive list of the data which must be recorded in the central database. Paragraph 2 provides, in the interests of data protection and security, for the destruction of the media used for transmitting fingerprint data to the Central Unit unless the Member State of origin has requested their return.

Article 6 – Data storage
This Article sets out a maximum period for which data on asylum applicants may be

stored in Eurodac. This is set at 10 years from the date on which the fingerprints were taken, after which the Central Unit is required to erase the data automatically from the central database.

In this Article, the frozen Convention text has been amended very slightly. The Convention text referred to a storage period of 10 years from the date on which fingerprints were last taken, implying that fingerprints could be stored for longer than 10 years if the individual to whom they related subsequently had their fingerprints recorded in the Eurodac central database a second time. In the current proposal, the word 'last' has been deleted, to ensure that there are no circumstances where fingerprint data could be kept for longer than 10 years.

The Commission's text reflects the fact that in negotiations on the draft Convention the Council agreed on a storage period of 10 years. Article 6(1)(e) of Directive 95/46/EC of the European Parliament and the Council of 24 October 1995 on the protection of individuals with regard to the processing of personal data and on the free movement of such data establishes the principle that data should be kept in a form which permits identification of data subjects for no longer than is necessary for the purposes for which the data were collected or for which they are further processed. A similar principle is contained in the Council of Europe Convention for the Protection of Individuals with regard to the Automatic Processing of Personal Data (Strasbourg, 1981). The Commission strongly recommends that the Council should examine again whether it is necessary to conserve data relating to asylum applicants for a 10-year period except in the one case where provision is made for advance data erasure by Article 7.

Article 7 – Advance data erasure
Makes provision for data relating to asylum applicants to be erased from the central database before the expiry of the 10 year storage period set out in Article 6 in cases where the person concerned acquires citizenship of the Union. This provision for advance data erasure also applies, by virtue of a reference in Article 10 of the draft regulation, to fingerprint data relating to persons apprehended in connection with the irregular crossing of an external border. The Dublin Convention is not applicable to citizens of the Union, so there can be no possible justification for storing fingerprint data on such persons within Eurodac.

The comments made by the Commission under Article 6 above – in relation to data erasure in accordance with principle that data should be kept in a form which permits identification of data subjects for no longer than is necessary for the purposes for which the data were collected or for which they are further processed – are equally applicable in relation to this Article. In particular, the Commission considers that the Council should seriously consider whether it is now able to agree on the immediate erasure of data relating to a person who is recognised as a refugee and admitted in a Member State, in which case Article 12 below could be deleted. The Commission also recommends that the Council consider whether there are circumstances in which data relating to an asylum applicant who is no longer present on the territory of the Member States should be erased in advance. It would also be appropriate to consider provision for advance data erasure in relation to asylum applicants who become long-term residents in a Member State.

CHAPTER III – ALIENS APPREHENDED IN CONNECTION WITH THE IRREGULAR CROSSING OF AN EXTERNAL BORDER

Article 8 – Collection and communication of fingerprint data
Paragraph 1 creates an obligation for each Member State to take the fingerprints of any third country national or stateless person aged fourteen years or over who is apprehended in connection with the irregular crossing of the border of that Member State with a third country. Paragraph 2 requires the Member State concerned to communicate to the Central Unit the fingerprints together with data on the Member State of origin, the gender of the person concerned, the applicable reference number, the date on which the fingerprints were taken and the date on which the fingerprints were transmitted to the Central Unit.

This Article corresponds to Article 3 of the frozen draft Eurodac Protocol text, although the general reference in paragraph 2 of the draft Protocol text to 'other relevant data' has been replaced with a specific reference cataloguing the relevant data. Articles 8 – 10 of the Regulation are designed to facilitate the implementation of Article 6 of the Dublin Convention, which provides that 'when it can be proved that an applicant for asylum has irregularly crossed the border into a Member State by land, sea or air, having come from a non-member State of the European Communities, the Member State thus entered shall be responsible for examining the application for asylum'. The purpose of Articles 8 – 10 of the Regulation is to build up a record of people apprehended in connection with the irregular crossing of the external border against which the fingerprints of people who subsequently claim asylum in the European Union can be checked.

In addition to freezing the text of the draft Protocol, the Council also agreed on the following draft statement for the Council minutes:

> 'The Member States declare that the obligation to take fingerprints of aliens apprehended "in connection with the irregular crossing of an external border" is not limited to the situation where an alien is apprehended at or close to the external border itself. This provision also covers cases where an alien is apprehended beyond the external border, where he/she is still en route and there is no doubt that he/she crossed the external border irregularly. This could be the case, for example, where, subsequently to the crossing of the external border, an alien on board a (high speed) train is detected during on board checks, or where an alien transported in a sealed commercial vehicle is apprehended at the moment of disembarkation from the vehicle.'

In the context of the current proposal for a Regulation, the Council will need to reflect on whether it wishes to agree on and publish a similar statement.

Article 9 – Recording of data
Article 9 sets out rules on the recording and comparison of fingerprint data on persons apprehended in connection with the irregular crossing of the external border. Article 9 provides that the data transmitted to the Central Unit under Article 8 must be recorded in the central database, and specifies clear limitation on the use of this data. It may be compared only with data on asylum applicants which is subsequently transmitted to the Central Unit. This is consistent with the purpose of facilitating the implementation of Article 6 of the Dublin Convention. This means that it may not be compared with any data – whether on asylum applicants or on other people apprehended in connection with the irregular crossing of the external border – which was previously transmitted to the Central Unit. Nor may it be compared with data on persons apprehended in connection with the irregular crossing of the external border which is subsequently transmitted to the Central

Unit. (The Commission notes that the final sentence of the first alinea is technically redundant.)

As far as the comparison which is permitted is concerned, the provisions set out in Article 4 of the Regulation apply.

Article 9 corresponds closely to Article 4 of the frozen draft Protocol text. Paragraph 2 of the frozen text has, however, been moved and included in the definition of 'Member State of origin' in Article 2 of the Regulation. The new reference in the text to the provisions laid down pursuant to Article 4 preserves the effect of Article 8 of the frozen Protocol text, which applied the provisions of the draft Eurodac Convention mutatis mutandis to the draft Eurodac Protocol.

Article 10 – Storage of data
Article 10 sets out the rules for storage and erasure of data relating to persons apprehended in connection with the irregular crossing of the external border of the European Union. Paragraph 1 provides that such data shall be stored for a maximum of two years, at the end of which the Central Unit shall automatically erase the data. Paragraph 2 sets out rules for advance data erasure before the expiry of the two-year period. There are three situations in which advanced erasure must be carried out.

The first is when the person concerned has been issued with a residence permit. In this context, it should be noted that the applicable definition of 'residence permit' is contained in Article 1(1)(e) of the Dublin Convention. If a person were to be issued with a residence permit, responsibility for any subsequent asylum application would in principle be governed by Article 5 rather than Article 6 of the Dublin Convention. In other words, the fact that the person has irregularly crossed an external border of the Union ceases to be a relevant factor in determining responsibility for any subsequent asylum claim, and so the corresponding data must be erased.

The second situation in which advance data erasure must take place is if the person has left the territory of the Member States. As soon as a person departs from the territory of the Member States, the fact that they previously crossed the external border irregularly ceases to be of relevance in determining responsibility for any future claim for asylum. If the person in question later returns to the territory of the Member States and claims asylum, the relevant factor in determining responsibility for considering their asylum application would in principle be which Member State was responsible for their presence on the territory of the Member States on that second occasion.

The third situation in which advance data erasure must take place is if the person in question acquires citizenship of the Union. The reasons for deleting data in these circumstances are set out in the explanatory note on Article 7.

The Article requires that erasure must be carried out as soon as the Member State of origin becomes aware that one of the three situations set out above has occurred.

Article 10 of the Regulation corresponds to Article 5 of the frozen Protocol text, with a small addition to make it clear that the rules on erasure of data on persons who have acquired citizenship also apply in this case. (This is in line with Article 8 of the frozen draft Protocol, which effectively applied Article 7 of the frozen Convention to data on persons apprehended in connection with the irregular crossing of the external border.)

The Commission repeats its comments on the need to examine whether additional provision can be made for advance data erasure. In particular, the Commission considers that the Council should consider whether provision could be made for fingerprint data relating to a person apprehended in connection with the irregular crossing of an external border to be erased from the central database if that person subsequently claims asylum in a Member State and one of the Member States accepts responsibility for considering the person's asylum application. In such cases, the fingerprint data taken in connection with the irregular crossing of the external border could be considered to have served its purpose.

CHAPTER IV – ALIENS FOUND ILLEGALLY PRESENT IN A MEMBER STATE

Article 11 – Comparison of fingerprints
Article 11 is concerned with facilitating the implementation of Articles 10(1)(c) and 10(1)(e) of the Dublin Convention. Article 10(1)(c) provides that the Member State responsible for considering an asylum application under the criteria set out in the Dublin Convention shall be obliged to readmit or take back an applicant whose application is under examination and who is irregularly in another Member State. Article 10(1)(e) provides that the Member State responsible for considering an asylum application under the criteria set out in the Dublin Convention shall be obliged to take back a person whose application it had rejected and who is illegally in another Member State.

Article 11 does not create an obligation or a power in Community legislation for a Member State to fingerprint persons found illegally present within its territory. The Member State in question can only take the fingerprints of the person in question if it is permitted to do so under its national law. The provisions of Article 11 on persons found illegally present within the territory of a Member State differ in this important respect from the provisions of Article 4 on applicants for asylum and the provisions of Article 8 on persons apprehended in connection with the irregular crossing of the external border.

Article 11 creates a facility for Member States to use Eurodac if they wish to do so to check whether a person found illegally present on its territory has previously claimed asylum in another Member State. Paragraph 1 sets out the circumstances in which, as a general rule, there are grounds for carrying out such checks. Three sets of circumstances are specified.

Paragraph 2 sets out the rules for the communication and comparison of fingerprint data relating to persons found illegally present within the territory of a Member State. The data in question can only be compared against data on applicants for asylum which has previously been transmitted to the Central Unit by other Member States and recorded in the central database. The data may not be compared with data on persons apprehended in connection with the irregular crossing of the external border communicated to the Central Unit under Article 8. Nor may the data be stored in the central database. Paragraph 4 provides that the Central Unit must destroy the fingerprints communicated to it under this Article as soon as the results of the comparison have been communicated to the Member State of origin.

Article 11 corresponds to Article 7 of the frozen Protocol text. The use of permissive language in places in the frozen text is, in the Commission's view, unorthodox in relation to a Community Regulation. Adaptation of the text into language which is legally more appropriate language would, however, appear to be incompatible with the compromise found in the Council on this point.

CHAPTER V – RECOGNISED REFUGEES

Article 12 – Blocking of data
This Article makes provision on how data relating to persons recognised as refugees should be treated. Paragraph 1 provides that data on such people will be blocked in the central database. For five years, the data would be used only for the purpose of compiling statistics on persons who have already been recognised as a refugee in one Member State but nevertheless go on to claim asylum in another Member State. During this period, Member States would not be informed of matches identified by the Central Unit relating to persons who have been recognised as a refugee.

Paragraph 2 provides that five years after Eurodac starts operations, a decision would be taken on whether data relating to persons who have been recognised as refugees but subsequently claimed asylum in another Member State should (a) be treated in the same way as data relating to any other asylum applicant, or (b) be erased in advance as soon as the person has been recognised and admitted as a refugee. In each case, the Article makes provision for the appropriate changes in the procedure for handling such data to be made.

Although Article 12 corresponds broadly to Article 8 of the frozen Convention text, three changes have been introduced in paragraph 2. First, a reference has been introduced to the new arrangements for Eurodac to start operations which are set out in Article 26 of the Regulation. Secondly, the provisions relating to the procedure for the decision which will be made after five years have been brought into line with the Treaty establishing the European Community. An explicit reference to Article 67 TEC has been introduced. The Article no longer refers to a decision by the Council, because it is possible that, by the time the decision is taken on what to do with data relating to refugees, the appropriate procedure under Article 67 will be the co-decision procedure set out in Article 251 of the TEC. The third change to paragraph 2 is the insertion in the third subparagraph, point (b), of a full statement of the applicable arrangements for erasure.

Paragraph 3 provides for the adoption of implementing rules concerning the compilation of statistics on people who have been recognised as refugees in one Member State but who have subsequently applied for asylum in another Member State. The frozen Convention text envisaged that these implementing rules would be adopted by the Council by two-thirds majority. This has been amended in the light of the communitarisation of asylum policy. The paragraph now envisages delegation of this implementing power to the Commission in accordance with Article 202 of the Treaty establishing the European Community. The comitology procedure selected and set out in Article 22 of this Regulation is Procedure III(a) in Council Decision 87/373/EEC of 13 July 1987 laying down the procedures for the exercise of implementing powers conferred on the Commission.

The comments made under Article 7 above are again applicable. The Commission recommends that the case for immediate deletion of data relating to recognised refugees should be re-examined. If the Council were able to agree on such a solution, Article 12 could be deleted and provision could be made in Article 7 for advance erasure of the relevant data.

CHAPTER VI – DATA USE, DATA PROTECTION, SECURITY AND LIABILITY
(...)

CHAPTER VII – FINAL PROVISIONS
(...)

Article 26 – Entry into force and applicability
This Article provides for the Regulation to enter into force on the day of its publication in the Official Journal of the European Communities, from which date Member States will be required to implement it. Due to the technical requirements involved in establishing the Eurodac system, it is not possible to provide for simultaneous entry into force and applicability of the Regulation. This requires specific provision in the Regulation, whereas such explicit provision was not necessary in the 'frozen' draft Convention text because it was envisaged that technical preparations would be undertaken between the signing of the Convention and the completion of its ratification by Member States. The present Article therefore provides for a notification mechanism under which the Commission will publish in the Official Journal the date on which Eurodac will apply at the point at which each Member State has notified the Commission that it has made the necessary technical arrangements and the Central Unit is in a position to begin operations.

Proposal for a COUNCIL REGULATION (EC) concerning the establishment of 'Eurodac' for the comparison of the fingerprints of applicants for asylum and certain other aliens

THE COUNCIL OF THE EUROPEAN UNION,
Having regard to the Treaty establishing the European Community, and in particular Article 63(1)(a) thereof,
Having regard to the proposal from the Commission
Having regard to the opinion of the European Parliament
Whereas:
(1) Member States have concluded the Dublin Convention determining the State responsible for examining applications for asylum lodged in one of the Member States of the European Communities, signed in Dublin on 15 June 1990 (hereinafter referred to as 'the Dublin Convention')
(2) For the purposes of applying the Dublin Convention, it is necessary to establish the identity of applicants for asylum and of persons apprehended in connection with the unlawful crossing of the external borders of the Community. It is also desirable in order to effectively apply the Dublin Convention, and in particular points (c) and (e) of Article 10(1) thereof, to allow each Member State to check whether an alien found illegally present on its territory has applied for asylum in another Member State.
(3) Fingerprints constitute an important element in establishing the exact identity of such persons; whereas it is necessary to set up a system for the comparison of their fingerprints.
(4) To this end, it is necessary to set up a system known as 'Eurodac', consisting of a Central Unit, to be established within the Commission and which will operate a computerized central database of fingerprints, as well as of the electronic means of transmission between the Member States and the central database.
(5) It is also necessary to require the Member States promptly to take fingerprints of every applicant for asylum and of every alien who is apprehended in connection with the irregular crossing of an external Community border, if they are at least 14 years of age.
(6) It is necessary to lay down precise rules on the transmission of such fingerprint data to the Central Unit, the recording of such fingerprint data and other relevant data in the

central database, their storage, their comparison with other fingerprint data, the transmission of the results of such comparison and the blocking and erasure of the recorded data; such rules may be different for, and should be specifically adapted to, the situation of different categories of aliens.

(7) Aliens who have requested asylum in one Member State may have the option of requesting asylum in another Member State for many years to come; whereas, therefore, the maximum period during which fingerprint data should be kept by the Central Unit should be of considerable length; whereas, given that most aliens who have stayed in the Community for several years will have obtained a settled status or even citizenship of the Union after that period, a period of 10 years should be considered a reasonable period for the conservation of fingerprint data.

(8) The conservation period should be shorter in certain special situations where there is no need to keep fingerprint data for that length of time: fingerprint data should be erased immediately once aliens obtain Union citizenship.

(9) It is necessary to lay down clearly the respective responsibilities of the Commission, in respect of the Central Unit, and of the Member States, as regards data use, data security, access to and correction of recorded data.

(10) While the non-contractual liability of the Community in connection with the operation of the Eurodac system will be governed by the relevant provisions of the Treaty, it is necessary to lay down specific rules for the non-contractual liability of the Member States in connection with the operation of the system.

(11) Directive 95/46/EC of the European Parliament and of the Council of 24 October 1995 on the protection of individuals with regard to the processing of personal data and on the free movement of such data) applies to the processing of personal data by the Member States within the framework of the Eurodac system.

(12) In accordance with the principles of subsidiarity and proportionality as set out in Article 5 of the Treaty, the objective of the proposed measures, namely the creation within the Commission of a system for the comparison of fingerprints to assist the implementation of the Community's asylum policy, cannot, by its very nature, be sufficiently achieved by the Member States and can therefore be better achieved by the Community: this Regulation confines itself to the minimum required in order to achieve those objectives and does not go beyond what is necessary for that purpose.

(13) By virtue of Article 286 of the Treaty, Directive 95/46/EC also applies to the Community institutions and bodies; whereas, the Central Unit being established within the Commission, that Directive applies to the processing of personal data by that Unit.

(14) The principles set out in Directive 95/46/EC regarding the protection of the rights and freedoms of individuals, notably their right to privacy, with regard to the processing of personal data should be supplemented or clarified, in particular as far as certain sectors are concerned.

(15) It is appropriate to monitor and evaluate the performance of Eurodac.

(16) Member States should provide for a system of sanctions for infringements of this Regulation.

(17) It is appropriate to restrict the territorial scope of this Regulation so as to align it on the territorial scope of the Dublin Convention.

(18) This Regulation should enter into force on the day of its publication in the Official Journal of the European Communities in order to serve as legal basis for the implementing rules which, with a view to its rapid application, are required for the establishment of

the necessary technical arrangements by the Member States and the Commission; the Commission should therefore be charged with verifying that those conditions are fulfilled.

HAS ADOPTED THIS REGULATION:

Chapter I – General provisions

Article 1
Purpose of 'Eurodac'
1. A system known as 'Eurodac' is hereby established, the purpose of which shall be to assist in determining which Member State is to be responsible pursuant to the Dublin Convention for examining an application for asylum lodged in a Member State, and otherwise to facilitate the application of the Dublin Convention under the conditions set out in this Regulation.
2. Eurodac shall consist of:
(a) the Central Unit referred to in Article 3,
(b) a computerized central database in which the data referred to in Article 5(1), Article 8(2) and Article 11(2) are processed for the purpose of comparing the fingerprints of applicants for asylum and certain other aliens,
(c) means of data transmission between the Member States and the central database.
The rules governing Eurodac shall also apply to operations effected by the Member States as from the transmission of data to the Central Unit until use is made of the results of the comparison.
3. Without prejudice to the use of data intended for Eurodac by the Member State of origin in databases set up under the latter's national law, fingerprints and other personal data may be processed in Eurodac only for the purposes set out in Article 15(1) of the Dublin Convention.

Article 2
Definitions
1. For the purposes of this Regulation:
(a) 'The Dublin Convention' means the Convention determining the State responsible for examining applications for asylum lodged in one of the Member States of the European Communities, signed at Dublin on 15 June 1990.
(b) An 'applicant for asylum' means an alien who has made an application for asylum or on whose behalf such an application has been made.
(c) 'Personal data' means any information relating to an identified or identifiable natural person ('data subject'); an identifiable person is one who can be identified, directly or indirectly, in particular by reference to an identification number or to one or more factors specific to his physical, physiological, mental, economic, cultural or social identity.
(d) 'Processing of personal data' ('processing') means any operation or set of operations which is performed on personal data, whether or not by automatic means, such as collection, recording, organisation, storage, adaptation or alteration, retrieval, consultation, use, disclosure by transmission, dissemination or otherwise making available, alignment or combination, blocking, erasure or destruction.
(e) 'Transmission of data' means:
(i) communication of personal data from Member States to the Central Unit for recording

in the central database and communication to Member States of the results of the comparison made by the Central Unit; and

(ii) recording of personal data directly by Member States in the central database and direct communication of the results of the comparison to such Member States.

(f) 'Member State of origin' means:

(i) in relation to an applicant for asylum or a person covered by Article 11, the Member State which transmits the personal data to the Central Unit and receives the results of the comparison;

(ii) in relation to a person covered by Article 8, the Member State which communicates such data to the Central Unit.

(g) 'Refugee' means a person who has been recognised as a refugee in accordance with the Geneva Convention on Refugees of 28 July 1951, as amended by the New York Protocol of 31 January 1967.

2. Unless stated otherwise, the terms defined in Article 1 of the Dublin Convention shall have the same meaning in this Regulation.

Article 3
Central Unit
1. A Central Unit shall be established within the Commission which shall be responsible for operating the central database of fingerprints on behalf of the Member States. The Central Unit shall be equipped with a computerized fingerprint recognition system.
2. Data on applicants for asylum, persons covered by Article 8 and persons covered by Article 11 which are processed at the Central Unit shall be processed on behalf of the Member State of origin.
3. Pursuant to the procedure laid down in Article 22, the Central Unit may be charged with carrying out certain statistical tasks on the basis of the data processed at the Unit.

Chapter II – Applicants for asylum

Article 4
Collection, transmission and comparison of fingerprints
1. Each Member State shall promptly take the fingerprints of every applicant for asylum of at least 14 years of age and shall promptly transmit the data referred to in points (a) to (f) of Article 5(1) to the Central Unit. The procedure for taking fingerprints shall be determined in accordance with the national practice of the Member State concerned.
2. The data referred to in Article 5(1) shall be immediately recorded in the central database by the Central Unit, or, provided that the technical conditions for such purposes are met, directly by the Member State of origin.
3. Fingerprint data within the meaning of point (b) of Article 5(1), transmitted by any Member State, shall be compared by the Central Unit with the fingerprint data transmitted by other Member States and already stored in the central database.
(...)

Article 5
Recording of data
1. Only the following data shall be recorded in the central database:
(...)

Article 6
Data storage
Each set of data, as referred to in Article 5(1), shall be stored in the central database for ten years from the date on which the fingerprints were taken.
Upon expiry of this period, the Central Unit shall automatically erase the data from the central database.

Article 7
Advance data erasure
Data relating to a person who has acquired citizenship of the Union before expiry of the period referred to in Article 6 shall be erased from the central database, in accordance with Article 15(3) as soon as the Member State of origin becomes aware that the person has acquired citizenship of the Union.

Chapter III – Aliens apprehended in connection with the irregular crossing of an external border

Article 8
Collection and communication of fingerprint data
1. Each Member State shall promptly take the fingerprints of every alien of at least 14 years of age who is apprehended by the competent control authorities in connection with the irregular crossing by land, sea or air of the border of that Member State having come from a third country and who is not turned back
2. The Member State concerned shall promptly communicate to the Central Unit the following data in relation to any alien as referred to in paragraph 1: (...)

Article 9
Recording of data (...)

Article 10
Storage of data (...)

Chapter IV – Aliens found illegally present in a Member State

Article 11
Comparison of fingerprints
1. With a view to checking whether an alien found illegally present within its territory has previously lodged an application for asylum in another Member State, each Member State may communicate to the Central Unit any fingerprints which it may have taken of any such alien of at least 14 years of age together with the reference number used by that Member State.
As a general rule there are grounds for checking whether the alien has previously lodged an application for asylum in another Member State where:
(a) the alien declares that he/she has lodged an application for asylum but without indicating the Member State in which he/she made the application;
(b) the alien does not request asylum but objects to being returned to his/her country of origin by claiming that he/she would be in danger, or

(c) the alien otherwise seeks to prevent his/her removal by refusing to cooperate in establishing his/her identity, in particular by showing no, or false, identity papers.
2. The fingerprints of an alien as referred to in paragraph 1 shall be communicated to the Central Unit solely for the purpose of comparison with the fingerprints of applicants for asylum transmitted by other Member States and already recorded in the central database. The fingerprints of such an alien shall not be stored in the central database, nor shall they be compared with the data communicated to the Central Unit pursuant to Article 8(2). (...)

Chapter V – Recognised refugees

Article 12
Blocking of data
1. Data relating to a person who has been recognised and admitted as a refugee in a Member State shall be blocked in the central database. Such blocking shall be carried out by the Central Unit on the instructions of the Member State of origin. (...)

Chapter VI – Data use, data protection, security and liability (...)

5.7

UNHCR'S EXECUTIVE COMMITTEE: CONCLUSIONS

No. 1	(XXVI)	1975	Establishment of the Sub-Committee and General
No. 2	(XXVII)	1976	Functioning of the Sub-Committee and General
No. 3	(XXVIII)	1977	General Conclusion on International Protection
No. 4	(XXVIII)	1977	International Instruments
No. 5	(XXVIII)	1977	Asylum
No. 6	(XXVIII)	1977	Non-Refoulement
No. 7	(XXVIII)	1977	Expulsion
No. 8	(XXVIII)	1977	Determination of Refugee Status
No. 9	(XXVIII)	1977	Family Reunion
No.10	(XXVIII)	1977	Protection Staff
No.11	(XXIX)	1978	General Conclusion on International Protection
No.12	(XXIX)	1978	Extraterritorial Effect on the Determination of Refugee Status
No.13	(XXIX)	1978	Travel Documents for Refugees
No.14	(XXX)	1979	General Conclusion on International Protection
No.15	(XXX)	1979	Refugees Without an Asylum Country
No.16	(XXXI)	1980	General Conclusion on International Protection
No.17	(XXXI)	1980	Problems of Extradition Affecting Refugees
No.18	(XXXI)	1980	Voluntary Repatriation
No.19	(XXXI)	1980	Temporary Refuge
No.20	(XXXI)	1980	Protection of Asylum-Seekers at Sea
No.21	(XXXII)	1981	General Conclusion on International Protection
No.22	(XXXII)	1981	Protection of Asylum-Seekers in Situations of Large-Scale Influx

No.23 (XXXII)	1981	Problems Related to the Rescue of Asylum-Seekers in Distress at Sea
No.24 (XXXII)	1981	Family Reunification
No.25 (XXXIII)	1982	General Conclusion on International Protection
No.26 (XXXIII)	1982	Report of the Working Group on Problems Related to the Rescue of Asylum-Seekers in Distress at Sea
No.27 (XXXIII)	1982	Military Attacks on Refugee Camps and Settlements in Southern Africa and Elsewhere
No.28 (XXXIII)	1982	Follow-up on Earlier Conclusions of the Sub-Committee of the Whole on International Protection on the Determination of Refugee Status, Inter Alia, with Reference to the Role of UNHCR in National Refugee Status Determination Procedures
No.29 (XXXIV)	1983	General Conclusion on International Protection
No.30 (XXXIV)	1983	The Problem of Manifestly Unfounded or Abusive Applications for Refugee Status or Asylum
No.31 (XXXIV)	1983	Rescue of Asylum-Seekers in Distress at Sea
No.32 (XXXIV)	1983	Military Attacks on Refugee Camps and Settlements in Southern Africa and Elsewhere
No.33 (XXXV)	1984	General Conclusion on International Protection
No.34 (XXXV)	1984	Problems Related to the Rescue of Asylum-Seekers in Distress at Sea
No.35 (XXXV)	1984	Identity Documents for Refugees
No.36 (XXXVI)	1985	General Conclusion on International Protection
No.37 (XXXVI)	1985	Central American Refugees and the Cartagena Declaration
No.38 (XXXVI)	1985	Rescue of Asylum-Seekers in Distress at Sea
No.39 (XXXVI)	1985	Refugee Women and International Protection
No.40 (XXXVI)	1985	Voluntary Repatriation
No.41 (XXXVII)	1986	General Conclusion on International Protection
No.42 (XXXVII)	1986	Accession to International Instruments and Their Implementation
No.43 (XXXVII)	1986	Geneva Declaration on the 1951 United Nations Convention and the 1967 Protocol Relating to the Status of Refugees
No.44 (XXXVII)	1986	Detention of Refugees and Asylum-Seekers
No.45 (XXXVII)	1986	Military and Armed Attacks on Refugee Camps and Settlements
No.46 (XXXVIII)	1987	General Conclusion on International Protection
No.47 (XXXVIII)	1987	Refugee Children
No.48 (XXXVIII)	1987	Military or Armed Attacks on Refugee Camps and Settlements
No.49 (XXXVIII)	1987	Travel Documents for Refugees
No.50 (XXXIX)	1988	General Conclusion on International Protection
No.51 (XXXIX)	1988	Promotion and Dissemination of Refugee Law
No.52 (XXXIX)	1988	International Solidarity and Refugee Protection
No.53 (XXXIX)	1988	Stowaway Asylum-Seekers
No.54 (XXXIX)	1988	Refugee Women
No.55 (XL)	1989	General Conclusion on International Protection
No.56 (XL)	1989	Durable Solutions and Refugee Protection
No.57 (XL)	1989	Implementation of the 1951 Convention and the 1967 Protocol Relating to the Status of Refugees

No.58 (XL)	1989	Problem of Refugees and Asylum-Seekers Who Move in an Irregular Manner from a Country in Which They Had Already Found Protection
No.59 (XL)	1989	Refugee Children
No.60 (XL)	1989	Refugee Women
No.61 (XLI)	1990	General Conclusion on International Protection
No.62 (XLI)	1990	Note on International Protection
No.63 (XLI)	1990	Solutions and Protection
No.64 (XLI)	1990	Refugee Women and International Protection
No.65 (XLII)	1991	General Conclusion on International Protection
No.66 (XLII)	1991	Report of the Working Group on Solutions and Protection
No.67 (XLII)	1991	Resettlement as an Instrument of Protection
No.68 (XLIII)	1992	General Conclusion on International Protection
No.69 (XLIII)	1992	Cessation of Status
No.70 (XLIII)	1992	Decision on Inter-Sessional Meetings
No.71 (XLIV)	1993	General Conclusion on International Protection
No.72 (XLIV)	1993	Personal Security of Refugees
No.73 (XLIV)	1993	Refugee Protection and Sexual Violence
No.74 (XLV)	1994	General Conclusion on International Protection
No.75 (XLV)	1994	Internally Displaced Persons
No.76 (XLV)	1994	Recommendations of the OAU/UNHCR Commemorative Symposium on Refugees and Forced Population Displacements in Africa
No.77 (XLVI)	1995	General Conclusion on International Protection
No.78 (XLVI)	1995	Conclusion on the Prevention and Reduction of Statelessness and the Protection of Stateless Persons
No.79 (XLVII)	1996	General Conclusion on International Protection
No.80 (XLVII)	1996	Comprehensive and Regional Approaches Within a Protection Framework
No.81 (XLVIII)	1997	General Conclusion on International Protection
No.82 (XLVIII)	1997	Conclusion on safeguarding asylum
No.83 (XLVIII)	1997	Conclusion on safety of UNHCR staff and other humanitarian personnel
No.84 (XLVIII)	1997	Conclusion on refugee children and adolescents
No.85 (XLIX)	1998	Conclusion on International Protection
No.86 (XLIX)	1998	Decision on Informal Consultations on Protection Issues
No.87 (L)	1999	Conclusion on International Protection

5.8

UNHCR HANDBOOK, INTRODUCTION AND CONCLUSION

INTRODUCTION

International instruments defining the term 'refugee'

A. **Early instruments (1921-1946)**

1. Early in the twentieth century, the refugee problem became the concern of the international community, which, for humanitarian reasons, began to assume responsibility for protecting and assisting refugees.

2. The pattern of international action on behalf of refugees was established by the League of Nations and led to the adoption of a number of international agreements for their benefit. These instruments are referred to in Article 1 A (1) of the 1951 Convention relating to the Status of Refugees (see paragraph 32 below).

3. The definitions in these instruments relate each category of refugees to their national origin, to the territory that they left and to the lack of diplomatic protection by their former home country. With this type of definition 'by categories' interpretation was simple and caused no great difficulty in ascertaining who was a refugee.

4. Although few persons covered by the terms of the early instruments are likely to request a formal determination of refugee status at the present time ... such cases could occasionally arise. They are dealt with below in Chapter II, A. Persons who meet the definitions of international instruments prior to the 1951 Convention are usually referred to as 'statutory refugees'.

B. **1951 Convention relating to the Status of Refugees**

5. Soon after the Second World War, as the refugee problem had not been solved, the need was felt for a new international instrument to define the legal status of refugees. Instead of ad hoc agreements adopted in relation to specific refugee situations, there was a call for an instrument containing a general definition of who was to be considered a refugee. The Convention relating to the Status of Refugees was adopted by a Conference of Plenipotentiaries of the United Nations on 28 July 1951, and entered into force on 21 April 1954. In the following paragraphs it is referred to as 'the 1951 Convention'. (The text of the 1951 Convention will be found in Annex II.)

C. **Protocol relating to the Status of Refugees**

6. According to the general definition contained in the 1951 Convention, a refugee is a person who:

'As a result of events occurring before 1 January 1951 and owing to well-founded fear of being persecuted ... is outside his country of nationality ...'

7. The 1951 dateline originated in the wish of Governments, at the time the Convention was adopted, to limit their obligations to refugee situations that were known to exist at that time, or to those which might subsequently arise from events that had already occurred.

8. With the passage of time and the emergence of new refugee situations, the need was increasingly felt to make the provisions of the 1951 Convention applicable to such new refugees. As a result, a Protocol relating to the Status of Refugees was prepared. After consideration by the General Assembly of the United Nations, it was opened for accession on 31 January 1967 and entered into force on 4 October 1967.

9. By accession to the 1967 Protocol, States undertake to apply the substantive provisions of the 1951 Convention to refugees as defined in the Convention, but without the 1951 dateline. Although related to the Convention in this way, the Protocol is an independent instrument, accession to which is not limited to States parties to the Convention.

10. In the following paragraphs, the 1967 Protocol relating to the Status of Refugees is referred to as 'the 1967 Protocol'. (The text of the Protocol will be found in Annex III.)

11. At the time of writing, 78 States are parties to the 1951 Convention or to the 1967 Protocol or to both instruments. (A list of the States parties will be found in Annex IV.)

D. **Main provisions of the 1951 Convention and the 1967 Protocol**

12. The 1951 Convention and the 1967 Protocol contain three types of provisions:
(i) Provisions giving the basic definition of who is (and who is not) a refugee and who, having been a refugee, has ceased to be one. The discussion and interpretation of these provisions constitute the main body of the present Handbook, intended for the guidance of those whose task it is to determine refugee status.
(ii) Provisions that define the legal status of refugees and their rights and duties in their country of refuge. Although these provisions have no influence on the process of determination of refugee status, the authority entrusted with this process should be aware of them, for its decision may indeed have far-reaching effects for the individual or family concerned.
(iii) Other provisions dealing with the implementation of the instruments from the administrative and diplomatic standpoint. Article 35 of the 1951 Convention and Article 11 of the 1967 Protocol contain an undertaking by Contracting States to co-operate with the Office of the United Nations High Commissioner for Refugees in the exercise of its functions and, in particular, to facilitate its duty of supervising the application of the provisions of these instruments.

E. **Statute of the Office of the United Nations High Commissioner for Refugees**

13. The instruments described above under A-C define the persons who are to be considered refugees and require the parties to accord a certain status to refugees in their respective territories.

14. Pursuant to a decision of the General Assembly, the Office of the United Nations High Commissioner for Refugees ('UNHCR') was established as of 1 January 1951. The Statute of the Office is annexed to Resolution 428 (V), adopted by the General Assembly on 14 December 1950. According to the Statute, the High Commissioner is called upon – inter alia – to provide international protection, under the auspices of the United Nations, to refugees falling within the competence of his Office.

15. The Statute contains definitions of those persons to whom the High Commissioner's competence extends, which are very close to, though not identical with, the definition contained in the 1951 Convention. By virtue of these definitions the High Commissioner is competent for refugees irrespective of any dateline 2 or geographic limitation. 3

16. Thus, a person who meets the criteria of the UNHCR Statute qualifies for the protection of the United Nations provided by the High Commissioner, regardless of whether or not he is in a country that is a party to the 1951 Convention or the 1967 Protocol or whether or not he has been recognized by his host country as a refugee under either of these instruments. Such refugees, being within the High Commissioner's mandate, are usually referred to as 'mandate refugees'.

17. From the foregoing, it will be seen that a person can simultaneously be both a mandate refugee and a refugee under the 1951 Convention or the 1967 Protocol. He may, however, be in a country that is not bound by either of these instruments, or he may be excluded from recognition as a Convention refugee by the application of the dateline or the geographic limitation. In such cases he would still qualify for protection by the High Commissioner under the terms of the Statute.

18. The above mentioned Resolution 428 (V) and the Statute of the High Commissioner's Office call for co-operation between Governments and the High Commissioner's Office in dealing with refugee problems. The High Commissioner is designated as the authority charged with providing inter-national protection to refugees, and is required inter alia to promote the conclusion and ratification of international conventions for the protection of refugees, and to supervise their application.

19. Such co-operation, combined with his supervisory function, forms the basis for the High Commissioner's fundamental interest in the process of determining refugee status under the 1951 Convention and the 1967 Protocol. The part played by the High Commissioner is reflected, to varying degrees, in the procedures for the determination of refugee status established by a number of Governments.

F. **Regional instruments relating to refugees**

20. In addition to the 1951 Convention and the 1967 Protocol, and the Statute of the Office of the United Nations High Commissioner for Refugees, there are a number of regional agreements, conventions and other instruments relating to refugees, particularly in Africa, the Americas and Europe. These regional instruments deal with such matters as the granting of asylum, travel documents and travel facilities, etc. Some also contain a definition of the term 'refugee', or of persons entitled to asylum.

21. In Latin America, the problem of diplomatic and territorial asylum is dealt with in a number of regional instruments including the Treaty on International Penal Law, (Montevideo, 1889); the Agreement on Extradition, (Caracas, 1911); the Convention on Asylum, (Havana, 1928); the Convention on Political Asylum, (Montevideo, 1933); the Convention on Diplomatic Asylum, (Caracas, 1954); and the Convention on Territorial Asylum, (Caracas, 1954).

22. A more recent regional instrument is the Convention Governing the Specific Aspects of Refugee Problems in Africa, adopted by the Assembly of Heads of State and Government of the Organization of African Unity on 10 September 1969. This Convention contains a definition of the term 'refugee', consisting of two parts: the first part is identical with the definition in the 1967 Protocol (i.e. the definition in the 1951 Convention without the dateline or geographic limitation). The second part applies the term 'refugee' to:
'every person who, owing to external aggression, occupation, foreign domination or events seriously disturbing public order in either part or the whole of his country of origin or nationality, is compelled to leave his place of habitual residence in order to seek refuge in another place outside his country of origin or nationality'.

23. The present Handbook deals only with the determination of refugee status under the two international instruments of universal scope: the 1951 Convention and the 1967 Protocol.

G. Asylum and the treatment of refugees

24. The Handbook does not deal with questions closely related to the determination of refugee status e.g. the granting of asylum to refugees or the legal treatment of refugees after they have been recognized as such.

25. Although there are references to asylum in the Final Act of the Conference of Plenipotentiaries as well as in the Preamble to the Convention, the granting of asylum is not dealt with in the 1951 Convention or the 1967 Protocol. The High Commissioner has always pleaded for a generous asylum policy in the spirit of the Universal Declaration of Human Rights and the Declaration on Territorial Asylum, adopted by the General Assembly of the United Nations on 10 December 1948 and on 14 December 1967 respectively.

26. With respect to the treatment within the territory of States, this is regulated as regards refugees by the main provisions of the 1951 Convention and 1967 Protocol (see paragraph 12(ii) above). Furthermore, attention should be drawn to Recommendation E contained in the Final Act of the Conference of Plenipotentiaries which adopted the 1951 Convention:
'The Conference Expresses the hope that the Convention relating to the Status of Refugees will have value as an example exceeding its contractual scope and that all nations will be guided by it in granting so far as possible to persons in their territory as refugees and who would not be covered by the terms of the Convention. the treatment for which it provides.'

27. This recommendation enables States to solve such problems as may arise with regard to persons who are not regarded as fully satisfying the criteria of the definition of the term 'refugee'.

(...)

CONCLUSION

220. In the present Handbook an attempt has been made to define certain guidelines that, in the experience of UNHCR, have proved useful in determining refugee status for the purposes of the 1951 Convention and the 1967 Protocol relating to the Status of Refugees. In so doing, particular attention has been paid to the definitions of the term 'refugee' in these two instruments, and to various problems of interpretation arising out of these definitions. It has also been sought to show how these definitions may be applied in concrete cases and to focus attention on various procedural problems arising in regard to the determination of refugee status.

221. The Office of the High Commissioner is fully aware of the shortcomings inherent in a Handbook of this nature, bearing in mind that it is not possible to encompass every situation in which a person may apply for refugee status. Such situations are manifold and depend upon the infinitely varied conditions prevailing in countries of origin and on the special personal factors relating to the individual applicant.

222. The explanations given have shown that the determination of refugee status is by no means a mechanical and routine process. On the contrary, it calls for specialized knowledge, training and experience and – what is more important – an understanding of the particular situation of the applicant and of the human factors involved.

223. Within the above limits it is hoped that the present Handbook may provide some guidance to those who in their daily work are called upon to determine refugee status.

CROSS REFERENCES

Hereinunder an overview will be given of exact places where references are made to the subjects concerned. The references will be followed by a short commentary/summary, and where relevant by references to case-law of the Strasbourg Court/Commission (ECHR) and/or authoritative literature. This list does not claim to be exhaustive: it only indicates the more relevant cross references, with the aim to enable practitioners to focus more easily on the basic acquis material available.

Abbreviations
C'51: Geneva Convention of 28 July 1951 Relating to the Status of Refugees
CoO: London Conclusions concerning Countries in Which there is Generally No Serious Risk of Persecution [T.8]
Dublin: Convention determining the State responsible for Examining Applications for Asylum lodged in one of the Member States of the European Communities
ExCom: the Executive Committee of the Programme of the United Nations High Commissioner for Refugees
HCR Handbook: UNHCR Handbook on Procedures and Criteria for Determining Refugee Status
JP: Joint Position defined by the Council on the basis of Article K.3 of the Treaty on European Union on the Harmonized Application of the Definition of the Term 'Refugee' in Article 1 of the Geneva Convention of 28 July 1951 Relating to the Status of Refugees [T.4]
MG: Resolution on Minimum Guarantees for Asylum Procedures [T.12]
MUA: London Resolution on Manifestly Unfounded Applications for Asylum [T.7]
[T.]: TAIEX List
ToA: (Treaty of Amsterdam =) Consolidated Version of the Treaty Establishing the European Community
UM: Council Resolution on Unaccompanied Minors who are Nationals of Third Countries [T.31]

Accelerated Procedure
 – CoO para 3
 – ExCom 8 (1977)
 – ExCom 30 1983)
 – ExCom 59 (1989)

P.J. van Krieken (Ed.), The Asylum Acquis Handbook
© 2000, T.M.C.Asser Press, The Hague, the Röling Foundation and the authors

- HCR Handbook para 192
- MG
- MUA para 2, para 3, para 6, para 11
- see also the Brussels Commentaries

Agent of Persecution
- Commission, 3 March 1999, working document
- HCR Handbook para 65
- Joint Position (JP) para 5

Airport Procedure
- Dublin art. 7.3
- Joint Action 4 March 1996 passim
- Strasbourg case-law: Amuut
- [T.16]

Appeal Procedure
- ExCom
- HCR Handbook para 192
- MG
- MUA para 3
- ToA art. 63
- see also Brussels Commentaries

Border Procedure
- Dublin Art. 3.1
- MG para 23-25

Cessation
- C'51 art.1C
- ExCom 69 (1992)
- JP para 11
- ToA Art. 63.1.d

Children
- ExCom 47 (1987)
- ExCom 59 (1989)
- ExCom 84 (1997)
- (CRC)
- MG
- see also: unaccompanied minors
- see also: family (unity/reunion/reunification)

Civil War
- HCR Handbook para 91, 98
- JP para 6
- [T.13]
- [T.14]

Country of Origin
- CoO passim
- MUA para 8
- Tampere para 12 (HLWG) [also: CIREA]

Degrading or Inhuman Treatment, see: Torture

Detention
- C'51, art. 31
- ExCom 44 (1986)
- ExCom 85 (1998) para (cc)-(ee)
- European Series (UNHCR), Vol 1, No 4, 1995

Determination of Refugee Status (Procedure)
- CoO para 2.1
- ExCom 8 (1977)
- ExCom 28 (1982)
- ExCom 30 (1983)
- HCR Handbook 189-219
- HTC para 1
- JP para 2
- MG passim
- MUA para 2
- Tampere para 14 and 15
- ToA Art. 63.1.a and 63.1.d

Documents (ID/Travel)
- C'51, Art. 31
- ExCom 13 (1978), 35 (1984), 49 (1987)
- ExCom 58 (1989)
- MG (para 18 refers to MUA)
- MUA para 9.a; 9.c;

Dublin Procedures
- CoO para 1
- Dublin Convention *cs* passim
- HTC para 3, 4

Exclusion/Expulsion/Extradition
- ExCom 7 (1977)
- ExCom 17 (1980)
- C'51 art.1F
- JP para 13
- MUA para 9.e; para 11
- HTC para 2
- HCR Handbook 147-163

Family Members; Unity; Reunification
- ToA Art. 63.3.a
- Dublin, artt. 4, 9
- C'51, final act
- ExCom 9 (1977)
- ExCom 24 (1981)
- ExCom 85 (1995) para (u)-(x)
- ExCom 1999 (B)
- HCR Handbook para 181-188, 213

Handbook
- Joint Position, preambule ('valuable aid')

Health
- C'51 final act (C)
- ExCom 22 (1981), para II.B.2.c

Host Third Countries
- Dublin art.3.5
- HTC passim
- MUA para 9.g

Illegal Entry
- C'51 art.31
- Dublin art.6
- ExCom 58 (1989)
- HCR Handbook

Inclusion
- C'51, Art. 1A
- HCR Handbook, passim
- JP, passim
- Tampere
- ToA Art. 63.1.c

Internal Flight Alternative
- ExCom 75 (1994)
- HCR Handbook para 91
- JP para 8
- MUA para 7

Irregular Movements
- ExCom 58 (1989)
- Dublin, implementing guidelines, art. 12
- HTC preambule

Manifestly Unfounded Applications
- CoO para 1; para 2

- ExCom 8 (1977)
- ExCom 28 (1982)
- ExCom 30 (1983)
- HCR Handbook para 192
- HTC para 1
- MG para 18-22
- MUA, passim

Military
- HCR Handbook para 167-171; 174-180
- JP para 10

Misuse (also: abuse) of Asylum Procedure
- ExCom (1996) para (l)
- ExCom 85 (1998) para (s)

Procedure: see determination of refugee status

Reception
- C'51, final act
- ExCom 22 (1981)
- Tampere para 14 and 20
- ToA Art. 63.1.b

Return/Repatriation
- ExCom 18 (1980)
- ExCom 40 (1985)
- ExCom (1996) para (q) and (u)
- ExCom 81 (1997) para (s)
- ExCom 85 (1998) para (y)-(bb)
- Readmission Agreements (specimen) passim
- [T.33-36]

Safe Third Countries (STC)
- see under Host Third Countries (HTC)

Safe Countries of Origin
- CoO passim

Statelessness
- ExCom 78 (1995)
- ExCom 85 (1998) para (m)
- HCR Handbook para 101-102, 104-105, 137-139

Temporary Protection
- ExCom 22 (1981)
- Tampere para 14
- ToA Art. 63.2.a

(– Resolution of 1 and 2 June 1993 on Certain Common Guidelines as Regards the Admission of particularly Vulnerable persons from the Former Yugoslavia, passim; not officially included in the acquis)
- [T.13] Burden Sharing Resolution 25 September 1995
- [T.14] Council Decision 4 March 1996
- (see also: civil war)

Torture (and degrading or inhuman treatment)
- CAT case-law on Art. 3
- ExCom 79 (1996) para (j)
- ExCom 81 (1997) para (i)
- Strasbourg case-law on Art. 3

Unaccompanied Minors
- MG para 26-27
- Handbook para 182, 213-219
- UAM passim
- [T.31] (1997) passim

Women
- ExCom 39 (1985)
- ExCom 54 (1988)
- ExCom 60 (1989)
- ExCom 64 (1990)
- ExCom 79 (1996) para (o)
- MG para 28